USING BIBLICAL SIMULATIONS

Donald E. Miller
Graydon F. Snyder
Robert W. Neff

JUDSON PRESS • Valley Forge

To Scott, Heather, Jonathan, Anna Christine,
Stephen, Bryan, Lisa, and Bruce,
who have taught us how to learn by playing.

USING BIBLICAL SIMULATIONS

Copyright © 1973
Judson Press, Valley Forge, PA 19481

Third Printing, 1975

Library of Congress Cataloging in Publication Data

Miller, Donald Eugene.
    Using Biblical simulations.

    SUMMARY: Instructions for the reenactment of events from the Bible with a
guide for subsequent discussion by the participants.
    1. Bible plays. 2. Drama in religious education. [1. Bible plays] I. Snyder,
Graydon F., joint author. II. Neff, Robert W., joint author. III. Title.
BVI534.4M55   220'.07   72-9569
ISBN 0-8170-0580-3

Printed in the U.S.A.

CONTENTS

PREFACE

The use of simulation as a part of Bible study is very new in one way and very old in another. It is new in that biblical simulation as a learning tool has become widespread only recently. It is old in that dramatic representation of biblical stories has been employed wherever the Bible has been studied. Simulation offers a dramatic and interesting approach to the Bible without focusing upon the viewpoint of the teacher. It allows participants to make their own discoveries about the truths of the Bible.

The simulations included in this collection provide material for a full-year's course of study, or they may add interest and variety to another study plan. Retreats and conferences can be designed around these simulations, or they may be used to supplement other retreat and conference plans. Because they do not push a point of view, they have an objectivity that may allow many of them to be used in a public school or college setting. Furthermore they provide a dramatic setting where youth and adults can enjoy being together.

All three authors conferred at every point in the development of these simulations, and the influence of all is to be found throughout.

However, Donald Miller is responsible for the overall editing; for the educational theory developed in chapters 1, 2, 3, and 4; and for simulations 13, 14, and 15. Graydon Snyder originated simulations 6, 7, 11, and 12; and he was the first to use the simulation model of Bible study in a conference setting. Robert Neff developed simulations 5, 8, 9, and 10; and he has been most original in varying the design.

We wish to express appreciation to our classes at Bethany Theological Seminary, who acted out many of these simulations, offering criticisms and new ideas. The same is true of those at the 1972 Bethany Extension School at Elizabethtown College in Pennsylvania, the Community Presbyterian Church of Clarendon Hills and the Naperville Church of the Brethren, both in Illinois. We are always indebted to our fellow faculty members, who constantly stimulate us in all that we do. Finally we want to thank Ann Risden for her generous help in typing a somewhat complicated manuscript.

Our hope is that the simulations included in this book will allow the Bible to come richly alive for many people.

1. WHAT IS A BIBLICAL SIMULATION?

WHAT IS A SIMULATION?

When we speak of simulation, we mean any reenactment of an event in which there is an attempt to portray accurately some selected elements of that event. Only recently has simulation come to have this meaning. Formerly it connoted feigning, mimicking, or hiding one's own identity. Currently simulation has taken on the highly positive meaning of reenacting an event so as to bring certain features of that event directly and powerfully before us. Simulation has often proven to be more effective in putting us into a situation than description, lecture, movie, discussion, or other methods of presentation where participants talk about an event rather than live in it.

The power of simulation was brought compellingly to anyone who watched the telecasts of the astronauts' voyages to the moon. First the viewer was impressed by the fact that every conceivable eventuality had been rehearsed beforehand. Simulation is able to bring future events before us so that we can prepare for them. The telecasts also showed mock-ups of the astronauts in flight when they could not be photographed directly. Therein we see how a simulation may bring a present event to us when it cannot otherwise be experienced firsthand. Just as simulation brought future and present events into the immediacy of present experience, the biblical simulations described in the following pages are designed to bring certain past events into the living reality of the present.

Simulation is closely related to both games and drama. Indeed it is difficult to draw sharp lines between the three. Drama portrays an actual or imaginary human event in order to feature some fundamental truth. Simulation begins by portraying a situation accurately in order that whatever truth is there may be perceived and further explored. Simulation is initially controlled by an event in a way that is not necessary to drama. Yet simulations may be dramatic. The simulations in these pages are meant to be dramatic, and they will lose a great deal if the dramatic quality is not developed.

Simulation is also very close to games. A game has behavioral rules that define the conditions under which a person may or may not act in certain ways until a predetermined goal is reached. It is important that the rules of the simulation be clear in everyone's mind. It is also important that the goal be mutually agreed upon. However, the aim of the simulation is not necessarily to win or to achieve a predetermined goal; it is rather to achieve a fuller experience of an event in order to learn from it. Of course, such learning may also occur in a game, and thus arises the difficulty of drawing a sharp line between games and simulations. Our point is that simulations have both dramatic and gaming qualities.

WHAT IS A BIBLICAL SIMULATION?

A biblical simulation is the reenactment of some particular biblical event in an attempt to portray accurately some selected features of that event. In brief, the purpose is to bring a biblical event into a present lived moment. If we examine each part of our definition, perhaps we shall better understand what a biblical simulation is.

A simulation is before all else a *reenactment*. In the moon landing the television audience saw a model of the lunar module apparently being controlled by someone who was playing the part of an astronaut. The biblical simulations in this book also have many situations in which those who carry out the simulation will act out the part of someone else. Someone may play the part of Peter or Paul discussing the missionary strategy for the early church. It helps to know something of the opinions of Peter and Paul to carry out such a discussion. Our simulations offer background information and suggested readings to make those attitudes more clear.

The reenactment takes place as a person acts out his idea of what Paul or Peter might have said. We know from the book of Acts that Peter thought newly converted Christians should follow the Hebrew dietary laws. Paul did not agree to this, and they apparently argued about the matter. A person playing the role of Peter might say, "But you know that the food laws were commanded by God and that Jesus himself kept them." Paul might answer, "You are wrong, Peter. Jesus didn't stress that kind of law. He picked grain on the sabbath. He taught that what is in a man's heart rather than what is in his stomach defiles him." We don't know that either Peter or Paul said these things, but they might have. Knowing what we do about Peter and Paul, such dialogue is quite possible.

To play a role means to begin with some idea of a person's attitude and then to carry out the conversation and action however it might occur. A person playing Paul might answer, "The more you talk to me, Peter, the more I think you are right." The simulation might conclude with Paul being persuaded by Peter. The book of Acts tells us that the change of opinion went the other direction, Peter being the one who was convinced. Nevertheless, a group could have a highly effective simulation with Paul changing his mind. A simulation is not a literal replay. It is rather an attempt to reenact or role-play a situation to see what happens. Since the conversation may go in whatever way seems fitting, Paul may very well change his mind. The group may then have a lively discussion about why the events recorded in Acts went in a different direction.

Our definition of a biblical simulation indicates that it focuses upon *particular events*. The setting for a simulation is a real situation in which different points of view are being worked out. We can begin to appreciate the different strands of tradition that make up Scripture when we act them out. A simulation about the entering of the Promised Land allows participants to take the points of view of the priestly class, the Yahwists, the Egyptians, and the nomads. A simulation about choosing a king for Israel lets us act out the opinions of the priests, the judges, the prophets, and the seers. In each instance the setting is a particular event recorded in Scripture, and the points of view are those actually described there.

The simulation allows us to explore critical events by living through them. The decision of Israel to occupy the Promised Land was critical in biblical history, as was the decision to appoint a king. The decision about what to do with Jesus after he had been captured and the early church's decision about the standards for admission into the church are both critical in the biblical narrative. There are many such critical situations, so that the simulations we have drawn up are only a beginning. The important thing is to get a situation that is actually recorded and then to reenact the different points of view. A reenactment of the dispute between God and Satan as they consider Job's fate is just as appropriate as the debate between Peter and Paul.

Our definition suggests that a simulation is an *accurate portrayal*. In the telecast of the moon landing, the simulated model was so accurate visually that the viewers had a real sense of seeing the event happen. One could attempt a visual simulation of a biblical event, but that is not primarily what we want to feature here. Rather we want to be accurate in portraying the attitudes and points of view represented in a biblical account. It doesn't matter what one wears during the simulation, although a group might develop real historical costumes if they like. Far more important is the appreciation of the convictions of the persons being portrayed.

It is not necessary to simulate the clothing of Caiaphas during the trial of Jesus although that can be interesting and instructive. More important is some understanding of Caiaphas's attitude toward Jesus. One can gain information about that attitude by studying certain passages of Scripture that describe the Sadducees, e.g., Mark 12:18-27; Acts 4:1-4, etc. Someone who planned to play the part of Caiaphas would do well to know that the Sadducees had a high reverence for Moses, but that they did not believe in resurrection. Sayings about resurrection annoyed the Sadducees (Acts 4:1-4).

The simulations we have included give many sources that may be consulted so that the role playing may be accurate to the part being played. Anyone who plays the role of Caiaphas will gain some new understanding about his attitudes, and therefore a better understanding about the trial and crucifixion of Jesus.

Finally, our definition of biblical simulation focuses upon the *selected elements* of an event. We have just said that we are more interested in the attitudes of the persons being portrayed than in other features, e.g., their clothing. The role play is also designed to allow the point of view to come into genuine dialogue and controversy. The Jerusalem Council recorded in Acts 15 may not have occurred in just the manner described in our simulation, but the conflict of points of view must have happened in a similar manner. We have therefore suggested rules for each simulation that will allow for maximum exploration of the background of the event and for contact between various opinions. The rules and procedure are preestablished, so that everyone knows what is happening and when the simulation is concluded. Clarity of procedure will allow everyone to participate more fully in the actual discussion.

Again it is important to remember that once the situation is established, it may go where it will. One could simulate the exact sequence of events as described in Scripture, and that might be instructive. We are more interested in allowing for the living interplay of different points of view. Whichever direction the simulation goes, it will throw new light on the passages being studied. A living dialogue between real points of view will be much more instructive than merely mimicking the sequence as recorded.

2. WHY USE BIBLICAL SIMULATIONS?

One may very well ask, "Why use biblical simulations?" Are there not better ways of studying the Scriptures? We might answer that it is an interesting procedure for most persons, but that would hardly suffice as an answer, even though it is true. We might answer that young and old can take part together, which is equally true, but also not a sufficient answer. A really adequate answer must go to the heart of the interpretation of Scripture. It must show that there is a hermeneutical basis for simulation, or else we simply have another interesting innovation.

HERMENEUTICS AND PLAY

Hermeneutics is the science of interpreting the Scripture. There are many different ways to interpret Scripture, although the moral approach is likely the most prevalent in our day. The moral approach requires that some moral truth be drawn from whatever passage is being considered. If Jesus wept, then we ought also to weep. You can furnish many examples of your own.

The early church preferred allegory. Persons, groups, and events were considered to be hidden references to the spiritual journey of the soul or of the church. For example, Israel in the wilderness was often thought to be an allegory of the human soul searching its way through a barren world to reach its promised destination in heaven.

Many believers today prefer the method of critical interpretation. The effort in this case is to establish the circumstances of fact and the intentions of the writer clearly enough that the meaning can be understood. The purpose of the critical approach is to seek to establish which of the Gospels was written first and which depended upon the other so as to gain a better idea of what was added or changed in each. Such study is done in order to ascertain the special intention of each Gospel writer, and thereby tie down the original meaning. However, the critical method cannot provide the answer to the question of what the passage should mean to us today.

When the Scripture is understood to be a set of facts to be unearthed, then we are following the critical approach. The quest for the historical Jesus was just such an effort. Various scholars tried to establish the facts of Jesus' life and the *ipsissima verba*, the actual words he spoke. In his magnificent study, *The Quest of the Historical Jesus*, Albert Schweitzer demonstrated that each of these efforts disclosed more about the presuppositions of the researcher than they did about Jesus himself. Current scholarly opinion holds that it is impossible to separate the hard facts about Jesus' life from the more fanciful, but faith-inspired, interpretations of those who wrote about him.

Faith is a play of the imagination. It is imagining and hoping in what is not yet seen. It is the fanciful hope of an Abraham whose wife is barren. It is the imaginative vision of a Moses whose people are held in Egyptian captivity. It is the dream of a John who records his vision of the end of the age in the book of Revelation. There is a playfulness in the Scriptures that more than anything in Western history has served to release man from the drudgery of his circumstances, from the fatedness of his existence.

The great and first commandment, to love the Lord your God with all your heart, soul, mind, and strength (Matthew 22:37), is sure to release the human imagination from bondage to the present moment. The second of the Ten

Commandments, not to make any graven images (Exodus 20:4), guarantees that the human imagination will not be permanently fixed upon any one item of the creation. If the Scripture itself is a record of the playfulness of faith, it would seem that we ought to be more imaginative in our own interpretation of it. Playfulness encourages creativity. Play is not bound by the hard necessities of the work world. Play is more appropriate as an approach to the larger context of life than is work, which is largely means-end activity. It would therefore seem that we ought to be more playful in our interpretation of Scripture, less prone to make work of it. Simulation is a more playful, imaginative, nevertheless serious, approach to the interpretation of Scripture.

The objection to such an approach is that play is usually considered to be frivolous, not serious. Such an objection would be most appropriate in an era when every bit of time were of necessity filled with labor to stave off starvation, when play were a way of avoiding life, or when drunkenness and destructiveness were to be equated with play. But we must remember that children learn to be persons by playing, and that the play of the imagination has been equally as important as work in freeing men from the threat of starvation.

Perhaps we can become more rather than less serious in our study of Scripture if we introduce a note of playfulness. We hope that such an attitude will not be divorced from disciplined critical study. But discipline itself can be a joy when set within the context of play, as every good teacher of children knows. Biblical simulation is an effort to combine a playful and a serious, disciplined note.

THE USE OF IMAGINATION
Our interpretation of Scripture must discover anew the interplay of imagination and discipline. We have become so enamored of the scientific method and of technological procedures that exercise of the imagination has dwindled. In a previous age it was the dreariness of work that stifled the imagination. Today it is the machine quality of all of life that kills flights of fancy. A boy who dreams in school is considered to be maladjusted. Like Joseph's brothers we have squelched the dreamer of our times.

Paradoxically were we to succeed in killing the dreamer, we would also extinguish our own chances for survival. Imagination is healing; it is the way to a deeper quality of life. Imagination and fantasy are able to keep other options before us when we are totally compelled by present ones. By so-called "dreaming" we are able to find wholly new ways of understanding our own situations. Reason forced into the narrows of rigorous logic can produce complex computers and elaborate principles, but it cannot bring them to life. Creative imagination is as important to our normal thinking processes as are the methods of induction and deduction.

Imagination is a gateway to the past. In a time when so many believe the past to be an albatross around the neck of the present, we should consider again what we mean by the past. The past is not merely a set of facts to be verified. One could not know Jesus by documenting all the facts of his life year by year. Nor is the past simply a tradition to be broken, a prison to be escaped, an ignorance to be forgotten. Rather the past is an open possibility to be regained by fantasy and imagination as well as hard research. Celebration and storytelling are how we recover who we are and where we are going.

Imagination is a healer of the present. The Gestalt psychologists have taught us that experience is a jumble until we are oriented. Anyone who travels at all has had the experience of waking in the morning and being disoriented about where he is. In those moments it becomes evident that more than the facticity of the bed or the mirror we need the orientation within which those items become useful. Psychotherapists have discovered that severe emotional conflicts can be healed by an altered self-image. The mind has a way of throwing up images during both night and day dreaming, some of which are able to reconcile conflicts within our lives. Fantasy and imagination have tremendous healing power in the present.

Imagination is a door to the future. We may find it less surprising to consider the relation of imagination to the future than to past and present. We are all aware that we anticipate the future by imagining various possibilities and by choosing from among them. Surely it is true that some people are more adept at such imagining than are others. When the images dry up, when there seem to be no possibilities but those which already exist, when the future is opaque to our glance, then the stream of our life dries up. Every institution lives by imagining and choosing its way into the future, as does every individual. The range, variety, and playfulness of imagining the future thus become highly important for the quality of life.

These considerations impress upon us the healing power of imagination. When imagination is limited to the means-end meat grinder, then life becomes terribly impoverished. At the same time it is well to note those ages when demonic imagination ran rampant in witch-hunting and orgy. Such periods are equally destructive to the quality of life. Perhaps we need a balance of disciplined thought and fertile imagination, but the latter seems to suffer most in our day. We need to recover the healing relationship of imagination and discipline in our interpretation of Scripture. Simulation is planned to stimulate imaginative interpretation without abandoning method.

LIVING THE PAST
A more playful and imaginative attitude toward Scripture is one in which the Scripture is not so much an idea to be debated as a situation to be lived. Human beings have the capacity imaginatively to put themselves in another time or place and actually feel and experience those situations. Thus literature, movies, and recordings do much more than remind us of an idea. They may become the vehicles by which we live the experience of another age or anticipate the experience of another tomorrow.

To know objectively that an event occurred at a certain time may be useful in its own way. It is, however, a kind of knowing that is more appropriate to the world of sticks and stones. Of persons we may know a great deal more, because each of us is one with every other human being in our ability to sense, feel, appreciate, fear, and decide. We not only know something about another person, but we also can put ourselves in his place. To put oneself in the place of another is the beginning of all genuine morality. The ability imaginatively to put ourselves in the place of another, to play at being the other, is one of the most deeply human capacities by which all of us come to be the persons we are.

Whereas in recent years we have searched after the historical Jesus by trying to ascertain the facts of his life and the actual words he spoke, a much longer tradition has sought the *imitatio Christi*, the imitation of Jesus. Such an imitation has sometimes fallen into a sandal-wearing, thou-speaking pantomime, but more often it has risen imaginatively to pick up and play out the life attitudes of Jesus as they might be lived in our time. Perhaps Francis of Assisi is the person who did this most completely, and incidentally most playfully. It is not unusual to hear a group of secular, non-church-attending persons, at a time of intimate soul searching, say to one another that deeply within themselves they fancy themselves to be like Jesus. Such is far more than a search for the facts of Jesus' life. It is a kind of playfulness, often suppressed, in which persons are most seriously themselves.

To play out the lived moment of the past is to enlarge our own lived moment. It is to exercise the marvelous human capacity for feeling and imagining. We may simulate the time of decision when Israel had to find a new leader to replace Moses and had to decide whether to enter the land of Canaan. From a factual point of view we already know what happened; at least we have a fair idea. We know from archeological as well as scriptural evidence that Saul became the first of a succession of kings of Israel. We can debate about the meaning of one or another verse, but for all practical purposes we feel that we know what happened. The matter is fundamentally closed, dead, and that is the end of it.

If we put ourselves imaginatively, playfully into that situation, our whole attitude can change. Allow ourselves to imagine the decision about who would become king. Be one or another of the persons present and sense how he felt. Play out the discussions and decisions with others. Forget for the moment how history records the outcome and play out the conversation anew. Let it happen as it will. Now life may surge into the drama; the decisions become real. The emotions are real, often so much so that we are embarrassed by them. Now the past becomes a present moment rather than a closed book.

The power of play, imagination, fantasy, and drama lies in the fact that they allow us to overcome distance and time in a way that objective understanding never can. The knowledge of certain objective facts is highly important for any imaginative reconstruction. But the time comes when the playfulness of the situation must run its own course. The script must be cast aside and real thought and emotion must be put into the event. So we recover the lived moment of the past, and it becomes one with this lived moment now. Furthermore, it opens our future to new possibilities, since every lived moment is an anticipation of the future. The living of the past may become a powerful way of studying the Scriptures.

THE MOVEMENT OF THE SPIRIT
Spirit is what moves us. We find ourselves moved to tears or to indignation. We are moved by children's innocence. John Wesley felt his heart strangely moved while Luther's *Preface to*

the Epistle to the Romans was being read aloud. The prophets were moved to prophesy by the Spirit. Jesus was driven by the Spirit into the wilderness to fast and to pray. The Spirit of God fell upon the early church, and they went forth to preach and to baptize. The distinctive mark of the Spirit is that it moves us.

The black criticism of the white church is that it lacks "soul." It is dead, the form of religion, but without the Spirit. People are often reluctant to put themselves into a situation in which they are moved by what happens. This repression of the Spirit is the mark of Victorianism in the church. Churches become far more important for what they will teach to the children than for their capacity to move us. Pentecostalism has thrived on the insight that people must be moved if the Spirit is present, but Pentecostalism is highly suspect in the more established churches. Paralysis becomes safer than being moved when all physical needs are cared for.

On every side there is also the attempt to recover the moving quality of life. The psychoanalysts tell their patients to "free associate," letting the words come as they will. Many artists have given up recognizable images in order to let the form and colors express what they will. John Cage lets the structure of the music at a concert be determined by casting dice. Rock music reaches deeply to move the listener. James Joyce put words together beyond the rules of grammar to elicit unusual feelings. The search for what deeply moves us goes on at every hand.

The Spirit that moves us is forever unexpected in his coming. His coming invariably has a surprise quality; he comes "in such a day as ye think not." So in our study of Scripture and our conduct of worship we need to put ourselves in a position to experience novelty and to be moved. When we always know the outcome and when the expected answer is always evident, the Spirit is seldom present. The Spirit comes by moving us in new and surprising ways. We may then put ourselves in dramatic situations, express feelings that we have, even when they may come as a surprise.

There is, of course, the possibility that we will open ourselves to an undesirable spirit. Speaking in tongues and faith healing have gained much popularity and have been much criticized recently. They both let the person be moved in a manner spoken of above. However, when such emotion no longer contributes to understandable speech, when it no longer testifies of Christ, it becomes suspect. When faith healing tries in any manner to replace medical science or no longer trusts it at all, then such healing is very untrustworthy.

We know that not every spirit is of God. The valley of dry bones in Ezekiel, which seemed not to be of God, was lifted up and moved by the Spirit of God. If we turn away from the moving Spirit because the power of evil can also move us, then we prefer death to life. In a company where no one is moved by worship and study, God seems to be dead. But God is a God of the living, and to worship Him, to study the Scriptures is to be moved. Biblical simulation is designed to be a moving experience.

CONFLICT AND TRUST

To put oneself in the lived moment of the past is to open oneself to conflict. The decision about who was to succeed Moses as the leader of Israel was one of struggle. If you have any doubt about the struggle of Israel in the wilderness, read again of the way the people rebelled against Moses and of the anger Moses often felt toward the people. To enter into the lived moment of the choice of a first king for Israel is to enter into conflict. The emotions for and against Saul ran high. To stand in the Roman courtroom in which Jesus was tried is to enter a moment of electrifying high tension. If that tension is not recaptured in our own replay, we can be sure we have not thoroughly put ourselves into the drama. To study the Scripture as a present, living moment is to risk conflict.

Many of us have been taught too well to be dispassionate and to avoid conflict. Can an approach to Scripture that reintroduces passion possibly be acceptable in God's sight? The separation of personality into reason and emotion, with faith on the side of reason to the exclusion of emotion, is of Greek origin. The Hebrew approach to life is with "heart, soul, mind, and strength." We have to be willing to enter into conflict if we want to feel the living character of the biblical faith.

On the other hand, Christians know what it is to be torn apart by conflict. The stubbornness and hostility of church members have driven many not only from study groups, but also from every meeting of the church. Where is there a congregation that does not have serious conflicts? To open the door to conflict would seem to let nothing in that is not already present.

Conflict has both positive and negative potential. To enter into positive conflict is to feel at odds with another, but to appreciate fully the way the other feels and to make way for change. It is to set one's face toward the difficulties of the wilderness of controversy for the sake of the promise of better understanding that lies beyond. Negative conflict is that type in which participants give expression to their own frustration and hostility without any willingness to appreciate the feelings of those who are the object of their hostility. Negative conflict means to be consumed in one's own anger, locked into one's own point of view, incapable of compassion, hard of heart.

Persons in positive conflict acknowledge and express anger, but at the same time allow and hear the feelings of their opponents. Simulation and role play offer an opportunity for positive conflict because the persons involved realize that emotions are being expressed only for the sake of the simulation. Feelings that might not otherwise be acceptable can now be expressed in playfulness. The simulation also sets helpful limits. The situation is acted out for a certain time and then clearly stopped. Time is then given for participants to reflect upon what happened to them in the process. The simulation therefore allows a person to express and acknowledge conflict indirectly without pointedly intending to contradict another. It can be a doorway to positive conflict and new understanding.

While many people realize that a sense of guilt accompanies suppressed sexual feelings, it is not so commonly understood that the suppression of aggressive feelings can also lead to a strong sense of guilt. Many Christians have been so well taught to avoid all conflict that they feel very guilty about any inclination to debate or argue. This attitude does not eliminate arguments, as any church member knows, but it does make people feel very guilty whenever conflict occurs. Consequently, suppressed conflict takes the form of backbiting and gossip.

The forgiveness of sins releases us and frees us to argue with those with whom we disagree. It also frees us to hear and accept their dissatisfaction and disagreements with us. It allows conflict to lead to closer intimacy between persons. Suppressed hostility can lead only to coldness and distance. To permit the expression of conflict between persons is to show a large measure of trust in God's forgiveness and his power to reconcile. Taking the initiative to speak to one with whom we disagree is taking the eighteenth chapter of Matthew seriously. It is running the risk of negative conflict in the hope of reconciliation.

Willingness to accept interpersonal conflict is a part of trusting in God.

The Bible speaks often of hardness of heart. Is not such hardness an unwillingness to acknowledge the feelings within ourselves, both hostile and compassionate? Acknowledging hostile feelings is often the only door to feeling compassionate. Hardness of heart may take the form of expressing hostility without acknowledging that feeling. A person may be destructive and punitive without being aware of his own deepest feelings. Hardness of heart is overcome only with the open expression of trust and gratitude that is intrinsic to life. To trust deeply is to praise God, to express appreciation or anger to my neighbor without shutting out his response. Since simulations are an indirect way of expressing feelings and understanding other persons, they can be the first step toward overcoming hardness of heart.

BIBLICAL EXPECTANCY

Recent studies have uncovered the important role of eschatological expectation in the faith of those whose deeds are recorded in Scripture. To put it another way, trust in God has always meant an intense sense of what God is bringing about in the world. Jesus came announcing that the New Age was at hand. That sense of the imminence of the New Age is of critical importance for Christian faith.

Discussing expectancy and hope exhibits at the very least a secondary kind of knowledge. On the other hand, being caught in the decisions we have to make with their implicit hopes and doubts is becoming more fully aware of our own expectations. The advantage of a simulation is that we are put into the situation of a biblical event and asked to play out that event without being bound by how it actually turned out. The debate about whether or not to have a king in Israel becomes very real just because the outcome is not predetermined in a simulation. In that sense it becomes like the original event. The mixture of feelings, the hopes, and doubts begin to play in our own experience as they must have originally.

One cannot play out the events of the Bible without beginning to feel the high sense of expectancy they must have felt. One cannot enter into those events deeply without beginning to feel, perhaps ever so remotely, the trust in God's providence that allowed those decisions to be made. In a word the events of the Bible can become less mystical and never-never. They can be linked to the kinds of attitudes that each of us feels day by day. Our own sense of expectancy can be related to what God is doing in history. We may reject such expectancy but nevertheless it beckons us as we play out the biblical events. The simulation may become so powerful that many cherished ideas are challenged. Yet we cannot avoid such challenges when moved in the depths of our faith.

There is a widespread call for the renewal of hope in our day. That hope will come as we recover the sense of biblical expectancy in what is coming to be in the midst and at the end of our history. As it has been in the past, the study of Scripture is the key to the renewal of our lives. Scripture is the most important source in the renewal of the vitality of Christian faith. Life and Scripture belong to one another. The use of simulation may be one way of expressing and acting out that relationship.

IN SUMMARY

Why then use biblical simulations? What is their purpose? Far beyond curiosity and novelty their purpose is to allow scriptural events to be lived deeply, imaginatively, and intensely. They are designed to combine playfulness with discipline, imagination with study, not so much because such an approach is new, but rather because the Holy Spirit himself exhibits these qualities throughout the Bible. Simulations are designed to help us feel the biblical events, to identify with biblical personalities, to sense their dilemmas and choices, their hopes and expectations. Their purpose is to encourage within us a trust that can tolerate conflict and a hope that finds God's kingdom breaking in among us. Their purpose is to let the past be present in order that the future may be ours. Simulation is based upon a hermeneutic of the lived moment permeated with historical understanding. When in the past people have been able to identify closely with Scripture, there has been a renewal of faith. Our hope for renewal again lies in a deeper understanding of the meaning and power of the biblical message.

3. HOW TO PREPARE FOR A BIBLICAL SIMULATION

Once a group has decided to conduct a biblical simulation, it would do well to make the preparations we are about to describe. Very early some person or group will have to be selected to serve as coordinator. Let us speak of this role in the singular even though several persons may be filling it.

THE COORDINATOR

We speak of a coordinator rather than a "leader" or a "director" in order to make it clear that a simulation is not required to come out at a certain point. Whereas certain procedures must be followed, what happens in the process depends more upon the group than upon the coordinator. The coordinator must help the group understand the procedures, but he must not impose a straitjacket upon the process. His role in the process is to facilitate, stimulate, and enable persons to make their own discoveries. Participants' learnings come out of their own experiences in the simulation. Unless the coordinator has a vision of inductive, experiential learning, the exercise may become very mechanical.

Every simulation must have a coordinator who is thoroughly familiar with the purpose and design of the exercise. He should therefore read all the instructions carefully. It would be well for him to walk through the procedure with a number of people so that he becomes thoroughly familiar with it. We shall have more to say about the staff in a moment. It is axiomatic that the coordinator's doubts will be reflected by the participants; so it might be well to wait until he is enthusiastic about simulations before trying any. At least let him study the instructions carefully.

SELECTING A SIMULATION

One of the first questions to be considered is that of which simulation to use. You can base your choice upon the special interests of your group. If you are interested in church-state relationships, you might consider "Jeremiah's Trial" or "Josiah's Dilemma." "What's in a Word?" is designed to help people understand the reason for various versions of Scripture. What it means to be a Christian is a question raised by "The Council of Jerusalem." Usually several subjects are interwoven in the same simulation. "The Gifts of the Spirit" treats the charismatic movement, but the women's liberation question is there, too. Reading a simulation over will help you decide whether it touches upon your special interest.

You may want to make your choice upon the basis of the biblical passages under consideration. You will not likely find a better introduction to the study of the Book of Job than to simulate "Job and His Friends." "Josiah's Dilemma" is intended to be an introduction to the book of Deuteronomy. The simulation could be used as an introduction or a conclusion to weeks of study of that book. The subtitle in each case gives the primary scriptural passage upon which the exercise is based. The directions for small groups give dozens of additional passages that may be studied.

Other considerations may affect your choice. You may want to choose a simulation that illustrates a theme or a lesson you are already studying. Archibald MacLeish's play *J.B.* would go together beautifully with "Job and His Friends." Some of the exercises are more cognitive and some more dramatic. The group will have to have some interest in translation to do "What's in a Word?" Persons with no such aptitude or interests may be turned off by "What's in a Word?" "What Shall We Do with Jesus?" is highly dramatic and may be very emotional for some; it is therefore also highly interesting. Some of the simulations treat materials that are very familiar, such as "What Happened in the Garden?" Everyone knows something about Adam and Eve. However, very few know anything about seventh-century Judah, and they may therefore have difficulty with "Josiah's Dilemma" unless they do serious study. The size of the group and the setting may also affect your choice, but these matters are discussed below.

PARTICIPANTS

The divergence of interests of participants raises the more fundamental question of who can take part in a biblical simulation. The simulations in this book were designed for youth and adults. The instructions and procedures have a complexity that stimulates most young people and adults. High school youth are usually very eager to take part. Their willingness to throw themselves into dramatic roles adds a marvelous liveliness to the procedures. While adults may be more reserved, the purposefulness of the study picks up many people very quickly. People who do not like to be in the limelight may take a more retiring role without disrupting the procedure.

The youngest group to enjoy these simulations would probably be junior high age youth. Seventh and eighth graders are more and more able to make their own decisions, which is a central assumption of each simulation. If a junior high group can understand the subtleties of procedure, and if they are willing to do some serious study, they will enjoy taking part. Many junior highs are capable of simulating; you must assess your own group. It is even possible that with a resourceful teacher a group of advanced nine- to eleven-year-olds could enjoy simulation. Some teachers may want to try their own adaptations with that age group.

A special comment should be made here about college and seminary classes or retreats. While the simulations are designed to instruct people with no special training in Bible, they also may be used to raise very sophisticated questions. The simulation of "The Upper Room" can lead to a very advanced discussion of the synoptic problem. "What Shall We Do with Jesus?" can raise the most profound christological questions. "What's in a Word?" is worthy the study of any group of seminarians who are not already taking Greek. The authors have used several of these simulations in their seminary classes and know that they can be a tool for college and graduate education.

The objectivity of simulation lends itself to use by the public schools. While the exercises developed here do present various points of view represented within a biblical passage, they do not themselves promote a special point of view. They are rather a way of experiencing what happened. Though highly involving, they represent an objective approach to the study of religion. Public school classes in social studies and culture could use these simulations well within the guidelines set up by the Supreme Court about the "objective study of religion." In that case, of course, any suggestion about worship contained herein would have to be ignored.

The fact that simulations can be used by a variety of age levels and with various degrees of sophistication points to a very interesting characteristic. Youth and adults enjoy doing them together. The drama overcomes the generation gap. A teenage son upon seeing his father take the role of God can say to him, "That's a good role for you, since you do it all the time anyhow." In a playful setting the truth becomes more tolerable. We have often seen the generation gap disappear. We have seen youth and adults enjoying a simulation together when they would not otherwise attend church together.

A SERIES OF SIMULATIONS

You may wonder whether to use more than one simulation during a weekend retreat, during a week's conference, or, for that matter, as a part of a longer course. In our judgment it is better not to use two simulations on the same day. To do so means that each of them is being pared down to several hours. You certainly derive more benefit by using a longer schedule of six hours or more for one simulation. A full day could very profitably be spent by using the morning for small-group preparation, the afternoon for simulation, and the evening for debriefing. You will need study aids and art materials to do this, but a full day makes for an excellent experience.

Two or more simulations should be conducted on different days. You might have one each day of the week during a conference or a camp. Such an experience could be very intensive. Your plan ought to be announced well ahead of time so that participants have some idea of what to expect. If only a short time is given to simulation each day, then you may want to reduce the number of simulations used to allow more adequate treatment of each.

A series of simulations may be used as a part

of an ongoing course. One or several may be mixed into a course to increase motivation and interest in the problem being considered. This raises the question of a course built entirely upon simulations. Our collection is designed with such a course in mind. A group meeting for one or two hours a week could profitably spend up to four weeks on each exercise, or a total of forty-four weeks in all. In effect they could have a year's course in Bible on the basis of this collection of simulations.

Such a course would cover many of the basic biblical themes. The Pentateuch is treated in "What Happened in the Garden?" "Josiah's Dilemma," and "The Taking of the Land." Biblical history is treated in "Josiah's Dilemma" and "The Making of a King." "Jeremiah's Trial" is the study of a major prophet, and "Job and His Friends" is the heart of wisdom literature. The Gospels are the focus of "What Shall We Do with Jesus?" and "The Upper Room." The letters of Paul are the subject of "The Gifts of the Spirit," and Acts is studied in "The Council of Jerusalem." In addition the problem of translation is the focus of "What's in a Word?" and "The Upper Room" cannot but raise the question of the canonization of Scripture. Were a class to use all of these simulations in a serious study, they would have a good introduction to the whole Bible.

THE SETTING

Really to appreciate the different settings in which simulations may be used, one must also be aware of how they may be adapted to fit different schedules. Of that we shall be concerned in a moment. Let it only be said here that they can be varied from one hour to more than six hours.

While one hour is not the most effective schedule, since so little can be done in that time, nevertheless it is what many groups have available to them. A one-hour schedule fits well into a school period. Continuing the same simulation over three or four sessions also allows its use within one-hour periods.

We have used simulations during the Sunday morning worship service. In one case the congregation set aside the whole morning of three hours for the event. We used "The Upper Room" and concluded with the Breaking of Bread that had been planned as a part of that simulation. "The Gifts of the Spirit" also concludes with a very high moment of worship. See the comments on worship in the next chapter.

A two-hour adaptation lends itself well to an evening meeting, e.g., a Sunday evening. With two hours a group can have a much more satisfactory experience than with one hour. Two- or three-hour adaptations can also be used in retreat, camping, or conference settings. Different simulations could be done on successive evenings. The retreat or camping setting usually allows a four- to six-hour schedule, which everyone will find to be the most satisfactory. All the decisions called for in the instructions can at least be touched upon in that time.

We have already mentioned that study groups, schools, and colleges can use these exercises for more serious study. They are designed for intensive study and become highly effective when good study aids are available. The same simulation may be continued over several periods to get the best use of it.

One final possibility is to develop a six- to twelve-week study group around one simulation. A study group could easily use the format of "The Upper Room" to study the eucharistic account in close detail for many weeks. Such a study could be the basis for a worship renewal in a congregation.

STAFF

If only a dozen persons are to be involved in the simulation, the coordinator can likely carry it himself. However, when larger numbers are involved, i.e., from twenty to one hundred or more, then the coordinator by all means ought to select a staff of at least one person for every ten participants. For example, were thirty persons to take part, then the coordinator ought to have at least three staff persons to help him. The coordinator may want a larger number of staff helpers, but he will probably find it unwieldy to work with a staff of more than twelve persons. If the simulation is to be done at a youth conference or some other setting where the coordinator cannot choose a staff ahead of time, then he might very well pick some people on the spot to help him. He may orient them at a meal together.

The coordinator and the staff should go through each part of the simulation and get it clearly in mind before introducing it to the whole group. Let the staff look up the biblical passages and role-play some of the situations so that they feel at home with what is about to be done. It is important that the staff do more than talk about the simulation. Whatever you expect to happen in the actual event should begin to happen with the staff. If the simulation is to be enjoyed, as it should be, then the staff meeting ought to be joyful. Suggestions from the staff ought to be tried out by the staff itself. If the staff members cannot get enthusiastic about what they are doing, there is little chance that anyone else will be inspired.

We recommend that the staff members' orientation not exclude them from taking part in the simulation; they should take part like anyone else. They must understand very well the assignments of the small groups, because it is there that they will be most helpful. The staff meeting should therefore include a careful look at the roles of the various small groups. The staff should also know the rules of the simulation itself. It will undoubtedly go much smoother if several participants are already aware of the rules.

SCHEDULE

The adaptation of the schedule to fit their own situation will be one of the key responsibilities of coordinator and staff. Let us consider first single sessions of different lengths, and then multiple sessions.

All the simulations have a brief introduction, time for small-group preparation, the actual simulation period, and finally the debriefing period. The simulation will go much better if there is adequate time for preparation. Also keep in mind that the debriefing period is so important that it should never be omitted. The following table offers schedules.

	Hour	Two Hours	Four Hours	Six Hours
Introduction	10 min.	15 min.	20 min.	½ hr.
Small groups	20 min.	45 min.	100 min.	2½ hrs.
Simulation	15 min.	30 min.	60 min.	2 hrs.
Debriefing	15 min.	30 min.	60 min.	1 hr.

These times can be varied somewhat as long as you remember that all four periods are essential. Periods of two hours or more may require a break. A brief interval for relaxation comes best between the small groups and the simulation. Refreshments can be served then. However, the study groups may be informal enough that anyone may have coffee and cookies at any time, if available.

Multiple sessions present still another problem. The schedule breaks nicely into two sessions with the introduction and small groups during the first session, and the simulation and debriefing during the second. If you want three sessions, begin with the introduction and small groups. During the second session give the small groups a few minutes to review their strategies, then move into one of the simulation decisions, and finally spend a few minutes debriefing. In the last session begin with a second simulation problem and allow ample time for debriefing. Four sessions allow two periods for small-group study, one for the simulation, and one for debriefing. In the case of multiple sessions the reports of the chroniclers will be useful during debriefing.

The longer periods allow more time for study and more time for making symbols or any other art work the group may want to do. Multiple sessions permit participants to do more serious study on their own. The longer simulation periods allow for the complications of the decision process to develop. Any group can easily be involved in the simulation period for two or three hours, not to mention the small-group preparation time. One caution—role playing of longer than two or three hours is difficult for some people to carry out. The simulation period ordinarily ought not be extended beyond that time.

GROUPING

Each of the simulations included here requires small-group preparation. For example, "The Council of Jerusalem" has the following four groups: Suffering Servants, Apocalypticists, Zealots, and Hellenists. Everyone will take part in one or another of these groups as preparation is made for the simulation. Each group is asked to play out a certain point of view, so that when all come together, the differences inevitably produce dramatic conflict. The heart of the simulation is the resolution of those differences between groups. Most of the simulations use four groups, but "What Happened in the Garden?" needs only three, and "Job and His Friends" may be played with six. "What Happened in the Garden?" is designed as a trial; so the small groups will be preparing briefs for prosecution and defense. "Josiah's Dilemma" follows a debate format, and the small groups are to prepare their cases. Most of the simulations are in the format of a conference, with voting delegates from each small group around a table. The small groups must use the preparation time to develop their positions and strategy.

The following table will help you set up the small groups:

Total no. of persons	No. of groups	Number in each group	Voting delegates in each group
8- 48	4	2-12	3
49- 96	8	6-12	2
97-144	12	8-12	1

The smallest number of persons for most of the simulations is eight. Fewer will not have the dramatic effect; groups might have only one member. Twelve to fifty seems to be a very good number. Our experience is that when the group exceeds fifty persons, it becomes difficult for everyone to participate actively. A helping staff then becomes very important.

If you have more than fifty persons, you have the option of running two simulations at once. They could be run in separate places and then be brought together to compare notes. Still another option is to break the whole assembly into clusters of twelve and let each cluster run its own simulation. This would be an especially good plan for "What's in a Word?" or "Job and His Friends." "Job and His Friends" allows for intensive conversations between friends, and "What's in a Word?" illustrates how different translations come about. You may, of course, see still other possibilities for design variations.

SPACE

Every simulation included in this collection requires a room in which all the participants can be assembled at one time. Furthermore, it will be far better if you can use a room with movable chairs and tables so that the space can be arranged for whatever size assembly you may have. In most of the exercises there will be much movement around the room, in and out of chairs. There should be enough space that each person can get to any other person in the room. Movable chairs and plenty of walking space will help.

You may have the chairs arranged in semicircular rows or other lecture arrangements for the coordinator's opening introductory remarks. This will mean that the chairs must be rearranged while everyone is in small groups. It is an unnecessary delay to try to direct members of a large group to arrange their own chairs when they return for the simulation period. It is better to have the chairs properly arranged when the group reenters.

The proper arrangement for the conference format is to have delegate chairs around a table in the center of the room. The table is actually optional, but it does help note takers. The chairs are then arranged so that each small group is seated immediately behind its delegates. Aisles should separate the groups from one another. The purpose of this arrangement is to let the members of any small group caucus among themselves whenever they choose, while at the same time permitting them to move around to speak to other persons

whenever they like. For "The Council of Jerusalem" each of the groups (Suffering Servants, Apocalypticists, Zealots, and Hellenists) should be able to caucus with its own representatives before a vote. The representatives should be seated around a table so that they can carry on the debate. Each person should be able to move to other persons in the room for purposes of lobbying.

Not all the simulations follow a conference format. However, in each instance it is important that the members of the same small group be seated together during the simulation period. In the trial scene for "What Happened in the Garden?" members of each small group will be seated together to allow prosecution and defense to call witnesses from their own groups. There must of course be a witness stand, as well as a group of chairs for those who are the judges.

In "Josiah's Dilemma" a debate takes place before the king; so the groups should be arranged around the king. In "Job and His Friends" each of the friends must be close enough to Job to speak intimately with him and yet be allowed to counsel with his own group when he chooses.

The seating principles are these:

a. Small groups must be seated close enough that all members of that group can confer with each other.
b. Representatives must be a part of the small group and yet a part of the central action of the simulation (trial, debate, etc.).
c. There must be enough separation for persons to move around.

It is highly desirable that there be a separate homeroom for each small group. The groups need the privacy of developing their plans without the knowledge of other groups. Each small-group room ought to have one or more tables, enough chairs, and space to move around. There ought to be space and facilities for each group to make symbols and banners. You may also want the group to have access to refreshments.

The final debriefing period will be done with the whole group, following the simulation periods. It is recommended that you rearrange seating in order to symbolize that roles are being dropped. That is done simply by asking people to set the chairs in semicircular rows and to seat themselves near someone from another small group. During debriefing you may use micro-groups of two, three, or four, but the micro-groups can be formed by a simple shifting of chairs. In this case it does not matter that the microgroups overhear each other.

You may wonder whether a simulation can be carried out if you are confined to the use of one single room. It certainly can, if you are able to separate the groups far enough that they do not overhear each other's planning.

But suppose you are confined to a room with nonmovable furniture, e.g., the church sanctuary. Such a room is a major obstacle, but you may be able to use it. Can the small groups be separated far enough to plan privately? Can the small groups be seated in such a way that they may confer with themselves and still take part in the simulation action? Can the simulated action (trial, council, etc.) take place? If the answer is yes in all three cases, you may proceed, even though the fixed furniture may inhibit spontaneity.

Perhaps you will want to try a simulation in the out-of-doors, or around a campfire. If you can comfortably see to study the Scripture passages, and if you don't mind standing or sitting on the ground, you may try it. "What Happened in the Garden?" is made to order for the out-of-doors. However, should you not be able to read and study the biblical passages, you should not proceed with any simulation.

Finally there is the question of the decoration of the main room. Certain accessories can help create a mood, although they are not at all essential. The setting for "Josiah's Dilemma" could be made to look like the king's throne room. The room for "Job and His Friends" could be made to appear like the city dump. The room for "What Happened in the Garden?" could appear to be a courtroom or, of course, a garden. The text for "What's in a Word?" could be printed on a large poster in actual Greek script. The room for "The Gifts of the Spirit" might give evidence of being in Corinth, an ancient Mediterranean seaport. Such preparations add mood, but you should not lose sight of the larger purpose of the simulation.

MATERIALS

Materials will vary from simulation to simulation, but certain materials are almost always called for. Every person will need a Bible. These simulations cannot be done unless there are Bibles for all, or almost all persons. Sometimes you will need various versions, and sometimes, the same version. It would be ideal for you to have a single version for everyone with many different versions available for reference, e.g., King James, Revised Standard, New English, Moffatt, Phillips, American Standard, etc.

You should also have Bible study aids

available for each group. Such aids include Bible dictionaries, concordances, and commentaries. Paper and pencils should be available for everyone, but especially for the chroniclers.

Each group is asked to make a symbol or poster. You should furnish construction paper, poster board, oak-tag, burlap, felt scraps, scissors, glue, felt-tipped pens, and anything else that will help them in this task.

Special interest can be created by making costume materials available. Cloth draped to simulate ancient clothing, choir robes, veils, hair coverings, early Christian symbols, and anything reminiscent of the period is useful.

Finally you may want to provide refreshments. We have already mentioned that something to eat or munch on during the study period or during the break adds a good note of informality. For "The Upper Room" you may want to have bread and wine as well as other foods available if the groups decide to carry out their service.

VARYING THE DESIGN

You are encouraged to create additional roles to help add interest during the simulation. In "The Taking of the Land" you may introduce one of the spies who was sent to Jericho. Titus may be brought forward in "The Council of Jerusalem." Jesus may appear in "What Shall We Do with Jesus?" These examples are written into the simulations, but you may come up with suggestions of your own. Such persons can add an interesting dramatic note. You may want to give thought to such roles ahead of time.

You may also want to try other variations. The simulations are balanced so that decision upon any issue will likely begin with a deadlock. The challenge is to work through the problem. If your variation destroys that balance of differences, you will abandon the key element of the design. The design may then lose its dynamic quality. That will happen, for example, should you drop from four to three small groups. Everything can then be decided in the first several minutes with no debate or discussion. Nevertheless we encourage you to try out your own variations.

The conference and the council model can easily be interchanged. The conference uses group representatives and gives each group the same number of votes. The council lets everyone speak and vote, but requires a two-thirds vote to pass anything. Most of our simulations follow the conference model, but you may prefer the council model.

A FINAL WORD

We recommend that you announce the simulation well in advance so that the people present have actively chosen to come. If participants feel that something was sprung upon them, they may resent it.

Reading all these notes, you may decide that a simulation needs too much preparation to be worth the effort. Such is not the case. The most important thing is to get a sense of what is to happen. This you can get only by trying your wings. Once you have experienced one or two simulations, you will find it quite easy to get the next one started. Of course larger groups and longer periods require more preparation, but the greater effort also pays off in greater benefits.

4. HOW TO CONDUCT A BIBLICAL SIMULATION

WRITTEN INSTRUCTIONS

The coordinator should begin with an introductory explanation of the meaning and purpose of biblical simulation as well as the special procedures to be followed. Even though group members may have taken part in many simulations, they still need to know the special procedures of the one in which they are about to take part. Sometime during the introduction the coordinator will want to pass out printed copies of the rules and instructions. It is best to make a general statement of introduction and then to divide into groups. When the groups have been formed, then the proper guidesheet of instructions can be given to each group.

You can get by with one set of general instructions per group, but everything will be better understood if you are able to have several copies per group. Of course it is best to have one copy of the instructions available for each person. In this book one tear-out sheet of instructions is provided for each group, in addition to a set for the coordinator. Additional copies may be made as needed. To rely only upon oral instructions is treacherous. If you have only a few copies of the general instructions, you would do better to copy the essential points on newsprint for all.

The simulations are written so that each small group has a different guidesheet of special instructions. The whole process will move more dramatically if no group is aware of the other group's special instructions. You must therefore have at least one set of special instructions for each small group. We recommend that you do not read each small group's instructions before the whole assembly. The problem of informing everyone is best resolved by having copies of special instructions available for every member of each group.

Again, in this book one set of special instructions is provided for each group; these special instructions are found on the reverse side of the general instructions for each group. Additional copies of the special instructions may also be made as needed.

Some groups may want to have the instructions passed out ahead of time, perhaps a week before the simulation is to begin. We know of one instance in which participants insisted upon having copies of every group's special instructions passed out well in advance. They said that they found it useful to know the various instructions so as to plan their own strategies. However, we recommend that you give each group only its own special instructions. After the simulation is completed, you can distribute all the instructions to everyone.

If you do plan to pass out instructions in advance of the simulation, then you must divide into groups so that each group will receive the proper set of instructions. You could pass out the sets of instructions at random, letting all those who receive the same guidesheet constitute a group. Whenever the simulation is to be carried on over two or more successive weeks, everyone will, of course, receive written instructions during the first session. The biblical passages may be studied between sessions, although the most effective study will be done together in small groups. The reason for this is that the study itself is part and parcel of the group's coming to a sense of identity while forming its own strategies.

INTRODUCTORY COMMENTS

All simulations begin with some introductory remarks. These may be brief or more extended, according to the previous experience of the participants, but some comment will be needed. Unless the group is very experienced, you should begin with some explanation of what a simulation is, how to participate, and what to expect. You might begin in the following manner:

This afternoon and this evening we are going to play out a biblical simulation. We shall reenact a certain biblical scene in order that we may study and appreciate it by being directly involved with the events described there. The purpose of a simulation is to make a passage of Scripture vivid, powerful, and compelling to us.

Each of you will be assigned to one of several groups which will interact with one another during the simulation. We shall then discuss what we have learned from our experience together. In a moment we will divide into groups, each of which will receive a special set of instructions. However, before we do that, let me say a few words about how to take part.

For the simulation you will be playing the role of a certain person or group of people who are described in the Bible. It is your task to represent the attitudes of those people as nearly as you can. To do so we suggest that you approach the role somewhat playfully and imaginatively. Try to find out what these persons thought and believed, but be free enough to interpret for our simulated setting. If you will enjoy yourself, use some imagination, and follow some of your own spontaneous hunches, you will find that the situation will come to life for you. You are to try to be true to your group identity as we begin, but you are also to follow whatever changes in attitude you may have as you play the role.

Please remember that a simulation does not necessarily come to the same conclusion as that described in the passage of Scripture we are studying. You are to represent truly the attitudes of the people involved, but you are to let the events develop as they will. Indeed you are to be creative and alive in your plans to get your point of view accepted by the other groups.

Since we do not know how the simulation will turn out, it should be far more genuine and alive than were we simply to mimic the biblical events. As you plan and decide, you may find that you suddenly understand why people acted the way they did. This is true even though you reach different conclusions than they did. The living reality of your own simulated decision helps you appreciate the living reality of the original. So let your decisions be real and genuine; do not let them be overly bound by what happened in the original event. In this way we will be able to better appreciate and learn from what is described in Scripture.

You may adapt the above comments to your own situation, or you may develop your own. In either case you should certainly read the chapters entitled "What Is a Biblical Simulation?" and "Why Use Biblical Simulations?" They explain in greater detail what is only summarized above, and they will give you a better background from which to answer questions.

After the more general comments of purpose and procedures, you should proceed to a consideration of the particular simulation before you. You might read the "situation" aloud and explain the schedule to be followed. You may then divide into small groups and distribute the instructions. Briefly indicate the tasks for the whole group and for the small groups. Allow time for questions, and then give each group its room assignment.

Let us take as an example "The Gifts of the Spirit." You should read the section entitled "The Situation" together:

The purpose of this simulation is to gain a greater appreciation for the gifts of the Spirit and to celebrate the working of the Spirit in your own group. You are to simulate the Corinthian church in a council meeting in which they are to decide whether to permit speaking in tongues to be a part of the regular worship service. You are then to name some of the gifts of the Spirit in your group and to celebrate their presence.

If you were to use a two-hour schedule, you might then continue in this way:

For the remainder of the time we have this evening we shall spend forty-five minutes in small groups preparing for the Corinthian council meeting. We will then have thirty minutes for the council meeting itself, and thirty minutes to discuss what happened to us (the debriefing period). Your task during the council meeting will be to decide whether or not to allow speaking in tongues, and if so in what manner it should be allowed.

(You have decided that there is not time to debate whether or not Paul's letter will be read, although the matter may come up without your introducing it.)

To prepare for the council meeting, you will spend the next forty-five minutes in one of four small groups: the Paulinists are those who sympathize with Paul; the Petrine group follows the views of Peter; the Apollos group follows after Apollos; and the Christ group has special knowledge that comes with belief in Christ.

You should now proceed with the division into groups. This can be done in at least three ways.
1. People may choose the groups they want to

join. Freedom of choice heightens motivation for many, but it also often leaves one group especially weak.

2. You may simply assign people into groups. The staff members can make the assignments ahead of time if they know who will be there. This allows the staff to be sure that there are active, expressive people in each group. However, some people feel manipulated by this procedure. A variation is to ask two or three people to be in each group, and then let others choose their own group. The disadvantage is the obvious favoritism shown.

3. Finally you may simply assign people at random, e.g., by counting off in fours. This usually works out very well with most people satisfied. Should one group be short of youth or men, simply ask several people to exchange. Another variation of random assignment is to have people take name tags of different colors as they arrive. All persons with the same color tag make up a group. You could mix the instruction sheets at random, and then simply pass them out. Whoever gets a certain sheet then becomes a member of that group. You could also let everyone sitting in one part of the room be a certain group.

Having divided into groups, you should get all persons of the same group together and seated again. Then you will be able to pass out the proper instruction sheets to each group. Go over the tasks for each small group and for the simulation itself and let people know about the debriefing period.

For example, after the division into groups, you might make the following comment:

When you come together as a small group, you should appoint a leader who will direct your preparation. You should also appoint a chronicler to record what happens in your group.

In a moment I shall pass out to you an instruction sheet which will give you biblical passages for you to examine together in order to establish your group identity. You should decide what your view is about speaking in tongues, being as true to your group as you can. You may want to prepare a symbol to represent your group. Poster paper and felt pens are in your room for that purpose. You should also give some thought to how you will persuade other groups to your view and where you are willing to make concessions. Please return to this room in forty-five minutes for the council meeting.

When we have completed the council meeting, we shall rearrange our chairs, drop our roles, and discuss together what we have learned.

You should allow time for questions of clarification. Be sure to encourage such questions, because lack of clarity can be a great impediment. On the other hand, some things are best answered by beginning. Give the groups their room assignments and send them out for the preparation period.

THE SMALL GROUPS

Much of the value of a simulation comes in the work of the small groups. They study various biblical passages together and try to come to some common interpretation of those passages. The study is purposive, being directed to immediate use in the simulation situation. The voice of every person finally counts in what is decided.

The coordinator should very quickly visit each of the small groups to see that directions are well understood. If you are working with a staff, at least one staff member should be in each small group. Staff could possibly be assigned to more than one group. The point is that someone should be available to clarify directions for the small groups. The coordinator or staff member may want to visit each group to check on progress. The groups should not only study Scripture passages, but also should make plans for their points of view and strategies during the simulation.

The first task of each small group will be to select a leader to chair its preparation and to lead participants during the simulation. This in itself sometimes can be an agonizing decision, but the process is important because the basis for leadership in the simulation is being established. The chronicler may want to record the process by which the leader is appointed.

Nearly all the simulations call for the appointment of a chronicler. The chronicler makes notes on what happens during the group preparation and also during the simulation itself. He records from the point of view of his own group so that the contrasts between groups can be brought out during the debriefing period. The chronicler should record not only the decisions made, but he should also note the process by which they were made. His notes need not be elaborate, but they should be sufficient to be helpful during the debriefing period. The chronicler becomes even more important when the simulation is split into sessions that occur on different days.

After the preliminary appointments the group begins to establish its identity by examining the biblical texts. Should they be following an abbreviated schedule, the group members will find that they cannot possibly study all the passages listed. We suggest that the various passages be assigned to different persons, each of whom is to read through a passage and summarize it for the whole group. In that way many passages can be touched upon in a few minutes.

A longer schedule of several hours permits the group to make a much more relaxed and thorough study of each passage. In effect the group must adapt its approach to the time available. Suggestions by staff or coordinator can be very helpful at this point. The longer period allows the group to refer to Bible dictionaries, commentaries, various versions, and other aids. Here again the group may proceed more efficiently if individuals or pairs study a particular passage thoroughly and then report to the others.

From its study the small group should arrive at a common identity and should then turn to consider its position regarding the major decisions to be made during the simulation. For example, in "What Shall We Do with Jesus?" the Sadducees under Caiaphas's leadership will need to decide who Jesus is and what his purpose is, what should be done with Jesus, and who is to carry out this decision. The coordinator or staff member should see that the small groups allow about half of their preparation time for strategizing.

The guidesheet for each small group will give suggestions about that group's position. In the example above, the guidesheet for the Sadducees explains why they considered Jesus to be a threat. The group should take these clues and forge out its own position. They may take some liberty in doing this, but should they stray too far from the actual position of the Sadducees, the simulation will lose its power.

Each group should also consider where it will or will not make concessions. The simulations are set up for the most part so that issues are deadlocked; someone must make concessions. Each group should consider what means of influence it can bring upon other groups. This process of give-and-take often becomes the heart of the exercise. The chronicler should record important shifts in strategy in his own group.

One of the most interesting parts of the simulation can be the making and displaying of symbols. With a brief schedule a hastily crayoned sign, such as SADDUCEAN POWER, can be displayed. Longer schedules allow for more thoughtful symbols. A song may be composed; a banner constructed; a costume developed. The use of costumes, signs, banners, and other symbols adds much vitality to the whole process. There is much room for creativity at this point.

THE SIMULATION

After a period of preparation the small groups are called together to begin the simulation itself. You may have a problem getting the groups to assemble in that they may have still further preparations to make. A five-minute notice will help them complete their work on time. The coordinator should be sure that the chairs are properly arranged beforehand, especially if a large group is involved. Each group is to be seated so that the members of that group can confer with each other at any time. For further comments on scheduling and seating refer to chapter 3. Be sure that a table is present if it is called for. You may also want to decorate the room in an appropriate way, although decoration is certainly not essential.

In each of our simulations someone must play the role of chairman, leader, king, etc. Sometimes the choice of the leader becomes a major task of the simulation. We have found it best in that instance for the coordinator to direct the group until the leader is chosen. You could also allow the group to resolve the problem as best it can with no outside direction. When you have only a few minutes for the simulation, you are well advised simply to ask someone to serve as leader. Sometimes the coordinator or a staff member should serve as leader, e.g., when the groups are small and evenly balanced as they stand. In any event the coordinator must see that the problem of a leader is cared for. You may also want to have the leader appropriately costumed.

As the groups assemble, the coordinator should review with everyone "The Tasks of the Simulation" and "The Rules of the Simulation," both of which are to be found on the guidesheets for each group. For example, in "Jeremiah's Trial for Treason" the group is to decide:

a. whether Jeremiah is guilty of treason;

b. if so, what penalty should be enacted;

c. if not, whether his activity be curtailed.

The group may or may not get all of these tasks done within the time limit. It is far more important that time be left for debriefing than that the tasks be finished.

The rules of the simulation vary according to the basic design. There are five different basic designs, namely: conference, council, debate, trial, and counseling. More of the simulations follow the conference design than any other; so let us consider that one first.

The conference model is set up so that each group has one or several representatives seated at the table or in a central circle. Only the representatives may vote and only they may speak to the issues being discussed. However, any member of a group may tap out his own representative and take his place. If the small-group leader is replaced, he still retains his role as leader. Small groups may caucus together before any vote is taken.

The conference model is designed so that the vote on most issues will result in a tie. An even distribution of power is achieved by giving each group the same number of votes. The simulation leader should not break a tie by casting his own vote, else the issues could be too easily resolved. When a tie vote is reached, the coordinator may have to suggest that the small groups get together to decide what to do.

Most issues can be resolved only by some kind of bargaining between groups. One group may give on one point if another group gives on a different point. To enhance such bargaining, several members of each small group not seated at the table may try to persuade those of another group, or they may try to work out an agreement with them. Once everyone sees the impasse in voting, someone will likely come up with some way around. The heart of the simulation is grappling with the deadlock. For example, in "The Taking of the Land," the priestly class under Levi may agree to vote for Joshua if he in turn will follow their directions in the conquest of Jericho. A few suggestions by the coordinator can enliven the process at this point.

The coordinator may also suggest that certain special witnesses are present. In "The Taking of the Land," the spy who visited Rahab in Jericho might be brought after a leader is selected. Further suggestions are given in "The Instructions to the Coordinator." No final blueprint can be given for the decision process, since the imagination of the group and of the staff will finally make the simulation go.

A second model is that of a council. It is very similar to the conference model except that everyone may speak to the issue and everyone may vote. All decisions should be made by two-thirds vote in the council model to insure that a genuine exchange of views takes place. Any small group may call for a caucus before a vote, and several delegates from each group are free to lobby with other groups.

With the council model as with the

conference model, the groups will reach an impasse in voting. The two-thirds voting rule guarantees that should the groups vary slightly in number, further negotiation will still be necessary. At the point of impasse the coordinator may find it necessary to suggest that the groups negotiate with one another. Once they catch a vision of the possibilities, they will begin actively to find ways around the impasse. The introduction of special roles, such as the spy to Jericho, is very appropriate for the council model.

"The Upper Room" and "The Gifts of the Spirit" are written according to the council model, but you can adapt any of the conference simulations to fit the council model. You will want to use the model that brings the greatest involvement and exchange of opinion in your group.

A third model is that of the debate. Here each of the small groups presents a case and has an opportunity for rebuttal. The judge or the king hears the arguments and makes a decision. The small group will likely designate someone or several persons to present the case, but there is no reason that others from that group cannot speak up as long as time remains. You will need a timekeeper in this model. If time allows, the formal debate may then be followed by open debate, as is suggested in "Josiah's Dilemma." Encouragement by the coordinator, publicly or privately, can add to the liveliness of the open debate.

A fourth model is that of the trial. "What Happened in the Garden?" is carried out as a trial. One group plays the part of God, deciding what punishment should be given. The prosecution must prepare a case against Adam, Eve, and the serpent. The defense seeks to defend them. Someone from prosecution and someone from defense will act as lawyers, although anyone from either group may replace his own lawyer. Those playing the parts of Adam, Eve, and the serpent must remain in those roles throughout the simulation. As coordinator you may help the groups plan their cases and carry out the court procedure. Trials are commonly enough understood that people enter easily into the trial model.

A fifth model is the counseling relationship. "Job and His Friends" is designed in this way. Each group takes a certain point of view in trying to counsel Job. No group decision is being made, except as the small groups decide how to approach Job. Each group will have one representative counseling Job. You can encourage the counselors to speak when they will; the exchange can be very intense. Anyone in a small group may take the place of his representative, and that includes the Job group. You may have to encourage people at this point, since there is often a reluctance to take someone else's place.

In summary the coordinator should be sure that the rules and the tasks are understood by everyone. He should get the simulation started, either by seeing that the group selects a leader or by acting as temporary leader himself. He should offer procedural suggestions to the group or to individuals to keep the process moving. His suggestions will depend a great deal upon whether the simulation is designed upon the model of a conference, council, debate, trial, or counseling relationship. Finally, he will bring the simulation to a close.

SPECIAL PROBLEMS

Participants will often ask whether to "give in" so that a decision can be made. The question comes up especially from persons who cannot wholeheartedly play the role assigned to them. They begin to ask whether they can vote their convictions. There is no clear answer to this question. Each person is to be as true to his role as he can, but he also should allow his mind to be changed when he really feels it changing. If people do not play their roles, there will be no simulation; and if they do not change their minds, there will be no resolution to the problems posed. Be sure that the assigned attitudes are given expression, and then let people change their minds as they feel led.

Often people will want to interject current materials into the simulation. Participants will be very inclined to interject their own eucharistic tradition into "The Upper Room" drama. They should be reminded that they are in the second century and that current ideas were not even known then. A tactful reminder can open up whole new realms of understanding for those playing the roles.

The coordinator and staff will inevitably be faced with the problem of when to intervene. Two appropriate times for intervention are when there is a misunderstanding of procedure or when the process is lagging. However, the group can sometimes resolve such difficulties itself. Intervention should enhance rather than stifle the group's creativity.

Groups are often at a loss when they come up against a tie vote. Struggling with deadlock is critical to the simulation model. However, should the group fall into lethargy, a simple suggestion about caucusing or bargaining with another group may help the process along. A few suggested stratagems may advance the process. Suggesting to one person that his group may want to work out an exchange of concessions with another group can add new life to the drama. Asking a person to play the role of Moses or someone relevant to the situation can add interest. The coordinator himself may play such a role.

Improvisation is to be encouraged. Occasionally the rules may be changed, although that should not be done too easily. If the conflict that is built into the design is lost, then the drama and much of the potential learning may also be lost. Still the group should be encouraged to improvise and find its own direction, perhaps even to the point of changing rules.

A special kind of intervention is that of bringing the simulation to a close. The most obvious time to close is according to the prearranged schedule. Often the group is in the middle of a decision and does not wish to close. It is better to give the group an additional five minutes and then close than to forgo the debriefing period. The decisions do not have to be made, but it is very important to summarize what has been learned.

Should all the decisions be completed, something that will seldom happen, you may bring the simulation to a close. Again, it is not unusual for people to begin dropping out of their roles and to start analyzing what is happening. In effect they have begun the debriefing process. Should that happen to any large degree, the coordinator may officially close the simulation and begin the debriefing.

Another special problem is that of observers. Some may want to observe rather than take part. Observers generally do not appreciate the drama, since much of the action takes place in private conversation. Many people will take part if they can be assured that they will not have to make a speech. Indeed anyone may take a more passive role in a group if he likes. You can allow a few to be an audience, if they insist, but a larger audience simply will not appreciate what is happening. Simulation, unlike traditional drama, is not designed for audiences.

One reason that some persons do not participate actively is that they feel poorly informed about the biblical passage being discussed. They would rather not speak than to show their ignorance. The better informed begin to take the more active roles. This is inevitable but can be modified. The coordinator may suggest that taking part does not depend upon how much one knows, but upon one's willingness to put oneself in the role.

The opposite problem is that of those who become overly involved. Should people begin to show emotional reactions, it is time to intervene. You may talk privately to such a person or persons, or you may have to terminate the simulation and begin the debriefing.

DEBRIEFING

The final period of a simulation is called the debriefing session. It is a time when people express how they feel and what they have learned. Suggestions for debriefing are to be found on the guidesheets. The coordinator's role is that of giving people an opportunity to express themselves. He should not predetermine what they are to learn, but he should see that what has been learned be expressed and summarized. If this is not done, much excitement but little that is actually remembered will result from the simulation.

The first thing to be done in the debriefing is to instruct people to drop the roles they have been playing. The words of instruction are not enough in themselves. Changing the seating arrangement, laying aside costumes and symbols, and changing whatever has been set up to promote the simulation will be necessary. Changing the seating is important in order to get people out of their own small groups and beside someone from a different group. The dropping of roles should be acted out in one of the dramatic ways just mentioned.

The coordinator should encourage two kinds of expressions: feelings and learnings. Simply ask questions, such as "What happened to you?" and "How did you feel?" Encourage expression of feeling in every way that you can. Such expression helps people to get out of the role. Expression of feeling should go on as long as people desire to talk.

The next important question is "What did you learn?" Here a chalkboard or newsprint is useful. If learnings are not voiced and summarized, they are less likely to be remembered. One effective way to allow everyone to express feelings or learnings is to work in microgroups of two, three, or four. You can also assign each microgroup a different learning question. After five or ten minutes in microgroups let those who wish report what they have been talking about. It is

not so important to hear from each group as to keep the discussion lively, open, and centered.

Following the microgroup discussions, you should call upon the chroniclers. Their observations should stimulate much discussion and further observations. The coordinator will do well if he gives the discussion a definite direction without controlling what is said. It is very important to summarize what was learned from the passage. You may want to compare or contrast the events of your simulation to what happened in the biblical account. What are the reasons for differences or similarities? To let questions like these guide the discussion will give a far better sense of accomplishment than simply talking without plan or direction.

The summarization of what was learned may be the high point and conclusion of the simulation. However, you may wish to conclude with worship. The whole event, even with the hilarity that is often involved, can be done in an attitude of worship. Worship need not be tacked on but can grow with the experience. "The Upper Room" and "The Gifts of the Spirit" are intended to be worship experiences.

After feelings and learnings have been expressed, the group will be ready for a prayer catching up the feelings of the moment. Should there be a mood of spontaneity, an invitation to open prayer can be very meaningful. A resourceful coordinator can mold the feelings and learnings into a litany with everyone giving a group response to each thought expressed. All might say in unison, "For this we give thanks, O Lord." Such a litany is suggested in the directions for "The Gifts of the Spirit."

The use of Scripture for worship can be very powerful after such an extensive study. Ask each person to quote the verse that was most meaningful to him. Have the group read one of the study passages in unison. Give many people opportunity to express the meaning of a certain verse or passage. Have persons read the same passage from different translations.

The singing of hymns belongs in the worship. It is not difficult to find hymns related to the Scripture being studied. Hymnals or printed words may be needed at this point. You may also want to allow people to express confession or new convictions they may have come to. A hymn, a verse of Scripture, or a simple statement can serve as benediction. With that the simulation is concluded.

5. WHAT HAPPENED IN THE GARDEN?

A Simulation Based upon Genesis 2-3

INSTRUCTIONS TO THE COORDINATOR

Preparation

Read through the whole simulation to get a good understanding of its purpose and direction. If you expect a large number of persons to take part, then you ought to involve some "leaders" in a discussion of goals and procedures prior to the simulation itself. You and they should read through the chapter "How to Conduct a Biblical Simulation" if you have not already done so.

Schedule

This simulation can be done very effectively in an hour or two, although you may use four hours or more. The time can be continuous or split up over several different sessions (see chapter 3). If you are using only a single hour, the court briefs will have to be sketchy at best, and you should limit the presentation of the prosecution and the defense to seven minutes each and the summations to one minute each. Two hours is an optimum time block for this simulation, and you should be able to complete most of the tasks within that time.

If you are breaking the time into three sessions, begin with the introduction and small groups. During the second session you should give the small groups a few minutes to collect their thoughts and to review their positions. Then move to the trial, allowing for debriefing at the end of the hour. During the third session, you will undoubtedly want to discuss the theological questions raised by the simulation. As coordinator, you should determine how much time the judges will be given to reach a decision. Depending on your schedule, this might last from three to ten minutes. You are also in a position to limit the presentations of the prosecution and the defense, if you find this necessary. The presentation of cases might last from seven to thirty minutes each. We recommend the following schedule:

	One Hour	Two Hours
Introduction	10 min.	15 min.
Preparation of case	15 min.	25 min.
Prosecution of case	7 min.	20 min.
Cross-examination	2 min.	4 min.
Defense of case	7 min.	20 min.
Cross-examination	2 min.	4 min.
Summation (half for each)	2 min.	4 min.
Recess for judges	3 min.	5 min.
Debriefing	10 min.	20 min.

Grouping

You will need a minimum of twelve people to do this simulation. You might reduce this to eight by collapsing the roles of God into one person and limiting the group for the prosecution to three. However, the design will work best for a group of twelve to thirty-six people. In groups of twenty or more you may wish to expand the panel of judges to eight; then divide the remainder of the participants evenly between the defense and the prosecution. In groups of less than twenty, you will want to hold the panel of judges to four; then divide the remainder of the participants evenly between the defense and the prosecution.

Space and Equipment

Your preparation should include obtaining each of the following items (see chapter 3 for fuller explanation): a large room, three small rooms, chairs, tables, Bibles, study aids, paper, pencils, and refreshments. Certain special preparations will help this simulation:
1. A sufficient number of Bibles is important, and various translations will be helpful.

2. The room arrangements should include a table for the judges, a witness stand, a table for the prosecution, and a table for the defense. The meeting room should give the appearance of a courtroom.
3. You may wish to provide certain art supplies which might be used in the preparation of exhibits for the defense or prosecution.

You will be greatly aided in the preparation if you allow your mind to imagine what a trial scene would have looked like in the Garden of Eden.

Facilitation

Your first facilitating task is to read the suggestions in chapter 4 on how to introduce the simulation. There you will find a discussion of the following items which should be explained to everyone before beginning: what a biblical simulation is, how to participate, purposes and tasks of this simulation, schedule, small-group tasks, materials, and division into groups. After allowing time for questions, divide the participants into three groups and proceed.

This simulation is designed to give people a better understanding of what happened in the Garden of Eden. The theological issues raised in Genesis 3 are pertinent to all time and have always been debated by the church and the synagogue. You will want to indicate to the participants that the trial hinges on an interpretation of what actually occurred. What did the man and woman do when they ate of the tree of the knowledge of good and evil? Don't allow the trial to become a question of whether they ate of the tree or not, but rather let the focus be upon what that act means.

One of the fundamental questions in the interpretation of Genesis 3 centers in the meaning of the knowledge of good and evil. Several options emerge: sexual knowledge, universal knowledge, moral knowledge, the knowledge of opposites. The group's authority for the resolution of the meaning is Genesis 3 itself. You must direct the attention of the participants to this text alone. However, you should be aware that some theologians have seen the Fall as blessed. In their view the Fall was essential for man and woman to become fully human, to possess the power to decide for themselves. You and the participants will discover in the course of the trial what Thomas Mann has said so ably, "These things never were, they always are."

Debriefing

As coordinator you should conduct the debriefing session. Here is a list of suggestions to be followed:
1. Rearrange the chairs so that everyone is aware that he has dropped his role.
2. In groups of four discuss what you have learned. Make sure that each group of four includes participants from more than one small group.
3. Ask for volunteers to share their observations with the whole group.
4. Ask the chroniclers to share their observations.
5. Try to summarize what you have been hearing.

Since some of the most heated arguments may have taken place among the judges when they adjourned to make their decision, you may ask them how they arrived at their decision and what their feelings were.

To conclude on a note of worship, have a prayer, litany, and hymn centered on the theme of confession of sin.

WHAT HAPPENED IN THE GARDEN? A Simulation Based upon Genesis 2 - 3

THE SITUATION

In order that everyone may understand the situation which has led to the trial, one person shall read aloud Genesis 2:15-17 and 3:1-13. Man and woman have eaten of the fruit of the tree of the knowledge of good and evil. The serpent has been an accessory to the fact. A trial has been ordered by the Divine Council to determine two things: (1) the exact crime which has been committed and (2) the penalty for that crime in the event the parties are found guilty. The case will be presented before a panel of judges consisting of the God of Justice, the God of Love, the God of Wrath, and the God of Mercy. As in any trial the prosecution will prepare a court brief in order to convict the man, the woman, and the serpent. The defense will seek to show that no crime of consequence has been committed and that all charges leveled against the defendants should be dropped. The participants in the trial will be:

1. the panel of judges
2. the prosecution
3. the defense.

Everyone should be assigned to one of these three groups.

TASKS OF GROUPS PRIOR TO THE SIMULATION

1. Appoint a chairman who will—
   a. lead in the preparation for the simulation,
   b. lead the prosecution, the defense, or the judges during the simulation.
2. Appoint a chronicler who will—
   a. record briefly the process of the group,
   b. record the action of the simulation from the perspective of his group,
   c. report to the debriefing session.
3. Examine carefully the deposition of the court (see Scripture references and explanation under "The Situation") to determine what crime has been committed and what penalty should be assessed in the event the accused are found guilty.
4. Prepare your case for trial. In the case of the judges, determine your role from the

passages assigned. (See background data sheet.)

5. The defendants should be clearly identified by the defense: Adam, Eve, and the serpent whom we might call Cecil. Other witnesses may be identified by either the defense or the prosecution should they wish to call further witnesses to the stand.
6. Remember that this is a courtroom situation and the simulation will assume the form of a trial.

PROCEDURE DURING THE SIMULATION

1. The panel of judges will determine courtroom procedure and may wish to select a bailiff to keep order in the court and to swear in witnesses.
2. The chief judge, who shall be selected by the panel of judges from among themselves, will open the trial by giving any opening remarks he sees fit to make. He will adjudicate all matters of procedure just as in a court of law.
3. The prosecution will then present its case. The defense has the right to cross-examine.
4. After the prosecution has finished presenting its case, the defense will then present its case. The prosecution has the right to cross-examine.
5. When the defense rests, the prosecution will be permitted a summary statement.
6. The defense may make a summary statement.
7. The panel of judges will decide the case and render a verdict of guilty or not guilty. In the case of guilt, they must determine the penalty for the crime.

TASKS FOR DEBRIEFING

1. Rearrange seating to symbolize the end of the simulation.
2. Ask people to describe how they felt during the trial.
3. Hear the reports from the chroniclers.
4. Discuss any questions that may be raised by the simulation.
5. Pose the following questions: How did you

feel in your role? Where did the most important exchanges take place in the simulation? What did you learn about Genesis 3 that you didn't know before? What did you learn about yourself? What theological issues did the simulation raise? For an extended discussion period you may wish to ask questions of content. Was the serpent right? Did the man or woman die? Does the writer explain the origin of evil?

How would you define the knowledge of good and evil?

The debriefing period could be the most important session. You will need to be sensitive to the thoughts and emotions of others as you discuss what happened during the simulation. You will find that this period can be a deeply personal one in which you, the participants, will learn something about yourselves.

1. The Panel of Judges

Your identity for the simulation will be four judges; each judge will play a distinct role on the basis of his character. You will want to appoint one person to lead the proceedings during the trial. It is your task to hear the case and to render a decision on the basis of your roles as described in the background data below. You should identify yourselves as the God of Justice, the God of Love, the God of Wrath, and the God of Mercy, and each of you should read the following passages:

God of Justice—Amos 1-2; 5:21-26
God of Love—Deuteronomy 7:7-8; Hosea 11:1-9
God of Wrath—Deuteronomy 28:15-46
God of Mercy—Hosea 1-3

BACKGROUND DATA
We encounter many different faces of God in the Old Testament. What we have done here is to break them into four separate roles. For the Hebrew mind justice is not an ideal but the meeting of the concrete demands of life. The God of Justice requires that men and women meet the requirements of the Law which are already clear to them. The God of Love binds himself to men and women for inexplicable reasons. Election love cannot be explained or rationalized; it simply exists. The God of Wrath is associated with the Covenant. Wherever the Covenant (social contract) is broken, the curse reigns. Breaking the law brings judgment. Mercy for many of us denotes an emotional feeling of tenderness. For the Hebrew it is a much stronger term. Mercy (hesed) means the steadfastness of God even in the face of collapse and brokenness in the human community. The God of Mercy remains faithful to his contract even when the partner has broken the bargain struck between them.

WHAT HAPPENED IN THE GARDEN? A Simulation Based upon Genesis 2 - 3

THE SITUATION

In order that everyone may understand the situation which has led to the trial, one person shall read aloud Genesis 2:15-17 and 3:1-13. Man and woman have eaten of the fruit of the tree of the knowledge of good and evil. The serpent has been an accessory to the fact. A trial has been ordered by the Divine Council to determine two things: (1) the exact crime which has been committed and (2) the penalty for that crime in the event the parties are found guilty. The case will be presented before a panel of judges consisting of the God of Justice, the God of Love, the God of Wrath, and the God of Mercy. As in any trial the prosecution will prepare a court brief in order to convict the man, the woman, and the serpent. The defense will seek to show that no crime of consequence has been committed and that all charges leveled against the defendants should be dropped. The participants in the trial will be:

1. the panel of judges
2. the prosecution
3. the defense.

Everyone should be assigned to one of these three groups.

TASKS OF GROUPS PRIOR TO THE SIMULATION

1. Appoint a chairman who will—
   a. lead in the preparation for the simulation,
   b. lead the prosecution, the defense, or the judges during the simulation.
2. Appoint a chronicler who will—
   a. record briefly the process of the group,
   b. record the action of the simulation from the perspective of his group,
   c. report to the debriefing session.
3. Examine carefully the deposition of the court (see Scripture references and explanation under "The Situation") to determine what crime has been committed and what penalty should be assessed in the event the accused are found guilty.
4. Prepare your case for trial. In the case of the judges, determine your role from the

passages assigned. (See background data sheet.)
5. The defendants should be clearly identified by the defense: Adam, Eve, and the serpent whom we might call Cecil. Other witnesses may be identified by either the defense or the prosecution should they wish to call further witnesses to the stand.
6. Remember that this is a courtroom situation and the simulation will assume the form of a trial.

PROCEDURE DURING THE SIMULATION

1. The panel of judges will determine courtroom procedure and may wish to select a bailiff to keep order in the court and to swear in witnesses.
2. The chief judge, who shall be selected by the panel of judges from among themselves, will open the trial by giving any opening remarks he sees fit to make. He will adjudicate all matters of procedure just as in a court of law.
3. The prosecution will then present its case. The defense has the right to cross-examine.
4. After the prosecution has finished presenting its case, the defense will then present its case. The prosecution has the right to cross-examine.
5. When the defense rests, the prosecution will be permitted a summary statement.
6. The defense may make a summary statement.
7. The panel of judges will decide the case and render a verdict of guilty or not guilty. In the case of guilt, they must determine the penalty for the crime.

TASKS FOR DEBRIEFING

1. Rearrange seating to symbolize the end of the simulation.
2. Ask people to describe how they felt during the trial.
3. Hear the reports from the chroniclers.
4. Discuss any questions that may be raised by the simulation.
5. Pose the following questions: How did you

feel in your role? Where did the most important exchanges take place in the simulation? What did you learn about Genesis 3 that you didn't know before? What did you learn about yourself? What theological issues did the simulation raise? For an extended discussion period you may wish to ask questions of content. Was the serpent right? Did the man or woman die? Does the writer explain the origin of evil?

How would you define the knowledge of good and evil?

The debriefing period could be the most important session. You will need to be sensitive to the thoughts and emotions of others as you discuss what happened during the simulation. You will find that this period can be a deeply personal one in which you, the participants, will learn something about yourselves.

1. The Panel of Judges

Your identity for the simulation will be four judges; each judge will play a distinct role on the basis of his character. You will want to appoint one person to lead the proceedings during the trial. It is your task to hear the case and to render a decision on the basis of your roles as described in the background data below. You should identify yourselves as the God of Justice, the God of Love, the God of Wrath, and the God of Mercy, and each of you should read the following passages:

God of Justice—Amos 1-2; 5:21-26
God of Love—Deuteronomy 7:7-8; Hosea 11:1-9
God of Wrath—Deuteronomy 28:15-46
God of Mercy—Hosea 1-3

BACKGROUND DATA
We encounter many different faces of God in the Old Testament. What we have done here is to break them into four separate roles. For the Hebrew mind justice is not an ideal but the meeting of the concrete demands of life. The God of Justice requires that men and women meet the requirements of the Law which are already clear to them. The God of Love binds himself to men and women for inexplicable reasons. Election love cannot be explained or rationalized; it simply exists. The God of Wrath is associated with the Covenant. Wherever the Covenant (social contract) is broken, the curse reigns. Breaking the law brings judgment. Mercy for many of us denotes an emotional feeling of tenderness. For the Hebrew it is a much stronger term. Mercy *(hesed)* means the steadfastness of God even in the face of collapse and brokenness in the human community. The God of Mercy remains faithful to his contract even when the partner has broken the bargain struck between them.

WHAT HAPPENED IN THE GARDEN? A Simulation Based upon Genesis 2 - 3

THE SITUATION

In order that everyone may understand the situation which has led to the trial, one person shall read aloud Genesis 2:15-17 and 3:1-13. Man and woman have eaten of the fruit of the tree of the knowledge of good and evil. The serpent has been an accessory to the fact. A trial has been ordered by the Divine Council to determine two things: (1) the exact crime which has been committed and (2) the penalty for that crime in the event the parties are found guilty. The case will be presented before a panel of judges consisting of the God of Justice, the God of Love, the God of Wrath, and the God of Mercy. As in any trial the prosecution will prepare a court brief in order to convict the man, the woman, and the serpent. The defense will seek to show that no crime of consequence has been committed and that all charges leveled against the defendants should be dropped. The participants in the trial will be:

1. the panel of judges
2. the prosecution
3. the defense.

Everyone should be assigned to one of these three groups.

TASKS OF GROUPS PRIOR TO THE SIMULATION

1. Appoint a chairman who will—
   a. lead in the preparation for the simulation,
   b. lead the prosecution, the defense, or the judges during the simulation.
2. Appoint a chronicler who will—
   a. record briefly the process of the group,
   b. record the action of the simulation from the perspective of his group,
   c. report to the debriefing session.
3. Examine carefully the deposition of the court (see Scripture references and explanation under "The Situation") to determine what crime has been committed and what penalty should be assessed in the event the accused are found guilty.
4. Prepare your case for trial. In the case of the judges, determine your role from the passages assigned. (See background data sheet.)
5. The defendants should be clearly identified by the defense: Adam, Eve, and the serpent whom we might call Cecil. Other witnesses may be identified by either the defense or the prosecution should they wish to call further witnesses to the stand.
6. Remember that this is a courtroom situation and the simulation will assume the form of a trial.

PROCEDURE DURING THE SIMULATION

1. The panel of judges will determine courtroom procedure and may wish to select a bailiff to keep order in the court and to swear in witnesses.
2. The chief judge, who shall be selected by the panel of judges from among themselves, will open the trial by giving any opening remarks he sees fit to make. He will adjudicate all matters of procedure just as in a court of law.
3. The prosecution will then present its case. The defense has the right to cross-examine.
4. After the prosecution has finished presenting its case, the defense will then present its case. The prosecution has the right to cross-examine.
5. When the defense rests, the prosecution will be permitted a summary statement.
6. The defense may make a summary statement.
7. The panel of judges will decide the case and render a verdict of guilty or not guilty. In the case of guilt, they must determine the penalty for the crime.

TASKS FOR DEBRIEFING

1. Rearrange seating to symbolize the end of the simulation.
2. Ask people to describe how they felt during the trial.
3. Hear the reports from the chroniclers.
4. Discuss any questions that may be raised by the simulation.
5. Pose the following questions: How did you

feel in your role? Where did the most important exchanges take place in the simulation? What did you learn about Genesis 3 that you didn't know before? What did you learn about yourself? What theological issues did the simulation raise? For an extended discussion period you may wish to ask questions of content. Was the serpent right? Did the man or woman die? Does the writer explain the origin of evil?

How would you define the knowledge of good and evil?

The debriefing period could be the most important session. You will need to be sensitive to the thoughts and emotions of others as you discuss what happened during the simulation. You will find that this period can be a deeply personal one in which you, the participants, will learn something about yourselves.

2. The Prosecution

Your identity for the simulation will be that of the staff of the state's attorney for the Divine Council. You will want to prepare a case which will lead to the conviction of Adam, Eve, and the serpent. You will contend that they have willfully committed a crime against the High God and should be expelled from the Garden of Eden. You will want to appoint at least one prosecuting attorney, perhaps more if you desire. You may want to have members of your group function as witnesses for the prosecution. (Use your imagination here. Perhaps someone from your group will want to play the tree or an animal or a member of the Divine Council.) It is your task to convict Adam, Eve, and the Serpent Cecil, and to secure the highest penalty, expulsion from the garden. Passages for you to read are:

Genesis 2 - 3
Job 1 - 2

BACKGROUND DATA
A prosecuting attorney is often a part of the Divine Council in the Old Testament. The most

notable example is to be found in the Book of Job, chapters 1 and 2. Your role then is clear. You must, however, create your case on the basis of narrative material in Genesis 2 - 3. You will undoubtedly want to show that Adam, Eve, and the Serpent Cecil had the power to make ethical decisions and therefore did not act out of ignorance. Furthermore, they had been specifically warned in Genesis 2:15-17 not to eat the fruit of the tree. They did willfully intend to subvert the basic law of the land. You may want to claim that Adam, Eve, and the Serpent Cecil set out to displace the High God and place themselves at the center of the universe. That is only one possible interpretation of their motives. Other interpretations are the desire for one of the following: sexual knowledge, universal knowledge, or moral knowledge. You will want to determine your own interpretation from the chapter itself. What is their crime? You may wish to indict only the Serpent Cecil, or both the Serpent Cecil and Eve, or all three defendants. The determination of the crime and the character of indictment is in your hands.

WHAT HAPPENED IN THE GARDEN? A Simulation Based upon Genesis 2 - 3

THE SITUATION

In order that everyone may understand the situation which has led to the trial, one person shall read aloud Genesis 2:15-17 and 3:1-13. Man and woman have eaten of the fruit of the tree of the knowledge of good and evil. The serpent has been an accessory to the fact. A trial has been ordered by the Divine Council to determine two things: (1) the exact crime which has been committed and (2) the penalty for that crime in the event the parties are found guilty. The case will be presented before a panel of judges consisting of the God of Justice, the God of Love, the God of Wrath, and the God of Mercy. As in any trial the prosecution will prepare a court brief in order to convict the man, the woman, and the serpent. The defense will seek to show that no crime of consequence has been committed and that all charges leveled against the defendants should be dropped. The participants in the trial will be:

1. the panel of judges
2. the prosecution
3. the defense.

Everyone should be assigned to one of these three groups.

TASKS OF GROUPS PRIOR TO THE SIMULATION

1. Appoint a chairman who will—
   a. lead in the preparation for the simulation,
   b. lead the prosecution, the defense, or the judges during the simulation.
2. Appoint a chronicler who will—
   a. record briefly the process of the group,
   b. record the action of the simulation from the perspective of his group,
   c. report to the debriefing session.
3. Examine carefully the deposition of the court (see Scripture references and explanation under "The Situation") to determine what crime has been committed and what penalty should be assessed in the event the accused are found guilty.
4. Prepare your case for trial. In the case of the judges, determine your role from the passages assigned. (See background data sheet.)
5. The defendants should be clearly identified by the defense: Adam, Eve, and the serpent whom we might call Cecil. Other witnesses may be identified by either the defense or the prosecution should they wish to call further witnesses to the stand.
6. Remember that this is a courtroom situation and the simulation will assume the form of a trial.

PROCEDURE DURING THE SIMULATION

1. The panel of judges will determine courtroom procedure and may wish to select a bailiff to keep order in the court and to swear in witnesses.
2. The chief judge, who shall be selected by the panel of judges from among themselves, will open the trial by giving any opening remarks he sees fit to make. He will adjudicate all matters of procedure just as in a court of law.
3. The prosecution will then present its case. The defense has the right to cross-examine.
4. After the prosecution has finished presenting its case, the defense will then present its case. The prosecution has the right to cross-examine.
5. When the defense rests, the prosecution will be permitted a summary statement.
6. The defense may make a summary statement.
7. The panel of judges will decide the case and render a verdict of guilty or not guilty. In the case of guilt, they must determine the penalty for the crime.

TASKS FOR DEBRIEFING

1. Rearrange seating to symbolize the end of the simulation.
2. Ask people to describe how they felt during the trial.
3. Hear the reports from the chroniclers.
4. Discuss any questions that may be raised by the simulation.
5. Pose the following questions: How did you

feel in your role? Where did the most important exchanges take place in the simulation? What did you learn about Genesis 3 that you didn't know before? What did you learn about yourself? What theological issues did the simulation raise? For an extended discussion period you may wish to ask questions of content. Was the serpent right? Did the man or woman die? Does the writer explain the origin of evil?

How would you define the knowledge of good and evil?

The debriefing period could be the most important session. You will need to be sensitive to the thoughts and emotions of others as you discuss what happened during the simulation. You will find that this period can be a deeply personal one in which you, the participants, will learn something about yourselves.

2. The Prosecution

Your identity for the simulation will be that of the staff of the state's attorney for the Divine Council. You will want to prepare a case which will lead to the conviction of Adam, Eve, and the serpent. You will contend that they have willfully committed a crime against the High God and should be expelled from the Garden of Eden. You will want to appoint at least one prosecuting attorney, perhaps more if you desire. You may want to have members of your group function as witnesses for the prosecution. (Use your imagination here. Perhaps someone from your group will want to play the tree or an animal or a member of the Divine Council.) It is your task to convict Adam, Eve, and the Serpent Cecil, and to secure the highest penalty, expulsion from the garden. Passages for you to read are:

Genesis 2 - 3
Job 1 - 2

BACKGROUND DATA

A prosecuting attorney is often a part of the Divine Council in the Old Testament. The most notable example is to be found in the Book of Job, chapters 1 and 2. Your role then is clear. You must, however, create your case on the basis of narrative material in Genesis 2 - 3. You will undoubtedly want to show that Adam, Eve, and the Serpent Cecil had the power to make ethical decisions and therefore did not act out of ignorance. Furthermore, they had been specifically warned in Genesis 2:15-17 not to eat the fruit of the tree. They did willfully intend to subvert the basic law of the land. You may want to claim that Adam, Eve, and the Serpent Cecil set out to displace the High God and place themselves at the center of the universe. That is only one possible interpretation of their motives. Other interpretations are the desire for one of the following: sexual knowledge, universal knowledge, or moral knowledge. You will want to determine your own interpretation from the chapter itself. What is their crime? You may wish to indict only the Serpent Cecil, or both the Serpent Cecil and Eve, or all three defendants. The determination of the crime and the character of indictment is in your hands.

WHAT HAPPENED IN THE GARDEN? A Simulation Based upon Genesis 2 - 3

THE SITUATION

In order that everyone may understand the situation which has led to the trial, one person shall read aloud Genesis 2:15-17 and 3:1-13. Man and woman have eaten of the fruit of the tree of the knowledge of good and evil. The serpent has been an accessory to the fact. A trial has been ordered by the Divine Council to determine two things: (1) the exact crime which has been committed and (2) the penalty for that crime in the event the parties are found guilty. The case will be presented before a panel of judges consisting of the God of Justice, the God of Love, the God of Wrath, and the God of Mercy. As in any trial the prosecution will prepare a court brief in order to convict the man, the woman, and the serpent. The defense will seek to show that no crime of consequence has been committed and that all charges leveled against the defendants should be dropped. The participants in the trial will be:

1. the panel of judges
2. the prosecution
3. the defense.

Everyone should be assigned to one of these three groups.

TASKS OF GROUPS PRIOR TO THE SIMULATION

1. Appoint a chairman who will—
   a. lead in the preparation for the simulation,
   b. lead the prosecution, the defense, or the judges during the simulation.
2. Appoint a chronicler who will—
   a. record briefly the process of the group,
   b. record the action of the simulation from the perspective of his group,
   c. report to the debriefing session.
3. Examine carefully the deposition of the court (see Scripture references and explanation under "The Situation") to determine what crime has been committed and what penalty should be assessed in the event the accused are found guilty.
4. Prepare your case for trial. In the case of the judges, determine your role from the passages assigned. (See background data sheet.)
5. The defendants should be clearly identified by the defense: Adam, Eve, and the serpent whom we might call Cecil. Other witnesses may be identified by either the defense or the prosecution should they wish to call further witnesses to the stand.
6. Remember that this is a courtroom situation and the simulation will assume the form of a trial.

PROCEDURE DURING THE SIMULATION

1. The panel of judges will determine courtroom procedure and may wish to select a bailiff to keep order in the court and to swear in witnesses.
2. The chief judge, who shall be selected by the panel of judges from among themselves, will open the trial by giving any opening remarks he sees fit to make. He will adjudicate all matters of procedure just as in a court of law.
3. The prosecution will then present its case. The defense has the right to cross-examine.
4. After the prosecution has finished presenting its case, the defense will then present its case. The prosecution has the right to cross-examine.
5. When the defense rests, the prosecution will be permitted a summary statement.
6. The defense may make a summary statement.
7. The panel of judges will decide the case and render a verdict of guilty or not guilty. In the case of guilt, they must determine the penalty for the crime.

TASKS FOR DEBRIEFING

1. Rearrange seating to symbolize the end of the simulation.
2. Ask people to describe how they felt during the trial.
3. Hear the reports from the chroniclers.
4. Discuss any questions that may be raised by the simulation.
5. Pose the following questions: How did you

feel in your role? Where did the most important exchanges take place in the simulation? What did you learn about Genesis 3 that you didn't know before? What did you learn about yourself? What theological issues did the simulation raise? For an extended discussion period you may wish to ask questions of content. Was the serpent right? Did the man or woman die? Does the writer explain the origin of evil?

How would you define the knowledge of good and evil?

The debriefing period could be the most important session. You will need to be sensitive to the thoughts and emotions of others as you discuss what happened during the simulation. You will find that this period can be a deeply personal one in which you, the participants, will learn something about yourselves.

3. The Defense

Your identity for the simulation will be that of a defense attorney and the defendants. You will want to prepare a case that will lead to the acquittal of Adam, Eve, and the Serpent Cecil, since you believe them to be innocent of any grave crime against the order of the universe. You will want to appoint at least one defense attorney, perhaps more, depending upon the size of the group. You will want to identify Adam, Eve, and the Serpent Cecil. You may want to have members of your group function as secondary witnesses for the defense. Use your imagination here. Perhaps someone from your group will want to play a character witness or an expert in moral law. It is your task to secure the release of the defendants, Adam, Eve, and the Serpent Cecil. Your primary written source is:

Genesis 2 - 3.

BACKGROUND DATA
In the history of the interpretation of good and evil in this chapter, five major positions have emerged. The knowledge of good and evil is the power to make ethical decisions, sexual

knowledge, universal wisdom, a knowledge of the polarities of life, or the experience of independence. You may take any of these interpretations and develop a case to show that eating of the tree is essential for maturity, for independence, and for man and woman to reach the full measure of their humanity. Again you may find an interpretation not listed here. You will be helped by the use of a concordance, since the phrase "good and evil" appears in a number of passages in the Old Testament. On the other hand, you may simply rely on the passage itself for new insights into the meaning of the phrase. You will want to show that the knowledge of good and evil, whatever your interpretation, is essential for life and a necessary part of the created order. Of course, you may wish to make the case on the order of blame. In that instance, you might fight for the acquittal of the man and the woman and the conviction of the serpent. Another possibility is to hold God accountable on the basis that he created the world and thus must be held responsible for it. The determination of the case and the character of the acquittal you seek is in your hands.

WHAT HAPPENED IN THE GARDEN? A Simulation Based upon Genesis 2 - 3

THE SITUATION

In order that everyone may understand the situation which has led to the trial, one person shall read aloud Genesis 2:15-17 and 3:1-13. Man and woman have eaten of the fruit of the tree of the knowledge of good and evil. The serpent has been an accessory to the fact. A trial has been ordered by the Divine Council to determine two things: (1) the exact crime which has been committed and (2) the penalty for that crime in the event the parties are found guilty. The case will be presented before a panel of judges consisting of the God of Justice, the God of Love, the God of Wrath, and the God of Mercy. As in any trial the prosecution will prepare a court brief in order to convict the man, the woman, and the serpent. The defense will seek to show that no crime of consequence has been committed and that all charges leveled against the defendants should be dropped. The participants in the trial will be:

1. the panel of judges
2. the prosecution
3. the defense.

Everyone should be assigned to one of these three groups.

TASKS OF GROUPS PRIOR TO THE SIMULATION

1. Appoint a chairman who will—
   a. lead in the preparation for the simulation,
   b. lead the prosecution, the defense, or the judges during the simulation.
2. Appoint a chronicler who will—
   a. record briefly the process of the group,
   b. record the action of the simulation from the perspective of his group,
   c. report to the debriefing session.
3. Examine carefully the deposition of the court (see Scripture references and explanation under "The Situation") to determine what crime has been committed and what penalty should be assessed in the event the accused are found guilty.
4. Prepare your case for trial. In the case of the judges, determine your role from the passages assigned. (See background data sheet.)
5. The defendants should be clearly identified by the defense: Adam, Eve, and the serpent whom we might call Cecil. Other witnesses may be identified by either the defense or the prosecution should they wish to call further witnesses to the stand.
6. Remember that this is a courtroom situation and the simulation will assume the form of a trial.

PROCEDURE DURING THE SIMULATION

1. The panel of judges will determine courtroom procedure and may wish to select a bailiff to keep order in the court and to swear in witnesses.
2. The chief judge, who shall be selected by the panel of judges from among themselves, will open the trial by giving any opening remarks he sees fit to make. He will adjudicate all matters of procedure just as in a court of law.
3. The prosecution will then present its case. The defense has the right to cross-examine.
4. After the prosecution has finished presenting its case, the defense will then present its case. The prosecution has the right to cross-examine.
5. When the defense rests, the prosecution will be permitted a summary statement.
6. The defense may make a summary statement.
7. The panel of judges will decide the case and render a verdict of guilty or not guilty. In the case of guilt, they must determine the penalty for the crime.

TASKS FOR DEBRIEFING

1. Rearrange seating to symbolize the end of the simulation.
2. Ask people to describe how they felt during the trial.
3. Hear the reports from the chroniclers.
4. Discuss any questions that may be raised by the simulation.
5. Pose the following questions: How did you

feel in your role? Where did the most important exchanges take place in the simulation? What did you learn about Genesis 3 that you didn't know before? What did you learn about yourself? What theological issues did the simulation raise? For an extended discussion period you may wish to ask questions of content. Was the serpent right? Did the man or woman die? Does the writer explain the origin of evil?

How would you define the knowledge of good and evil?

The debriefing period could be the most important session. You will need to be sensitive to the thoughts and emotions of others as you discuss what happened during the simulation. You will find that this period can be a deeply personal one in which you, the participants, will learn something about yourselves.

3. The Defense

Your identity for the simulation will be that of a defense attorney and the defendants. You will want to prepare a case that will lead to the acquittal of Adam, Eve, and the Serpent Cecil, since you believe them to be innocent of any grave crime against the order of the universe. You will want to appoint at least one defense attorney, perhaps more, depending upon the size of the group. You will want to identify Adam, Eve, and the Serpent Cecil. You may want to have members of your group function as secondary witnesses for the defense. Use your imagination here. Perhaps someone from your group will want to play a character witness or an expert in moral law. It is your task to secure the release of the defendants, Adam, Eve, and the Serpent Cecil. Your primary written source is:

Genesis 2 - 3.

BACKGROUND DATA
In the history of the interpretation of good and evil in this chapter, five major positions have emerged. The knowledge of good and evil is the power to make ethical decisions, sexual

knowledge, universal wisdom, a knowledge of the polarities of life, or the experience of independence. You may take any of these interpretations and develop a case to show that eating of the tree is essential for maturity, for independence, and for man and woman to reach the full measure of their humanity. Again you may find an interpretation not listed here. You will be helped by the use of a concordance, since the phrase "good and evil" appears in a number of passages in the Old Testament. On the other hand, you may simply rely on the passage itself for new insights into the meaning of the phrase. You will want to show that the knowledge of good and evil, whatever your interpretation, is essential for life and a necessary part of the created order. Of course, you may wish to make the case on the order of blame. In that instance, you might fight for the acquittal of the man and the woman and the conviction of the serpent. Another possibility is to hold God accountable on the basis that he created the world and thus must be held responsible for it. The determination of the case and the character of the acquittal you seek is in your hands.

6. THE TAKING OF THE LAND

A Simulation of Numbers 14

INSTRUCTIONS TO THE COORDINATOR

Preparation

The coordinator should read over the simulation so as to familiarize himself with the instructions and purposes. The intent of this simulation is to lift up the problems of freedom and violence. It would profit the group if these purposes were shared with some participants ahead of time so that time is not wasted on useless side issues. Since this simulation deals with a lesser known biblical story, the events which surround the taking of Jericho, it would be wise to read through relevant passages from the Bible prior to the simulation. Check with the information in the category "Facilitation" to see if there is information needed regarding ancient cities of Palestine or the history of Egypt.

Schedule

For shorter or longer simulations the following schedules will be feasible:

	Short	Long
Introduction	5 min.	15 min.
Study of biblical passages and simulation material	25 min.	60 min.
Formulation of strategy	30 min.	45 min.
Break		
Tribal meeting	45 min.	90 min.
Debriefing	15 min.	30 min.

For a shorter simulation you could have a two-hour session or two one-hour sessions. The shorter schedule will require that you limit the biblical study to three or four passages, and the decision making at the plenary session may have to be limited to one decision. In such a case it might be valuable to appoint a tribal leader so that the actual decision about violence to the town of Jericho can be made. For various scheduling possibilities see chapter 3.

Space and Equipment

In order to carry out this simulation the participants must have copies of the Old Testament, pencil or pen, and paper. For the articulation of the small groups some poster and banner materials, such as felt pens, newsprint, and even cloth and burlap would be helpful. The Egyptians might be more persuasive if they had some of the food of Egypt, such as onions, cucumbers, or garlic. The priests would enjoy using paper horns and the nomads cloth turbans.

For the plenary session you will need a large room with a center table large enough to seat twelve. The representatives will sit at the table with the other team members behind them. For the small-group work you need either four rooms with smaller tables or four corners of the large room and sufficient privacy for the teams to formulate their plans without being overheard.

Facilitation

Knowledge of the Old Testament differs from group to group, of course, but experience has shown that stories from the Old Testament are often more difficult to simulate than those from the New Testament simply because people are not familiar with the details. If your group does not know the story of the wilderness and the taking of Jericho, then you should take extra steps to insure better acquaintance. The participants might read the passages in advance, or they could be read as the first item of the simulation, as a part of the introduction. (Both chapters 13 and 14 of Numbers are helpful as well as chapters 2 and 6 of Joshua.)

Because detail is not known for a simulation like this, the extra witnesses are especially important. In the simulation the spy who visited Rahab in Jericho is to appear. Since such a witness is not to be the pawn of any group, this part should be played by the coordinator or someone not participating in one of the groups. The spy can have considerable influence on the plenary session and at the same time will add interest and excitement to the simulation. As with other witnesses it is best if the story the spy tells is either equivocal or inconsequential. For example, he might say that the city is well protected but the soldiers are drunk most of the time. Or he might report that Rahab's apartment has walls a foot thick.

Needless to say, in this kind of simulation the matter of witnesses can be extended indefinitely. The group might consider calling Rahab herself for a testimony about life in Jericho. The Egyptians might present a messenger who reports that the present Pharaoh has died so that the Hebrew people can return to Egypt without fear of reprisal or slavery. The problem of theological violence might be tested by hearing from Balaam who was hired by Balak to curse the Hebrew tribes and thus prevent them from entering Palestine (Numbers 22 - 24).

Debriefing

In a situation where the material is not as well known, the emotional involvement may not be so great as with the Adam and Eve story or the crucifixion of Jesus. Debriefing then may be more of an articulation of the learning than an attempt to lose the role. If there has been considerable conflict and emotion, then the simulation should be stopped by methods indicated in chapter 4. In this simulation, where roles are identified with places at the table, changing seats might be helpful. Members of each group could tell how they felt about the strategy of the other three groups. If the struggle has not been overly emotional, you can turn directly to articulating the meaning and value of the simulation. Issues that may appear are faith in biblical miracles (e.g., the collapse of the walls of Jericho or the miraculous feeding in the wilderness) and the use of violence by God's people, especially by priests. There are no final answers to these questions, but the value of the simulation is to allow them to be worked through. Another feeling likely to arise is some sympathy for the Egyptians, who, despite their rather negative role in the simulation, do represent those preferring the security of the tradition to the unknown of a new venture. This is especially likely if several age groups are present. One of the proven values of such a simulation is to allow young and old to grapple with such issues as security and freedom through the medium of a "game."

THE TAKING OF THE LAND A Simulation Based upon Numbers 14

THE SITUATION

You are to simulate a tribal meeting of the Israelites on the banks of the Jordan River after years of wandering in the wilderness. Moses has just died, and you are faced with several difficult decisions:

1. You must elect a leader to replace Moses.

    The leadership of Moses during the wilderness period was incredibly rocky. In the first place some of the Hebrews apparently joined the Exodus under protest (the group that murmured). From time to time there arose leaders who could mount a severe challenge to Moses. The most famous rebellion was that of Korah in Numbers 16, but the most striking is that of Moses' own brother and sister, Aaron and Miriam, in Numbers 12. Moses had tried to settle the leadership question by gathering seventy elders upon whom the Lord passed the spirit, but that apparently did not solve all the problems (Numbers 11). The critical challenge came when the decision to take Palestine was made. Joshua became the leader because he favored the taking of the land.

2. You must decide whether to cross over the Jordan or not.

    The crossing of the Red Sea, freedom from Egypt, and the taking of the Promised Land are the major elements of the formation of Israel as a people and a nation. Despite this central action of God, there were variations in the wishes of the people. Not all of the Hebrews wanted to leave Egypt (the murmurers in the wilderness); some did not wish to settle in the Fertile Crescent but wished to remain on the edge of the desert (sons of Reuben and sons of Gad). Historically the taking of Palestine was probably more gradual (as Judges indicates) than simply the one attack on Jericho, but that does not affect the simulation.

3. You must decide whether to defend yourselves by conventional military means or otherwise.

    In this section of the Old Testament there are two distinct ways of approaching the conquest. One is to depend entirely on the power of God. One can see this in the battle of Jericho, later in the battles led by Gideon, and even much later in the battle of David with Goliath. In sharp contrast are the battles which are sheer military endeavors and which end with bloody defeat of the enemy. Even some of those conquests which in the beginning were entirely dependent on the power of God ended with the bloody defeat of the enemy. Scholars also are not agreed on which was the method used in the conquest of Palestine or even on which is the dominant message of the Old Testament. It may be the intent was to depend on the power of God, but in moments of doubt man used his own might. At least most of the military stories of the Old Testament show how man in his weakness was saved by the overwhelming miraculous power of God.

TASKS OF ALL GROUPS
PRIOR TO THE SIMULATION

1. Appoint a leader who will—
    a. chair in the preparation for the simulation,
    b. lead the group during the simulation,
    For purposes of the simulation the leader of the groups will have the following identities:

The Priestly Class	Levi
The Jahwists	Joshua
The Egyptians	Achan
The Nomads	Gad

2. Appoint a chronicler who will—
    a. record briefly the process of the group,
    b. record the action of the simulation from the perspective of his group,
    c. report to the debriefing session.
3. Examine those texts of the Old Testament which establish the identity of your particular group.
4. Articulate your identity to each other by a song or a gesture or a banner.
5. Decide how your group will act in the simulated decisions. (See the background

data sheet.)

6. Discuss what means of group persuasion are available to you, given the group identity you have.

7. Assist the chronicler in recording, especially by articulating your plans as you project them prior to the simulation.

RULES OF THE SIMULATION

1. Each group will be allowed three representatives at the tribal meeting.

2. Other members of the group will be arranged behind the three representatives.

3. Any member of the group may replace one of his table representatives at will.

4. Each group will be allowed two roving politicians who may—
   a. discover the character and purposes of the other groups,
   b. facilitate or disrupt the procedures,
   c. consult with the background resource person.

TASKS OF THE SIMULATION

1. The coordinator will act as Moses until a new leader can be elected.

2. Under the direction of the newly elected leader the tribes will make the following decisions:
   a. Shall the tribes cross over the Jordan River and take Jericho?
   b. If they do try to take Jericho, what method will be used?
   c. If they choose to remain in the wilderness, or return to Egypt, what method of defense should be used against the hostile Amalekites, Amorites, and Moabites?

TASKS FOR DEBRIEFING

1. Make some change of the room arrangement to symbolize the end of the simulation.

2. Discuss with one another how you felt during the simulation.

3. Hear the reports from the chroniclers.

4. Discuss any questions that may be raised by the experience together.

1. The Priestly Class

Your group identity for the simulation will be that of the priestly class whose influence can be seen so clearly in the narrative of the Exodus and the taking of Palestine. In the simulation there will be other groups helping to make the decision about crossing over the Jordan. It is your task to determine how to use your specific interests and powers in the decision-making process. The following are some Old Testament texts which will help you establish your identity:

> Exodus 4:10-17
> Exodus 4:27-31
> Exodus 28:1-4
> Exodus 32:1-35
> Numbers 15:1-40
> Joshua 5:1 - 6:27

BACKGROUND DATA

The priestly class owes its origin to the line of Aaron, the brother and religious assistant of Moses. Its concerns as a group are correct cultic practices, religious purity, and absolute dependence on God in all of life including political and military aspects. The cultic practices and laws can be found in the large sections from Exodus 25 through Leviticus. In regard to the taking of Palestine, the priestly influence can be seen in the ritual which preceded the taking of Jericho: the role of the ark, the miraculous crossing of the Jordan River, circumcision, and the celebration of the Passover. Following the destruction of Jericho, the priestly class insisted on the rule of *cherem*, the destruction of all things alien to God (Joshua 7). God is holy and always to be obeyed. While the point is disputed by readers of the Old Testament, it would appear that the priestly group supported military conquest but rejected conventional military methods. At least in the case of Jericho it was the priestly method which was utilized.

THE TAKING OF THE LAND A Simulation Based upon Numbers 14

THE SITUATION

You are to simulate a tribal meeting of the Israelites on the banks of the Jordan River after years of wandering in the wilderness. Moses has just died, and you are faced with several difficult decisions:

1. You must elect a leader to replace Moses.

    The leadership of Moses during the wilderness period was incredibly rocky. In the first place some of the Hebrews apparently joined the Exodus under protest (the group that murmured). From time to time there arose leaders who could mount a severe challenge to Moses. The most famous rebellion was that of Korah in Numbers 16, but the most striking is that of Moses' own brother and sister, Aaron and Miriam, in Numbers 12. Moses had tried to settle the leadership question by gathering seventy elders upon whom the Lord passed the spirit, but that apparently did not solve all the problems (Numbers 11). The critical challenge came when the decision to take Palestine was made. Joshua became the leader because he favored the taking of the land.

2. You must decide whether to cross over the Jordan or not.

    The crossing of the Red Sea, freedom from Egypt, and the taking of the Promised Land are the major elements of the formation of Israel as a people and a nation. Despite this central action of God, there were variations in the wishes of the people. Not all of the Hebrews wanted to leave Egypt (the murmurers in the wilderness); some did not wish to settle in the Fertile Crescent but wished to remain on the edge of the desert (sons of Reuben and sons of Gad). Historically the taking of Palestine was probably more gradual (as Judges indicates) than simply the one attack on Jericho, but that does not affect the simulation.

3. You must decide whether to defend yourselves by conventional military means or otherwise.

    In this section of the Old Testament there are two distinct ways of approaching the conquest. One is to depend entirely on the power of God. One can see this in the battle of Jericho, later in the battles led by Gideon, and even much later in the battle of David with Goliath. In sharp contrast are the battles which are sheer military endeavors and which end with bloody defeat of the enemy. Even some of those conquests which in the beginning were entirely dependent on the power of God ended with the bloody defeat of the enemy. Scholars also are not agreed on which was the method used in the conquest of Palestine or even on which is the dominant message of the Old Testament. It may be the intent was to depend on the power of God, but in moments of doubt man used his own might. At least most of the military stories of the Old Testament show how man in his weakness was saved by the overwhelming miraculous power of God.

TASKS OF ALL GROUPS
PRIOR TO THE SIMULATION

1. Appoint a leader who will—
    a. chair in the preparation for the simulation,
    b. lead the group during the simulation,
    For purposes of the simulation the leader of the groups will have the following identities:

The Priestly Class	Levi
The Jahwists	Joshua
The Egyptians	Achan
The Nomads	Gad

2. Appoint a chronicler who will—
    a. record briefly the process of the group,
    b. record the action of the simulation from the perspective of his group,
    c. report to the debriefing session.
3. Examine those texts of the Old Testament which establish the identity of your particular group.
4. Articulate your identity to each other by a song or a gesture or a banner.
5. Decide how your group will act in the simulated decisions. (See the background

data sheet.)

6. Discuss what means of group persuasion are available to you, given the group identity you have.
7. Assist the chronicler in recording, especially by articulating your plans as you project them prior to the simulation.

RULES OF THE SIMULATION

1. Each group will be allowed three representatives at the tribal meeting.
2. Other members of the group will be arranged behind the three representatives.
3. Any member of the group may replace one of his table representatives at will.
4. Each group will be allowed two roving politicians who may—
   a. discover the character and purposes of the other groups,
   b. facilitate or disrupt the procedures,
   c. consult with the background resource person.

TASKS OF THE SIMULATION

1. The coordinator will act as Moses until a new leader can be elected.
2. Under the direction of the newly elected leader the tribes will make the following decisions:
   a. Shall the tribes cross over the Jordan River and take Jericho?
   b. If they do try to take Jericho, what method will be used?
   c. If they choose to remain in the wilderness, or return to Egypt, what method of defense should be used against the hostile Amalekites, Amorites, and Moabites?

TASKS FOR DEBRIEFING

1. Make some change of the room arrangement to symbolize the end of the simulation.
2. Discuss with one another how you felt during the simulation.
3. Hear the reports from the chroniclers.
4. Discuss any questions that may be raised by the experience together.

1. The Priestly Class

Your group identity for the simulation will be that of the priestly class whose influence can be seen so clearly in the narrative of the Exodus and the taking of Palestine. In the simulation there will be other groups helping to make the decision about crossing over the Jordan. It is your task to determine how to use your specific interests and powers in the decision-making process. The following are some Old Testament texts which will help you establish your identity:

> Exodus 4:10-17
> Exodus 4:27-31
> Exodus 28:1-4
> Exodus 32:1-35
> Numbers 15:1-40
> Joshua 5:1 - 6:27

BACKGROUND DATA

The priestly class owes its origin to the line of Aaron, the brother and religious assistant of Moses. Its concerns as a group are correct cultic practices, religious purity, and absolute dependence on God in all of life including political and military aspects. The cultic practices and laws can be found in the large sections from Exodus 25 through Leviticus. In regard to the taking of Palestine, the priestly influence can be seen in the ritual which preceded the taking of Jericho: the role of the ark, the miraculous crossing of the Jordan River, circumcision, and the celebration of the Passover. Following the destruction of Jericho, the priestly class insisted on the rule of *cherem*, the destruction of all things alien to God (Joshua 7). God is holy and always to be obeyed. While the point is disputed by readers of the Old Testament, it would appear that the priestly group supported military conquest but rejected conventional military methods. At least in the case of Jericho it was the priestly method which was utilized.

THE TAKING OF THE LAND A Simulation Based upon Numbers 14

THE SITUATION

You are to simulate a tribal meeting of the Israelites on the banks of the Jordan River after years of wandering in the wilderness. Moses has just died, and you are faced with several difficult decisions:

1. You must elect a leader to replace Moses.

 The leadership of Moses during the wilderness period was incredibly rocky. In the first place some of the Hebrews apparently joined the Exodus under protest (the group that murmured). From time to time there arose leaders who could mount a severe challenge to Moses. The most famous rebellion was that of Korah in Numbers 16, but the most striking is that of Moses' own brother and sister, Aaron and Miriam, in Numbers 12. Moses had tried to settle the leadership question by gathering seventy elders upon whom the Lord passed the spirit, but that apparently did not solve all the problems (Numbers 11). The critical challenge came when the decision to take Palestine was made. Joshua became the leader because he favored the taking of the land.

2. You must decide whether to cross over the Jordan or not.

 The crossing of the Red Sea, freedom from Egypt, and the taking of the Promised Land are the major elements of the formation of Israel as a people and a nation. Despite this central action of God, there were variations in the wishes of the people. Not all of the Hebrews wanted to leave Egypt (the murmurers in the wilderness); some did not wish to settle in the Fertile Crescent but wished to remain on the edge of the desert (sons of Reuben and sons of Gad). Historically the taking of Palestine was probably more gradual (as Judges indicates) than simply the one attack on Jericho, but that does not affect the simulation.

3. You must decide whether to defend yourselves by conventional military means or otherwise.

 In this section of the Old Testament there are two distinct ways of approaching the conquest. One is to depend entirely on the power of God. One can see this in the battle of Jericho, later in the battles led by Gideon, and even much later in the battle of David with Goliath. In sharp contrast are the battles which are sheer military endeavors and which end with bloody defeat of the enemy. Even some of those conquests which in the beginning were entirely dependent on the power of God ended with the bloody defeat of the enemy. Scholars also are not agreed on which was the method used in the conquest of Palestine or even on which is the dominant message of the Old Testament. It may be the intent was to depend on the power of God, but in moments of doubt man used his own might. At least most of the military stories of the Old Testament show how man in his weakness was saved by the overwhelming miraculous power of God.

TASKS OF ALL GROUPS
PRIOR TO THE SIMULATION

1. Appoint a leader who will—
   a. chair in the preparation for the simulation,
   b. lead the group during the simulation,
   For purposes of the simulation the leader of the groups will have the following identities:

The Priestly Class	Levi
The Jahwists	Joshua
The Egyptians	Achan
The Nomads	Gad

2. Appoint a chronicler who will—
   a. record briefly the process of the group,
   b. record the action of the simulation from the perspective of his group,
   c. report to the debriefing session.
3. Examine those texts of the Old Testament which establish the identity of your particular group.
4. Articulate your identity to each other by a song or a gesture or a banner.
5. Decide how your group will act in the simulated decisions. (See the background

data sheet.)

6. Discuss what means of group persuasion are available to you, given the group identity you have.

7. Assist the chronicler in recording, especially by articulating your plans as you project them prior to the simulation.

RULES OF THE SIMULATION

1. Each group will be allowed three representatives at the tribal meeting.

2. Other members of the group will be arranged behind the three representatives.

3. Any member of the group may replace one of his table representatives at will.

4. Each group will be allowed two roving politicians who may—
   a. discover the character and purposes of the other groups,
   b. facilitate or disrupt the procedures,
   c. consult with the background resource person.

TASKS OF THE SIMULATION

1. The coordinator will act as Moses until a new leader can be elected.

2. Under the direction of the newly elected leader the tribes will make the following decisions:
   a. Shall the tribes cross over the Jordan River and take Jericho?
   b. If they do try to take Jericho, what method will be used?
   c. If they choose to remain in the wilderness, or return to Egypt, what method of defense should be used against the hostile Amalekites, Amorites, and Moabites?

TASKS FOR DEBRIEFING

1. Make some change of the room arrangement to symbolize the end of the simulation.

2. Discuss with one another how you felt during the simulation.

3. Hear the reports from the chroniclers.

4. Discuss any questions that may be raised by the experience together.

2. The Jahwists

Your group identity for the simulation will be that of the Jahwists, a name given to that group which resulted from the revelation of the Lord recorded in Exodus 3. In the simulation there will be other groups helping to make the decision about crossing over the Jordan River. It is your task to determine how to use your specific interests and powers in the decision-making process. The following are some Old Testament texts which will help you establish your identity:

Exodus 3:1-15
Numbers 13:1-20
Numbers 14:20-38
Joshua 1:1 - 2:24

BACKGROUND DATA

The Jahwist group is to be identified with the program of Moses. In Exodus, when God reveals his name to Moses as Jahweh (see 3:14 in which the Hebrew letters for "I AM" are YHWH or JHWH, hence Jahweh), he proposes to lead the Hebrew people out of bondage in Egypt and to take them to a new land flowing with milk and honey. As the narrative continues, all goes well when the Hebrew people are obedient to the commandments of the Lord (Ten Commandments) and move toward that goal which he has set (the taking of Palestine). It is the Jahwist group which spies out the land and prepares for military action against it. Much of Numbers and Joshua tells in detail the military preparations and might of the twelve tribes. This military action and spying (with Rahab in Jericho) stands in sharp contrast to the priestly group which also advocated conquest but proceeded by means of ritual. Both methods are recorded in the early history of Israel and the conquest of Palestine. But it is primarily the Jahwist group which is responsible for the picture of Holy War in the Old Testament. For them God is the Lord of Hosts who led them out of Egypt by a pillar of cloud and who will lead them victoriously against their enemies. Those things which belong to the enemy are *cherem* (devoted to an alien god) and must be destroyed for the sake of Jahweh. So it is the very fanatical devotion to Jahweh which accounts for the bloody destruction of Canaanite cities and people.

THE TAKING OF THE LAND A Simulation Based upon Numbers 14

THE SITUATION

You are to simulate a tribal meeting of the Israelites on the banks of the Jordan River after years of wandering in the wilderness. Moses has just died, and you are faced with several difficult decisions:

1. You must elect a leader to replace Moses.

   The leadership of Moses during the wilderness period was incredibly rocky. In the first place some of the Hebrews apparently joined the Exodus under protest (the group that murmured). From time to time there arose leaders who could mount a severe challenge to Moses. The most famous rebellion was that of Korah in Numbers 16, but the most striking is that of Moses' own brother and sister, Aaron and Miriam, in Numbers 12. Moses had tried to settle the leadership question by gathering seventy elders upon whom the Lord passed the spirit, but that apparently did not solve all the problems (Numbers 11). The critical challenge came when the decision to take Palestine was made. Joshua became the leader because he favored the taking of the land.

2. You must decide whether to cross over the Jordan or not.

   The crossing of the Red Sea, freedom from Egypt, and the taking of the Promised Land are the major elements of the formation of Israel as a people and a nation. Despite this central action of God, there were variations in the wishes of the people. Not all of the Hebrews wanted to leave Egypt (the murmurers in the wilderness); some did not wish to settle in the Fertile Crescent but wished to remain on the edge of the desert (sons of Reuben and sons of Gad). Historically the taking of Palestine was probably more gradual (as Judges indicates) than simply the one attack on Jericho, but that does not affect the simulation.

3. You must decide whether to defend yourselves by conventional military means or otherwise.

   In this section of the Old Testament there are two distinct ways of approaching the conquest. One is to depend entirely on the power of God. One can see this in the battle of Jericho, later in the battles led by Gideon, and even much later in the battle of David with Goliath. In sharp contrast are the battles which are sheer military endeavors and which end with bloody defeat of the enemy. Even some of those conquests which in the beginning were entirely dependent on the power of God ended with the bloody defeat of the enemy. Scholars also are not agreed on which was the method used in the conquest of Palestine or even on which is the dominant message of the Old Testament. It may be the intent was to depend on the power of God, but in moments of doubt man used his own might. At least most of the military stories of the Old Testament show how man in his weakness was saved by the overwhelming miraculous power of God.

TASKS OF ALL GROUPS
PRIOR TO THE SIMULATION

1. Appoint a leader who will—
   a. chair in the preparation for the simulation,
   b. lead the group during the simulation,

   For purposes of the simulation the leader of the groups will have the following identities:

The Priestly Class	Levi
The Jahwists	Joshua
The Egyptians	Achan
The Nomads	Gad

2. Appoint a chronicler who will—
   a. record briefly the process of the group,
   b. record the action of the simulation from the perspective of his group,
   c. report to the debriefing session.
3. Examine those texts of the Old Testament which establish the identity of your particular group.
4. Articulate your identity to each other by a song or a gesture or a banner.
5. Decide how your group will act in the simulated decisions. (See the background

data sheet.)

6. Discuss what means of group persuasion are available to you, given the group identity you have.

7. Assist the chronicler in recording, especially by articulating your plans as you project them prior to the simulation.

RULES OF THE SIMULATION

1. Each group will be allowed three representatives at the tribal meeting.

2. Other members of the group will be arranged behind the three representatives.

3. Any member of the group may replace one of his table representatives at will.

4. Each group will be allowed two roving politicians who may—
   a. discover the character and purposes of the other groups,
   b. facilitate or disrupt the procedures,
   c. consult with the background resource person.

TASKS OF THE SIMULATION

1. The coordinator will act as Moses until a new leader can be elected.

2. Under the direction of the newly elected leader the tribes will make the following decisions:
   a. Shall the tribes cross over the Jordan River and take Jericho?
   b. If they do try to take Jericho, what method will be used?
   c. If they choose to remain in the wilderness, or return to Egypt, what method of defense should be used against the hostile Amalekites, Amorites, and Moabites?

TASKS FOR DEBRIEFING

1. Make some change of the room arrangement to symbolize the end of the simulation.

2. Discuss with one another how you felt during the simulation.

3. Hear the reports from the chroniclers.

4. Discuss any questions that may be raised by the experience together.

2. The Jahwists

Your group identity for the simulation will be that of the Jahwists, a name given to that group which resulted from the revelation of the Lord recorded in Exodus 3. In the simulation there will be other groups helping to make the decision about crossing over the Jordan River. It is your task to determine how to use your specific interests and powers in the decision-making process. The following are some Old Testament texts which will help you establish your identity:

> Exodus 3:1-15
> Numbers 13:1-20
> Numbers 14:20-38
> Joshua 1:1 - 2:24

BACKGROUND DATA

The Jahwist group is to be identified with the program of Moses. In Exodus, when God reveals his name to Moses as Jahweh (see 3:14 in which the Hebrew letters for "I AM" are YHWH or JHWH, hence Jahweh), he proposes to lead the Hebrew people out of bondage in Egypt and to take them to a new land flowing with milk and honey. As the narrative continues, all goes well when the Hebrew people are obedient to the commandments of the Lord (Ten Commandments) and move toward that goal which he has set (the taking of Palestine). It is the Jahwist group which spies out the land and prepares for military action against it. Much of Numbers and Joshua tells in detail the military preparations and might of the twelve tribes. This military action and spying (with Rahab in Jericho) stands in sharp contrast to the priestly group which also advocated conquest but proceeded by means of ritual. Both methods are recorded in the early history of Israel and the conquest of Palestine. But it is primarily the Jahwist group which is responsible for the picture of Holy War in the Old Testament. For them God is the Lord of Hosts who led them out of Egypt by a pillar of cloud and who will lead them victoriously against their enemies. Those things which belong to the enemy are *cherem* (devoted to an alien god) and must be destroyed for the sake of Jahweh. So it is the very fanatical devotion to Jahweh which accounts for the bloody destruction of Canaanite cities and people.

THE TAKING OF THE LAND A Simulation Based upon Numbers 14

THE SITUATION

You are to simulate a tribal meeting of the Israelites on the banks of the Jordan River after years of wandering in the wilderness. Moses has just died, and you are faced with several difficult decisions:

1. You must elect a leader to replace Moses.

   The leadership of Moses during the wilderness period was incredibly rocky. In the first place some of the Hebrews apparently joined the Exodus under protest (the group that murmured). From time to time there arose leaders who could mount a severe challenge to Moses. The most famous rebellion was that of Korah in Numbers 16, but the most striking is that of Moses' own brother and sister, Aaron and Miriam, in Numbers 12. Moses had tried to settle the leadership question by gathering seventy elders upon whom the Lord passed the spirit, but that apparently did not solve all the problems (Numbers 11). The critical challenge came when the decision to take Palestine was made. Joshua became the leader because he favored the taking of the land.

2. You must decide whether to cross over the Jordan or not.

   The crossing of the Red Sea, freedom from Egypt, and the taking of the Promised Land are the major elements of the formation of Israel as a people and a nation. Despite this central action of God, there were variations in the wishes of the people. Not all of the Hebrews wanted to leave Egypt (the murmurers in the wilderness); some did not wish to settle in the Fertile Crescent but wished to remain on the edge of the desert (sons of Reuben and sons of Gad). Historically the taking of Palestine was probably more gradual (as Judges indicates) than simply the one attack on Jericho, but that does not affect the simulation.

3. You must decide whether to defend yourselves by conventional military means or otherwise.

   In this section of the Old Testament there are two distinct ways of approaching the conquest. One is to depend entirely on the power of God. One can see this in the battle of Jericho, later in the battles led by Gideon, and even much later in the battle of David with Goliath. In sharp contrast are the battles which are sheer military endeavors and which end with bloody defeat of the enemy. Even some of those conquests which in the beginning were entirely dependent on the power of God ended with the bloody defeat of the enemy. Scholars also are not agreed on which was the method used in the conquest of Palestine or even on which is the dominant message of the Old Testament. It may be the intent was to depend on the power of God, but in moments of doubt man used his own might. At least most of the military stories of the Old Testament show how man in his weakness was saved by the overwhelming miraculous power of God.

TASKS OF ALL GROUPS
PRIOR TO THE SIMULATION

1. Appoint a leader who will—
   a. chair in the preparation for the simulation,
   b. lead the group during the simulation,
   For purposes of the simulation the leader of the groups will have the following identities:

The Priestly Class	Levi
The Jahwists	Joshua
The Egyptians	Achan
The Nomads	Gad

2. Appoint a chronicler who will—
   a. record briefly the process of the group,
   b. record the action of the simulation from the perspective of his group,
   c. report to the debriefing session.
3. Examine those texts of the Old Testament which establish the identity of your particular group.
4. Articulate your identity to each other by a song or a gesture or a banner.
5. Decide how your group will act in the simulated decisions. (See the background

data sheet.)

6. Discuss what means of group persuasion are available to you, given the group identity you have.

7. Assist the chronicler in recording, especially by articulating your plans as you project them prior to the simulation.

RULES OF THE SIMULATION

1. Each group will be allowed three representatives at the tribal meeting.
2. Other members of the group will be arranged behind the three representatives.
3. Any member of the group may replace one of his table representatives at will.
4. Each group will be allowed two roving politicians who may—
   a. discover the character and purposes of the other groups,
   b. facilitate or disrupt the procedures,
   c. consult with the background resource person.

TASKS OF THE SIMULATION

1. The coordinator will act as Moses until a new leader can be elected.
2. Under the direction of the newly elected leader the tribes will make the following decisions:
   a. Shall the tribes cross over the Jordan River and take Jericho?
   b. If they do try to take Jericho, what method will be used?
   c. If they choose to remain in the wilderness, or return to Egypt, what method of defense should be used against the hostile Amalekites, Amorites, and Moabites?

TASKS FOR DEBRIEFING

1. Make some change of the room arrangement to symbolize the end of the simulation.
2. Discuss with one another how you felt during the simulation.
3. Hear the reports from the chroniclers.
4. Discuss any questions that may be raised by the experience together.

3. The Egyptians

Your group identity for the simulation will be that of the Egyptians, a name given to that group which wished to return to Egypt rather than go on to the Promised Land. In the simulation there will be other groups helping to make the decision about crossing over the Jordan. It is your task to determine how to use your specific interests and powers in the decision-making process. The following are some Old Testament texts which will help you establish your identity:

> Exodus 14:10-12
> Exodus 15:22 - 16:3
> Exodus 17:1-7
> Numbers 11:1-23
> Numbers 13:31 - 14:5

BACKGROUND DATA

As one reads the Bible, it takes little imagination to see that the Hebrew people were hardly a monolithic body, all of one accord. Some were fanatical for Jahweh and the program of Moses. Others obviously could care less. Many adapted to the culture of which they were a part. While in Palestine many Hebrews adopted the ways of the Canaanites (to the utter disgust of the prophets). We know that even much later many Jews adopted the ways of the Babylonians during the Exile. The stay in Egypt had the same effect. Many of the Hebrew people had come to like Egypt and left only under duress. The same group protested during the wilderness period and likely was responsible for the many rebellions. While historical reconstruction is not possible in this regard, presumably the group which left Egypt reluctantly is the same group which took over Canaanite culture so quickly. The world at that time was divided primarily between the settled farmers and city dwellers on the one hand and the nomads on the other. The Hebrews once had been primarily nomads. The Egyptian group is one which had come to enjoy the security of farms and cities, however. In this sense they differed radically from the nomads who preferred a sheepherding existence in the nonsettled area across the Jordan.

THE TAKING OF THE LAND A Simulation Based upon Numbers 14

THE SITUATION
You are to simulate a tribal meeting of the Israelites on the banks of the Jordan River after years of wandering in the wilderness. Moses has just died, and you are faced with several difficult decisions:
1. You must elect a leader to replace Moses.

The leadership of Moses during the wilderness period was incredibly rocky. In the first place some of the Hebrews apparently joined the Exodus under protest (the group that murmured). From time to time there arose leaders who could mount a severe challenge to Moses. The most famous rebellion was that of Korah in Numbers 16, but the most striking is that of Moses' own brother and sister, Aaron and Miriam, in Numbers 12. Moses had tried to settle the leadership question by gathering seventy elders upon whom the Lord passed the spirit, but that apparently did not solve all the problems (Numbers 11). The critical challenge came when the decision to take Palestine was made. Joshua became the leader because he favored the taking of the land.
2. You must decide whether to cross over the Jordan or not.

The crossing of the Red Sea, freedom from Egypt, and the taking of the Promised Land are the major elements of the formation of Israel as a people and a nation. Despite this central action of God, there were variations in the wishes of the people. Not all of the Hebrews wanted to leave Egypt (the murmurers in the wilderness); some did not wish to settle in the Fertile Crescent but wished to remain on the edge of the desert (sons of Reuben and sons of Gad). Historically the taking of Palestine was probably more gradual (as Judges indicates) than simply the one attack on Jericho, but that does not affect the simulation.
3. You must decide whether to defend yourselves by conventional military means or otherwise.

In this section of the Old Testament there are two distinct ways of approaching the conquest. One is to depend entirely on the power of God. One can see this in the battle of Jericho, later in the battles led by Gideon, and even much later in the battle of David with Goliath. In sharp contrast are the battles which are sheer military endeavors and which end with bloody defeat of the enemy. Even some of those conquests which in the beginning were entirely dependent on the power of God ended with the bloody defeat of the enemy. Scholars also are not agreed on which was the method used in the conquest of Palestine or even on which is the dominant message of the Old Testament. It may be the intent was to depend on the power of God, but in moments of doubt man used his own might. At least most of the military stories of the Old Testament show how man in his weakness was saved by the overwhelming miraculous power of God.

TASKS OF ALL GROUPS
PRIOR TO THE SIMULATION
1. Appoint a leader who will—
   a. chair in the preparation for the simulation,
   b. lead the group during the simulation,

   For purposes of the simulation the leader of the groups will have the following identities:

The Priestly Class	Levi
The Jahwists	Joshua
The Egyptians	Achan
The Nomads	Gad
2. Appoint a chronicler who will—
   a. record briefly the process of the group,
   b. record the action of the simulation from the perspective of his group,
   c. report to the debriefing session.
3. Examine those texts of the Old Testament which establish the identity of your particular group.
4. Articulate your identity to each other by a song or a gesture or a banner.
5. Decide how your group will act in the simulated decisions. (See the background

data sheet.)

6. Discuss what means of group persuasion are available to you, given the group identity you have.

7. Assist the chronicler in recording, especially by articulating your plans as you project them prior to the simulation.

RULES OF THE SIMULATION

1. Each group will be allowed three representatives at the tribal meeting.

2. Other members of the group will be arranged behind the three representatives.

3. Any member of the group may replace one of his table representatives at will.

4. Each group will be allowed two roving politicians who may—
   a. discover the character and purposes of the other groups,
   b. facilitate or disrupt the procedures,
   c. consult with the background resource person.

TASKS OF THE SIMULATION

1. The coordinator will act as Moses until a new leader can be elected.

2. Under the direction of the newly elected leader the tribes will make the following decisions:
   a. Shall the tribes cross over the Jordan River and take Jericho?
   b. If they do try to take Jericho, what method will be used?
   c. If they choose to remain in the wilderness, or return to Egypt, what method of defense should be used against the hostile Amalekites, Amorites, and Moabites?

TASKS FOR DEBRIEFING

1. Make some change of the room arrangement to symbolize the end of the simulation.

2. Discuss with one another how you felt during the simulation.

3. Hear the reports from the chroniclers.

4. Discuss any questions that may be raised by the experience together.

3. The Egyptians

Your group identity for the simulation will be that of the Egyptians, a name given to that group which wished to return to Egypt rather than go on to the Promised Land. In the simulation there will be other groups helping to make the decision about crossing over the Jordan. It is your task to determine how to use your specific interests and powers in the decision-making process. The following are some Old Testament texts which will help you establish your identity:

> Exodus 14:10-12
> Exodus 15:22 - 16:3
> Exodus 17:1-7
> Numbers 11:1-23
> Numbers 13:31 - 14:5

BACKGROUND DATA

As one reads the Bible, it takes little imagination to see that the Hebrew people were hardly a monolithic body, all of one accord. Some were fanatical for Jahweh and the program of Moses. Others obviously could care less. Many adapted to the culture of which they were a part. While in Palestine many Hebrews adopted the ways of the Canaanites (to the utter disgust of the prophets). We know that even much later many Jews adopted the ways of the Babylonians during the Exile. The stay in Egypt had the same effect. Many of the Hebrew people had come to like Egypt and left only under duress. The same group protested during the wilderness period and likely was responsible for the many rebellions. While historical reconstruction is not possible in this regard, presumably the group which left Egypt reluctantly is the same group which took over Canaanite culture so quickly. The world at that time was divided primarily between the settled farmers and city dwellers on the one hand and the nomads on the other. The Hebrews once had been primarily nomads. The Egyptian group is one which had come to enjoy the security of farms and cities, however. In this sense they differed radically from the nomads who preferred a sheepherding existence in the nonsettled area across the Jordan.

THE TAKING OF THE LAND A Simulation Based upon Numbers 14

THE SITUATION

You are to simulate a tribal meeting of the Israelites on the banks of the Jordan River after years of wandering in the wilderness. Moses has just died, and you are faced with several difficult decisions:

1. You must elect a leader to replace Moses.

    The leadership of Moses during the wilderness period was incredibly rocky. In the first place some of the Hebrews apparently joined the Exodus under protest (the group that murmured). From time to time there arose leaders who could mount a severe challenge to Moses. The most famous rebellion was that of Korah in Numbers 16, but the most striking is that of Moses' own brother and sister, Aaron and Miriam, in Numbers 12. Moses had tried to settle the leadership question by gathering seventy elders upon whom the Lord passed the spirit, but that apparently did not solve all the problems (Numbers 11). The critical challenge came when the decision to take Palestine was made. Joshua became the leader because he favored the taking of the land.

2. You must decide whether to cross over the Jordan or not.

    The crossing of the Red Sea, freedom from Egypt, and the taking of the Promised Land are the major elements of the formation of Israel as a people and a nation. Despite this central action of God, there were variations in the wishes of the people. Not all of the Hebrews wanted to leave Egypt (the murmurers in the wilderness); some did not wish to settle in the Fertile Crescent but wished to remain on the edge of the desert (sons of Reuben and sons of Gad). Historically the taking of Palestine was probably more gradual (as Judges indicates) than simply the one attack on Jericho, but that does not affect the simulation.

3. You must decide whether to defend yourselves by conventional military means or otherwise.

In this section of the Old Testament there are two distinct ways of approaching the conquest. One is to depend entirely on the power of God. One can see this in the battle of Jericho, later in the battles led by Gideon, and even much later in the battle of David with Goliath. In sharp contrast are the battles which are sheer military endeavors and which end with bloody defeat of the enemy. Even some of those conquests which in the beginning were entirely dependent on the power of God ended with the bloody defeat of the enemy. Scholars also are not agreed on which was the method used in the conquest of Palestine or even on which is the dominant message of the Old Testament. It may be the intent was to depend on the power of God, but in moments of doubt man used his own might. At least most of the military stories of the Old Testament show how man in his weakness was saved by the overwhelming miraculous power of God.

TASKS OF ALL GROUPS
PRIOR TO THE SIMULATION

1. Appoint a leader who will—
    a. chair in the preparation for the simulation,
    b. lead the group during the simulation,
      For purposes of the simulation the leader of the groups will have the following identities:

The Priestly Class	Levi
The Jahwists	Joshua
The Egyptians	Achan
The Nomads	Gad

2. Appoint a chronicler who will—
    a. record briefly the process of the group,
    b. record the action of the simulation from the perspective of his group,
    c. report to the debriefing session.
3. Examine those texts of the Old Testament which establish the identity of your particular group.
4. Articulate your identity to each other by a song or a gesture or a banner.
5. Decide how your group will act in the simulated decisions. (See the background

data sheet.)

6. Discuss what means of group persuasion are available to you, given the group identity you have.

7. Assist the chronicler in recording, especially by articulating your plans as you project them prior to the simulation.

RULES OF THE SIMULATION

1. Each group will be allowed three representatives at the tribal meeting.

2. Other members of the group will be arranged behind the three representatives.

3. Any member of the group may replace one of his table representatives at will.

4. Each group will be allowed two roving politicians who may—

   a. discover the character and purposes of the other groups,

   b. facilitate or disrupt the procedures,

   c. consult with the background resource person.

TASKS OF THE SIMULATION

1. The coordinator will act as Moses until a new leader can be elected.

2. Under the direction of the newly elected leader the tribes will make the following decisions:

   a. Shall the tribes cross over the Jordan River and take Jericho?

   b. If they do try to take Jericho, what method will be used?

   c. If they choose to remain in the wilderness, or return to Egypt, what method of defense should be used against the hostile Amalekites, Amorites, and Moabites?

TASKS FOR DEBRIEFING

1. Make some change of the room arrangement to symbolize the end of the simulation.

2. Discuss with one another how you felt during the simulation.

3. Hear the reports from the chroniclers.

4. Discuss any questions that may be raised by the experience together.

4. The Nomads

Your group identity for the simulation will be that of the nomads, a name given to that group of Hebrews who did not wish to enter Palestine with the rest of the tribes. In the simulation there will be other groups helping to make the decision about crossing over the Jordan. It is your task to determine how to use your specific interests and powers in the decision-making process. The following are some Old Testament texts which will help you establish your identity:

> Genesis 47:1-7
> Numbers 32:1-32
> Joshua 1:12-18
> Micah 1:5-7
> Hosea 2:14f.
> Jeremiah 35

BACKGROUND DATA

The nomadic group represents one side of a struggle which was very intense at the time of Moses and continued to haunt the Jews even up to the time of Jesus. The conflict was between the wandering nomads and the settled farmers.

In Genesis particularly the struggle seems to lie underneath every story. It can be seen in the Cain and Abel story, the Abraham and Lot conflict, the quarrel between Esau and Jacob, and the hatred between Joseph and his brothers. Some of the Hebrews obviously had become acclimated to farms and cities and did not wish to leave Egypt (the Egyptians in our simulation). In sharp contrast the nomads were glad to leave Egypt, but did not share the enthusiasm of the priestly clan and the Jahwist group for settling in Palestine. Finally they made an agreement to remain seminomadic on the desert side of the Fertile Crescent. For this group the desert experience was the crucible of Hebrew history. It was there that the Hebrews learned to depend solely on God. The fall came when Israel entered into Palestine and became sedentary. This critique can be seen in many prophetic passages. The nomads shared a strong faith with the Jahwists, but for them Palestine was a theological trap to be avoided at all costs.

THE TAKING OF THE LAND A Simulation Based upon Numbers 14

THE SITUATION

You are to simulate a tribal meeting of the Israelites on the banks of the Jordan River after years of wandering in the wilderness. Moses has just died, and you are faced with several difficult decisions:

1. You must elect a leader to replace Moses.

   The leadership of Moses during the wilderness period was incredibly rocky. In the first place some of the Hebrews apparently joined the Exodus under protest (the group that murmured). From time to time there arose leaders who could mount a severe challenge to Moses. The most famous rebellion was that of Korah in Numbers 16, but the most striking is that of Moses' own brother and sister, Aaron and Miriam, in Numbers 12. Moses had tried to settle the leadership question by gathering seventy elders upon whom the Lord passed the spirit, but that apparently did not solve all the problems (Numbers 11). The critical challenge came when the decision to take Palestine was made. Joshua became the leader because he favored the taking of the land.

2. You must decide whether to cross over the Jordan or not.

   The crossing of the Red Sea, freedom from Egypt, and the taking of the Promised Land are the major elements of the formation of Israel as a people and a nation. Despite this central action of God, there were variations in the wishes of the people. Not all of the Hebrews wanted to leave Egypt (the murmurers in the wilderness); some did not wish to settle in the Fertile Crescent but wished to remain on the edge of the desert (sons of Reuben and sons of Gad). Historically the taking of Palestine was probably more gradual (as Judges indicates) than simply the one attack on Jericho, but that does not affect the simulation.

3. You must decide whether to defend yourselves by conventional military means or otherwise.

   In this section of the Old Testament there are two distinct ways of approaching the conquest. One is to depend entirely on the power of God. One can see this in the battle of Jericho, later in the battles led by Gideon, and even much later in the battle of David with Goliath. In sharp contrast are the battles which are sheer military endeavors and which end with bloody defeat of the enemy. Even some of those conquests which in the beginning were entirely dependent on the power of God ended with the bloody defeat of the enemy. Scholars also are not agreed on which was the method used in the conquest of Palestine or even on which is the dominant message of the Old Testament. It may be the intent was to depend on the power of God, but in moments of doubt man used his own might. At least most of the military stories of the Old Testament show how man in his weakness was saved by the overwhelming miraculous power of God.

TASKS OF ALL GROUPS
PRIOR TO THE SIMULATION

1. Appoint a leader who will—
   a. chair in the preparation for the simulation,
   b. lead the group during the simulation,
   For purposes of the simulation the leader of the groups will have the following identities:

The Priestly Class	Levi
The Jahwists	Joshua
The Egyptians	Achan
The Nomads	Gad

2. Appoint a chronicler who will—
   a. record briefly the process of the group,
   b. record the action of the simulation from the perspective of his group,
   c. report to the debriefing session.
3. Examine those texts of the Old Testament which establish the identity of your particular group.
4. Articulate your identity to each other by a song or a gesture or a banner.
5. Decide how your group will act in the simulated decisions. (See the background

61

data sheet.)

6. Discuss what means of group persuasion are available to you, given the group identity you have.

7. Assist the chronicler in recording, especially by articulating your plans as you project them prior to the simulation.

RULES OF THE SIMULATION

1. Each group will be allowed three representatives at the tribal meeting.

2. Other members of the group will be arranged behind the three representatives.

3. Any member of the group may replace one of his table representatives at will.

4. Each group will be allowed two roving politicians who may—

   a. discover the character and purposes of the other groups,

   b. facilitate or disrupt the procedures,

   c. consult with the background resource person.

TASKS OF THE SIMULATION

1. The coordinator will act as Moses until a new leader can be elected.

2. Under the direction of the newly elected leader the tribes will make the following decisions:

   a. Shall the tribes cross over the Jordan River and take Jericho?

   b. If they do try to take Jericho, what method will be used?

   c. If they choose to remain in the wilderness, or return to Egypt, what method of defense should be used against the hostile Amalekites, Amorites, and Moabites?

TASKS FOR DEBRIEFING

1. Make some change of the room arrangement to symbolize the end of the simulation.

2. Discuss with one another how you felt during the simulation.

3. Hear the reports from the chroniclers.

4. Discuss any questions that may be raised by the experience together.

4. The Nomads

Your group identity for the simulation will be that of the nomads, a name given to that group of Hebrews who did not wish to enter Palestine with the rest of the tribes. In the simulation there will be other groups helping to make the decision about crossing over the Jordan. It is your task to determine how to use your specific interests and powers in the decision-making process. The following are some Old Testament texts which will help you establish your identity:

Genesis 47:1-7
Numbers 32:1-32
Joshua 1:12-18
Micah 1:5-7
Hosea 2:14f.
Jeremiah 35

BACKGROUND DATA

The nomadic group represents one side of a struggle which was very intense at the time of Moses and continued to haunt the Jews even up to the time of Jesus. The conflict was between the wandering nomads and the settled farmers.

In Genesis particularly the struggle seems to lie underneath every story. It can be seen in the Cain and Abel story, the Abraham and Lot conflict, the quarrel between Esau and Jacob, and the hatred between Joseph and his brothers. Some of the Hebrews obviously had become acclimated to farms and cities and did not wish to leave Egypt (the Egyptians in our simulation). In sharp contrast the nomads were glad to leave Egypt, but did not share the enthusiasm of the priestly clan and the Jahwist group for settling in Palestine. Finally they made an agreement to remain seminomadic on the desert side of the Fertile Crescent. For this group the desert experience was the crucible of Hebrew history. It was there that the Hebrews learned to depend solely on God. The fall came when Israel entered into Palestine and became sedentary. This critique can be seen in many prophetic passages. The nomads shared a strong faith with the Jahwists, but for them Palestine was a theological trap to be avoided at all costs.

7. THE MAKING OF A KING

A Simulation Based upon 1 Samuel 8

INSTRUCTIONS TO
THE COORDINATOR

Preparation

The coordinator should read through the simulation in order to become acquainted with the details and the purposes. The particular theme of this simulation concerns the relationship between religion and the political life. It would be helpful for the simulation if some of the participants knew the goals and had a general idea about simulations prior to the actual session. This could prevent unnecessary delays and useless sidetracking.

Schedule

For a shorter or longer simulation the following schedules will be feasible:

	Short	Long
Introduction	5 min.	15 min.
Study of biblical passages and simulation material	25 min.	60 min.
Formulation of strategy	30 min.	45 min.
Break		
Tribal meeting	45 min.	90 min.
Debriefing	15 min.	30 min.

For the short schedule the biblical study should be limited to three or four passages and the decision making at the plenary session may have to be limited to one decision. In that case it might be valuable to appoint the leader of the tribes so that the issue of "church and state" could be discussed. See chapter 3 for other scheduling possibilities.

Space and Equipment

Each of the participants ought to have a Bible and pen or pencil and paper. For the identity articulation there should be available banner and poster materials, such as crayons, felt pens,

newsprint, and possibly felt or burlap for cloth banners. Props which establish identity are always useful in a simulation. The priests could wear choir robes; the seers could take on "hippie" or counter-culture attire. If a king is elected by the tribes, a special robe could be given to him.

For the plenary session you will need a large room with a center table large enough to seat twelve. The representatives will sit at the table with the other team members behind them. For the small-group work you will need either four rooms with smaller tables or four corners of the large room and sufficient privacy for the teams to formulate their plans without being overheard.

Facilitation

A major value of the simulation style of education is that various positions can be expressed in a game atmosphere. In this simulation sharply differing attitudes about "church and state" will likely emerge. If used with youth and adults together, it can be an expecially helpful introduction to the difficult problem of the generation gap. However, because the Old Testament stories are not as well known as those of the New Testament, it may be necessary to be rather creative in presenting the theme. As far as the story itself is concerned, it would be useful to ask the participants to read 1 Samuel 8 - 10. Minimally 1 Samuel 8 should be read as a part of the introduction.

Another method of introducing more information into the simulation is to call on witnesses. The groups should be informed by the coordinator that witnesses are available. We would suggest the possibility that some Hebrew converted from a non-Hebrew religion might give witness to the nature of a kingship in his religion. Any biblical encyclopedia will give information on "divine kingship" under the rubric "king." Lacking the opportunity for such preparation, the witness could utilize not only the information given in the simulation but also such passages as Judges 9:1-21 or Daniel 1 - 4. Psalm 24:7-10 could be cited as an example of the liturgy used for such a king.

If a king is elected, further educational benefits and interest could be obtained by crowning the king. Again, if time permits, consult encyclopedias under the rubrics "enthronement" or "king." If that is not possible, one could follow the enthronement described in Isaiah 6 utilizing such an enthronement psalm as Psalm 2.

Debriefing

Because this Old Testament simulation pertains to material not as well known as the Adam and Eve story, it is possible that not as much emotional energy will be spent in developing it. Experience indicates that when the cognitive demands are high, the encounters are not quite as sharp. If that is true in this case, then a stylized debriefing may be out of order. (If considerable emotional involvement has occurred, then debriefing should occur as described in chapter 4.)

The coordinator might move rather directly to the learning process itself. He can ask what was learned from the simulation. Persons who have had an exercise in self-education seem anxious to share that personally. In any simulation debriefing, the coordinator should allow every person a chance to articulate his impressions, either publicly or by talking to his "neighbor."

Particularly if the simulation was stopped because of a time limit, the groups will want to explain what their political strategy was. This will likely come out during the public expressions of impressions. If not, opportunity should be given the chronicler to tell what happened.

The value of some simulations is enhanced by the fact that form and content are united. This simulation fits that category. The election of a king parallels the problem of electing a leader for the tribal meeting. Some groups are to oppose the election of any administration. The spirit cares for that. In most groups that same attitude could be found today. In the debriefing, time should be allowed to let various persons respond to the issue of organization.

If the simulation is to be finished in a more worshipful mood, some affirmation of Jesus Christ as King would be a fitting close. A pairing of Psalm 2 with the baptism of Jesus (Matthew 3:13-17) would be both educational and faith affirming.

THE MAKING OF A KING A Simulation Based upon 1 Samuel 8

THE SITUATION

The leaders of Israel have come together in Ramah to decide whether or not to have a king. There are strong differences of opinion on the matter. As you simulate their decision, you will be faced with several questions:

1. You will need to select one of the group leaders to direct the whole group assembled in Ramah.

   There are times when one is tempted to say the history of Israel was a continuous struggle for leadership. Prior to the rise of David as king there were many kinds of leadership present: charismatic generals (Gideon), kings (Abimelech), judges (Jair), priests (Eli), and more frequently no one at all (Judges 21:25). From this Samuel emerges as the leader who is responsible for the decision about a king and then for the selection of Saul as first king. The problem is: Who was Samuel? He was raised by a priest and he scolded Saul for taking over his priestly functions (1 Samuel 13:8-15). He was well known as a seer and diviner (1 Samuel 9:6). He was called as a prophet (hearing the voice of the Lord in the night) and acted as a prophet by anointing both Saul and David king of Israel. And the text tells quite explicitly that Samuel was a judge (1 Samuel 7:15 - 8:3). Clearly all the major groups in Israel thought Samuel was "their man."

2. With the guidance of the chosen leader you will decide whether the twelve tribes should unite under one king.

   Because the association of the twelve tribes was a theological amphictyony (that is, organized by God), the various leaders obviously would oppose the creation of a monarchy. But the people began to insist on a king. After some debate the key seems to be that the prophets shifted positions (or, more technically, some seers became prophets) from opposition to a king to divine appointment of a king (1 Samuel 8:22). From that point on the conflict seems to be more in the method of choosing a king than the problem of having a king at all.

3. If a king is to be chosen, you should decide how it shall be done. If not, the problem of leadership must still be faced.

   While the narrator indicates only a few problems about who would be chosen king (see 1 Samuel 10:27 and 11:12), the story fairly bristles with the conflict about method. In fact Saul became king in four different ways. He was anointed by Samuel as the prophetic movement would have it; he was chosen by lot as the seers would have it (assisted by the priests, albeit); he was called by the Spirit of God and charismatically sent pieces of oxen to the tribes much as the judges would have it; and finally he performed the role of a priest-king much as the priests would like it. There is no historic way to determine whether Saul became king primarily through one method, or whether he satisfied all four power groups.

TASKS OF ALL GROUPS
PRIOR TO THE SIMULATION

1. Appoint a leader who will—
   a. chair in the preparation for the simulation,
   b. lead the group during the simulation.

   For purposes of the simulation the leaders of the groups will have the following historic identities:

The Priests	Eleazar
The Judges	Joel
The Prophets	Samuel
The Seers	Saul

2. Appoint a chronicler who will—
   a. record briefly the process of the group.
   b. record the action of the simulation from the perspective of his group,
   c. report to the debriefing session.

3. Examine those texts of the Old Testament which establish the identity of your particular group.

4. Articulate your identity to each other by a song or a gesture or a banner.

5. Project how your group will act in the simulated actions (consult your special instructions).

6. Discuss what means of group persuasion are available to you, given the group identity you have.
7. Assist the chronicler in recording, especially by articulating your plans as you project them prior to the simulation.

RULES OF THE SIMULATION
1. Each group will be allowed three representatives at the council table in Ramah.
2. Other members will be arranged behind the chairs of the three representatives.
3. Any member of the group may replace any one of his table representatives at will.
4. Each group will be allowed two roving politicians who may—
   a. discover the character and purpose of the other groups,
   b. facilitate or disrupt the procedures,
   c. consult with the background resource person.

TASKS OF THE SIMULATION
1. The coordinator will chair the session until the tribes are able to elect a leader.
2. Following the guidance of their chosen leader, the twelve tribes will attempt to deal with the following critical decisions:
   a. Should the tribes have a king?
   b. If so, how should he be chosen?
   c. If not, by what means will the tribes remain an organizational unit?

TASKS FOR THE DEBRIEFING
1. Make some change of your room arrangement to symbolize the end of the simulation.
2. Discuss with one another how you felt during the simulation.
3. Hear the reports from the chroniclers.
4. Discuss any questions that may be raised by the experience together.

1. The Priests

Your group identity for the simulation will be that of the priests, who were responsible for the cultic acts of the Hebrew tribes. In the simulation there will be other groups who are concerned about the organization of the tribes. Your task is to determine how your group can best utilize its special concern to bring about unification of the people. The following are some Old Testament texts which will help you establish your identity:

> Judges 17 - 18
> 1 Samuel 1 - 2
> 1 Samuel 4:1 - 7:14
> 1 Samuel 13:8-15
> 1 Samuel 14:1-5, 16-35

BACKGROUND DATA
The priests originated from the line of Aaron, brother of Moses, the great political leader. That is to say, in Israel religion and politics were nearly identical. So in the great moments of Israel's early history Moses and Aaron said and did the same things. The wars of Israel were religious wars in which the power of the God of Israel was placed against the power of other gods. This can be seen clearly in the above passages. It was the priest who had control of the sacred items, such as the ark of the covenant, which were used to defeat the enemy. Because this was a theocracy (rulership of God), it stands to reason any leader of the twelve tribes would have to be subservient to the priests. In the examples given, the king and his family were subject to the priest in matters of cultic practices and military or religious vows. It is highly probable the priests did not oppose the selection of a king for the tribes. But they undoubtedly insisted that a king would have to be subject to the laws of God as interpreted by the priests.

THE MAKING OF A KING A Simulation Based upon 1 Samuel 8

THE SITUATION

The leaders of Israel have come together in Ramah to decide whether or not to have a king. There are strong differences of opinion on the matter. As you simulate their decision, you will be faced with several questions:

1. You will need to select one of the group leaders to direct the whole group assembled in Ramah.

   There are times when one is tempted to say the history of Israel was a continuous struggle for leadership. Prior to the rise of David as king there were many kinds of leadership present: charismatic generals (Gideon), kings (Abimelech), judges (Jair), priests (Eli), and more frequently no one at all (Judges 21:25). From this Samuel emerges as the leader who is responsible for the decision about a king and then for the selection of Saul as first king. The problem is: Who was Samuel? He was raised by a priest and he scolded Saul for taking over his priestly functions (1 Samuel 13:8-15). He was well known as a seer and diviner (1 Samuel 9:6). He was called as a prophet (hearing the voice of the Lord in the night) and acted as a prophet by anointing both Saul and David king of Israel. And the text tells quite explicitly that Samuel was a judge (1 Samuel 7:15 - 8:3). Clearly all the major groups in Israel thought Samuel was "their man."

2. With the guidance of the chosen leader you will decide whether the twelve tribes should unite under one king.

   Because the association of the twelve tribes was a theological amphictyony (that is, organized by God), the various leaders obviously would oppose the creation of a monarchy. But the people began to insist on a king. After some debate the key seems to be that the prophets shifted positions (or, more technically, some seers became prophets) from opposition to a king to divine appointment of a king (1 Samuel 8:22). From that point on the conflict seems to be more in the method of choosing a king than the problem of having a king at all.

3. If a king is to be chosen, you should decide how it shall be done. If not, the problem of leadership must still be faced.

   While the narrator indicates only a few problems about who would be chosen king (see 1 Samuel 10:27 and 11:12), the story fairly bristles with the conflict about method. In fact Saul became king in four different ways. He was anointed by Samuel as the prophetic movement would have it; he was chosen by lot as the seers would have it (assisted by the priests, albeit); he was called by the Spirit of God and charismatically sent pieces of oxen to the tribes much as the judges would have it; and finally he performed the role of a priest-king much as the priests would like it. There is no historic way to determine whether Saul became king primarily through one method, or whether he satisfied all four power groups.

TASKS OF ALL GROUPS
PRIOR TO THE SIMULATION

1. Appoint a leader who will—
   a. chair in the preparation for the simulation,
   b. lead the group during the simulation.

   For purposes of the simulation the leaders of the groups will have the following historic identities:

The Priests	Eleazar
The Judges	Joel
The Prophets	Samuel
The Seers	Saul

2. Appoint a chronicler who will—
   a. record briefly the process of the group.
   b. record the action of the simulation from the perspective of his group,
   c. report to the debriefing session.

3. Examine those texts of the Old Testament which establish the identity of your particular group.

4. Articulate your identity to each other by a song or a gesture or a banner.

5. Project how your group will act in the simulated actions (consult your special instructions).

6. Discuss what means of group persuasion are available to you, given the group identity you have.
7. Assist the chronicler in recording, especially by articulating your plans as you project them prior to the simulation.

RULES OF THE SIMULATION

1. Each group will be allowed three representatives at the council table in Ramah.
2. Other members will be arranged behind the chairs of the three representatives.
3. Any member of the group may replace any one of his table representatives at will.
4. Each group will be allowed two roving politicians who may—
   a. discover the character and purpose of the other groups,
   b. facilitate or disrupt the procedures,
   c. consult with the background resource person.

TASKS OF THE SIMULATION

1. The coordinator will chair the session until the tribes are able to elect a leader.
2. Following the guidance of their chosen leader, the twelve tribes will attempt to deal with the following critical decisions:
   a. Should the tribes have a king?
   b. If so, how should he be chosen?
   c. If not, by what means will the tribes remain an organizational unit?

TASKS FOR THE DEBRIEFING

1. Make some change of your room arrangement to symbolize the end of the simulation.
2. Discuss with one another how you felt during the simulation.
3. Hear the reports from the chroniclers.
4. Discuss any questions that may be raised by the experience together.

1. The Priests

Your group identity for the simulation will be that of the priests, who were responsible for the cultic acts of the Hebrew tribes. In the simulation there will be other groups who are concerned about the organization of the tribes. Your task is to determine how your group can best utilize its special concern to bring about unification of the people. The following are some Old Testament texts which will help you establish your identity:

> Judges 17 - 18
> 1 Samuel 1 - 2
> 1 Samuel 4:1 - 7:14
> 1 Samuel 13:8-15
> 1 Samuel 14:1-5, 16-35

BACKGROUND DATA

The priests originated from the line of Aaron, brother of Moses, the great political leader. That is to say, in Israel religion and politics were nearly identical. So in the great moments of Israel's early history Moses and Aaron said and did the same things. The wars of Israel were religious wars in which the power of the God of Israel was placed against the power of other gods. This can be seen clearly in the above passages. It was the priest who had control of the sacred items, such as the ark of the covenant, which were used to defeat the enemy. Because this was a theocracy (rulership of God), it stands to reason any leader of the twelve tribes would have to be subservient to the priests. In the examples given, the king and his family were subject to the priest in matters of cultic practices and military or religious vows. It is highly probable the priests did not oppose the selection of a king for the tribes. But they undoubtedly insisted that a king would have to be subject to the laws of God as interpreted by the priests.

THE MAKING OF A KING A Simulation Based upon 1 Samuel 8

THE SITUATION

The leaders of Israel have come together in Ramah to decide whether or not to have a king. There are strong differences of opinion on the matter. As you simulate their decision, you will be faced with several questions:

1. You will need to select one of the group leaders to direct the whole group assembled in Ramah.

   There are times when one is tempted to say the history of Israel was a continuous struggle for leadership. Prior to the rise of David as king there were many kinds of leadership present: charismatic generals (Gideon), kings (Abimelech), judges (Jair), priests (Eli), and more frequently no one at all (Judges 21:25). From this Samuel emerges as the leader who is responsible for the decision about a king and then for the selection of Saul as first king. The problem is: Who was Samuel? He was raised by a priest and he scolded Saul for taking over his priestly functions (1 Samuel 13:8-15). He was well known as a seer and diviner (1 Samuel 9:6). He was called as a prophet (hearing the voice of the Lord in the night) and acted as a prophet by anointing both Saul and David king of Israel. And the text tells quite explicitly that Samuel was a judge (1 Samuel 7:15 - 8:3). Clearly all the major groups in Israel thought Samuel was "their man."

2. With the guidance of the chosen leader you will decide whether the twelve tribes should unite under one king.

   Because the association of the twelve tribes was a theological amphictyony (that is, organized by God), the various leaders obviously would oppose the creation of a monarchy. But the people began to insist on a king. After some debate the key seems to be that the prophets shifted positions (or, more technically, some seers became prophets) from opposition to a king to divine appointment of a king (1 Samuel 8:22). From that point on the conflict seems to be more in the method of choosing a king than the problem of having a king at all.

3. If a king is to be chosen, you should decide how it shall be done. If not, the problem of leadership must still be faced.

   While the narrator indicates only a few problems about who would be chosen king (see 1 Samuel 10:27 and 11:12), the story fairly bristles with the conflict about method. In fact Saul became king in four different ways. He was anointed by Samuel as the prophetic movement would have it; he was chosen by lot as the seers would have it (assisted by the priests, albeit); he was called by the Spirit of God and charismatically sent pieces of oxen to the tribes much as the judges would have it; and finally he performed the role of a priest-king much as the priests would like it. There is no historic way to determine whether Saul became king primarily through one method, or whether he satisfied all four power groups.

TASKS OF ALL GROUPS
PRIOR TO THE SIMULATION

1. Appoint a leader who will—
   a. chair in the preparation for the simulation,
   b. lead the group during the simulation.

   For purposes of the simulation the leaders of the groups will have the following historic identities:

The Priests	Eleazar
The Judges	Joel
The Prophets	Samuel
The Seers	Saul

2. Appoint a chronicler who will—
   a. record briefly the process of the group.
   b. record the action of the simulation from the perspective of his group,
   c. report to the debriefing session.

3. Examine those texts of the Old Testament which establish the identity of your particular group.

4. Articulate your identity to each other by a song or a gesture or a banner.

5. Project how your group will act in the simulated actions (consult your special instructions).

6. Discuss what means of group persuasion are available to you, given the group identity you have.
7. Assist the chronicler in recording, especially by articulating your plans as you project them prior to the simulation.

RULES OF THE SIMULATION

1. Each group will be allowed three representatives at the council table in Ramah.
2. Other members will be arranged behind the chairs of the three representatives.
3. Any member of the group may replace any one of his table representatives at will.
4. Each group will be allowed two roving politicians who may—
   a. discover the character and purpose of the other groups,
   b. facilitate or disrupt the procedures,
   c. consult with the background resource person.

TASKS OF THE SIMULATION

1. The coordinator will chair the session until the tribes are able to elect a leader.
2. Following the guidance of their chosen leader, the twelve tribes will attempt to deal with the following critical decisions:
   a. Should the tribes have a king?
   b. If so, how should he be chosen?
   c. If not, by what means will the tribes remain an organizational unit?

TASKS FOR THE DEBRIEFING

1. Make some change of your room arrangement to symbolize the end of the simulation.
2. Discuss with one another how you felt during the simulation.
3. Hear the reports from the chroniclers.
4. Discuss any questions that may be raised by the experience together.

2. The Judges

Your group identity for the simulation will be that of the judges who were the occasional, charismatic (spirit-led) leaders of Israel prior to the time of Saul. In the simulation there will be other groups helping to make the decision about organizing Israel. It is your task to determine how to use your specific interests and powers in the decision-making process. The following are some Old Testament texts which will help you establish your identity:

> Judges 2:16-23
> Judges 8:22 - 9:21
> Judges 10:1 - 11:33
> 1 Samuel 7:15 - 8:18
> 1 Samuel 11:1-15

BACKGROUND DATA

"Judges" is a rather inept or inappropriate English name for those leaders of the twelve tribes prior to the formation of the monarchy. It is inappropriate because it leaves the English-speaking reader with the impression that these were men and women in charge of the legal system of Israel. While it is true these persons did judge in cases of difficult decisions (1 Samuel 7:15-17), that is only a small part of the total picture we have of these early leaders. There is no single description which will satisfy the category "judges." Many of them were not leaders in the ordinary sense of the word. Especially the ones we know best, like Gideon, Samson, and Jephthah, seemed to come from nowhere, responding to a serious military situation. In fact the Old Testament often plays them up as "nobodies" who responded to the action of the Spirit of the Lord in a miraculous situation. Therefore we speak of the judges as charismatics (spirit-led). Yet, on the other hand, many of the judges were local leaders (Abimelech, Jair, Deborah) who in emergency situations temporarily led all the tribes. In that sense Saul acts like a judge in 1 Samuel 11 rather than a king. The judges would favor tribal organization, but they would resist any permanent "human" seat of that power. For the judges the formation of the amphictyony (league of twelve tribes) was an act of the Spirit, and they would fight vehemently any attempt to make that a human organization.

THE MAKING OF A KING A Simulation Based upon 1 Samuel 8

THE SITUATION

The leaders of Israel have come together in Ramah to decide whether or not to have a king. There are strong differences of opinion on the matter. As you simulate their decision, you will be faced with several questions:

1. You will need to select one of the group leaders to direct the whole group assembled in Ramah.

   There are times when one is tempted to say the history of Israel was a continuous struggle for leadership. Prior to the rise of David as king there were many kinds of leadership present: charismatic generals (Gideon), kings (Abimelech), judges (Jair), priests (Eli), and more frequently no one at all (Judges 21:25). From this Samuel emerges as the leader who is responsible for the decision about a king and then for the selection of Saul as first king. The problem is: Who was Samuel? He was raised by a priest and he scolded Saul for taking over his priestly functions (1 Samuel 13:8-15). He was well known as a seer and diviner (1 Samuel 9:6). He was called as a prophet (hearing the voice of the Lord in the night) and acted as a prophet by anointing both Saul and David king of Israel. And the text tells quite explicitly that Samuel was a judge (1 Samuel 7:15 - 8:3). Clearly all the major groups in Israel thought Samuel was "their man."

2. With the guidance of the chosen leader you will decide whether the twelve tribes should unite under one king.

   Because the association of the twelve tribes was a theological amphictyony (that is, organized by God), the various leaders obviously would oppose the creation of a monarchy. But the people began to insist on a king. After some debate the key seems to be that the prophets shifted positions (or, more technically, some seers became prophets) from opposition to a king to divine appointment of a king (1 Samuel 8:22). From that point on the conflict seems to be more in the method of choosing a king than the problem of having a king at all.

3. If a king is to be chosen, you should decide how it shall be done. If not, the problem of leadership must still be faced.

   While the narrator indicates only a few problems about who would be chosen king (see 1 Samuel 10:27 and 11:12), the story fairly bristles with the conflict about method. In fact Saul became king in four different ways. He was anointed by Samuel as the prophetic movement would have it; he was chosen by lot as the seers would have it (assisted by the priests, albeit); he was called by the Spirit of God and charismatically sent pieces of oxen to the tribes much as the judges would have it; and finally he performed the role of a priest-king much as the priests would like it. There is no historic way to determine whether Saul became king primarily through one method, or whether he satisfied all four power groups.

TASKS OF ALL GROUPS
PRIOR TO THE SIMULATION

1. Appoint a leader who will—
   a. chair in the preparation for the simulation,
   b. lead the group during the simulation.

   For purposes of the simulation the leaders of the groups will have the following historic identities:

The Priests	Eleazar
The Judges	Joel
The Prophets	Samuel
The Seers	Saul

2. Appoint a chronicler who will—
   a. record briefly the process of the group.
   b. record the action of the simulation from the perspective of his group,
   c. report to the debriefing session.

3. Examine those texts of the Old Testament which establish the identity of your particular group.

4. Articulate your identity to each other by a song or a gesture or a banner.

5. Project how your group will act in the simulated actions (consult your special instructions).

6. Discuss what means of group persuasion are available to you, given the group identity you have.
7. Assist the chronicler in recording, especially by articulating your plans as you project them prior to the simulation.

RULES OF THE SIMULATION

1. Each group will be allowed three representatives at the council table in Ramah.
2. Other members will be arranged behind the chairs of the three representatives.
3. Any member of the group may replace any one of his table representatives at will.
4. Each group will be allowed two roving politicians who may—
   a. discover the character and purpose of the other groups,
   b. facilitate or disrupt the procedures,
   c. consult with the background resource person.

TASKS OF THE SIMULATION

1. The coordinator will chair the session until the tribes are able to elect a leader.
2. Following the guidance of their chosen leader, the twelve tribes will attempt to deal with the following critical decisions:
   a. Should the tribes have a king?
   b. If so, how should he be chosen?
   c. If not, by what means will the tribes remain an organizational unit?

TASKS FOR THE DEBRIEFING

1. Make some change of your room arrangement to symbolize the end of the simulation.
2. Discuss with one another how you felt during the simulation.
3. Hear the reports from the chroniclers.
4. Discuss any questions that may be raised by the experience together.

2. The Judges

Your group identity for the simulation will be that of the judges who were the occasional, charismatic (spirit-led) leaders of Israel prior to the time of Saul. In the simulation there will be other groups helping to make the decision about organizing Israel. It is your task to determine how to use your specific interests and powers in the decision-making process. The following are some Old Testament texts which will help you establish your identity:

Judges 2:16-23
Judges 8:22 - 9:21
Judges 10:1 - 11:33
1 Samuel 7:15 - 8:18
1 Samuel 11:1-15

BACKGROUND DATA

"Judges" is a rather inept or inappropriate English name for those leaders of the twelve tribes prior to the formation of the monarchy. It is inappropriate because it leaves the English-speaking reader with the impression that these were men and women in charge of the legal system of Israel. While it is true these persons did judge in cases of difficult decisions (1 Samuel 7:15-17), that is only a small part of the total picture we have of these early leaders. There is no single description which will satisfy the category "judges." Many of them were not leaders in the ordinary sense of the word. Especially the ones we know best, like Gideon, Samson, and Jephthah, seemed to come from nowhere, responding to a serious military situation. In fact the Old Testament often plays them up as "nobodies" who responded to the action of the Spirit of the Lord in a miraculous situation. Therefore we speak of the judges as charismatics (spirit-led). Yet, on the other hand, many of the judges were local leaders (Abimelech, Jair, Deborah) who in emergency situations temporarily led all the tribes. In that sense Saul acts like a judge in 1 Samuel 11 rather than a king. The judges would favor tribal organization, but they would resist any permanent "human" seat of that power. For the judges the formation of the amphictyony (league of twelve tribes) was an act of the Spirit, and they would fight vehemently any attempt to make that a human organization.

THE MAKING OF A KING A Simulation Based upon 1 Samuel 8

THE SITUATION

The leaders of Israel have come together in Ramah to decide whether or not to have a king. There are strong differences of opinion on the matter. As you simulate their decision, you will be faced with several questions:

1. You will need to select one of the group leaders to direct the whole group assembled in Ramah.

   There are times when one is tempted to say the history of Israel was a continuous struggle for leadership. Prior to the rise of David as king there were many kinds of leadership present: charismatic generals (Gideon), kings (Abimelech), judges (Jair), priests (Eli), and more frequently no one at all (Judges 21:25). From this Samuel emerges as the leader who is responsible for the decision about a king and then for the selection of Saul as first king. The problem is: Who was Samuel? He was raised by a priest and he scolded Saul for taking over his priestly functions (1 Samuel 13:8-15). He was well known as a seer and diviner (1 Samuel 9:6). He was called as a prophet (hearing the voice of the Lord in the night) and acted as a prophet by anointing both Saul and David king of Israel. And the text tells quite explicitly that Samuel was a judge (1 Samuel 7:15 - 8:3). Clearly all the major groups in Israel thought Samuel was "their man."

2. With the guidance of the chosen leader you will decide whether the twelve tribes should unite under one king.

   Because the association of the twelve tribes was a theological amphictyony (that is, organized by God), the various leaders obviously would oppose the creation of a monarchy. But the people began to insist on a king. After some debate the key seems to be that the prophets shifted positions (or, more technically, some seers became prophets) from opposition to a king to divine appointment of a king (1 Samuel 8:22). From that point on the conflict seems to be more in the method of choosing a king than the problem of having a king at all.

3. If a king is to be chosen, you should decide how it shall be done. If not, the problem of leadership must still be faced.

   While the narrator indicates only a few problems about who would be chosen king (see 1 Samuel 10:27 and 11:12), the story fairly bristles with the conflict about method. In fact Saul became king in four different ways. He was anointed by Samuel as the prophetic movement would have it; he was chosen by lot as the seers would have it (assisted by the priests, albeit); he was called by the Spirit of God and charismatically sent pieces of oxen to the tribes much as the judges would have it; and finally he performed the role of a priest-king much as the priests would like it. There is no historic way to determine whether Saul became king primarily through one method, or whether he satisfied all four power groups.

TASKS OF ALL GROUPS
PRIOR TO THE SIMULATION

1. Appoint a leader who will—
   a. chair in the preparation for the simulation,
   b. lead the group during the simulation.

   For purposes of the simulation the leaders of the groups will have the following historic identities:

The Priests	Eleazar
The Judges	Joel
The Prophets	Samuel
The Seers	Saul

2. Appoint a chronicler who will—
   a. record briefly the process of the group.
   b. record the action of the simulation from the perspective of his group,
   c. report to the debriefing session.

3. Examine those texts of the Old Testament which establish the identity of your particular group.

4. Articulate your identity to each other by a song or a gesture or a banner.

5. Project how your group will act in the simulated actions (consult your special instructions).

6. Discuss what means of group persuasion are available to you, given the group identity you have.
7. Assist the chronicler in recording, especially by articulating your plans as you project them prior to the simulation.

RULES OF THE SIMULATION
1. Each group will be allowed three representatives at the council table in Ramah.
2. Other members will be arranged behind the chairs of the three representatives.
3. Any member of the group may replace any one of his table representatives at will.
4. Each group will be allowed two roving politicians who may—
   a. discover the character and purpose of the other groups,
   b. facilitate or disrupt the procedures,
   c. consult with the background resource person.

TASKS OF THE SIMULATION
1. The coordinator will chair the session until the tribes are able to elect a leader.
2. Following the guidance of their chosen leader, the twelve tribes will attempt to deal with the following critical decisions:
   a. Should the tribes have a king?
   b. If so, how should he be chosen?
   c. If not, by what means will the tribes remain an organizational unit?

TASKS FOR THE DEBRIEFING
1. Make some change of your room arrangement to symbolize the end of the simulation.
2. Discuss with one another how you felt during the simulation.
3. Hear the reports from the chroniclers.
4. Discuss any questions that may be raised by the experience together.

3. The Prophets

Your group identity for the simulation will be that of the prophets who began, at the time of Samuel, to play a leading role in the political decisions of the coming nations, Judah and Israel. In the simulation there will be other groups helping to make the decision about organizing the twelve tribes. It is your task to determine how to use your specific interests and powers in the decision-making process. The following are some Old Testament texts which will help you establish your identity:

> 1 Samuel 3:1 - 4:1
> 1 Samuel 8:4-22
> 1 Samuel 9:15 - 10:1
> 1 Samuel 10:17-19
> 1 Samuel 15:34 - 16:13

BACKGROUND DATA
As the narrator tells us (1 Samuel 9:9), the prophets were once seers and in these stories the distinction sometimes cannot be seen. Historically the origin of the prophetic movement and its relationship to the seers has never been explained satisfactorily. But for the simulation we might make these distinctions. Seers were charismatic (spirit-led) diviners who could create among themselves ecstatic "trips" by means of music, flagellation, or sex. In moments of ecstasy they became clairvoyant, able to find lost objects (1 Samuel 9:3-10), able to predict the future (1 Samuel 10:5), and even able to speak to the dead (1 Samuel 28:8). Such diviners or seers were common in the world at that time and even today can be found in Near Eastern villages. On the other hand, the prophetic movement is fairly unique to the Hebrew people. It arose from the seer movement about the time of the rise of the monarchy. In fact the two may be intimately related. In the books of Samuel and Kings it is the prophets who anoint kings in the name of the Lord. By the time of the great prophets they are critics of the king and his policies (Isaiah and Jeremiah). In any case the prophet stands close to the king. The prophet presents the Word of the Lord to the king much as the priest oversees his ritual purity. So for this simulation we would assume the prophet would take an active part in selecting the king but would oppose anyone who tried to become king apart from the Word of the Lord.

THE MAKING OF A KING A Simulation Based upon 1 Samuel 8

THE SITUATION

The leaders of Israel have come together in Ramah to decide whether or not to have a king. There are strong differences of opinion on the matter. As you simulate their decision, you will be faced with several questions:

1. You will need to select one of the group leaders to direct the whole group assembled in Ramah.

There are times when one is tempted to say the history of Israel was a continuous struggle for leadership. Prior to the rise of David as king there were many kinds of leadership present: charismatic generals (Gideon), kings (Abimelech), judges (Jair), priests (Eli), and more frequently no one at all (Judges 21:25). From this Samuel emerges as the leader who is responsible for the decision about a king and then for the selection of Saul as first king. The problem is: Who was Samuel? He was raised by a priest and he scolded Saul for taking over his priestly functions (1 Samuel 13:8-15). He was well known as a seer and diviner (1 Samuel 9:6). He was called as a prophet (hearing the voice of the Lord in the night) and acted as a prophet by anointing both Saul and David king of Israel. And the text tells quite explicitly that Samuel was a judge (1 Samuel 7:15 - 8:3). Clearly all the major groups in Israel thought Samuel was "their man."

2. With the guidance of the chosen leader you will decide whether the twelve tribes should unite under one king.

Because the association of the twelve tribes was a theological amphictyony (that is, organized by God), the various leaders obviously would oppose the creation of a monarchy. But the people began to insist on a king. After some debate the key seems to be that the prophets shifted positions (or, more technically, some seers became prophets) from opposition to a king to divine appointment of a king (1 Samuel 8:22). From that point on the conflict seems to be more in the method of choosing a king than the problem of having a king at all.

3. If a king is to be chosen, you should decide how it shall be done. If not, the problem of leadership must still be faced.

While the narrator indicates only a few problems about who would be chosen king (see 1 Samuel 10:27 and 11:12), the story fairly bristles with the conflict about method. In fact Saul became king in four different ways. He was anointed by Samuel as the prophetic movement would have it; he was chosen by lot as the seers would have it (assisted by the priests, albeit); he was called by the Spirit of God and charismatically sent pieces of oxen to the tribes much as the judges would have it; and finally he performed the role of a priest-king much as the priests would like it. There is no historic way to determine whether Saul became king primarily through one method, or whether he satisfied all four power groups.

TASKS OF ALL GROUPS
PRIOR TO THE SIMULATION

1. Appoint a leader who will—
   a. chair in the preparation for the simulation,
   b. lead the group during the simulation.

   For purposes of the simulation the leaders of the groups will have the following historic identities:

The Priests	Eleazar
The Judges	Joel
The Prophets	Samuel
The Seers	Saul

2. Appoint a chronicler who will—
   a. record briefly the process of the group.
   b. record the action of the simulation from the perspective of his group,
   c. report to the debriefing session.

3. Examine those texts of the Old Testament which establish the identity of your particular group.

4. Articulate your identity to each other by a song or a gesture or a banner.

5. Project how your group will act in the simulated actions (consult your special instructions).

6. Discuss what means of group persuasion are available to you, given the group identity you have.
7. Assist the chronicler in recording, especially by articulating your plans as you project them prior to the simulation.

RULES OF THE SIMULATION
1. Each group will be allowed three representatives at the council table in Ramah.
2. Other members will be arranged behind the chairs of the three representatives.
3. Any member of the group may replace any one of his table representatives at will.
4. Each group will be allowed two roving politicians who may—
   a. discover the character and purpose of the other groups,
   b. facilitate or disrupt the procedures,
   c. consult with the background resource person.

TASKS OF THE SIMULATION
1. The coordinator will chair the session until the tribes are able to elect a leader.
2. Following the guidance of their chosen leader, the twelve tribes will attempt to deal with the following critical decisions:
   a. Should the tribes have a king?
   b. If so, how should he be chosen?
   c. If not, by what means will the tribes remain an organizational unit?

TASKS FOR THE DEBRIEFING
1. Make some change of your room arrangement to symbolize the end of the simulation.
2. Discuss with one another how you felt during the simulation.
3. Hear the reports from the chroniclers.
4. Discuss any questions that may be raised by the experience together.

3. The Prophets

Your group identity for the simulation will be that of the prophets who began, at the time of Samuel, to play a leading role in the political decisions of the coming nations, Judah and Israel. In the simulation there will be other groups helping to make the decision about organizing the twelve tribes. It is your task to determine how to use your specific interests and powers in the decision-making process. The following are some Old Testament texts which will help you establish your identity:

> 1 Samuel 3:1 - 4:1
> 1 Samuel 8:4-22
> 1 Samuel 9:15 - 10:1
> 1 Samuel 10:17-19
> 1 Samuel 15:34 - 16:13

BACKGROUND DATA
As the narrator tells us (1 Samuel 9:9), the prophets were once seers and in these stories the distinction sometimes cannot be seen. Historically the origin of the prophetic movement and its relationship to the seers has never been explained satisfactorily. But for the simulation we might make these distinctions. Seers were charismatic (spirit-led) diviners who could create among themselves ecstatic "trips" by means of music, flagellation, or sex. In moments of ecstasy they became clairvoyant, able to find lost objects (1 Samuel 9:3-10), able to predict the future (1 Samuel 10:5), and even able to speak to the dead (1 Samuel 28:8). Such diviners or seers were common in the world at that time and even today can be found in Near Eastern villages. On the other hand, the prophetic movement is fairly unique to the Hebrew people. It arose from the seer movement about the time of the rise of the monarchy. In fact the two may be intimately related. In the books of Samuel and Kings it is the prophets who anoint kings in the name of the Lord. By the time of the great prophets they are critics of the king and his policies (Isaiah and Jeremiah). In any case the prophet stands close to the king. The prophet presents the Word of the Lord to the king much as the priest oversees his ritual purity. So for this simulation we would assume the prophet would take an active part in selecting the king but would oppose anyone who tried to become king apart from the Word of the Lord.

THE MAKING OF A KING A Simulation Based upon 1 Samuel 8

THE SITUATION

The leaders of Israel have come together in Ramah to decide whether or not to have a king. There are strong differences of opinion on the matter. As you simulate their decision, you will be faced with several questions:

1. You will need to select one of the group leaders to direct the whole group assembled in Ramah.

   There are times when one is tempted to say the history of Israel was a continuous struggle for leadership. Prior to the rise of David as king there were many kinds of leadership present: charismatic generals (Gideon), kings (Abimelech), judges (Jair), priests (Eli), and more frequently no one at all (Judges 21:25). From this Samuel emerges as the leader who is responsible for the decision about a king and then for the selection of Saul as first king. The problem is: Who was Samuel? He was raised by a priest and he scolded Saul for taking over his priestly functions (1 Samuel 13:8-15). He was well known as a seer and diviner (1 Samuel 9:6). He was called as a prophet (hearing the voice of the Lord in the night) and acted as a prophet by anointing both Saul and David king of Israel. And the text tells quite explicitly that Samuel was a judge (1 Samuel 7:15 - 8:3). Clearly all the major groups in Israel thought Samuel was "their man."

2. With the guidance of the chosen leader you will decide whether the twelve tribes should unite under one king.

   Because the association of the twelve tribes was a theological amphictyony (that is, organized by God), the various leaders obviously would oppose the creation of a monarchy. But the people began to insist on a king. After some debate the key seems to be that the prophets shifted positions (or, more technically, some seers became prophets) from opposition to a king to divine appointment of a king (1 Samuel 8:22). From that point on the conflict seems to be more in the method of choosing a king than the problem of having a king at all.

3. If a king is to be chosen, you should decide how it shall be done. If not, the problem of leadership must still be faced.

   While the narrator indicates only a few problems about who would be chosen king (see 1 Samuel 10:27 and 11:12), the story fairly bristles with the conflict about method. In fact Saul became king in four different ways. He was anointed by Samuel as the prophetic movement would have it; he was chosen by lot as the seers would have it (assisted by the priests, albeit); he was called by the Spirit of God and charismatically sent pieces of oxen to the tribes much as the judges would have it; and finally he performed the role of a priest-king much as the priests would like it. There is no historic way to determine whether Saul became king primarily through one method, or whether he satisfied all four power groups.

TASKS OF ALL GROUPS
PRIOR TO THE SIMULATION

1. Appoint a leader who will—
   a. chair in the preparation for the simulation,
   b. lead the group during the simulation.

   For purposes of the simulation the leaders of the groups will have the following historic identities:

The Priests	Eleazar
The Judges	Joel
The Prophets	Samuel
The Seers	Saul

2. Appoint a chronicler who will—
   a. record briefly the process of the group.
   b. record the action of the simulation from the perspective of his group,
   c. report to the debriefing session.

3. Examine those texts of the Old Testament which establish the identity of your particular group.

4. Articulate your identity to each other by a song or a gesture or a banner.

5. Project how your group will act in the simulated actions (consult your special instructions).

6. Discuss what means of group persuasion are available to you, given the group identity you have.
7. Assist the chronicler in recording, especially by articulating your plans as you project them prior to the simulation.

RULES OF THE SIMULATION
1. Each group will be allowed three representatives at the council table in Ramah.
2. Other members will be arranged behind the chairs of the three representatives.
3. Any member of the group may replace any one of his table representatives at will.
4. Each group will be allowed two roving politicians who may—
   a. discover the character and purpose of the other groups,
   b. facilitate or disrupt the procedures,
   c. consult with the background resource person.

TASKS OF THE SIMULATION
1. The coordinator will chair the session until the tribes are able to elect a leader.
2. Following the guidance of their chosen leader, the twelve tribes will attempt to deal with the following critical decisions:
   a. Should the tribes have a king?
   b. If so, how should he be chosen?
   c. If not, by what means will the tribes remain an organizational unit?

TASKS FOR THE DEBRIEFING
1. Make some change of your room arrangement to symbolize the end of the simulation.
2. Discuss with one another how you felt during the simulation.
3. Hear the reports from the chroniclers.
4. Discuss any questions that may be raised by the experience together.

4. The Seers

Your group identity for the simulation will be that of seers, a group of ecstatic diviners who could be found in Palestine as well as elsewhere in the ancient Near East. In the simulation there will be other groups helping to make the decision about organizing the twelve tribes. It is your task to determine how to use your specific interests and powers in the decision-making process. The following are some Old Testament texts which will help you establish your identity:

> 1 Samuel 8:4-18
> 1 Samuel 9:1-26
> 1 Samuel 10:2-16
> 1 Samuel 10:20-27
> 1 Samuel 16:14-18
> 2 Samuel 6:6-23
> Micah 3:7
> 1 Kings 18

BACKGROUND DATA
Seers are not mentioned much in the Old Testament other than in the first chapters of First Samuel. Their importance at that point lies in the fact that the prophetic movement originated with the seers (1 Samuel 9:9). The narrator of First Samuel indicates this was a chronological change of name, but one can detect more than that. Seers continued on through the prophetic period, as can be seen in the Micah passage. They may be closely related to the sons of the prophets, an ecstatic group of men associated in First and Second Kings with Elijah and Elisha. The seers likely banded together because of their common ability in clairvoyance and other ecstatic phenomena. Their contribution to the community was to discover lost objects (1 Samuel 9:6), predict the future (1 Samuel 10:5), and even speak to the dead (1 Samuel 28:8). Their "trips" were triggered by music (1 Samuel 10:5, 10), flagellation (1 Kings 18:28), or sex (2 Samuel 6:20). Prophets apparently had some of these same attributes, but strictly speaking they arose with the monarchy as leaders who brought the Word of the Lord to the king. They anointed kings and then also became their consciences (political critics). While the seers were the source of the prophets, they never carried out this function. It cannot be said from the Old Testament evidence that they absolutely would oppose a king (as would the judges). But like the judges they surely would have insisted on a "spiritual" election of the king. Presumably the election of Saul as king by lot (1 Samuel 10:20-27) would satisfy the seers, though it was likely a priest who cast the lots.

THE MAKING OF A KING A Simulation Based upon 1 Samuel 8

THE SITUATION

The leaders of Israel have come together in Ramah to decide whether or not to have a king. There are strong differences of opinion on the matter. As you simulate their decision, you will be faced with several questions:

1. You will need to select one of the group leaders to direct the whole group assembled in Ramah.

There are times when one is tempted to say the history of Israel was a continuous struggle for leadership. Prior to the rise of David as king there were many kinds of leadership present: charismatic generals (Gideon), kings (Abimelech), judges (Jair), priests (Eli), and more frequently no one at all (Judges 21:25). From this Samuel emerges as the leader who is responsible for the decision about a king and then for the selection of Saul as first king. The problem is: Who was Samuel? He was raised by a priest and he scolded Saul for taking over his priestly functions (1 Samuel 13:8-15). He was well known as a seer and diviner (1 Samuel 9:6). He was called as a prophet (hearing the voice of the Lord in the night) and acted as a prophet by anointing both Saul and David king of Israel. And the text tells quite explicitly that Samuel was a judge (1 Samuel 7:15 - 8:3). Clearly all the major groups in Israel thought Samuel was "their man."

2. With the guidance of the chosen leader you will decide whether the twelve tribes should unite under one king.

Because the association of the twelve tribes was a theological amphictyony (that is, organized by God), the various leaders obviously would oppose the creation of a monarchy. But the people began to insist on a king. After some debate the key seems to be that the prophets shifted positions (or, more technically, some seers became prophets) from opposition to a king to divine appointment of a king (1 Samuel 8:22). From that point on the conflict seems to be more in the method of choosing a king than the problem of having a king at all.

3. If a king is to be chosen, you should decide how it shall be done. If not, the problem of leadership must still be faced.

While the narrator indicates only a few problems about who would be chosen king (see 1 Samuel 10:27 and 11:12), the story fairly bristles with the conflict about method. In fact Saul became king in four different ways. He was anointed by Samuel as the prophetic movement would have it; he was chosen by lot as the seers would have it (assisted by the priests, albeit); he was called by the Spirit of God and charismatically sent pieces of oxen to the tribes much as the judges would have it; and finally he performed the role of a priest-king much as the priests would like it. There is no historic way to determine whether Saul became king primarily through one method, or whether he satisfied all four power groups.

TASKS OF ALL GROUPS
PRIOR TO THE SIMULATION

1. Appoint a leader who will—
   a. chair in the preparation for the simulation,
   b. lead the group during the simulation.

   For purposes of the simulation the leaders of the groups will have the following historic identities:

The Priests	Eleazar
The Judges	Joel
The Prophets	Samuel
The Seers	Saul

2. Appoint a chronicler who will—
   a. record briefly the process of the group.
   b. record the action of the simulation from the perspective of his group,
   c. report to the debriefing session.
3. Examine those texts of the Old Testament which establish the identity of your particular group.
4. Articulate your identity to each other by a song or a gesture or a banner.
5. Project how your group will act in the simulated actions (consult your special instructions).

6. Discuss what means of group persuasion are available to you, given the group identity you have.
7. Assist the chronicler in recording, especially by articulating your plans as you project them prior to the simulation.

RULES OF THE SIMULATION

1. Each group will be allowed three representatives at the council table in Ramah.
2. Other members will be arranged behind the chairs of the three representatives.
3. Any member of the group may replace any one of his table representatives at will.
4. Each group will be allowed two roving politicians who may—
   a. discover the character and purpose of the other groups,
   b. facilitate or disrupt the procedures,
   c. consult with the background resource person.

TASKS OF THE SIMULATION

1. The coordinator will chair the session until the tribes are able to elect a leader.
2. Following the guidance of their chosen leader, the twelve tribes will attempt to deal with the following critical decisions:
   a. Should the tribes have a king?
   b. If so, how should he be chosen?
   c. If not, by what means will the tribes remain an organizational unit?

TASKS FOR THE DEBRIEFING

1. Make some change of your room arrangement to symbolize the end of the simulation.
2. Discuss with one another how you felt during the simulation.
3. Hear the reports from the chroniclers.
4. Discuss any questions that may be raised by the experience together.

4. The Seers

Your group identity for the simulation will be that of seers, a group of ecstatic diviners who could be found in Palestine as well as elsewhere in the ancient Near East. In the simulation there will be other groups helping to make the decision about organizing the twelve tribes. It is your task to determine how to use your specific interests and powers in the decision-making process. The following are some Old Testament texts which will help you establish your identity:

> 1 Samuel 8:4-18
> 1 Samuel 9:1-26
> 1 Samuel 10:2-16
> 1 Samuel 10:20-27
> 1 Samuel 16:14-18
> 2 Samuel 6:6-23
> Micah 3:7
> 1 Kings 18

BACKGROUND DATA

Seers are not mentioned much in the Old Testament other than in the first chapters of First Samuel. Their importance at that point lies in the fact that the prophetic movement originated with the seers (1 Samuel 9:9). The narrator of First Samuel indicates this was a chronological change of name, but one can detect more than that. Seers continued on through the prophetic period, as can be seen in the Micah passage. They may be closely related to the sons of the prophets, an ecstatic group of men associated in First and Second Kings with Elijah and Elisha. The seers likely banded together because of their common ability in clairvoyance and other ecstatic phenomena. Their contribution to the community was to discover lost objects (1 Samuel 9:6), predict the future (1 Samuel 10:5), and even speak to the dead (1 Samuel 28:8). Their "trips" were triggered by music (1 Samuel 10:5, 10), flagellation (1 Kings 18:28), or sex (2 Samuel 6:20). Prophets apparently had some of these same attributes, but strictly speaking they arose with the monarchy as leaders who brought the Word of the Lord to the king. They anointed kings and then also became their consciences (political critics). While the seers were the source of the prophets, they never carried out this function. It cannot be said from the Old Testament evidence that they absolutely would oppose a king (as would the judges). But like the judges they surely would have insisted on a "spiritual" election of the king. Presumably the election of Saul as king by lot (1 Samuel 10:20-27) would satisfy the seers, though it was likely a priest who cast the lots.

8. JOSIAH'S DILEMMA

A Simulation Based upon 2 Kings 22-23

INSTRUCTIONS TO THE COORDINATOR

Preparation
Read through the whole simulation to get a good understanding of its purpose and direction. If you expect a large number of persons to take part, then you ought to involve some "leaders" in a discussion of goals and procedures prior to the simulation itself. You and they should read through the chapter "How to Conduct a Biblical Simulation" if you have not already done so.

Schedule
This simulation can very profitably fill a whole day, or it can be done in an hour or two. The time can be continuous or split up over several different sessions (see chapter 3).

For a single hour you will need to curtail preparation time and limit the presentations. No time can be allowed for getting final arguments in shape. A two-hour session gives you time for a more adequate experience.

The time schedules for one-hour, for two-hour, and six-hour sessions are as follows:

	One Hour	Two Hours	Six Hours
Introduction	10 min.	15 min.	½ hr.
Preparation	15 min.	45 min.	2½ hrs.
Simulation	20 min.	33 min.	1¾ hrs.
Decision of king	3 min.	5 min.	¼ hr.
Debriefing	12 min.	22 min.	1 hr.

In the one-hour session allow three minutes for each major presentation and two minutes for rebuttal for a total of twenty minutes as indicated above. The two-hour session permits five minutes for each major presentation, two minutes for rebuttal, and five minutes preparation time for rebuttal for a total of thirty-three minutes.

With a six-hour session you can enlarge the period for preparation and for making major speeches. If you are breaking the time into three sessions, during the second session give the small groups a chance to review arguments. Then move to the simulation allowing only a short time for debriefing. In the third session you can begin to examine learnings.

We have found this simulation to be an excellent climax to a study of the book of Deuteronomy. In that event, over a period of weeks the various groups can gather information in preparation for the simulation much as a debate team would gather information.

Grouping
You will need at least two or three persons working in each small group or a total of nine to thirteen persons. Since different persons within each small group can be assigned to prepare various parts of the argument, you will be able to include as many as fifty people in the simulation. Any group larger than this can better be handled by running simultaneous simulations.

Space and Equipment
Your preparation should include obtaining each of the following items (see chapter 3 for fuller explanation): a large room, small rooms, chairs, tables, Bibles, study aids, paper, pencils, materials for symbols (optional), and refreshments. Other materials which will help this simulation are:
1. A sufficient number of Bibles is important, and various translations will be helpful.
2. 3 x 5 cards will also be helpful for the debate style since they will enable the participants to keep better control of the arguments.

3. A crown and a scepter for the king if you wish to uphold a throne-room setting.
4. A large scroll to represent the book of Deuteronomy.
5. Robes for the priest.

The Jeremiah group has on occasion, when we have run the simulation, performed various symbolic acts recorded in the Book of Jeremiah, such as shattering a pot, ripping a shirt, or breaking a cardboard yoke. You may wish to provide a flower pot, an old shirt, and cardboard for making a yoke.

Facilitation

In your introduction of the simulation to a group you will want to explain the following items (see chapter 4): what a biblical simulation is, how to participate, purpose and tasks of this simulation, schedule, small-group tasks, materials, division into groups, and the function of the small-group chairman. Allow people time to ask questions. Appoint someone to serve as king and another person to be timekeeper.

As you already understand from reading the aids, this simulation will be run as a debate. Affirmative arguments and negative arguments will be given. We have simply divided the affirmative team and the negative team into two so that four groups emerge. However, the judge, in this case the king, will choose one of four positions, whereas in a debate situation he would choose one of two. This might suggest whom you will want to choose as king. It should be someone who can hear arguments and make a decision on the basis of reasons given.

You will find it helpful in your preparation to look in the *Interpreter's Dictionary of the Bible* under the headings "Josiah" and "Deuteronomy." Any Old Testament history will have a section on Josiah's reform which you might also wish to consult. The central issue for the simulation is the advisability of reform, given the historical situation of 622 B.C.

Debriefing

As coordinator you should conduct the debriefing session. Here is a list of suggestions to be followed:

1. Rearrange the chairs, or stand and stretch so that everyone is aware that the simulation has been concluded.
2. In groups of four discuss what you have learned. How did you feel in your role? Where did the most important argument occur? What did you learn about the book of Deuteronomy and reform? This simulation tends to stress content, so that questions about what individuals learned about themselves should not assume priority as they have in some other simulations.
3. Ask for volunteers to share their observations.
4. Ask the king to share with the group why he made his decision as he did.
5. Ask the chroniclers to share their observations.
6. Try to summarize what you have been hearing.
7. To conclude on a note of worship, have someone read Deuteronomy 6:4-9, and then let someone else read Matthew 22:35-40. Lead the group in a prayer in which you draw upon the common experience of the simulation. Finally, sing a hymn of tribute to God, such as "God of Grace and God of Glory."

JOSIAH'S DILEMMA A Simulation Based upon 2 Kings 22-23

THE SITUATION

It is the year 622 B.C. and King Josiah has just been given a reform document by the priesthood of Jerusalem (2 Kings 22 - 23). This document (which probably consisted of Deuteronomy 5 - 26) calls for a radical renewal of God's covenant with his people. Due to the character of the reform the king has scheduled a hearing of various parties in the capital. From their testimony the king will consider the advisability of adopting the reform. The hearing will take the form of a debate as suggested by one of the king's counselors. This will give everyone an opportunity to speak within certain specified time periods and it will also give each group a chance for rebuttal.

TASKS OF ALL GROUPS
PRIOR TO THE SIMULATION

After a few selected passages have been read from Second Kings (i.e., 22:3-10; 23:1-2), the coordinator will break the group into four smaller groups and choose a king and a timekeeper to maintain order.

The four smaller groups are these:

1. Jeremiah's followers—Jeremiah and his associates who feel that the reform offers a false hope.
2. Judean nationalists—The group which favors a direct break with Assyria and urges the adoption of the reform to dramatize Judah's increasing independence.
3. Southern priests—The Southern Israelite priests of the outlying districts of Judah who oppose the reform on practical and theological grounds.
4. Northern priests—Northern Israelite and Jerusalem priests who support the reform because it enhances their position of power in Jerusalem.

Following are the specific tasks each group should perform:

1. Appoint a leader who will—
   a. chair in the preparation for the simulation,
   b. make the major presentation for the group during the simulation.

2. Appoint a chronicler who will—
   a. record briefly the process of the group,
   b. record the action of the simulation from the perspective of his group.
   c. report to the interpretation session.
3. Examine those texts which establish the identity of your group.
4. Prepare a case which seeks to persuade the king either to adopt or to reject the reform.
5. Articulate your identity to each other by a song or a gesture or banner.
6. Anticipate responses and rebuttals to the other groups.

RULES OF THE SIMULATION

1. The king will open the meeting by asking Jeremiah's followers to speak. Each group will be allowed a predetermined time to present its case without interruption. Any group or individual who interferes with the presentation of another group will be evicted from the hearing room. At the end of the predetermined period the group must rest its case by finishing the sentence started when the timekeeper indicates that the time has elapsed. The order of presentations is: Jeremiah's followers, Judean nationalists, Southern priests, and Northern priests.
2. After the major presentations there will be a brief intermission.
3. Rebuttal speeches may be given in the following order: Southern priests, Jeremiah's followers, Northern priests, Judean nationalists; or you may have a free-for-all in which the king opens the meeting. No one should speak without being recognized. All members may speak and the order of the presentation will be established by the king as he sees fit. Obstreperous participants will be removed from the room. All arguments should be presented in such a way as to convince the king of your point of view and should not exceed two minutes in length.
4. When the time has elapsed according to a prearranged schedule or when the king has heard enough in the free-for-all, the king

will retire to decide whether to adopt or reject the reform. Whatever he chooses must be based upon the reasoning of one particular group. The king must decide and he must accept one of the group's arguments. He will state his decision in the following way, "I, King Josiah, (adopt or reject) the reform on the basis of (Jeremiah's followers', Judean nationalists', Southern priests', Northern priests') arguments.

TASKS OF THE SIMULATION
1. To reason cogently and effectively about the adoption or rejection of the reform.
2. To convince the king of the rightness of your position.

TASKS FOR DEBRIEFING
1. Rearrange the room to symbolize the termination of the simulation.
2. Let everyone, including the chronicler, share his observations with the whole group.
3. Let everyone express his feelings about what happened.
4. Let the whole group work at summarizing what was learned.

1. Jeremiah's Followers

Your group identity for the simulation will be Jeremiah and his followers, particularly Baruch, the amanuensis (secretary) of the prophet. You feel the reform is not necessarily bad, but it has come too late. You encourage repentance and waiting. For you the reform offers a false hope which appears to equate deliverance with obedience. You reject this conditional aspect on the ground that it attempts to control God. Therefore, you will argue for the rejection of the reform. You may wish to read Jeremiah 2 - 6, but the oracles listed below should provide a case (by inference) against the reform:

> Jeremiah 3:6-13
> Jeremiah 4:5-18
> Jeremiah 5:1-6

BACKGROUND DATA
The earliest oracles of Jeremiah would appear to suggest that Judah is doomed. She is more evil than the Northern Kingdom and therefore must suffer an even worse fate (Jeremiah 3:6-13).

Jeremiah has looked for virtue throughout Jerusalem and has not found one person who does justice (Jeremiah 5:1-6). Jeremiah's call for repentance is no guarantee that things will be better. All one can do is await the impending disaster (Jeremiah 4:5-18). Most scholars concede that these oracles stem from near the beginning of Jeremiah's ministry, perhaps soon after 626 B.C., which marks the first year of his prophetic utterances. We might conclude from these oracles that Jeremiah sees the judgment of God coming upon Judah, and there is no way this judgment can be averted. Although Jeremiah remains silent about the reform, we might infer that he fears its effect upon the lives of the people will be superficial. They will see it as a means of buying protection from God. The real issue for Judah is not reform but the announcement of the end. Only the judgment of an end time will give rise to a radical new beginning. To speak of reform allows people to hold onto the scraps of the past without changing their lives.

JOSIAH'S DILEMMA A Simulation Based upon 2 Kings 22-23

THE SITUATION

It is the year 622 B.C. and King Josiah has just been given a reform document by the priesthood of Jerusalem (2 Kings 22 - 23). This document (which probably consisted of Deuteronomy 5 - 26) calls for a radical renewal of God's covenant with his people. Due to the character of the reform the king has scheduled a hearing of various parties in the capital. From their testimony the king will consider the advisability of adopting the reform. The hearing will take the form of a debate as suggested by one of the king's counselors. This will give everyone an opportunity to speak within certain specified time periods and it will also give each group a chance for rebuttal.

TASKS OF ALL GROUPS
PRIOR TO THE SIMULATION

After a few selected passages have been read from Second Kings (i.e., 22:3-10; 23:1-2), the coordinator will break the group into four smaller groups and choose a king and a timekeeper to maintain order.

The four smaller groups are these:

1. Jeremiah's followers—Jeremiah and his associates who feel that the reform offers a false hope.
2. Judean nationalists—The group which favors a direct break with Assyria and urges the adoption of the reform to dramatize Judah's increasing independence.
3. Southern priests—The Southern Israelite priests of the outlying districts of Judah who oppose the reform on practical and theological grounds.
4. Northern priests—Northern Israelite and Jerusalem priests who support the reform because it enhances their position of power in Jerusalem.

Following are the specific tasks each group should perform:

1. Appoint a leader who will—
   a. chair in the preparation for the simulation,
   b. make the major presentation for the group during the simulation.

2. Appoint a chronicler who will—
   a. record briefly the process of the group,
   b. record the action of the simulation from the perspective of his group.
   c. report to the interpretation session.
3. Examine those texts which establish the identity of your group.
4. Prepare a case which seeks to persuade the king either to adopt or to reject the reform.
5. Articulate your identity to each other by a song or a gesture or banner.
6. Anticipate responses and rebuttals to the other groups.

RULES OF THE SIMULATION

1. The king will open the meeting by asking Jeremiah's followers to speak. Each group will be allowed a predetermined time to present its case without interruption. Any group or individual who interferes with the presentation of another group will be evicted from the hearing room. At the end of the predetermined period the group must rest its case by finishing the sentence started when the timekeeper indicates that the time has elapsed. The order of presentations is: Jeremiah's followers, Judean nationalists, Southern priests, and Northern priests.
2. After the major presentations there will be a brief intermission.
3. Rebuttal speeches may be given in the following order: Southern priests, Jeremiah's followers, Northern priests, Judean nationalists; or you may have a free-for-all in which the king opens the meeting. No one should speak without being recognized. All members may speak and the order of the presentation will be established by the king as he sees fit. Obstreperous participants will be removed from the room. All arguments should be presented in such a way as to convince the king of your point of view and should not exceed two minutes in length.
4. When the time has elapsed according to a prearranged schedule or when the king has heard enough in the free-for-all, the king

will retire to decide whether to adopt or reject the reform. Whatever he chooses must be based upon the reasoning of one particular group. The king must decide and he must accept one of the group's arguments. He will state his decision in the following way, "I, King Josiah, (adopt or reject) the reform on the basis of (Jeremiah's followers', Judean nationalists', Southern priests', Northern priests') arguments.

TASKS OF THE SIMULATION
1. To reason cogently and effectively about the adoption or rejection of the reform.
2. To convince the king of the rightness of your position.

TASKS FOR DEBRIEFING
1. Rearrange the room to symbolize the termination of the simulation.
2. Let everyone, including the chronicler, share his observations with the whole group.
3. Let everyone express his feelings about what happened.
4. Let the whole group work at summarizing what was learned.

1. Jeremiah's Followers

Your group identity for the simulation will be Jeremiah and his followers, particularly Baruch, the amanuensis (secretary) of the prophet. You feel the reform is not necessarily bad, but it has come too late. You encourage repentance and waiting. For you the reform offers a false hope which appears to equate deliverance with obedience. You reject this conditional aspect on the ground that it attempts to control God. Therefore, you will argue for the rejection of the reform. You may wish to read Jeremiah 2 - 6, but the oracles listed below should provide a case (by inference) against the reform:

> Jeremiah 3:6-13
> Jeremiah 4:5-18
> Jeremiah 5:1-6

BACKGROUND DATA
The earliest oracles of Jeremiah would appear to suggest that Judah is doomed. She is more evil than the Northern Kingdom and therefore must suffer an even worse fate (Jeremiah 3:6-13).

Jeremiah has looked for virtue throughout Jerusalem and has not found one person who does justice (Jeremiah 5:1-6). Jeremiah's call for repentance is no guarantee that things will be better. All one can do is await the impending disaster (Jeremiah 4:5-18). Most scholars concede that these oracles stem from near the beginning of Jeremiah's ministry, perhaps soon after 626 B.C., which marks the first year of his prophetic utterances. We might conclude from these oracles that Jeremiah sees the judgment of God coming upon Judah, and there is no way this judgment can be averted. Although Jeremiah remains silent about the reform, we might infer that he fears its effect upon the lives of the people will be superficial. They will see it as a means of buying protection from God. The real issue for Judah is not reform but the announcement of the end. Only the judgment of an end time will give rise to a radical new beginning. To speak of reform allows people to hold onto the scraps of the past without changing their lives.

JOSIAH'S DILEMMA A Simulation Based upon 2 Kings 22-23

THE SITUATION

It is the year 622 B.C. and King Josiah has just been given a reform document by the priesthood of Jerusalem (2 Kings 22 - 23). This document (which probably consisted of Deuteronomy 5 - 26) calls for a radical renewal of God's covenant with his people. Due to the character of the reform the king has scheduled a hearing of various parties in the capital. From their testimony the king will consider the advisability of adopting the reform. The hearing will take the form of a debate as suggested by one of the king's counselors. This will give everyone an opportunity to speak within certain specified time periods and it will also give each group a chance for rebuttal.

TASKS OF ALL GROUPS
PRIOR TO THE SIMULATION

After a few selected passages have been read from Second Kings (i.e., 22:3-10; 23:1-2), the coordinator will break the group into four smaller groups and choose a king and a timekeeper to maintain order.

The four smaller groups are these:

1. Jeremiah's followers—Jeremiah and his associates who feel that the reform offers a false hope.
2. Judean nationalists—The group which favors a direct break with Assyria and urges the adoption of the reform to dramatize Judah's increasing independence.
3. Southern priests—The Southern Israelite priests of the outlying districts of Judah who oppose the reform on practical and theological grounds.
4. Northern priests—Northern Israelite and Jerusalem priests who support the reform because it enhances their position of power in Jerusalem.

Following are the specific tasks each group should perform:

1. Appoint a leader who will—
   a. chair in the preparation for the simulation,
   b. make the major presentation for the group during the simulation.

2. Appoint a chronicler who will—
   a. record briefly the process of the group,
   b. record the action of the simulation from the perspective of his group.
   c. report to the interpretation session.
3. Examine those texts which establish the identity of your group.
4. Prepare a case which seeks to persuade the king either to adopt or to reject the reform.
5. Articulate your identity to each other by a song or a gesture or banner.
6. Anticipate responses and rebuttals to the other groups.

RULES OF THE SIMULATION

1. The king will open the meeting by asking Jeremiah's followers to speak. Each group will be allowed a predetermined time to present its case without interruption. Any group or individual who interferes with the presentation of another group will be evicted from the hearing room. At the end of the predetermined period the group must rest its case by finishing the sentence started when the timekeeper indicates that the time has elapsed. The order of presentations is: Jeremiah's followers, Judean nationalists, Southern priests, and Northern priests.
2. After the major presentations there will be a brief intermission.
3. Rebuttal speeches may be given in the following order: Southern priests, Jeremiah's followers, Northern priests, Judean nationalists; or you may have a free-for-all in which the king opens the meeting. No one should speak without being recognized. All members may speak and the order of the presentation will be established by the king as he sees fit. Obstreperous participants will be removed from the room. All arguments should be presented in such a way as to convince the king of your point of view and should not exceed two minutes in length.
4. When the time has elapsed according to a prearranged schedule or when the king has heard enough in the free-for-all, the king

will retire to decide whether to adopt or reject the reform. Whatever he chooses must be based upon the reasoning of one particular group. The king must decide and he must accept one of the group's arguments. He will state his decision in the following way, "I, King Josiah, (adopt or reject) the reform on the basis of (Jeremiah's followers', Judean nationalists', Southern priests', Northern priests') arguments.

TASKS OF THE SIMULATION
1. To reason cogently and effectively about the adoption or rejection of the reform.
2. To convince the king of the rightness of your position.

TASKS FOR DEBRIEFING
1. Rearrange the room to symbolize the termination of the simulation.
2. Let everyone, including the chronicler, share his observations with the whole group.
3. Let everyone express his feelings about what happened.
4. Let the whole group work at summarizing what was learned.

2. Judean Nationalists

Your group identity for the simulation will be Judean national army officers and counselors close to the king who encourage the adoption of the reform. Your best military intelligence tells you that Assyria is on the verge of collapse. The king's official course, charted in the eighth year of his reign (632 B.C.), has not met with any rebuff from Assyria. You feel the time is ripe for declaring independence, and the Deuteronomic Code provides a working document for that independence. You will find the following passages of the reform document particularly helpful for the formulation of a brief to present to the king:

Deuteronomy 20:1-20—The reform includes a new document for conscription and more humane treatment of soldiers, thus a boost in army morale.

Deuteronomy 8:7 - 9:6—The reform includes a new document for independence and the worship of one national God, thus a rejection of domination by a foreign power.

Deuteronomy 7:1-6—Israel has always been a people set apart and the need for separation from all foreign domination has never been more apparent.

BACKGROUND DATA
You have helped formulate a policy of growing independence from Assyria, as recorded in 2 Chronicles 34:3-11. You were convinced that the best way to show independence was by purging all elements of Assyrian ritual from the official worship of God. You particularly favor the reform since it has far-reaching implications for the reorganization of the army. You believe in universal military conscription in time of war, and you notice that the reform resurrects the ancient belief in holy warfare, which had its roots in the premonarchial period at the time of the judges (see Joshua 6 and Judges 4 - 8). But above all you have a fervent hope that your country might be free from the chains of bondage to a foreign power. You like the independent spirit of the document, which speaks of the recognition of Israel's God alone and the absolute rejection of all foreign power and domination. Your stance is clear: a free Judah and a return to the nationalism of the time of David. You see in Josiah a second David who will create a new empire and a new nationalism. You want to convince Josiah that it is politically sound to adopt the reform.

JOSIAH'S DILEMMA A Simulation Based upon 2 Kings 22-23

THE SITUATION

It is the year 622 B.C. and King Josiah has just been given a reform document by the priesthood of Jerusalem (2 Kings 22 - 23). This document (which probably consisted of Deuteronomy 5 - 26) calls for a radical renewal of God's covenant with his people. Due to the character of the reform the king has scheduled a hearing of various parties in the capital. From their testimony the king will consider the advisability of adopting the reform. The hearing will take the form of a debate as suggested by one of the king's counselors. This will give everyone an opportunity to speak within certain specified time periods and it will also give each group a chance for rebuttal.

TASKS OF ALL GROUPS
PRIOR TO THE SIMULATION

After a few selected passages have been read from Second Kings (i.e., 22:3-10; 23:1-2), the coordinator will break the group into four smaller groups and choose a king and a timekeeper to maintain order.

The four smaller groups are these:

1. Jeremiah's followers—Jeremiah and his associates who feel that the reform offers a false hope.
2. Judean nationalists—The group which favors a direct break with Assyria and urges the adoption of the reform to dramatize Judah's increasing independence.
3. Southern priests—The Southern Israelite priests of the outlying districts of Judah who oppose the reform on practical and theological grounds.
4. Northern priests—Northern Israelite and Jerusalem priests who support the reform because it enhances their position of power in Jerusalem.

Following are the specific tasks each group should perform:

1. Appoint a leader who will—
   a. chair in the preparation for the simulation,
   b. make the major presentation for the group during the simulation.

2. Appoint a chronicler who will—
   a. record briefly the process of the group,
   b. record the action of the simulation from the perspective of his group.
   c. report to the interpretation session.
3. Examine those texts which establish the identity of your group.
4. Prepare a case which seeks to persuade the king either to adopt or to reject the reform.
5. Articulate your identity to each other by a song or a gesture or banner.
6. Anticipate responses and rebuttals to the other groups.

RULES OF THE SIMULATION

1. The king will open the meeting by asking Jeremiah's followers to speak. Each group will be allowed a predetermined time to present its case without interruption. Any group or individual who interferes with the presentation of another group will be evicted from the hearing room. At the end of the predetermined period the group must rest its case by finishing the sentence started when the timekeeper indicates that the time has elapsed. The order of presentations is: Jeremiah's followers, Judean nationalists, Southern priests, and Northern priests.
2. After the major presentations there will be a brief intermission.
3. Rebuttal speeches may be given in the following order: Southern priests, Jeremiah's followers, Northern priests, Judean nationalists; or you may have a free-for-all in which the king opens the meeting. No one should speak without being recognized. All members may speak and the order of the presentation will be established by the king as he sees fit. Obstreperous participants will be removed from the room. All arguments should be presented in such a way as to convince the king of your point of view and should not exceed two minutes in length.
4. When the time has elapsed according to a prearranged schedule or when the king has heard enough in the free-for-all, the king

will retire to decide whether to adopt or reject the reform. Whatever he chooses must be based upon the reasoning of one particular group. The king must decide and he must accept one of the group's arguments. He will state his decision in the following way, "I, King Josiah, (adopt or reject) the reform on the basis of (Jeremiah's followers', Judean nationalists', Southern priests', Northern priests') arguments.

TASKS OF THE SIMULATION
1. To reason cogently and effectively about the adoption or rejection of the reform.
2. To convince the king of the rightness of your position.

TASKS FOR DEBRIEFING
1. Rearrange the room to symbolize the termination of the simulation.
2. Let everyone, including the chronicler, share his observations with the whole group.
3. Let everyone express his feelings about what happened.
4. Let the whole group work at summarizing what was learned.

2. Judean Nationalists

Your group identity for the simulation will be Judean national army officers and counselors close to the king who encourage the adoption of the reform. Your best military intelligence tells you that Assyria is on the verge of collapse. The king's official course, charted in the eighth year of his reign (632 B.C.), has not met with any rebuff from Assyria. You feel the time is ripe for declaring independence, and the Deuteronomic Code provides a working document for that independence. You will find the following passages of the reform document particularly helpful for the formulation of a brief to present to the king:

Deuteronomy 20:1-20—The reform includes a new document for conscription and more humane treatment of soldiers, thus a boost in army morale.

Deuteronomy 8:7 - 9:6—The reform includes a new document for independence and the worship of one national God, thus a rejection of domination by a foreign power.

Deuteronomy 7:1-6—Israel has always been a people set apart and the need for separation from all foreign domination has never been more apparent.

BACKGROUND DATA
You have helped formulate a policy of growing independence from Assyria, as recorded in 2 Chronicles 34:3-11. You were convinced that the best way to show independence was by purging all elements of Assyrian ritual from the official worship of God. You particularly favor the reform since it has far-reaching implications for the reorganization of the army. You believe in universal military conscription in time of war, and you notice that the reform resurrects the ancient belief in holy warfare, which had its roots in the premonarchial period at the time of the judges (see Joshua 6 and Judges 4 - 8). But above all you have a fervent hope that your country might be free from the chains of bondage to a foreign power. You like the independent spirit of the document, which speaks of the recognition of Israel's God alone and the absolute rejection of all foreign power and domination. Your stance is clear: a free Judah and a return to the nationalism of the time of David. You see in Josiah a second David who will create a new empire and a new nationalism. You want to convince Josiah that it is politically sound to adopt the reform.

JOSIAH'S DILEMMA A Simulation Based upon 2 Kings 22-23

THE SITUATION

It is the year 622 B.C. and King Josiah has just been given a reform document by the priesthood of Jerusalem (2 Kings 22 - 23). This document (which probably consisted of Deuteronomy 5 - 26) calls for a radical renewal of God's covenant with his people. Due to the character of the reform the king has scheduled a hearing of various parties in the capital. From their testimony the king will consider the advisability of adopting the reform. The hearing will take the form of a debate as suggested by one of the king's counselors. This will give everyone an opportunity to speak within certain specified time periods and it will also give each group a chance for rebuttal.

TASKS OF ALL GROUPS
PRIOR TO THE SIMULATION

After a few selected passages have been read from Second Kings (i.e., 22:3-10; 23:1-2), the coordinator will break the group into four smaller groups and choose a king and a timekeeper to maintain order.

The four smaller groups are these:

1. Jeremiah's followers—Jeremiah and his associates who feel that the reform offers a false hope.
2. Judean nationalists—The group which favors a direct break with Assyria and urges the adoption of the reform to dramatize Judah's increasing independence.
3. Southern priests—The Southern Israelite priests of the outlying districts of Judah who oppose the reform on practical and theological grounds.
4. Northern priests—Northern Israelite and Jerusalem priests who support the reform because it enhances their position of power in Jerusalem.

Following are the specific tasks each group should perform:

1. Appoint a leader who will—
   a. chair in the preparation for the simulation,
   b. make the major presentation for the group during the simulation.

2. Appoint a chronicler who will—
   a. record briefly the process of the group,
   b. record the action of the simulation from the perspective of his group.
   c. report to the interpretation session.
3. Examine those texts which establish the identity of your group.
4. Prepare a case which seeks to persuade the king either to adopt or to reject the reform.
5. Articulate your identity to each other by a song or a gesture or banner.
6. Anticipate responses and rebuttals to the other groups.

RULES OF THE SIMULATION

1. The king will open the meeting by asking Jeremiah's followers to speak. Each group will be allowed a predetermined time to present its case without interruption. Any group or individual who interferes with the presentation of another group will be evicted from the hearing room. At the end of the predetermined period the group must rest its case by finishing the sentence started when the timekeeper indicates that the time has elapsed. The order of presentations is: Jeremiah's followers, Judean nationalists, Southern priests, and Northern priests.
2. After the major presentations there will be a brief intermission.
3. Rebuttal speeches may be given in the following order: Southern priests, Jeremiah's followers, Northern priests, Judean nationalists; or you may have a free-for-all in which the king opens the meeting. No one should speak without being recognized. All members may speak and the order of the presentation will be established by the king as he sees fit. Obstreperous participants will be removed from the room. All arguments should be presented in such a way as to convince the king of your point of view and should not exceed two minutes in length.
4. When the time has elapsed according to a prearranged schedule or when the king has heard enough in the free-for-all, the king

will retire to decide whether to adopt or reject the reform. Whatever he chooses must be based upon the reasoning of one particular group. The king must decide and he must accept one of the group's arguments. He will state his decision in the following way, "I, King Josiah, (adopt or reject) the reform on the basis of (Jeremiah's followers', Judean nationalists', Southern priests', Northern priests') arguments.

TASKS OF THE SIMULATION
1. To reason cogently and effectively about the adoption or rejection of the reform.
2. To convince the king of the rightness of your position.

TASKS FOR DEBRIEFING
1. Rearrange the room to symbolize the termination of the simulation.
2. Let everyone, including the chronicler, share his observations with the whole group.
3. Let everyone express his feelings about what happened.
4. Let the whole group work at summarizing what was learned.

3. Southern Priests

Your group identity for the simulation will be priests who serve shrines in the outlying districts of Jerusalem. You see the reform as disturbing the religious practices of the past by its insistence that there should be only one place of worship, the temple in Jerusalem. You feel that this will give merchants in Jerusalem added advantages because all pilgrims to the city must purchase the animals for their sacrifices in the city itself. The closing of the shrines will force priests like yourselves to seek employment at the temple of Jerusalem, and such centralized control can have a deleterious effect on the religious life of the nation. Review the following texts to establish the position of your group:

Micah 1:5-9 and 3:9-12—Jerusalem is the center of apostasy.

Genesis 12:6-9; 28:10-19 and 1 Samuel 3—The local shrine preserves the traditions of the fathers.

BACKGROUND DATA
Since the earliest occupation of the land, shrines dedicated to religious events of the past have been preserved. Local priests managed these shrines and made sacrifices on behalf of the people at these locations. However, the reform seeks to change all that by insisting that Jerusalem is the only legitimate shrine (Deuteronomy 12). You will argue that such a drastic measure creates even greater distance between the non-Jerusalemites and the one true God. You may wish to quote Micah who asserts that the center of apostasy in the south is Jerusalem, not the small country parish (Micah 1:5-9 and 3:9-12). You will want to show that from the beginning God appeared at these local shrines (see Genesis 12:6-9, 28:10-19, 1 Samuel 3). To deny these shrines is to renounce some of Judah's and Israel's most significant tradition. If Jerusalem would become the center of Judah's religious life, the people would soon fail to support the worship of their God since he would appear remote and distant to them. You are the proponents of localism in this struggle. Imagine yourselves as local priests who will have everything taken away from you should the reform succeed. That should prompt a number of arguments.

JOSIAH'S DILEMMA A Simulation Based upon 2 Kings 22-23

THE SITUATION

It is the year 622 B.C. and King Josiah has just been given a reform document by the priesthood of Jerusalem (2 Kings 22 - 23). This document (which probably consisted of Deuteronomy 5 - 26) calls for a radical renewal of God's covenant with his people. Due to the character of the reform the king has scheduled a hearing of various parties in the capital. From their testimony the king will consider the advisability of adopting the reform. The hearing will take the form of a debate as suggested by one of the king's counselors. This will give everyone an opportunity to speak within certain specified time periods and it will also give each group a chance for rebuttal.

TASKS OF ALL GROUPS
PRIOR TO THE SIMULATION

After a few selected passages have been read from Second Kings (i.e., 22:3-10; 23:1-2), the coordinator will break the group into four smaller groups and choose a king and a timekeeper to maintain order.

The four smaller groups are these:

1. Jeremiah's followers—Jeremiah and his associates who feel that the reform offers a false hope.
2. Judean nationalists—The group which favors a direct break with Assyria and urges the adoption of the reform to dramatize Judah's increasing independence.
3. Southern priests—The Southern Israelite priests of the outlying districts of Judah who oppose the reform on practical and theological grounds.
4. Northern priests—Northern Israelite and Jerusalem priests who support the reform because it enhances their position of power in Jerusalem.

Following are the specific tasks each group should perform:

1. Appoint a leader who will—
   a. chair in the preparation for the simulation,
   b. make the major presentation for the group during the simulation.

2. Appoint a chronicler who will—
   a. record briefly the process of the group,
   b. record the action of the simulation from the perspective of his group.
   c. report to the interpretation session.
3. Examine those texts which establish the identity of your group.
4. Prepare a case which seeks to persuade the king either to adopt or to reject the reform.
5. Articulate your identity to each other by a song or a gesture or banner.
6. Anticipate responses and rebuttals to the other groups.

RULES OF THE SIMULATION

1. The king will open the meeting by asking Jeremiah's followers to speak. Each group will be allowed a predetermined time to present its case without interruption. Any group or individual who interferes with the presentation of another group will be evicted from the hearing room. At the end of the predetermined period the group must rest its case by finishing the sentence started when the timekeeper indicates that the time has elapsed. The order of presentations is: Jeremiah's followers, Judean nationalists, Southern priests, and Northern priests.
2. After the major presentations there will be a brief intermission.
3. Rebuttal speeches may be given in the following order: Southern priests, Jeremiah's followers, Northern priests, Judean nationalists; or you may have a free-for-all in which the king opens the meeting. No one should speak without being recognized. All members may speak and the order of the presentation will be established by the king as he sees fit. Obstreperous participants will be removed from the room. All arguments should be presented in such a way as to convince the king of your point of view and should not exceed two minutes in length.
4. When the time has elapsed according to a prearranged schedule or when the king has heard enough in the free-for-all, the king

will retire to decide whether to adopt or reject the reform. Whatever he chooses must be based upon the reasoning of one particular group. The king must decide and he must accept one of the group's arguments. He will state his decision in the following way, "I, King Josiah, (adopt or reject) the reform on the basis of (Jeremiah's followers', Judean nationalists', Southern priests', Northern priests') arguments.

TASKS OF THE SIMULATION

1. To reason cogently and effectively about the adoption or rejection of the reform.
2. To convince the king of the rightness of your position.

TASKS FOR DEBRIEFING

1. Rearrange the room to symbolize the termination of the simulation.
2. Let everyone, including the chronicler, share his observations with the whole group.
3. Let everyone express his feelings about what happened.
4. Let the whole group work at summarizing what was learned.

3. Southern Priests

Your group identity for the simulation will be priests who serve shrines in the outlying districts of Jerusalem. You see the reform as disturbing the religious practices of the past by its insistence that there should be only one place of worship, the temple in Jerusalem. You feel that this will give merchants in Jerusalem added advantages because all pilgrims to the city must purchase the animals for their sacrifices in the city itself. The closing of the shrines will force priests like yourselves to seek employment at the temple of Jerusalem, and such centralized control can have a deleterious effect on the religious life of the nation. Review the following texts to establish the position of your group:

Micah 1:5-9 and 3:9-12—Jerusalem is the center of apostasy.

Genesis 12:6-9; 28:10-19 and 1 Samuel 3—The local shrine preserves the traditions of the fathers.

BACKGROUND DATA

Since the earliest occupation of the land, shrines dedicated to religious events of the past have been preserved. Local priests managed these shrines and made sacrifices on behalf of the people at these locations. However, the reform seeks to change all that by insisting that Jerusalem is the only legitimate shrine (Deuteronomy 12). You will argue that such a drastic measure creates even greater distance between the non-Jerusalemites and the one true God. You may wish to quote Micah who asserts that the center of apostasy in the south is Jerusalem, not the small country parish (Micah 1:5-9 and 3:9-12). You will want to show that from the beginning God appeared at these local shrines (see Genesis 12:6-9, 28:10-19, 1 Samuel 3). To deny these shrines is to renounce some of Judah's and Israel's most significant tradition. If Jerusalem would become the center of Judah's religious life, the people would soon fail to support the worship of their God since he would appear remote and distant to them. You are the proponents of localism in this struggle. Imagine yourselves as local priests who will have everything taken away from you should the reform succeed. That should prompt a number of arguments.

JOSIAH'S DILEMMA A Simulation Based upon 2 Kings 22-23

THE SITUATION

It is the year 622 B.C. and King Josiah has just been given a reform document by the priesthood of Jerusalem (2 Kings 22 - 23). This document (which probably consisted of Deuteronomy 5 - 26) calls for a radical renewal of God's covenant with his people. Due to the character of the reform the king has scheduled a hearing of various parties in the capital. From their testimony the king will consider the advisability of adopting the reform. The hearing will take the form of a debate as suggested by one of the king's counselors. This will give everyone an opportunity to speak within certain specified time periods and it will also give each group a chance for rebuttal.

TASKS OF ALL GROUPS
PRIOR TO THE SIMULATION

After a few selected passages have been read from Second Kings (i.e., 22:3-10; 23:1-2), the coordinator will break the group into four smaller groups and choose a king and a timekeeper to maintain order.

The four smaller groups are these:

1. Jeremiah's followers—Jeremiah and his associates who feel that the reform offers a false hope.
2. Judean nationalists—The group which favors a direct break with Assyria and urges the adoption of the reform to dramatize Judah's increasing independence.
3. Southern priests—The Southern Israelite priests of the outlying districts of Judah who oppose the reform on practical and theological grounds.
4. Northern priests—Northern Israelite and Jerusalem priests who support the reform because it enhances their position of power in Jerusalem.

Following are the specific tasks each group should perform:

1. Appoint a leader who will—
   a. chair in the preparation for the simulation,
   b. make the major presentation for the group during the simulation.
2. Appoint a chronicler who will—
   a. record briefly the process of the group,
   b. record the action of the simulation from the perspective of his group.
   c. report to the interpretation session.
3. Examine those texts which establish the identity of your group.
4. Prepare a case which seeks to persuade the king either to adopt or to reject the reform.
5. Articulate your identity to each other by a song or a gesture or banner.
6. Anticipate responses and rebuttals to the other groups.

RULES OF THE SIMULATION

1. The king will open the meeting by asking Jeremiah's followers to speak. Each group will be allowed a predetermined time to present its case without interruption. Any group or individual who interferes with the presentation of another group will be evicted from the hearing room. At the end of the predetermined period the group must rest its case by finishing the sentence started when the timekeeper indicates that the time has elapsed. The order of presentations is: Jeremiah's followers, Judean nationalists, Southern priests, and Northern priests.
2. After the major presentations there will be a brief intermission.
3. Rebuttal speeches may be given in the following order: Southern priests, Jeremiah's followers, Northern priests, Judean nationalists; or you may have a free-for-all in which the king opens the meeting. No one should speak without being recognized. All members may speak and the order of the presentation will be established by the king as he sees fit. Obstreperous participants will be removed from the room. All arguments should be presented in such a way as to convince the king of your point of view and should not exceed two minutes in length.
4. When the time has elapsed according to a prearranged schedule or when the king has heard enough in the free-for-all, the king

will retire to decide whether to adopt or reject the reform. Whatever he chooses must be based upon the reasoning of one particular group. The king must decide and he must accept one of the group's arguments. He will state his decision in the following way, "I, King Josiah, (adopt or reject) the reform on the basis of (Jeremiah's followers', Judean nationalists', Southern priests', Northern priests') arguments.

TASKS OF THE SIMULATION

1. To reason cogently and effectively about the adoption or rejection of the reform.
2. To convince the king of the rightness of your position.

TASKS FOR DEBRIEFING

1. Rearrange the room to symbolize the termination of the simulation.
2. Let everyone, including the chronicler, share his observations with the whole group.
3. Let everyone express his feelings about what happened.
4. Let the whole group work at summarizing what was learned.

4. Northern Priests

Your group identity for the simulation will be priests from Jerusalem as well as priests from the Northern Kingdom who have found a home at the Jerusalem temple. You have been the architects of the reform, which for you represents a return to the tradition of Moses. You believe in strong central control and thus have argued for the "closing," a nice word for destruction, of all local shrines. You will press Josiah for the adoption of the reform. You may understand your role by reading the following sections of Deuteronomy which should give you the rationale for the reform:

> Deuteronomy 12
> Deuteronomy 6 - 9

BACKGROUND DATA

It may seem strange at first that priests from the north would join priests in Jerusalem for the purpose of creating a reform document. However, much of the tradition in Deuteronomy may have come to the south when the Northern Kingdom was destroyed. Thus, the book of Deuteronomy represents an amalgamation of material, preserving the covenant traditions of the past. At the forefront of this covenant tradition was loyalty to the One God who brought Israel out of bondage and gave her the Promised Land. Chapter 12 of Deuteronomy outlines this religious loyalty, which for you means the end of all syncretistic practices in Judah and a reaffirmation of the God of the past who revealed himself to Moses at Mount Horeb. To bring control over the religious life of the people must mean the end of all local shrines where all kinds of religious abuses have arisen. You believe that a new day of obedience can emerge in Judah if the reform document becomes the pattern and design for that new life.

JOSIAH'S DILEMMA A Simulation Based upon 2 Kings 22-23

THE SITUATION

It is the year 622 B.C. and King Josiah has just been given a reform document by the priesthood of Jerusalem (2 Kings 22 - 23). This document (which probably consisted of Deuteronomy 5 - 26) calls for a radical renewal of God's covenant with his people. Due to the character of the reform the king has scheduled a hearing of various parties in the capital. From their testimony the king will consider the advisability of adopting the reform. The hearing will take the form of a debate as suggested by one of the king's counselors. This will give everyone an opportunity to speak within certain specified time periods and it will also give each group a chance for rebuttal.

TASKS OF ALL GROUPS
PRIOR TO THE SIMULATION

After a few selected passages have been read from Second Kings (i.e., 22:3-10; 23:1-2), the coordinator will break the group into four smaller groups and choose a king and a timekeeper to maintain order.

The four smaller groups are these:

1. Jeremiah's followers—Jeremiah and his associates who feel that the reform offers a false hope.
2. Judean nationalists—The group which favors a direct break with Assyria and urges the adoption of the reform to dramatize Judah's increasing independence.
3. Southern priests—The Southern Israelite priests of the outlying districts of Judah who oppose the reform on practical and theological grounds.
4. Northern priests—Northern Israelite and Jerusalem priests who support the reform because it enhances their position of power in Jerusalem.

Following are the specific tasks each group should perform:

1. Appoint a leader who will—
   a. chair in the preparation for the simulation,
   b. make the major presentation for the group during the simulation.
2. Appoint a chronicler who will—
   a. record briefly the process of the group,
   b. record the action of the simulation from the perspective of his group.
   c. report to the interpretation session.
3. Examine those texts which establish the identity of your group.
4. Prepare a case which seeks to persuade the king either to adopt or to reject the reform.
5. Articulate your identity to each other by a song or a gesture or banner.
6. Anticipate responses and rebuttals to the other groups.

RULES OF THE SIMULATION

1. The king will open the meeting by asking Jeremiah's followers to speak. Each group will be allowed a predetermined time to present its case without interruption. Any group or individual who interferes with the presentation of another group will be evicted from the hearing room. At the end of the predetermined period the group must rest its case by finishing the sentence started when the timekeeper indicates that the time has elapsed. The order of presentations is: Jeremiah's followers, Judean nationalists, Southern priests, and Northern priests.
2. After the major presentations there will be a brief intermission.
3. Rebuttal speeches may be given in the following order: Southern priests, Jeremiah's followers, Northern priests, Judean nationalists; or you may have a free-for-all in which the king opens the meeting. No one should speak without being recognized. All members may speak and the order of the presentation will be established by the king as he sees fit. Obstreperous participants will be removed from the room. All arguments should be presented in such a way as to convince the king of your point of view and should not exceed two minutes in length.
4. When the time has elapsed according to a prearranged schedule or when the king has heard enough in the free-for-all, the king

will retire to decide whether to adopt or reject the reform. Whatever he chooses must be based upon the reasoning of one particular group. The king must decide and he must accept one of the group's arguments. He will state his decision in the following way, "I, King Josiah, (adopt or reject) the reform on the basis of (Jeremiah's followers', Judean nationalists', Southern priests', Northern priests') arguments.

TASKS OF THE SIMULATION
1. To reason cogently and effectively about the adoption or rejection of the
2. To convince the king of the rig... position.

TASKS FOR DEBRIEFING
1. Rearrange the room to symbolize the termination of the simulation.
2. Let everyone, including the chronicler, share his observations with the whole group.
3. Let everyone express his feelings about what happened.
4. Let the whole group work at summarizing what was learned.

4. Northern Priests

Your group identity for the simulation will be priests from Jerusalem as well as priests from the Northern Kingdom who have found a home at the Jerusalem temple. You have been the architects of the reform, which for you represents a return to the tradition of Moses. You believe in strong central control and thus have argued for the "closing," a nice word for destruction, of all local shrines. You will press Josiah for the adoption of the reform. You may understand your role by reading the following sections of Deuteronomy which should give you the rationale for the reform:

Deuteronomy 12
Deuteronomy 6 - 9

BACKGROUND DATA
It may seem strange at first that priests from the north would join priests in Jerusalem for the purpose of creating a reform document.

However, much of the tradition in Deuteronomy may have come to the south when the Northern Kingdom was destroyed. Thus, the book of Deuteronomy represents an amalgamation of material, preserving the covenant traditions of the past. At the forefront of this covenant tradition was loyalty to the One God who brought Israel out of bondage and gave her the Promised Land. Chapter 12 of Deuteronomy outlines this religious loyalty, which for you means the end of all syncretistic practices in Judah and a reaffirmation of the God of the past who revealed himself to Moses at Mount Horeb. To bring control over the religious life of the people must mean the end of all local shrines where all kinds of religious abuses have arisen. You believe that a new day of obedience can emerge in Judah if the reform document becomes the pattern and design for that new life.

9. JEREMIAH'S TRIAL FOR TREASON

A Simulation Based upon Jeremiah 26

INSTRUCTIONS TO THE COORDINATOR

Preparation

Read through the whole simulation to get a good understanding of its purpose and direction. If you expect a large number of persons to take part, then you ought to involve some "leaders" in a discussion of goals and procedures prior to the simulation itself. You and they should read through the chapter "How to Conduct a Biblical Simulation" if you have not already done so.

Schedule

This simulation can fill a whole day or it can be done in an hour or two. The time can be continuous or split up over several different sessions (see chapter 3). The following are possible options:

	One Hour	Two Hours	Six Hours
Introduction	10 min.	15 min.	½ hr.
Small groups	20 min.	45 min.	2½ hrs.
Simulation	15 min.	30 min.	2 hrs.
Debriefing	15 min.	30 min.	1 hr.

For a single hour you will only graze the surface of the issues involved in Jeremiah's trial for treason. In a two-hour period you should be able to grasp the essential nature of the trial. With six hours you gain more time for Bible study. If you are breaking the time into three sessions, begin with the introduction and small groups. During the second session you should give the small groups a few minutes. Then move to the trial setting and end with a short debriefing. During the third session give the small groups a few minutes and then work on what the participants have learned in regard to this situation and themselves.

Grouping

You will need two or three persons working in each small group and one person to play the role of king or a total of nine to thirteen persons. From the following list you can decide upon the number of small groups and the number of representatives from each small group to be seated at the table during the simulation:

Persons present	Number of small groups	Representatives at the table
9 - 49	4	3 per group
50 - 96	8	2 per group

However, should the group exceed fifty persons, we recommend that you run two simulations simultaneously.

Space and Equipment

Your preparation should include obtaining each of the following items (see chapter 3 for fuller explanation): one large room, small rooms according to the number of groups, chairs, tables, Bibles, study aids, paper, pencils, materials for symbols (optional), and refreshments. Certain special preparations will help this simulation:
1. A sufficient number of Bibles.
2. Special interesting touches can include swords for the army personnel, draped cloth or robes for clothing, a crown and a scepter for the king.
3. The large room might well be decorated as the throne room of the king.

Facilitation

You will begin the simulation by explaining the following items: what a biblical simulation is, how to participate, purpose and tasks of this simulation, schedule, small-group tasks, materials, and division into groups. (See chapter 4 for further discussion.) Allow people time to ask questions. Appoint someone to serve as king. Then ask someone to read Jeremiah 26:1-19 aloud to everyone. The groups are then sent to begin their preparation.

The simulation is designed to give people a better understanding of the events surrounding Jeremiah's ministry and in particular the critical event retold in Jeremiah 20:1-18, when he was threatened with death for his prophetic pronouncements. The question underlying the simulation can be stated simply: What constitutes true patriotism? Issues almost certain to arise include the following: the marks of the true prophet, the basis of national security, the necessity of securing the public good, and the need for speaking the truth in highly inflammable situations.

You may be pressed as the coordinator to defend the historical basis of the trial. In truth a trial such as we have outlined did not occur. Also, many of the names used in this simulation are fictitious names. However, the simulation creates an historically realistic setting in which to explore basic issues that were surfacing around the prophetic ministry of Jeremiah in Judah in the year 605 B.C. Clearly King Jehoiakim was hostile to Jeremiah and would have liked him banished or assassinated. Certain officials in the army and the priesthood felt that he was undermining the morale of the nation as can be seen from Jeremiah 20 and 26. Jeremiah, from his recorded oracles, understood his ministry for the good of Judah. As the role defined for the Deuteronomists indicates, their relationship with Jeremiah is unclear. This simulation attempts to allow these parties to speak from their historical perspective. In that sense we may say the simulation is set in the circumstances of 605 B.C. At the same time it points us to critical moments in our own national life as we attempt to deal with the problem of dissenting and prophetic voices within our culture. The simulation should lead to a consideration of what constitutes patriotism.

Debriefing

As coordinator you should conduct the debriefing session. Here is a list of tasks to be followed:

1. Rearrange the chairs so that everyone becomes aware that all have dropped their roles.
2. In groups of four discuss what you have learned.
3. Ask volunteers to share their observations with the whole group.
4. Ask the chroniclers to share their observations.
5. Try to summarize what you have been hearing.

The debriefing period could be the most important session. You must help people to understand their thoughts and emotions during the simulation. In that sense this period can be deeply personal since the participants will undoubtedly learn something about themselves. When this simulation was run in one church, an exchange occurred between the minister and a layman, entirely unrelated to the simulation but symptomatic of feelings which existed between them. The simulation helped them to come to terms with how they felt about each other. Emotions run high when we speak about dissent in this culture. The simulation helps people to work at their feelings about dissent around issues that seem more distant. In this way persons are enabled to gain new insight into themselves regarding this very hot issue in our culture. Remember there are no final answers. Encourage people to share about where they were in the simulation and how they feel now in the debriefing session.

JEREMIAH'S TRIAL FOR TREASON A Simulation Based upon Jeremiah 26

THE SITUATION
After the death of his father, Josiah, King Jehoiakim was placed on the throne by the Egyptian Pharaoh. Because of the great political unrest both within and outside Judah, King Jehoiakim fears open revolt at any moment. Therefore, he has called a council to determine what should be done with the prophet Jeremiah who has preached what might be labeled a treasonable sermon within the temple precincts. A number of people want to put him to death on the spot, but the king has called for a general hearing where all major parties might testify in relation to the case. These parties, the army, the priests, the Deuteronomic reformers, and Jeremiah himself, will determine his fate. In essence it is a trial, but in procedure it will follow the pattern of a general discussion. (To facilitate the discussion, a king should be selected before the groups are identified. After this selection, the king will read the various background data sheets while the four groups meet to determine strategy.) The situation for which Jeremiah is on trial is recorded in Jeremiah 26:1-15. An unabridged version of the sermon appears in Jeremiah 7, although some parties feel this official record does not reproduce Jeremiah's exact words. The task of the group is to determine whether Jeremiah has committed a treasonable act.

TASKS OF ALL GROUPS
PRIOR TO THE SIMULATION
After everyone has heard the story of Jeremiah's speech in Jeremiah 26, the coordinator will break the group into four smaller groups. These groups are:
1. Deuteronomic scholars—defenders of the Law.
2. Zionists—ardent priests who see Jerusalem as the symbol of the national identity.
3. Army officers—a group of officers who see Jeremiah as a direct threat to the morale of the nation.
4. Baruch and Jeremiah—both of whom believe that Jeremiah is a patriot.

Following are the specific tasks each group should perform:
1. Appoint a leader who will—
   a. chair in the preparation for the simulation,
   b. lead the group during the simulation.
2. Appoint a chronicler who will—
   a. record briefly the process of the group,
   b. record the action of the simulation from the perspective of his group,
   c. report to the debriefing session.
3. Examine those texts of the Old Testament which establish the identity of this particular group.
4. Articulate your identity to each other by a song or a gesture or a banner.
5. Prepare your case and decide how your group will act in the simulated decisions (see background data sheet).
6. You will want to appoint one other person to assume major responsibility with the leader at the conference table. Both the leader and the selected person will assume the names associated with your particular group.

RULES OF THE SIMULATION
1. The king will chair the meeting and should be recognized as absolute authority in the kingdom of Judah.
2. Each group will be allowed two representatives at the conference table.
3. Other members of the group will replace the table representatives at will after the initial presentations.
4. Each group will be allowed two roving politicians who may—
   a. discover the character and purposes of the other groups,
   b. consult with the resource person.

TASKS OF THE SIMULATION
1. The four groups will sit at the conference table and will have the following representatives:
   a. Deuteronomic scholars—Hilkiah and Huldah;
   b. Zionists—Zadok and Baalita;

c. Army—Captain Ratzach and General Mishpat;

d. Jeremiah—Baruch and Jeremiah.

2. Under the direction of the king, the assembled groups will make the following decisions:

   a. Is Jeremiah guilty of treason and upon what grounds?

   b. If he is guilty, what appropriate penalty should be exacted?

   c. If he is not guilty, should his activity in Jerusalem be curtailed?

   d. Each group should make an initial presentation before general debate begins. The king will determine the order of these presentations. No group should speak more than five minutes at one time.

3. The simulation will be terminated according to a previously arranged schedule, when the tasks have been accomplished, or if debriefing appears to be occurring prior to either of the above.

TASKS FOR DEBRIEFING

1. Rearrange the room to symbolize the termination of the simulation.

2. Let everyone, including the chroniclers, share his observations with the whole group.

3. Let everyone express his feelings about what happened.

4. You might wish to pose the following questions: How did you feel in your role? Where did the most important exchanges take place in the simulation? What new things did you learn about Jeremiah and the historical situation of 605 B.C.? What did you learn about yourself? What theological issues did the simulation raise? What constitutes true patriotism?

5. Summarize what was learned.

1. The Deuteronomic Scholars

Your group identity for the simulation will be that of distinguished scholars who have worked night and day on the Law. You are not sure about Jeremiah since the temple sermon (Jeremiah 7 and 26), but you have felt in the past that Jeremiah has supported a renewed faith and belief in Judah. You will want to appoint the prophetess Huldah and the scribe Hilkiah to represent you at the council of the king. It is your task to determine how to use your special interests and powers in the decision-making process. Read the following passages:

Deuteronomy 13
Deuteronomy 18:9-22

BACKGROUND DATA:

The Deuteronomic scholars were responsible for the reform of Josiah in 622 B.C. They actually date their ancestry from the time of Moses who instituted the Deuteronomic Code or the Covenant of Sinai. You have always felt that reform was essential if Judah was to survive as a nation, particularly after the dreadful King Manasseh who preceded Josiah in the kingly office. However, you question within your own minds whether or not Jeremiah constitutes a real threat to the nation since he may be going beyond reform. He seems to be announcing God's unconditional judgment of Judah. You have guidelines for considering a true prophet, and they are found in your own book of the Law, Deuteronomy 13 and 18:9-20. You are indeed reluctant to banish any prophet who claims to be speaking for God.

JEREMIAH'S TRIAL FOR TREASON   A Simulation Based upon Jeremiah 26

THE SITUATION
After the death of his father, Josiah, King Jehoiakim was placed on the throne by the Egyptian Pharaoh. Because of the great political unrest both within and outside Judah, King Jehoiakim fears open revolt at any moment. Therefore, he has called a council to determine what should be done with the prophet Jeremiah who has preached what might be labeled a treasonable sermon within the temple precincts. A number of people want to put him to death on the spot, but the king has called for a general hearing where all major parties might testify in relation to the case. These parties, the army, the priests, the Deuteronomic reformers, and Jeremiah himself, will determine his fate. In essence it is a trial, but in procedure it will follow the pattern of a general discussion. (To facilitate the discussion, a king should be selected before the groups are identified. After this selection, the king will read the various background data sheets while the four groups meet to determine strategy.) The situation for which Jeremiah is on trial is recorded in Jeremiah 26:1-15. An unabridged version of the sermon appears in Jeremiah 7, although some parties feel this official record does not reproduce Jeremiah's exact words. The task of the group is to determine whether Jeremiah has committed a treasonable act.

TASKS OF ALL GROUPS
PRIOR TO THE SIMULATION
After everyone has heard the story of Jeremiah's speech in Jeremiah 26, the coordinator will break the group into four smaller groups. These groups are:
1. Deuteronomic scholars—defenders of the Law.
2. Zionists—ardent priests who see Jerusalem as the symbol of the national identity.
3. Army officers—a group of officers who see Jeremiah as a direct threat to the morale of the nation.
4. Baruch and Jeremiah—both of whom believe that Jeremiah is a patriot.

Following are the specific tasks each group should perform:
1. Appoint a leader who will—
   a. chair in the preparation for the simulation,
   b. lead the group during the simulation.
2. Appoint a chronicler who will—
   a. record briefly the process of the group,
   b. record the action of the simulation from the perspective of his group,
   c. report to the debriefing session.
3. Examine those texts of the Old Testament which establish the identity of this particular group.
4. Articulate your identity to each other by a song or a gesture or a banner.
5. Prepare your case and decide how your group will act in the simulated decisions (see background data sheet).
6. You will want to appoint one other person to assume major responsibility with the leader at the conference table. Both the leader and the selected person will assume the names associated with your particular group.

RULES OF THE SIMULATION
1. The king will chair the meeting and should be recognized as absolute authority in the kingdom of Judah.
2. Each group will be allowed two representatives at the conference table.
3. Other members of the group will replace the table representatives at will after the initial presentations.
4. Each group will be allowed two roving politicians who may—
   a. discover the character and purposes of the other groups,
   b. consult with the resource person.

TASKS OF THE SIMULATION
1. The four groups will sit at the conference table and will have the following representatives:
   a. Deuteronomic scholars—Hilkiah and Huldah;
   b. Zionists—Zadok and Baalita;

c. Army—Captain Ratzach and General Mishpat;

d. Jeremiah—Baruch and Jeremiah.

2. Under the direction of the king, the assembled groups will make the following decisions:

   a. Is Jeremiah guilty of treason and upon what grounds?

   b. If he is guilty, what appropriate penalty should be exacted?

   c. If he is not guilty, should his activity in Jerusalem be curtailed?

   d. Each group should make an initial presentation before general debate begins. The king will determine the order of these presentations. No group should speak more than five minutes at one time.

3. The simulation will be terminated according to a previously arranged schedule, when the tasks have been accomplished, or if debriefing appears to be occurring prior to either of the above.

TASKS FOR DEBRIEFING

1. Rearrange the room to symbolize the termination of the simulation.

2. Let everyone, including the chroniclers, share his observations with the whole group.

3. Let everyone express his feelings about what happened.

4. You might wish to pose the following questions: How did you feel in your role? Where did the most important exchanges take place in the simulation? What new things did you learn about Jeremiah and the historical situation of 605 B.C.? What did you learn about yourself? What theological issues did the simulation raise? What constitutes true patriotism?

5. Summarize what was learned.

1. The Deuteronomic Scholars

Your group identity for the simulation will be that of distinguished scholars who have worked night and day on the Law. You are not sure about Jeremiah since the temple sermon (Jeremiah 7 and 26), but you have felt in the past that Jeremiah has supported a renewed faith and belief in Judah. You will want to appoint the prophetess Huldah and the scribe Hilkiah to represent you at the council of the king. It is your task to determine how to use your special interests and powers in the decision-making process. Read the following passages:

Deuteronomy 13

Deuteronomy 18:9-22

BACKGROUND DATA:

The Deuteronomic scholars were responsible for the reform of Josiah in 622 B.C. They actually date their ancestry from the time of Moses who instituted the Deuteronomic Code or the Covenant of Sinai. You have always felt that reform was essential if Judah was to survive as a nation, particularly after the dreadful King Manasseh who preceded Josiah in the kingly office. However, you question within your own minds whether or not Jeremiah constitutes a real threat to the nation since he may be going beyond reform. He seems to be announcing God's unconditional judgment of Judah. You have guidelines for considering a true prophet, and they are found in your own book of the Law, Deuteronomy 13 and 18:9-20. You are indeed reluctant to banish any prophet who claims to be speaking for God.

JEREMIAH'S TRIAL FOR TREASON A Simulation Based upon Jeremiah 26

THE SITUATION

After the death of his father, Josiah, King Jehoiakim was placed on the throne by the Egyptian Pharaoh. Because of the great political unrest both within and outside Judah, King Jehoiakim fears open revolt at any moment. Therefore, he has called a council to determine what should be done with the prophet Jeremiah who has preached what might be labeled a treasonable sermon within the temple precincts. A number of people want to put him to death on the spot, but the king has called for a general hearing where all major parties might testify in relation to the case. These parties, the army, the priests, the Deuteronomic reformers, and Jeremiah himself, will determine his fate. In essence it is a trial, but in procedure it will follow the pattern of a general discussion. (To facilitate the discussion, a king should be selected before the groups are identified. After this selection, the king will read the various background data sheets while the four groups meet to determine strategy.) The situation for which Jeremiah is on trial is recorded in Jeremiah 26:1-15. An unabridged version of the sermon appears in Jeremiah 7, although some parties feel this official record does not reproduce Jeremiah's exact words. The task of the group is to determine whether Jeremiah has committed a treasonable act.

TASKS OF ALL GROUPS
PRIOR TO THE SIMULATION

After everyone has heard the story of Jeremiah's speech in Jeremiah 26, the coordinator will break the group into four smaller groups. These groups are:

1. Deuteronomic scholars—defenders of the Law.
2. Zionists—ardent priests who see Jerusalem as the symbol of the national identity.
3. Army officers—a group of officers who see Jeremiah as a direct threat to the morale of the nation.
4. Baruch and Jeremiah—both of whom believe that Jeremiah is a patriot.

Following are the specific tasks each group should perform:

1. Appoint a leader who will—
   a. chair in the preparation for the simulation,
   b. lead the group during the simulation.
2. Appoint a chronicler who will—
   a. record briefly the process of the group,
   b. record the action of the simulation from the perspective of his group,
   c. report to the debriefing session.
3. Examine those texts of the Old Testament which establish the identity of this particular group.
4. Articulate your identity to each other by a song or a gesture or a banner.
5. Prepare your case and decide how your group will act in the simulated decisions (see background data sheet).
6. You will want to appoint one other person to assume major responsibility with the leader at the conference table. Both the leader and the selected person will assume the names associated with your particular group.

RULES OF THE SIMULATION

1. The king will chair the meeting and should be recognized as absolute authority in the kingdom of Judah.
2. Each group will be allowed two representatives at the conference table.
3. Other members of the group will replace the table representatives at will after the initial presentations.
4. Each group will be allowed two roving politicians who may—
   a. discover the character and purposes of the other groups,
   b. consult with the resource person.

TASKS OF THE SIMULATION

1. The four groups will sit at the conference table and will have the following representatives:
   a. Deuteronomic scholars—Hilkiah and Huldah;
   b. Zionists—Zadok and Baalita;

c. Army—Captain Ratzach and General Mishpat;

d. Jeremiah—Baruch and Jeremiah.

2. Under the direction of the king, the assembled groups will make the following decisions:

a. Is Jeremiah guilty of treason and upon what grounds?

b. If he is guilty, what appropriate penalty should be exacted?

c. If he is not guilty, should his activity in Jerusalem be curtailed?

d. Each group should make an initial presentation before general debate begins. The king will determine the order of these presentations. No group should speak more than five minutes at one time.

3. The simulation will be terminated according to a previously arranged schedule,

when the tasks have been accomplished, or if debriefing appears to be occurring prior to either of the above.

TASKS FOR DEBRIEFING

1. Rearrange the room to symbolize the termination of the simulation.

2. Let everyone, including the chroniclers, share his observations with the whole group.

3. Let everyone express his feelings about what happened.

4. You might wish to pose the following questions: How did you feel in your role? Where did the most important exchanges take place in the simulation? What new things did you learn about Jeremiah and the historical situation of 605 B.C.? What did you learn about yourself? What theological issues did the simulation raise? What constitutes true patriotism?

5. Summarize what was learned.

2. The Zionists

Your group identity for the simulation will be that of ardent Jerusalem priests who see in Jeremiah a direct threat to the national ideology that Jerusalem can not be conquered by force. Jeremiah's attack on the temple (Jeremiah 7 and 26) constitutes a violation of the official theology which has been in vogue since the days of David. You will want to appoint the priest Zadok and the priestess Baalita to represent you at the council of the king. It is your task to determine how to use your special interests and powers in the decision-making process. You may want to read the following passages:

Isaiah 2:1-4

2 Kings 18 - 19

BACKGROUND DATA:

Your ancestry dates from the time of Zadok, the

first priest appointed by David in Jerusalem. You believe that Zion is the sign of God's rule on earth. To proclaim, as Jeremiah does, that the temple can be destroyed is the same as saying, "God is dead." You believe that you must protect the official theology at all costs. If you don't defend the God of David and Jerusalem in these difficult times, who will? You know that for four hundred years God has defended Jerusalem and Zion. In fact, when Sennacherib invaded Judah in 701, God brought about a miraculous deliverance at the very moment that Jerusalem seemed fated to destruction. The God of history is on your side. Therefore, you feel that Jeremiah should be silenced and banished from the state of Judah, since he has blasphemed God.

JEREMIAH'S TRIAL FOR TREASON A Simulation Based upon Jeremiah 26

THE SITUATION

After the death of his father, Josiah, King Jehoiakim was placed on the throne by the Egyptian Pharaoh. Because of the great political unrest both within and outside Judah, King Jehoiakim fears open revolt at any moment. Therefore, he has called a council to determine what should be done with the prophet Jeremiah who has preached what might be labeled a treasonable sermon within the temple precincts. A number of people want to put him to death on the spot, but the king has called for a general hearing where all major parties might testify in relation to the case. These parties, the army, the priests, the Deuteronomic reformers, and Jeremiah himself, will determine his fate. In essence it is a trial, but in procedure it will follow the pattern of a general discussion. (To facilitate the discussion, a king should be selected before the groups are identified. After this selection, the king will read the various background data sheets while the four groups meet to determine strategy.) The situation for which Jeremiah is on trial is recorded in Jeremiah 26:1-15. An unabridged version of the sermon appears in Jeremiah 7, although some parties feel this official record does not reproduce Jeremiah's exact words. The task of the group is to determine whether Jeremiah has committed a treasonable act.

TASKS OF ALL GROUPS
PRIOR TO THE SIMULATION

After everyone has heard the story of Jeremiah's speech in Jeremiah 26, the coordinator will break the group into four smaller groups. These groups are:

1. Deuteronomic scholars—defenders of the Law.
2. Zionists—ardent priests who see Jerusalem as the symbol of the national identity.
3. Army officers—a group of officers who see Jeremiah as a direct threat to the morale of the nation.
4. Baruch and Jeremiah—both of whom believe that Jeremiah is a patriot.

Following are the specific tasks each group should perform:

1. Appoint a leader who will—
   a. chair in the preparation for the simulation,
   b. lead the group during the simulation.
2. Appoint a chronicler who will—
   a. record briefly the process of the group,
   b. record the action of the simulation from the perspective of his group,
   c. report to the debriefing session.
3. Examine those texts of the Old Testament which establish the identity of this particular group.
4. Articulate your identity to each other by a song or a gesture or a banner.
5. Prepare your case and decide how your group will act in the simulated decisions (see background data sheet).
6. You will want to appoint one other person to assume major responsibility with the leader at the conference table. Both the leader and the selected person will assume the names associated with your particular group.

RULES OF THE SIMULATION

1. The king will chair the meeting and should be recognized as absolute authority in the kingdom of Judah.
2. Each group will be allowed two representatives at the conference table.
3. Other members of the group will replace the table representatives at will after the initial presentations.
4. Each group will be allowed two roving politicians who may—
   a. discover the character and purposes of the other groups,
   b. consult with the resource person.

TASKS OF THE SIMULATION

1. The four groups will sit at the conference table and will have the following representatives:
   a. Deuteronomic scholars—Hilkiah and Huldah;
   b. Zionists—Zadok and Baalita;

107

c. Army—Captain Ratzach and General Mishpat;

d. Jeremiah—Baruch and Jeremiah.

2. Under the direction of the king, the assembled groups will make the following decisions:

   a. Is Jeremiah guilty of treason and upon what grounds?

   b. If he is guilty, what appropriate penalty should be exacted?

   c. If he is not guilty, should his activity in Jerusalem be curtailed?

   d. Each group should make an initial presentation before general debate begins. The king will determine the order of these presentations. No group should speak more than five minutes at one time.

3. The simulation will be terminated according to a previously arranged schedule, when the tasks have been accomplished, or if debriefing appears to be occurring prior to either of the above.

TASKS FOR DEBRIEFING

1. Rearrange the room to symbolize the termination of the simulation.

2. Let everyone, including the chroniclers, share his observations with the whole group.

3. Let everyone express his feelings about what happened.

4. You might wish to pose the following questions: How did you feel in your role? Where did the most important exchanges take place in the simulation? What new things did you learn about Jeremiah and the historical situation of 605 B.C.? What did you learn about yourself? What theological issues did the simulation raise? What constitutes true patriotism?

5. Summarize what was learned.

2. The Zionists

Your group identity for the simulation will be that of ardent Jerusalem priests who see in Jeremiah a direct threat to the national ideology that Jerusalem can not be conquered by force. Jeremiah's attack on the temple (Jeremiah 7 and 26) constitutes a violation of the official theology which has been in vogue since the days of David. You will want to appoint the priest Zadok and the priestess Baalita to represent you at the council of the king. It is your task to determine how to use your special interests and powers in the decision-making process. You may want to read the following passages:

Isaiah 2:1-4

2 Kings 18 - 19

BACKGROUND DATA:

Your ancestry dates from the time of Zadok, the first priest appointed by David in Jerusalem. You believe that Zion is the sign of God's rule on earth. To proclaim, as Jeremiah does, that the temple can be destroyed is the same as saying, "God is dead." You believe that you must protect the official theology at all costs. If you don't defend the God of David and Jerusalem in these difficult times, who will? You know that for four hundred years God has defended Jerusalem and Zion. In fact, when Sennacherib invaded Judah in 701, God brought about a miraculous deliverance at the very moment that Jerusalem seemed fated to destruction. The God of history is on your side. Therefore, you feel that Jeremiah should be silenced and banished from the state of Judah, since he has blasphemed God.

JEREMIAH'S TRIAL FOR TREASON A Simulation Based upon Jeremiah 26

THE SITUATION

After the death of his father, Josiah, King Jehoiakim was placed on the throne by the Egyptian Pharaoh. Because of the great political unrest both within and outside Judah, King Jehoiakim fears open revolt at any moment. Therefore, he has called a council to determine what should be done with the prophet Jeremiah who has preached what might be labeled a treasonable sermon within the temple precincts. A number of people want to put him to death on the spot, but the king has called for a general hearing where all major parties might testify in relation to the case. These parties, the army, the priests, the Deuteronomic reformers, and Jeremiah himself, will determine his fate. In essence it is a trial, but in procedure it will follow the pattern of a general discussion. (To facilitate the discussion, a king should be selected before the groups are identified. After this selection, the king will read the various background data sheets while the four groups meet to determine strategy.) The situation for which Jeremiah is on trial is recorded in Jeremiah 26:1-15. An unabridged version of the sermon appears in Jeremiah 7, although some parties feel this official record does not reproduce Jeremiah's exact words. The task of the group is to determine whether Jeremiah has committed a treasonable act.

TASKS OF ALL GROUPS
PRIOR TO THE SIMULATION

After everyone has heard the story of Jeremiah's speech in Jeremiah 26, the coordinator will break the group into four smaller groups. These groups are:

1. Deuteronomic scholars—defenders of the Law.
2. Zionists—ardent priests who see Jerusalem as the symbol of the national identity.
3. Army officers—a group of officers who see Jeremiah as a direct threat to the morale of the nation.
4. Baruch and Jeremiah—both of whom believe that Jeremiah is a patriot.

Following are the specific tasks each group should perform:

1. Appoint a leader who will—
   a. chair in the preparation for the simulation,
   b. lead the group during the simulation.
2. Appoint a chronicler who will—
   a. record briefly the process of the group,
   b. record the action of the simulation from the perspective of his group,
   c. report to the debriefing session.
3. Examine those texts of the Old Testament which establish the identity of this particular group.
4. Articulate your identity to each other by a song or a gesture or a banner.
5. Prepare your case and decide how your group will act in the simulated decisions (see background data sheet).
6. You will want to appoint one other person to assume major responsibility with the leader at the conference table. Both the leader and the selected person will assume the names associated with your particular group.

RULES OF THE SIMULATION

1. The king will chair the meeting and should be recognized as absolute authority in the kingdom of Judah.
2. Each group will be allowed two representatives at the conference table.
3. Other members of the group will replace the table representatives at will after the initial presentations.
4. Each group will be allowed two roving politicians who may—
   a. discover the character and purposes of the other groups,
   b. consult with the resource person.

TASKS OF THE SIMULATION

1. The four groups will sit at the conference table and will have the following representatives:
   a. Deuteronomic scholars—Hilkiah and Huldah;
   b. Zionists—Zadok and Baalita;

109

c. Army—Captain Ratzach and General Mishpat;

d. Jeremiah—Baruch and Jeremiah.

2. Under the direction of the king, the assembled groups will make the following decisions:

a. Is Jeremiah guilty of treason and upon what grounds?

b. If he is guilty, what appropriate penalty should be exacted?

c. If he is not guilty, should his activity in Jerusalem be curtailed?

d. Each group should make an initial presentation before general debate begins. The king will determine the order of these presentations. No group should speak more than five minutes at one time.

3. The simulation will be terminated according to a previously arranged schedule, when the tasks have been accomplished, or if debriefing appears to be occurring prior to either of the above.

TASKS FOR DEBRIEFING

1. Rearrange the room to symbolize the termination of the simulation.

2. Let everyone, including the chroniclers, share his observations with the whole group.

3. Let everyone express his feelings about what happened.

4. You might wish to pose the following questions: How did you feel in your role? Where did the most important exchanges take place in the simulation? What new things did you learn about Jeremiah and the historical situation of 605 B.C.? What did you learn about yourself? What theological issues did the simulation raise? What constitutes true patriotism?

5. Summarize what was learned.

3. The Army

Your group identity for the simulation will be that of army officers who see in Jeremiah a direct threat to the already sagging morale of the nation. His temple sermon (Jeremiah 7 and 26) constitutes a treasonous act since Jerusalem is close to a state of war. You will want to appoint a Captain Ratzach and a General Mishpat to represent you at the council of the king. It is your task to determine how to use your special interests and powers in the decision-making process. Read the following support documents:

Joshua 6
Exodus 15
Judges 4 - 8

BACKGROUND DATA:

You date your ancestry to the Israelite Revolution of the thirteenth century B.C., when Israel was freed from Egypt. You believe that since that time God has continually defeated Israel's enemies in times of national crisis. Although the idea of the Holy War had been pushed into the background in recent times, you favored the reinstitution of the Holy War under Josiah who ruled Judah from 640 - 609 B.C. You believe that God will fight for Israel against the Babylonians and give you victory as he did against the Assyrians just a century before. Therefore, the real issue is to encourage the people to believe in God's deliverance which will vanquish the enemy. Jeremiah undermines this faith because he feels that the nation can no longer rely on God to deliver her because she has sinned and must expect the judgment of God. He speaks an untruth and should be banned from public life so that the people might rally to the cause of freedom and the spirit of the Holy War.

JEREMIAH'S TRIAL FOR TREASON A Simulation Based upon Jeremiah 26

THE SITUATION
After the death of his father, Josiah, King Jehoiakim was placed on the throne by the Egyptian Pharaoh. Because of the great political unrest both within and outside Judah, King Jehoiakim fears open revolt at any moment. Therefore, he has called a council to determine what should be done with the prophet Jeremiah who has preached what might be labeled a treasonable sermon within the temple precincts. A number of people want to put him to death on the spot, but the king has called for a general hearing where all major parties might testify in relation to the case. These parties, the army, the priests, the Deuteronomic reformers, and Jeremiah himself, will determine his fate. In essence it is a trial, but in procedure it will follow the pattern of a general discussion. (To facilitate the discussion, a king should be selected before the groups are identified. After this selection, the king will read the various background data sheets while the four groups meet to determine strategy.) The situation for which Jeremiah is on trial is recorded in Jeremiah 26:1-15. An unabridged version of the sermon appears in Jeremiah 7, although some parties feel this official record does not reproduce Jeremiah's exact words. The task of the group is to determine whether Jeremiah has committed a treasonable act.

TASKS OF ALL GROUPS
PRIOR TO THE SIMULATION
After everyone has heard the story of Jeremiah's speech in Jeremiah 26, the coordinator will break the group into four smaller groups. These groups are:
1. Deuteronomic scholars—defenders of the Law.
2. Zionists—ardent priests who see Jerusalem as the symbol of the national identity.
3. Army officers—a group of officers who see Jeremiah as a direct threat to the morale of the nation.
4. Baruch and Jeremiah—both of whom believe that Jeremiah is a patriot.

Following are the specific tasks each group should perform:
1. Appoint a leader who will—
   a. chair in the preparation for the simulation,
   b. lead the group during the simulation.
2. Appoint a chronicler who will—
   a. record briefly the process of the group,
   b. record the action of the simulation from the perspective of his group,
   c. report to the debriefing session.
3. Examine those texts of the Old Testament which establish the identity of this particular group.
4. Articulate your identity to each other by a song or a gesture or a banner.
5. Prepare your case and decide how your group will act in the simulated decisions (see background data sheet).
6. You will want to appoint one other person to assume major responsibility with the leader at the conference table. Both the leader and the selected person will assume the names associated with your particular group.

RULES OF THE SIMULATION
1. The king will chair the meeting and should be recognized as absolute authority in the kingdom of Judah.
2. Each group will be allowed two representatives at the conference table.
3. Other members of the group will replace the table representatives at will after the initial presentations.
4. Each group will be allowed two roving politicians who may—
   a. discover the character and purposes of the other groups,
   b. consult with the resource person.

TASKS OF THE SIMULATION
1. The four groups will sit at the conference table and will have the following representatives:
   a. Deuteronomic scholars—Hilkiah and Huldah;
   b. Zionists—Zadok and Baalita;

111

c. Army—Captain Ratzach and General Mishpat;

  d. Jeremiah—Baruch and Jeremiah.

2. Under the direction of the king, the assembled groups will make the following decisions:

  a. Is Jeremiah guilty of treason and upon what grounds?

  b. If he is guilty, what appropriate penalty should be exacted?

  c. If he is not guilty, should his activity in Jerusalem be curtailed?

  d. Each group should make an initial presentation before general debate begins. The king will determine the order of these presentations. No group should speak more than five minutes at one time.

3. The simulation will be terminated according to a previously arranged schedule, when the tasks have been accomplished, or if debriefing appears to be occurring prior to either of the above.

TASKS FOR DEBRIEFING

1. Rearrange the room to symbolize the termination of the simulation.

2. Let everyone, including the chroniclers, share his observations with the whole group.

3. Let everyone express his feelings about what happened.

4. You might wish to pose the following questions: How did you feel in your role? Where did the most important exchanges take place in the simulation? What new things did you learn about Jeremiah and the historical situation of 605 B.C.? What did you learn about yourself? What theological issues did the simulation raise? What constitutes true patriotism?

5. Summarize what was learned.

3. The Army

Your group identity for the simulation will be that of army officers who see in Jeremiah a direct threat to the already sagging morale of the nation. His temple sermon (Jeremiah 7 and 26) constitutes a treasonous act since Jerusalem is close to a state of war. You will want to appoint a Captain Ratzach and a General Mishpat to represent you at the council of the king. It is your task to determine how to use your special interests and powers in the decision-making process. Read the following support documents:

Joshua 6
Exodus 15
Judges 4 - 8

BACKGROUND DATA:

You date your ancestry to the Israelite Revolution of the thirteenth century B.C., when Israel was freed from Egypt. You believe that since that time God has continually defeated Israel's enemies in times of national crisis. Although the idea of the Holy War had been pushed into the background in recent times, you favored the reinstitution of the Holy War under Josiah who ruled Judah from 640 - 609 B.C. You believe that God will fight for Israel against the Babylonians and give you victory as he did against the Assyrians just a century before. Therefore, the real issue is to encourage the people to believe in God's deliverance which will vanquish the enemy. Jeremiah undermines this faith because he feels that the nation can no longer rely on God to deliver her because she has sinned and must expect the judgment of God. He speaks an untruth and should be banned from public life so that the people might rally to the cause of freedom and the spirit of the Holy War.

JEREMIAH'S TRIAL FOR TREASON A Simulation Based upon Jeremiah 26

THE SITUATION

After the death of his father, Josiah, King Jehoiakim was placed on the throne by the Egyptian Pharaoh. Because of the great political unrest both within and outside Judah, King Jehoiakim fears open revolt at any moment. Therefore, he has called a council to determine what should be done with the prophet Jeremiah who has preached what might be labeled a treasonable sermon within the temple precincts. A number of people want to put him to death on the spot, but the king has called for a general hearing where all major parties might testify in relation to the case. These parties, the army, the priests, the Deuteronomic reformers, and Jeremiah himself, will determine his fate. In essence it is a trial, but in procedure it will follow the pattern of a general discussion. (To facilitate the discussion, a king should be selected before the groups are identified. After this selection, the king will read the various background data sheets while the four groups meet to determine strategy.) The situation for which Jeremiah is on trial is recorded in Jeremiah 26:1-15. An unabridged version of the sermon appears in Jeremiah 7, although some parties feel this official record does not reproduce Jeremiah's exact words. The task of the group is to determine whether Jeremiah has committed a treasonable act.

TASKS OF ALL GROUPS
PRIOR TO THE SIMULATION

After everyone has heard the story of Jeremiah's speech in Jeremiah 26, the coordinator will break the group into four smaller groups. These groups are:

1. Deuteronomic scholars—defenders of the Law.
2. Zionists—ardent priests who see Jerusalem as the symbol of the national identity.
3. Army officers—a group of officers who see Jeremiah as a direct threat to the morale of the nation.
4. Baruch and Jeremiah—both of whom believe that Jeremiah is a patriot.

Following are the specific tasks each group should perform:

1. Appoint a leader who will—
   a. chair in the preparation for the simulation,
   b. lead the group during the simulation.
2. Appoint a chronicler who will—
   a. record briefly the process of the group,
   b. record the action of the simulation from the perspective of his group,
   c. report to the debriefing session.
3. Examine those texts of the Old Testament which establish the identity of this particular group.
4. Articulate your identity to each other by a song or a gesture or a banner.
5. Prepare your case and decide how your group will act in the simulated decisions (see background data sheet).
6. You will want to appoint one other person to assume major responsibility with the leader at the conference table. Both the leader and the selected person will assume the names associated with your particular group.

RULES OF THE SIMULATION

1. The king will chair the meeting and should be recognized as absolute authority in the kingdom of Judah.
2. Each group will be allowed two representatives at the conference table.
3. Other members of the group will replace the table representatives at will after the initial presentations.
4. Each group will be allowed two roving politicians who may—
   a. discover the character and purposes of the other groups,
   b. consult with the resource person.

TASKS OF THE SIMULATION

1. The four groups will sit at the conference table and will have the following representatives:
   a. Deuteronomic scholars—Hilkiah and Huldah;
   b. Zionists—Zadok and Baalita;

113

c. Army—Captain Ratzach and General Mishpat;

d. Jeremiah—Baruch and Jeremiah.

2. Under the direction of the king, the assembled groups will make the following decisions:

   a. Is Jeremiah guilty of treason and upon what grounds?

   b. If he is guilty, what appropriate penalty should be exacted?

   c. If he is not guilty, should his activity in Jerusalem be curtailed?

   d. Each group should make an initial presentation before general debate begins. The king will determine the order of these presentations. No group should speak more than five minutes at one time.

3. The simulation will be terminated according to a previously arranged schedule, when the tasks have been accomplished, or if debriefing appears to be occurring prior to either of the above.

TASKS FOR DEBRIEFING

1. Rearrange the room to symbolize the termination of the simulation.

2. Let everyone, including the chroniclers, share his observations with the whole group.

3. Let everyone express his feelings about what happened.

4. You might wish to pose the following questions: How did you feel in your role? Where did the most important exchanges take place in the simulation? What new things did you learn about Jeremiah and the historical situation of 605 B.C.? What did you learn about yourself? What theological issues did the simulation raise? What constitutes true patriotism?

5. Summarize what was learned.

4. Baruch and Jeremiah

You are a party of two; perhaps others sitting at the council of the king will side with you. You, of course, believe that Jeremiah is a faithful supporter of the nation. For background data you may wish to read the following chapters:

> Jeremiah 7
>
> Jeremiah 26 (27 - 28)

BACKGROUND DATA:

You wholeheartedly believe that Jeremiah is a super patriot who is interpreting the covenant that God has established with Judah. He realistically seeks the easiest way out for Judah by proclaiming judgment: namely, she will escape with her skin. You know that Jeremiah is fighting against the idea that naïve belief is enough to deliver a people who have continued to perpetuate the sins of their fathers. You will want to show that Jeremiah is misunderstood. He is not a traitor, but a prophet who calls the people to a new obedience while accepting the impending judgment of God. You, of course, have the whole book of Jeremiah as a resource. For understanding Baruch and his relationship to the prophet, you will find Jeremiah 36 and 45 particularly helpful. You will also want to remember that Jeremiah sees himself standing in a line of true prophecy, particularly as represented by the prophet Hosea.

JEREMIAH'S TRIAL FOR TREASON A Simulation Based upon Jeremiah 26

THE SITUATION

After the death of his father, Josiah, King Jehoiakim was placed on the throne by the Egyptian Pharaoh. Because of the great political unrest both within and outside Judah, King Jehoiakim fears open revolt at any moment. Therefore, he has called a council to determine what should be done with the prophet Jeremiah who has preached what might be labeled a treasonable sermon within the temple precincts. A number of people want to put him to death on the spot, but the king has called for a general hearing where all major parties might testify in relation to the case. These parties, the army, the priests, the Deuteronomic reformers, and Jeremiah himself, will determine his fate. In essence it is a trial, but in procedure it will follow the pattern of a general discussion. (To facilitate the discussion, a king should be selected before the groups are identified. After this selection, the king will read the various background data sheets while the four groups meet to determine strategy.) The situation for which Jeremiah is on trial is recorded in Jeremiah 26:1-15. An unabridged version of the sermon appears in Jeremiah 7, although some parties feel this official record does not reproduce Jeremiah's exact words. The task of the group is to determine whether Jeremiah has committed a treasonable act.

TASKS OF ALL GROUPS
PRIOR TO THE SIMULATION

After everyone has heard the story of Jeremiah's speech in Jeremiah 26, the coordinator will break the group into four smaller groups. These groups are:

1. Deuteronomic scholars—defenders of the Law.
2. Zionists—ardent priests who see Jerusalem as the symbol of the national identity.
3. Army officers—a group of officers who see Jeremiah as a direct threat to the morale of the nation.
4. Baruch and Jeremiah—both of whom believe that Jeremiah is a patriot.

Following are the specific tasks each group should perform:

1. Appoint a leader who will—
   a. chair in the preparation for the simulation,
   b. lead the group during the simulation.
2. Appoint a chronicler who will—
   a. record briefly the process of the group,
   b. record the action of the simulation from the perspective of his group,
   c. report to the debriefing session.
3. Examine those texts of the Old Testament which establish the identity of this particular group.
4. Articulate your identity to each other by a song or a gesture or a banner.
5. Prepare your case and decide how your group will act in the simulated decisions (see background data sheet).
6. You will want to appoint one other person to assume major responsibility with the leader at the conference table. Both the leader and the selected person will assume the names associated with your particular group.

RULES OF THE SIMULATION

1. The king will chair the meeting and should be recognized as absolute authority in the kingdom of Judah.
2. Each group will be allowed two representatives at the conference table.
3. Other members of the group will replace the table representatives at will after the initial presentations.
4. Each group will be allowed two roving politicians who may—
   a. discover the character and purposes of the other groups,
   b. consult with the resource person.

TASKS OF THE SIMULATION

1. The four groups will sit at the conference table and will have the following representatives:
   a. Deuteronomic scholars—Hilkiah and Huldah;
   b. Zionists—Zadok and Baalita;

115

c. Army—Captain Ratzach and General Mishpat;

d. Jeremiah—Baruch and Jeremiah.

2. Under the direction of the king, the assembled groups will make the following decisions:

   a. Is Jeremiah guilty of treason and upon what grounds?

   b. If he is guilty, what appropriate penalty should be exacted?

   c. If he is not guilty, should his activity in Jerusalem be curtailed?

   d. Each group should make an initial presentation before general debate begins. The king will determine the order of these presentations. No group should speak more than five minutes at one time.

3. The simulation will be terminated according to a previously arranged schedule, when the tasks have been accomplished, or if debriefing appears to be occurring prior to either of the above.

TASKS FOR DEBRIEFING

1. Rearrange the room to symbolize the termination of the simulation.

2. Let everyone, including the chroniclers, share his observations with the whole group.

3. Let everyone express his feelings about what happened.

4. You might wish to pose the following questions: How did you feel in your role? Where did the most important exchanges take place in the simulation? What new things did you learn about Jeremiah and the historical situation of 605 B.C.? What did you learn about yourself? What theological issues did the simulation raise? What constitutes true patriotism?

5. Summarize what was learned.

4. Baruch and Jeremiah

You are a party of two; perhaps others sitting at the council of the king will side with you. You, of course, believe that Jeremiah is a faithful supporter of the nation. For background data you may wish to read the following chapters:

Jeremiah 7
Jeremiah 26 (27 - 28)

BACKGROUND DATA:

You wholeheartedly believe that Jeremiah is a super patriot who is interpreting the covenant that God has established with Judah. He realistically seeks the easiest way out for Judah by proclaiming judgment: namely, she will escape with her skin. You know that Jeremiah is fighting against the idea that naïve belief is enough to deliver a people who have continued to perpetuate the sins of their fathers. You will want to show that Jeremiah is misunderstood. He is not a traitor, but a prophet who calls the people to a new obedience while accepting the impending judgment of God. You, of course, have the whole book of Jeremiah as a resource. For understanding Baruch and his relationship to the prophet, you will find Jeremiah 36 and 45 particularly helpful. You will also want to remember that Jeremiah sees himself standing in a line of true prophecy, particularly as represented by the prophet Hosea.

10. JOB AND HIS FRIENDS

A Simulation Based upon the Book of Job

INSTRUCTIONS TO THE COORDINATOR

Preparation

Read through the whole simulation to get a good understanding of its purpose and direction. If you expect a large number of persons to take part, then you ought to involve some "leaders" in a discussion of goals and procedures prior to the simulation itself. You and they should read through the chapter "How to Conduct a Biblical Simulation" if you have not already done so.

Schedule

This simulation can be done in an hour or two, but it also can be profitably extended to four or six hours. The time can be continuous or split up over several sessions (see chapter 3). For a single-hour session, you will want to allow ten minutes for introduction, thirty minutes for preparation, ten minutes for the simulation, and ten minutes for debriefing. You need not allow a great length of time for the simulation since the issues will emerge immediately. With two hours you will want to allow fifteen minutes for the introduction, forty-five minutes for preparation, fifteen minutes for the simulation, and forty-five minutes for the debriefing. If you are breaking the time into three sessions, begin with the introduction and small-group preparation. During the second session you should give the small groups a few minutes to reorient themselves to their roles, then move to the simulation and debriefing. During the third session you will want to raise the basic theological problems of the Book of Job and the way we meet people in distress or grief situations.

Grouping

You need a minimum of four people to do this simulation, in which case there will be only one orthodox theologian instead of three. However, the design permits as many as fifty participants. There are two ways you could handle the larger number. One way is to have several simulations going on simultaneously. If you have forty-eight participants, you might divide them into eight groups of six and have each group carry out its own simulation independently from all other groups. Participants in every group of six can meet separately in a small room, do their study together, play out all the roles of the simulation, and discuss what they have learned. Finally all eight groups can return to the total group setting to discuss together what happened to them during their mini-simulations. The other way to handle the large group is to have everyone involved in the same simulation. In this case you would simply divide the forty-eight people into four different groups with twelve in each group. Each group would have one representative at the table when the counseling session with Job begins, with the exception of the orthodox theologians, who would have three. You, of course, can determine what modifications are needed for groups of people numbering between six and forty-eight.

SPACE AND EQUIPMENT

Your preparation should include obtaining each of the following items (see chapter 3 for fuller explanation): a large room, small rooms, chairs, tables, Bibles, study aids, paper, pencils, and refreshments. Certain special preparations will help this simulation:

1. A sufficient number of Bibles is important, and various translations will be helpful.

2. Materials which might be used to construct the city dump on which Job might sit should be provided.
3. Special interesting touches might include makeup to give Job the semblance of a man in distress and deep physical discomfort.

Facilitation

To introduce a simulation, you ought to explain the following items: what a biblical simulation is, how to participate, purposes and tasks of this simulation, schedule, small-group tasks, materials, division into groups, and the function of the small-group chairman (when necessary).

This simulation is designed to give people a better awareness of how they speak to those in distress situations. You may find, as we have, that the orthodox theologians behave the way many church men and women do today, striving to make people hold their faith at all cost while masking any other feelings that they may have. Therefore, it will not be difficult for people to play this role.

Since in the central section of the Book of Job (the section assigned for reading), Job, himself, behaves so much differently from what we expect, the choice of the person to play this role is critical. Job's role is not as easy as the other roles in the simulation. Much of the dramatic effect will depend upon the person who plays this role. Therefore, you will want to choose an aggressive and forceful person to play Job, one who can speak with anger and distress about his plight.

You should keep in mind certain theological issues. The Book of Job does not give ultimate answers to the question of why men suffer. In fact the simulation seeks to discover the measure of God's justice, the relation between what a man does and what he receives. Although some authorities would argue that Job should be condemned because of his arrogance, one should be reminded that the premise of the book is Job's innocence and guiltlessness. In other words, it is possible within the context of Hebrew thought for man to do the will of God as Job asserts in chapter 31. A man can become angry against injustice and berate God for what has befallen him. Job has spoken the truth (Job 42:7). Keep these thoughts in mind as you proceed, although we believe that these issues will take care of themselves in the course of the simulation and the debriefing period.

Debriefing

As coordinator you should conduct the debriefing session. Here is a list of suggestions to be followed:

1. Rearrange the chairs so that everyone is aware that he has dropped his role. (If you are running several simulations on Job simultaneously, you may want to give these instructions during the introduction.)
2. In small groups discuss what you have learned—in this instance, groups of four or six.
3. Ask volunteers to share their observations with the whole group.
4. Ask the chroniclers to share their observations.
5. Try to summarize what you have been hearing.
6. If you are to close on a worshipful note, you may read Job 42:1-6 and offer a prayer that catches up the mood of the discussion. Finally, conclude with a hymn that catches up God's majesty, such as "Holy, Holy, Holy."

JOB AND HIS FRIENDS A Simulation Based upon the Book of Job

THE SITUATION

Job, Bildad, Eliphaz, Zophar, and Elihu are all gathered at Job's dump sometime in the fifth century B.C. The four men have come to comfort Job and convince him of their points of view in reference to his suffering. So that all participants will have a chance to understand the predicament of Job, one person from the total group should be chosen to read aloud Job 1 - 2.

TASKS OF ALL GROUPS
PRIOR TO THE SIMULATION

After everyone has heard the story, the coordinator should divide the group into four smaller groups:

1. Job—defender of his position as a righteous man.
2. Eliphaz, Bildad, Zophar—representatives of the orthodox theology of the time. (Have at least three members in this group.)
3. Elihu—a young upstart who sees suffering as God's discipline for maturity.
4. God—describer of the mystery of the universe.

Specific tasks which the small groups should perform follow:

1. Appoint a leader who will—
    a. chair in the preparation for the simulation,
    b. play the role of one of the principle participants during the simulation.
2. Appoint a chronicler who will—
    a. record briefly the process of the group,
    b. record the action of the simulation from the perspective of his group,
    c. report to the debriefing session.
3. Examine those texts of the Old Testament which establish the identity of the group, and in the case of Job prepare a paraphrase of Job 3.
4. Prepare your response to Job and his situation. In the case of Job prepare the defense of your innocence. You will create a more lively discussion if you fill the role with freedom and spontaneity.

RULES OF THE SIMULATION

1. Job will begin the simulation with an expression of his lament (paraphrase of Job 3).
2. Anyone at the table may speak after Job finishes his lament, with the exception of the God group, who must not speak until the concluding statement.
3. Only those who have assumed the role of one of the chief participants at the table should speak. However, during the simulation you may want to follow a tap-in-tap-out procedure where other persons in the group take the place of the one who was originally designated to play the principal role for that group.
4. The discussion should follow the lines of any heated debate. People may interrupt, shout, or do anything else appropriate for such a discussion which is in accordance with their roles.
5. At a time designated by the leader, the God group will make a final answer to all other groups, based upon its findings from Job 38 - 40.
6. The simulation ends when the God group finishes its presentation. No one is permitted to speak after the God group.

TASKS OF THE SIMULATION

1. Job is to convince everyone that he is innocent and that his position is basically correct.
2. All other groups are to convince Job of the rightness of their positions.

TASKS FOR DEBRIEFING

1. Rearrange the room to symbolize the termination of the simulation.
2. Let everyone, including the chronicler, share his observations with the whole group.
3. Let everyone express his feelings about what happened.
4. You may wish to consider the following questions: How did you feel in your role? Where did the most important exchanges take place? What did you learn about the

Book of Job that you didn't know before? What theological issues did the simulation raise for you? What does this simulation say about the way in which we approach people in distress? If you were given the opportunity to rewrite chapters 38 - 41 of Job, what would you write?

5. Let the whole group work at summarizing what was learned.

1. Job

Your identity for the simulation will be that of Job who has lost possessions and family. The possessions symbolize his stature in the community, and his children symbolize his future. Job becomes a man without a future and without dignity. Unlike the orthodox theologians of his day, he decides to protest by proclaiming his innocence and by railing against God. Your group will appoint one representative, Job, to defend Job's innocence. It is your task to determine how to present your case in such a way as to convince your friends of the rightness of your position. Since you will begin the simulation, you should rewrite Job 3 in your own words so that those who seek to counsel you will have something to react against. You will find it helpful to read the following chapters:

> Job 3
> Job 6 - 7
> Job 12 - 14

BACKGROUND DATA

In chapter 3, Job denies the day of his birth by recounting creation in reverse. He contemplates death and the hope for release from oppression (Job 3:11-19). Suicide becomes the alternative to life and the only possibility for escape. However, wherever the issue of death is raised, the seriousness of life also emerges. Death presses man to the question about the meaning and the urgency of life so that Job next considers the question about God and the possibility of meaning (Job 3:20-26). One finds in this chapter the reflections of a person in profound grief. After you rewrite the chapter in your own words, you are ready to follow the argument of Job. Job pictures God as a hostile presence who treats man with sadistic pleasure, toying with him but never delivering the final blow so that he can escape his misery (Job 6:2-14). His friends also present a hostile presence since they are like a wadi that gives the traveler hope for water; but when he depends upon it, the wadi is dry and unyielding. Instead of life the friends give him despair and death (6:15-30). Job speaks not in the gentle tones that the wise have come to expect from him, but in the forceful, angry words of a man who has been wounded by the misery of life (Job 7). It is not necessary to read all of Job's speeches to find out what he is saying.

JOB AND HIS FRIENDS A Simulation Based upon the Book of Job

THE SITUATION

Job, Bildad, Eliphaz, Zophar, and Elihu are all gathered at Job's dump sometime in the fifth century B.C. The four men have come to comfort Job and convince him of their points of view in reference to his suffering. So that all participants will have a chance to understand the predicament of Job, one person from the total group should be chosen to read aloud Job 1 - 2.

TASKS OF ALL GROUPS
PRIOR TO THE SIMULATION

After everyone has heard the story, the coordinator should divide the group into four smaller groups:

1. Job—defender of his position as a righteous man.
2. Eliphaz, Bildad, Zophar—representatives of the orthodox theology of the time. (Have at least three members in this group.)
3. Elihu—a young upstart who sees suffering as God's discipline for maturity.
4. God—describer of the mystery of the universe.

Specific tasks which the small groups should perform follow:

1. Appoint a leader who will—
   a. chair in the preparation for the simulation,
   b. play the role of one of the principle participants during the simulation.
2. Appoint a chronicler who will—
   a. record briefly the process of the group,
   b. record the action of the simulation from the perspective of his group,
   c. report to the debriefing session.
3. Examine those texts of the Old Testament which establish the identity of the group, and in the case of Job prepare a paraphrase of Job 3.
4. Prepare your response to Job and his situation. In the case of Job prepare the defense of your innocence. You will create a more lively discussion if you fill the role with freedom and spontaneity.

RULES OF THE SIMULATION

1. Job will begin the simulation with an expression of his lament (paraphrase of Job 3).
2. Anyone at the table may speak after Job finishes his lament, with the exception of the God group, who must not speak until the concluding statement.
3. Only those who have assumed the role of one of the chief participants at the table should speak. However, during the simulation you may want to follow a tap-in-tap-out procedure where other persons in the group take the place of the one who was originally designated to play the principal role for that group.
4. The discussion should follow the lines of any heated debate. People may interrupt, shout, or do anything else appropriate for such a discussion which is in accordance with their roles.
5. At a time designated by the leader, the God group will make a final answer to all other groups, based upon its findings from Job 38 - 40.
6. The simulation ends when the God group finishes its presentation. No one is permitted to speak after the God group.

TASKS OF THE SIMULATION

1. Job is to convince everyone that he is innocent and that his position is basically correct.
2. All other groups are to convince Job of the rightness of their positions.

TASKS FOR DEBRIEFING

1. Rearrange the room to symbolize the termination of the simulation.
2. Let everyone, including the chronicler, share his observations with the whole group.
3. Let everyone express his feelings about what happened.
4. You may wish to consider the following questions: How did you feel in your role? Where did the most important exchanges take place? What did you learn about the

Book of Job that you didn't know before? What theological issues did the simulation raise for you? What does this simulation say about the way in which we approach people in distress? If you were given the opportunity to rewrite chapters 38 - 41 of Job, what would you write?

5. Let the whole group work at summarizing what was learned.

1. Job

Your identity for the simulation will be that of Job who has lost possessions and family. The possessions symbolize his stature in the community, and his children symbolize his future. Job becomes a man without a future and without dignity. Unlike the orthodox theologians of his day, he decides to protest by proclaiming his innocence and by railing against God. Your group will appoint one representative, Job, to defend Job's innocence. It is your task to determine how to present your case in such a way as to convince your friends of the rightness of your position. Since you will begin the simulation, you should rewrite Job 3 in your own words so that those who seek to counsel you will have something to react against. You will find it helpful to read the following chapters:

> Job 3
> Job 6 - 7
> Job 12 - 14

BACKGROUND DATA

In chapter 3, Job denies the day of his birth by recounting creation in reverse. He contemplates death and the hope for release from oppression (Job 3:11-19). Suicide becomes the alternative to life and the only possibility for escape. However, wherever the issue of death is raised, the seriousness of life also emerges. Death presses man to the question about the meaning and the urgency of life so that Job next considers the question about God and the possibility of meaning (Job 3:20-26). One finds in this chapter the reflections of a person in profound grief. After you rewrite the chapter in your own words, you are ready to follow the argument of Job. Job pictures God as a hostile presence who treats man with sadistic pleasure, toying with him but never delivering the final blow so that he can escape his misery (Job 6:2-14). His friends also present a hostile presence since they are like a wadi that gives the traveler hope for water; but when he depends upon it, the wadi is dry and unyielding. Instead of life the friends give him despair and death (6:15-30). Job speaks not in the gentle tones that the wise have come to expect from him, but in the forceful, angry words of a man who has been wounded by the misery of life (Job 7). It is not necessary to read all of Job's speeches to find out what he is saying.

JOB AND HIS FRIENDS A Simulation Based upon the Book of Job

THE SITUATION

Job, Bildad, Eliphaz, Zophar, and Elihu are all gathered at Job's dump sometime in the fifth century B.C. The four men have come to comfort Job and convince him of their points of view in reference to his suffering. So that all participants will have a chance to understand the predicament of Job, one person from the total group should be chosen to read aloud Job 1 - 2.

TASKS OF ALL GROUPS
PRIOR TO THE SIMULATION

After everyone has heard the story, the coordinator should divide the group into four smaller groups:

1. Job—defender of his position as a righteous man.
2. Eliphaz, Bildad, Zophar—representatives of the orthodox theology of the time. (Have at least three members in this group.)
3. Elihu—a young upstart who sees suffering as God's discipline for maturity.
4. God—describer of the mystery of the universe.

Specific tasks which the small groups should perform follow:

1. Appoint a leader who will—
   a. chair in the preparation for the simulation,
   b. play the role of one of the principle participants during the simulation.
2. Appoint a chronicler who will—
   a. record briefly the process of the group,
   b. record the action of the simulation from the perspective of his group,
   c. report to the debriefing session.
3. Examine those texts of the Old Testament which establish the identity of the group, and in the case of Job prepare a paraphrase of Job 3.
4. Prepare your response to Job and his situation. In the case of Job prepare the defense of your innocence. You will create a more lively discussion if you fill the role with freedom and spontaneity.

RULES OF THE SIMULATION

1. Job will begin the simulation with an expression of his lament (paraphrase of Job 3).
2. Anyone at the table may speak after Job finishes his lament, with the exception of the God group, who must not speak until the concluding statement.
3. Only those who have assumed the role of one of the chief participants at the table should speak. However, during the simulation you may want to follow a tap-in-tap-out procedure where other persons in the group take the place of the one who was originally designated to play the principal role for that group.
4. The discussion should follow the lines of any heated debate. People may interrupt, shout, or do anything else appropriate for such a discussion which is in accordance with their roles.
5. At a time designated by the leader, the God group will make a final answer to all other groups, based upon its findings from Job 38 - 40.
6. The simulation ends when the God group finishes its presentation. No one is permitted to speak after the God group.

TASKS OF THE SIMULATION

1. Job is to convince everyone that he is innocent and that his position is basically correct.
2. All other groups are to convince Job of the rightness of their positions.

TASKS FOR DEBRIEFING

1. Rearrange the room to symbolize the termination of the simulation.
2. Let everyone, including the chronicler, share his observations with the whole group.
3. Let everyone express his feelings about what happened.
4. You may wish to consider the following questions: How did you feel in your role? Where did the most important exchanges take place? What did you learn about the

Book of Job that you didn't know before? What theological issues did the simulation raise for you? What does this simulation say about the way in which we approach people in distress? If you were given the opportunity to rewrite chapters 38 - 41 of Job, what would you write?

5. Let the whole group work at summarizing what was learned.

2. Eliphaz, Bildad, and Zophar

For the simulation you will be a group of theologians who defend the orthodoxy of the day. Eliphaz would appear to be the elder statesman who speaks with dignity and caution. Bildad is a conservative who states simply the maxims of the past. Zophar speaks with a certainty untested by experience and attempts to belittle and shame Job by slams and intimidation. Your group will want to appoint three representatives who will play the respective roles of Eliphaz, Bildad, and Zophar. In your study, you might find it advantageous to break into subgroups, although the basic arguments will be much the same. It is your task to determine how to present your case to Job in such a way as to convince him of the rightness of your own position. The following passages will help you establish your identity:

Eliphaz—Job 4 - 5
Bildad—Job 8
Zophar—Job 11

BACKGROUND DATA
The three friends are defenders of a system of thought which can be found in the wisdom of the Old Testament, such as the book of Proverbs. In some instances their expressed opinions are an oversimplification of three basic tenets of this system: (1) all men should be humble and never show emotion even during extreme adversity, (2) God has created a moral universe in which there is a one-to-one correlation between a man's deed and its reward, and (3) a man who suffers adversity must be receiving recompense for some evil which he has done. The better arguments state that there is indeed a veil between God's order and man's life so that there can never be a simple correlation between the situation of a man and his moral life. Thus we find in Proverbs the admonition that one should not mock the poor. Also in the Book of Job Eliphaz states in his first speech that if Job is innocent, he has nothing to worry about. God will finally rectify the situation of an innocent man. However, as the speeches go on, Job's guilt is assumed by all three parties so that his situation becomes evidence that he has done something wrong. The friends attempt to prove Job's guilt by arguing that all men are guilty and no man can claim innocence, or by asserting that Job has committed a heinous crime. You may wish to read all the speeches of each of the three counselors, but it is not necessary. You will find that they are repetitive and that the chapters listed above give the basic arguments.

JOB AND HIS FRIENDS A Simulation Based upon the Book of Job

THE SITUATION

Job, Bildad, Eliphaz, Zophar, and Elihu are all gathered at Job's dump sometime in the fifth century B.C. The four men have come to comfort Job and convince him of their points of view in reference to his suffering. So that all participants will have a chance to understand the predicament of Job, one person from the total group should be chosen to read aloud Job 1 - 2.

TASKS OF ALL GROUPS
PRIOR TO THE SIMULATION

After everyone has heard the story, the coordinator should divide the group into four smaller groups:

1. Job—defender of his position as a righteous man.
2. Eliphaz, Bildad, Zophar—representatives of the orthodox theology of the time. (Have at least three members in this group.)
3. Elihu—a young upstart who sees suffering as God's discipline for maturity.
4. God—describer of the mystery of the universe.

Specific tasks which the small groups should perform follow:

1. Appoint a leader who will—
   a. chair in the preparation for the simulation,
   b. play the role of one of the principle participants during the simulation.
2. Appoint a chronicler who will—
   a. record briefly the process of the group,
   b. record the action of the simulation from the perspective of his group,
   c. report to the debriefing session.
3. Examine those texts of the Old Testament which establish the identity of the group, and in the case of Job prepare a paraphrase of Job 3.
4. Prepare your response to Job and his situation. In the case of Job prepare the defense of your innocence. You will create a more lively discussion if you fill the role with freedom and spontaneity.

RULES OF THE SIMULATION

1. Job will begin the simulation with an expression of his lament (paraphrase of Job 3).
2. Anyone at the table may speak after Job finishes his lament, with the exception of the God group, who must not speak until the concluding statement.
3. Only those who have assumed the role of one of the chief participants at the table should speak. However, during the simulation you may want to follow a tap-in-tap-out procedure where other persons in the group take the place of the one who was originally designated to play the principal role for that group.
4. The discussion should follow the lines of any heated debate. People may interrupt, shout, or do anything else appropriate for such a discussion which is in accordance with their roles.
5. At a time designated by the leader, the God group will make a final answer to all other groups, based upon its findings from Job 38 - 40.
6. The simulation ends when the God group finishes its presentation. No one is permitted to speak after the God group.

TASKS OF THE SIMULATION

1. Job is to convince everyone that he is innocent and that his position is basically correct.
2. All other groups are to convince Job of the rightness of their positions.

TASKS FOR DEBRIEFING

1. Rearrange the room to symbolize the termination of the simulation.
2. Let everyone, including the chronicler, share his observations with the whole group.
3. Let everyone express his feelings about what happened.
4. You may wish to consider the following questions: How did you feel in your role? Where did the most important exchanges take place? What did you learn about the

Book of Job that you didn't know before? What theological issues did the simulation raise for you? What does this simulation say about the way in which we approach people in distress? If you were given the opportunity to rewrite chapters 38 - 41 of Job, what would you write?

5. Let the whole group work at summarizing what was learned.

2. Eliphaz, Bildad, and Zophar

For the simulation you will be a group of theologians who defend the orthodoxy of the day. Eliphaz would appear to be the elder statesman who speaks with dignity and caution. Bildad is a conservative who states simply the maxims of the past. Zophar speaks with a certainty untested by experience and attempts to belittle and shame Job by slams and intimidation. Your group will want to appoint three representatives who will play the respective roles of Eliphaz, Bildad, and Zophar. In your study, you might find it advantageous to break into subgroups, although the basic arguments will be much the same. It is your task to determine how to present your case to Job in such a way as to convince him of the rightness of your own position. The following passages will help you establish your identity:

Eliphaz—Job 4 - 5
Bildad—Job 8
Zophar—Job 11

BACKGROUND DATA

The three friends are defenders of a system of thought which can be found in the wisdom of the Old Testament, such as the book of Proverbs. In some instances their expressed opinions are an oversimplification of three basic tenets of this system: (1) all men should be humble and never show emotion even during extreme adversity, (2) God has created a moral universe in which there is a one-to-one correlation between a man's deed and its reward, and (3) a man who suffers adversity must be receiving recompense for some evil which he has done. The better arguments state that there is indeed a veil between God's order and man's life so that there can never be a simple correlation between the situation of a man and his moral life. Thus we find in Proverbs the admonition that one should not mock the poor. Also in the Book of Job Eliphaz states in his first speech that if Job is innocent, he has nothing to worry about. God will finally rectify the situation of an innocent man. However, as the speeches go on, Job's guilt is assumed by all three parties so that his situation becomes evidence that he has done something wrong. The friends attempt to prove Job's guilt by arguing that all men are guilty and no man can claim innocence, or by asserting that Job has committed a heinous crime. You may wish to read all the speeches of each of the three counselors, but it is not necessary. You will find that they are repetitive and that the chapters listed above give the basic arguments.

JOB AND HIS FRIENDS A Simulation Based upon the Book of Job

THE SITUATION

Job, Bildad, Eliphaz, Zophar, and Elihu are all gathered at Job's dump sometime in the fifth century B.C. The four men have come to comfort Job and convince him of their points of view in reference to his suffering. So that all participants will have a chance to understand the predicament of Job, one person from the total group should be chosen to read aloud Job 1 - 2.

TASKS OF ALL GROUPS
PRIOR TO THE SIMULATION

After everyone has heard the story, the coordinator should divide the group into four smaller groups:

1. Job—defender of his position as a righteous man.
2. Eliphaz, Bildad, Zophar—representatives of the orthodox theology of the time. (Have at least three members in this group.)
3. Elihu—a young upstart who sees suffering as God's discipline for maturity.
4. God—describer of the mystery of the universe.

Specific tasks which the small groups should perform follow:

1. Appoint a leader who will—
   a. chair in the preparation for the simulation,
   b. play the role of one of the principle participants during the simulation.
2. Appoint a chronicler who will—
   a. record briefly the process of the group,
   b. record the action of the simulation from the perspective of his group,
   c. report to the debriefing session.
3. Examine those texts of the Old Testament which establish the identity of the group, and in the case of Job prepare a paraphrase of Job 3.
4. Prepare your response to Job and his situation. In the case of Job prepare the defense of your innocence. You will create a more lively discussion if you fill the role with freedom and spontaneity.

RULES OF THE SIMULATION

1. Job will begin the simulation with an expression of his lament (paraphrase of Job 3).
2. Anyone at the table may speak after Job finishes his lament, with the exception of the God group, who must not speak until the concluding statement.
3. Only those who have assumed the role of one of the chief participants at the table should speak. However, during the simulation you may want to follow a tap-in-tap-out procedure where other persons in the group take the place of the one who was originally designated to play the principal role for that group.
4. The discussion should follow the lines of any heated debate. People may interrupt, shout, or do anything else appropriate for such a discussion which is in accordance with their roles.
5. At a time designated by the leader, the God group will make a final answer to all other groups, based upon its findings from Job 38 - 40.
6. The simulation ends when the God group finishes its presentation. No one is permitted to speak after the God group.

TASKS OF THE SIMULATION

1. Job is to convince everyone that he is innocent and that his position is basically correct.
2. All other groups are to convince Job of the rightness of their positions.

TASKS FOR DEBRIEFING

1. Rearrange the room to symbolize the termination of the simulation.
2. Let everyone, including the chronicler, share his observations with the whole group.
3. Let everyone express his feelings about what happened.
4. You may wish to consider the following questions: How did you feel in your role? Where did the most important exchanges take place? What did you learn about the

Book of Job that you didn't know before? What theological issues did the simulation raise for you? What does this simulation say about the way in which we approach people in distress? If you were given the opportunity to rewrite chapters 38 - 41 of Job, what would you write?

5. Let the whole group work at summarizing what was learned.

3. Elihu

Your identity for the simulation will be that of an arrogant young man who sees Job attacking the orthodox theology of the day and who therefore appoints himself as the defender of God's justice. (See the masterful caricature of Elihu in Job 32:1-6.) You want to prove that God's universe is guided by a moral purpose and that Job must admit his guilt before God. Your group will appoint one person to be Elihu and to confront Job during the counseling session. It is your group's task to determine how Elihu is to present his case to Job in such a way as to convince him of your position. The text for your identity is found in Job 32 - 37, but special attention should be given to the following passages:

Job 33:19-33
Job 37

BACKGROUND DATA

When you listen to the three friends, who appear first in the Book of Job, you will say that they sound much like Elihu's position. However, there are notable exceptions. For example, in Job 33:19-33, Elihu seems to be extending the case of the three friends by saying that suffering chastens and instructs man. In other words, "Job, accept your suffering as a lesson in life. Learn from the situation which now confronts you." Beyond this dimension of the argument, Elihu seems to anticipate the answer of God in Job 38 - 41, when he describes the glory of God's universe (Job 37). God's majesty stands outside our experience and cannot readily be comprehended by mortal flesh. Since God's purpose is distant from man, one should behold Him with awe and fear. Elihu says to Job, "Who can tell how God controls the universe?" Your reading will show that apart from these variations Elihu upholds the official theology of his day. He feels that man should be humble, recognize his guilt, and proclaim the justice of God.

JOB AND HIS FRIENDS A Simulation Based upon the Book of Job

THE SITUATION

Job, Bildad, Eliphaz, Zophar, and Elihu are all gathered at Job's dump sometime in the fifth century B.C. The four men have come to comfort Job and convince him of their points of view in reference to his suffering. So that all participants will have a chance to understand the predicament of Job, one person from the total group should be chosen to read aloud Job 1 - 2.

TASKS OF ALL GROUPS
PRIOR TO THE SIMULATION

After everyone has heard the story, the coordinator should divide the group into four smaller groups:

1. Job—defender of his position as a righteous man.
2. Eliphaz, Bildad, Zophar—representatives of the orthodox theology of the time. (Have at least three members in this group.)
3. Elihu—a young upstart who sees suffering as God's discipline for maturity.
4. God—describer of the mystery of the universe.

Specific tasks which the small groups should perform follow:

1. Appoint a leader who will—
   a. chair in the preparation for the simulation,
   b. play the role of one of the principle participants during the simulation.
2. Appoint a chronicler who will—
   a. record briefly the process of the group,
   b. record the action of the simulation from the perspective of his group,
   c. report to the debriefing session.
3. Examine those texts of the Old Testament which establish the identity of the group, and in the case of Job prepare a paraphrase of Job 3.
4. Prepare your response to Job and his situation. In the case of Job prepare the defense of your innocence. You will create a more lively discussion if you fill the role with freedom and spontaneity.

RULES OF THE SIMULATION

1. Job will begin the simulation with an expression of his lament (paraphrase of Job 3).
2. Anyone at the table may speak after Job finishes his lament, with the exception of the God group, who must not speak until the concluding statement.
3. Only those who have assumed the role of one of the chief participants at the table should speak. However, during the simulation you may want to follow a tap-in-tap-out procedure where other persons in the group take the place of the one who was originally designated to play the principal role for that group.
4. The discussion should follow the lines of any heated debate. People may interrupt, shout, or do anything else appropriate for such a discussion which is in accordance with their roles.
5. At a time designated by the leader, the God group will make a final answer to all other groups, based upon its findings from Job 38 - 40.
6. The simulation ends when the God group finishes its presentation. No one is permitted to speak after the God group.

TASKS OF THE SIMULATION

1. Job is to convince everyone that he is innocent and that his position is basically correct.
2. All other groups are to convince Job of the rightness of their positions.

TASKS FOR DEBRIEFING

1. Rearrange the room to symbolize the termination of the simulation.
2. Let everyone, including the chronicler, share his observations with the whole group.
3. Let everyone express his feelings about what happened.
4. You may wish to consider the following questions: How did you feel in your role? Where did the most important exchanges take place? What did you learn about the

Book of Job that you didn't know before? What theological issues did the simulation raise for you? What does this simulation say about the way in which we approach people in distress? If you were given the opportunity to rewrite chapters 38 - 41 of Job, what would you write?

5. Let the whole group work at summarizing what was learned.

3. Elihu

Your identity for the simulation will be that of an arrogant young man who sees Job attacking the orthodox theology of the day and who therefore appoints himself as the defender of God's justice. (See the masterful caricature of Elihu in Job 32:1-6.) You want to prove that God's universe is guided by a moral purpose and that Job must admit his guilt before God. Your group will appoint one person to be Elihu and to confront Job during the counseling session. It is your group's task to determine how Elihu is to present his case to Job in such a way as to convince him of your position. The text for your identity is found in Job 32 - 37, but special attention should be given to the following passages:

Job 33:19-33
Job 37

BACKGROUND DATA
When you listen to the three friends, who appear first in the Book of Job, you will say that they sound much like Elihu's position. However, there are notable exceptions. For example, in Job 33:19-33, Elihu seems to be extending the case of the three friends by saying that suffering chastens and instructs man. In other words, "Job, accept your suffering as a lesson in life. Learn from the situation which now confronts you." Beyond this dimension of the argument, Elihu seems to anticipate the answer of God in Job 38 - 41, when he describes the glory of God's universe (Job 37). God's majesty stands outside our experience and cannot readily be comprehended by mortal flesh. Since God's purpose is distant from man, one should behold Him with awe and fear. Elihu says to Job, "Who can tell how God controls the universe?" Your reading will show that apart from these variations Elihu upholds the official theology of his day. He feels that man should be humble, recognize his guilt, and proclaim the justice of God.

JOB AND HIS FRIENDS A Simulation Based upon the Book of Job

THE SITUATION

Job, Bildad, Eliphaz, Zophar, and Elihu are all gathered at Job's dump sometime in the fifth century B.C. The four men have come to comfort Job and convince him of their points of view in reference to his suffering. So that all participants will have a chance to understand the predicament of Job, one person from the total group should be chosen to read aloud Job 1 - 2.

TASKS OF ALL GROUPS
PRIOR TO THE SIMULATION

After everyone has heard the story, the coordinator should divide the group into four smaller groups:

1. Job—defender of his position as a righteous man.
2. Eliphaz, Bildad, Zophar—representatives of the orthodox theology of the time. (Have at least three members in this group.)
3. Elihu—a young upstart who sees suffering as God's discipline for maturity.
4. God—describer of the mystery of the universe.

Specific tasks which the small groups should perform follow:

1. Appoint a leader who will—
   a. chair in the preparation for the simulation,
   b. play the role of one of the principle participants during the simulation.
2. Appoint a chronicler who will—
   a. record briefly the process of the group,
   b. record the action of the simulation from the perspective of his group,
   c. report to the debriefing session.
3. Examine those texts of the Old Testament which establish the identity of the group, and in the case of Job prepare a paraphrase of Job 3.
4. Prepare your response to Job and his situation. In the case of Job prepare the defense of your innocence. You will create a more lively discussion if you fill the role with freedom and spontaneity.

RULES OF THE SIMULATION

1. Job will begin the simulation with an expression of his lament (paraphrase of Job 3).
2. Anyone at the table may speak after Job finishes his lament, with the exception of the God group, who must not speak until the concluding statement.
3. Only those who have assumed the role of one of the chief participants at the table should speak. However, during the simulation you may want to follow a tap-in-tap-out procedure where other persons in the group take the place of the one who was originally designated to play the principal role for that group.
4. The discussion should follow the lines of any heated debate. People may interrupt, shout, or do anything else appropriate for such a discussion which is in accordance with their roles.
5. At a time designated by the leader, the God group will make a final answer to all other groups, based upon its findings from Job 38 - 40.
6. The simulation ends when the God group finishes its presentation. No one is permitted to speak after the God group.

TASKS OF THE SIMULATION

1. Job is to convince everyone that he is innocent and that his position is basically correct.
2. All other groups are to convince Job of the rightness of their positions.

TASKS FOR DEBRIEFING

1. Rearrange the room to symbolize the termination of the simulation.
2. Let everyone, including the chronicler, share his observations with the whole group.
3. Let everyone express his feelings about what happened.
4. You may wish to consider the following questions: How did you feel in your role? Where did the most important exchanges take place? What did you learn about the

Book of Job that you didn't know before? What theological issues did the simulation raise for you? What does this simulation say about the way in which we approach people in distress? If you were given the opportunity to rewrite chapters 38 - 41 of Job, what would you write?

5. Let the whole group work at summarizing what was learned.

4. God

Your identity for the simulation will be that of God, who has the final word in the session. You will want to wait until the counselors have presented their positions in full detail before you speak. You have the authority of the universe on your side and the majesty of the cosmos. Your group will appoint one representative to present your point of view. It is your task to determine how to present your case in such a way as to convince Job of the truth of your position. You will want to study the following chapters.

Job 38 - 41

BACKGROUND DATA

If one looks for an answer to Job's suffering in the speeches of God (Job 38 - 41), he will be utterly disappointed since no such answer appears. The misery and the brokenness of Job are overlooked. Therefore the speeches have been a puzzle to all who have sought to interpret them. Some argue for a bitter irony here. Job has said from the beginning that God would overshadow him with His might. From this perspective God has a callous disregard for man and his situation. Another view holds that heretofore Job had known God only in a secondary way and God now confronts him at the primary root of his existence. For the first time in his life Job comes to know God firsthand and this frees him to repent of the arrogance of his statements, which presuppose a deeper knowledge than he actually had possessed. Robert Frost in his *A Masque of Reason* argues that God shows himself to be beyond good and evil. The speeches show that God is not bound by the normal conventions of justice that men seek to place upon God. God is free from the yoke of good and evil which demands that a man's moral life have a direct link to his destiny. This position would seem to suggest that Job has been called upon to look at his life from a totally different perspective. God calls Job in these speeches to view life from the divine situation. In other words, God tells Job that he must look at the world from a universal perspective in which the ordinary concept of justice collapses. You are now in a position to seek your own answer to the riddle of these speeches by assessing for yourself God's answer to Job.

JOB AND HIS FRIENDS A Simulation Based upon the Book of Job

THE SITUATION

Job, Bildad, Eliphaz, Zophar, and Elihu are all gathered at Job's dump sometime in the fifth century B.C. The four men have come to comfort Job and convince him of their points of view in reference to his suffering. So that all participants will have a chance to understand the predicament of Job, one person from the total group should be chosen to read aloud Job 1 - 2.

TASKS OF ALL GROUPS
PRIOR TO THE SIMULATION

After everyone has heard the story, the coordinator should divide the group into four smaller groups:

1. Job—defender of his position as a righteous man.
2. Eliphaz, Bildad, Zophar—representatives of the orthodox theology of the time. (Have at least three members in this group.)
3. Elihu—a young upstart who sees suffering as God's discipline for maturity.
4. God—describer of the mystery of the universe.

Specific tasks which the small groups should perform follow:

1. Appoint a leader who will—
   a. chair in the preparation for the simulation,
   b. play the role of one of the principle participants during the simulation.
2. Appoint a chronicler who will—
   a. record briefly the process of the group,
   b. record the action of the simulation from the perspective of his group,
   c. report to the debriefing session.
3. Examine those texts of the Old Testament which establish the identity of the group, and in the case of Job prepare a paraphrase of Job 3.
4. Prepare your response to Job and his situation. In the case of Job prepare the defense of your innocence. You will create a more lively discussion if you fill the role with freedom and spontaneity.

RULES OF THE SIMULATION

1. Job will begin the simulation with an expression of his lament (paraphrase of Job 3).
2. Anyone at the table may speak after Job finishes his lament, with the exception of the God group, who must not speak until the concluding statement.
3. Only those who have assumed the role of one of the chief participants at the table should speak. However, during the simulation you may want to follow a tap-in-tap-out procedure where other persons in the group take the place of the one who was originally designated to play the principal role for that group.
4. The discussion should follow the lines of any heated debate. People may interrupt, shout, or do anything else appropriate for such a discussion which is in accordance with their roles.
5. At a time designated by the leader, the God group will make a final answer to all other groups, based upon its findings from Job 38 - 40.
6. The simulation ends when the God group finishes its presentation. No one is permitted to speak after the God group.

TASKS OF THE SIMULATION

1. Job is to convince everyone that he is innocent and that his position is basically correct.
2. All other groups are to convince Job of the rightness of their positions.

TASKS FOR DEBRIEFING

1. Rearrange the room to symbolize the termination of the simulation.
2. Let everyone, including the chronicler, share his observations with the whole group.
3. Let everyone express his feelings about what happened.
4. You may wish to consider the following questions: How did you feel in your role? Where did the most important exchanges take place? What did you learn about the

133

Book of Job that you didn't know before? What theological issues did the simulation raise for you? What does this simulation say about the way in which we approach people in distress? If you were given the opportunity to rewrite chapters 38 - 41 of Job, what would you write?

5. Let the whole group work at summarizing what was learned.

4. God

Your identity for the simulation will be that of God, who has the final word in the session. You will want to wait until the counselors have presented their positions in full detail before you speak. You have the authority of the universe on your side and the majesty of the cosmos. Your group will appoint one representative to present your point of view. It is your task to determine how to present your case in such a way as to convince Job of the truth of your position. You will want to study the following chapters.

Job 38 - 41

BACKGROUND DATA

If one looks for an answer to Job's suffering in the speeches of God (Job 38 - 41), he will be utterly disappointed since no such answer appears. The misery and the brokenness of Job are overlooked. Therefore the speeches have been a puzzle to all who have sought to interpret them. Some argue for a bitter irony here. Job has said from the beginning that God would overshadow him with His might. From this perspective God has a callous disregard for man and his situation. Another view holds that heretofore Job had known God only in a secondary way and God now confronts him at the primary root of his existence. For the first time in his life Job comes to know God firsthand and this frees him to repent of the arrogance of his statements, which presuppose a deeper knowledge than he actually had possessed. Robert Frost in his *A Masque of Reason* argues that God shows himself to be beyond good and evil. The speeches show that God is not bound by the normal conventions of justice that men seek to place upon God. God is free from the yoke of good and evil which demands that a man's moral life have a direct link to his destiny. This position would seem to suggest that Job has been called upon to look at his life from a totally different perspective. God calls Job in these speeches to view life from the divine situation. In other words, God tells Job that he must look at the world from a universal perspective in which the ordinary concept of justice collapses. You are now in a position to seek your own answer to the riddle of these speeches by assessing for yourself God's answer to Job.

11. WHAT SHALL WE DO WITH JESUS?

A Simulation Based upon John 11

INSTRUCTIONS TO THE COORDINATOR

Preparation

Read the simulation through so that you will be familiar with the directions and purposes. The intent of this simulation is to acquaint the group with various attitudes toward Jesus as an historical person. However, it would be difficult to do the simulation without facing one's own Christology. With larger groups the coordinator should involve some of the leadership in joint planning of the simulation to prevent straying into useless sidelines.

Schedule

For the longer and shorter schedules the following timetable should be adequate:

	2 Hours	4 Hours
Introduction	5 min.	15 min.
Study of the passages	25 min.	60 min.
Strategy planning	30 min.	45 min.
Sanhedrin simulation	45 min.	90 min.
Debriefing	15 min.	30 min.

For the shorter simulation we suggest that only three or four passages be discussed. If a series of shorter periods is used, the most obvious dividing place is between the small-group experience and the plenary session. However, the participants should be warned not to play their roles during the intervening period. It can be interesting and entertaining to play the roles prior to the plenary session, but experience indicates that this will seriously impair the dynamics of the simulation.

For various ways of doing this simulation in successive shorter sessions, see chapter 3. If a very short time is allotted, then the coordinator should appoint a "high priest" so that the crucifixion problem can be faced immediately.

Grouping

This simulation was designed for a large group, and it works well because there are so many political variations possible. If the group is small, however, simply reduce the number of representatives at the table (see chapter 3). This simulation should not be adapted to a smaller group by eliminating one of the positions.

Space and Equipment

A large room with a conference table arrangement (sixteen chairs around it with each group situated directly behind its representatives) will be needed. In addition four smaller and somewhat private spaces are needed for the small groups. Each of these also should be equipped with a table and chairs.

Each participant will need a New Testament, pencil, and paper. Materials for banners and posters will also be helpful. In this simulation the Zealots often have wanted some weapons; so a few mock swords would add reality. Pictures of Jesus are also useful.

Facilitation

You will begin by introducing what a simulation is, how to participate, the focus of this simulation, the division into small groups, small-group assignments, space arrangements, and materials. After the groups have divided and begun their preparation, you will want to circulate among the groups to see that they understand the procedure.

The only person required other than those named in the directions is "Jesus." Normally the Sanhedrin will want to question him. It would be possible to assume that Jesus is not available for such a trial, but it has been facilitating to let Jesus appear. That role can be played by someone asked to stay out of the simulation or by the coordinator himself. Much of the simulation can be a discussion of the merits of such an appearance by Jesus. When he does appear, a good approach would be for him to remain silent or to reply with an occasional "You say that I am" to various questions about who Jesus is. If pressed very hard, Jesus could also give answers which are unsatisfactory to all groups concerned. For example, the statement from John 18:36, "If my kingdom were of this world, my servants would fight . . ." will throw new light and confusion on the problem of violence.

This simulation is potentially the most dramatic and most dangerous of those we have outlined. The subject of Christology arouses deep emotions so that some who are required to advocate the death of Jesus find the role almost frightening. Unfortunately "Jesus" means Law and Authority to many. The simulation allows the unusual possibility of attacking such a Father-figure. The leader should be especially prepared for a thorough debriefing and a significant discussion of feelings about Jesus.

Debriefing
As already indicated, this simulation has the possibility of very strong emotional involvement. It would be well to be prepared for expressions of emotion as the simulation progresses. The reaction to Jesus and his crucifixion can be remarkable. Some, such as the Zealots, take on a "crusader" role. They can easily become violent in their defense of Jesus, completely negating the teachings of love and concern for neighbor which otherwise characterize Jesus. At the same time those who are responsible for the death of Jesus may take on an unusual delight in their job. This might indicate, as noted above, that Jesus has replaced the "Father-God" and no longer operates as a reconciler in our culture. In the debriefing the coordinator could allow these normally forbidden feelings to be expressed and discussed. In fact, if these feelings do become manifest, another session could well be spent on the theology of "crusades" and/or the conflict between Creator-Father and Reconciler-Son.

A third motif may very well emerge, that of anti-Semitism. The importance of the form of execution lies in the placing of responsibility for the death of Jesus. Probably few problems have received more attention in the last decade than this. Many Jewish authors have written to show that Christian writers, wanting to attract Romans (see Luke 1:1-4), tried to place the blame for the crucifixion on the Jews. This in turn has fostered the intense anti-Semitism in the Western Christian world. In any normal gathering of Christians this ordinarily subterranean feeling might very well emerge during such a simulation.

Because of these unusual involvements, the debriefing has to be done with sensitivity. The following procedure might serve as a guideline:

1. Ask each group to tell about its plan and motivations. Then ask individuals within the group to describe how they feel about the role assigned them.
2. Break up the seating arrangement and then allow persons to express what they have gained, especially in regard to their attitude toward Jesus.
3. Conclude the session with some type of affirmation, such as a hymn like "O Sacred Head, Now Wounded" or a series of affirmations of faith.

WHAT SHALL WE DO WITH JESUS? A Simulation Based upon John 11

THE SITUATION

You are to simulate the members of the Sanhedrin who have been called together by the high priest because of the disturbances that Jesus of Nazareth is causing throughout the land. Many in the Sanhedrin feel that something must be done immediately. You are faced with several problems:

1. You must select a chairman for the meeting.

   Since the Sadducees were largely the aristocracy of Jerusalem, it was their party which usually furnished the high priest and/or president of the Sanhedrin. However, after the purge of this group by Herod the Great in 37 B.C., Herodians, inserted into power by Herod himself, and then also Pharisees could furnish the leader of the Jewish council. Presumably the more radical Jews, such as Essenes, Qumranites, and Zealots, would not be interested in the Sanhedrin, nor would they likely be elected to office.

2. You will inevitably express your views about who Jesus is.

   The confession of Peter in Mark 8:27-30 shows that Jesus was quite differently regarded by various groups in Palestine. Herod and his followers thought Jesus was John the Baptist come back to haunt them and criticize their political policies (Mark 6:14). The apocalypticists likely thought he was the forerunner of the kingdom and so spoke of him as Elijah. Others, such as the Pharisees and Sadducees, must have seen him as a prophet (John 4:19, 44) or a rabbi (Mark 1:27). Most dangerous, however, was the belief in Jesus as a Messiah. The intent of the high priest and the Sanhedrin was to trap him into admitting he was a messianic pretender (Son of God or King of the Jews). This was finally done (Mark 15:26) and Jesus was killed as a threat to Rome.

3. You must decide what to do with Jesus.

   The meeting of the Sanhedrin, recorded in John 11:45-53, was called by the high priests to determine what they should do with this popular leader named Jesus. We can see that the high priest and the Sadducees wished

him killed, while the Pharisees were more tolerant. The Sadducees were disturbed by his growing political power, while the more faith-oriented Pharisees recognized that he might be "of God." Jesus was finally trapped when his affirmations convinced both parties that he was a political revolutionary and also a religious blasphemer. He was killed for pretending to be the King of the Jews.

4. You must decide how to carry out your plan.

   There are two basic problems in the death of Jesus:

   a. Who was responsible—the Jews or the Romans? Pro-Roman sources say it was the Jews (Luke), while pro-Jewish sources say it was the Romans (Mark). Did the Sanhedrin issue a death warrant which the Romans carried out, or did they trick the Romans into passing sentence on Jesus? We cannot say for sure.

   b. Could the Jews have held an execution? This, too, cannot be answered. Many suppose that since it was a religious court, they could not have condemned Jesus to death and then carried it out. At least a Jewish execution would have been by stoning, while crucifixion is a Roman means of execution.

TASKS OF ALL GROUPS
PRIOR TO THE SIMULATION

1. Appoint a leader who will—
   a. chair in the preparation for the simulation,
   b. lead the group during the simulation.

   For purposes of the simulation the leaders of the groups will have the following identities:

The Sadducees	Caiaphas
The Pharisees	Nicodemus
Herodians	Antipater
Apocalypticists	Saul

2. Appoint a chronicler who will—
   a. record briefly the process of the group.
   b. record the action of the simulation from the perspective of his group,

c. report to the debriefing session.
3. Examine those texts of the New Testament which establish the identity of your particular group.
4. Articulate your identity to each other by a song or a gesture or a banner.
5. Decide how your group will act in the simulated decision.
6. Discuss what means of group persuasion are available to you, given the group identity you have.
7. Assist the chronicler in recording, especially by articulating your plans as you project them prior to the simulation.

RULES OF THE SIMULATION
1. Each group will be allowed four representatives at the official Sanhedrin conference table.
2. Other members of the group will be arranged behind the four representatives.
3. Any member of the group may replace his table representative at will.

4. Each group will be allowed two roving politicians who may—
   a. discover the character and purposes of the other groups,
   b. facilitate or disrupt the procedures,
   c. consult with the background resource person.

TASKS OF THE SIMULATION
1. The coordinator will chair the meeting until a chairman of the Sanhedrin can be elected.
2. Under the guidance of the chairman of the Sanhedrin the Jewish leaders will attempt to deal with the following critical decisions:
   a. Who is Jesus and what is his purpose?
   b. What should be done with Jesus?
   c. Who will carry out the decision about Jesus?

TASKS FOR DEBRIEFING
Follow the suggestions of the coordinator. (For a detailed explanation of the debriefing process, see chapter 4, page 29.)

1. The Sadducees

Your group identity for the simulation will be that of a major party of the Jewish people at the time of Jesus, known as Sadducees. In the simulation there will be other Jewish parties with views quite different from your own. It is your task to determine how your group would deal with Jesus and what means of persuasion would be suitable for you to use in the simulation exercise. The following are some New Testament texts which will help you with your identity:

> Mark 12:18-27
> Acts 4:1-4
> Acts 5:17-28
> Acts 23:6-8
> Matthew 16:21
> Matthew 26:3-5, 14-16, 57-68

BACKGROUND DATA
The Sadducees stem from a priestly family in Jerusalem known in the intertestamental period as the Hasmoneans. Apparently they held considerable power in Jerusalem, so that the Romans continued to appoint them as high priests. From the New Testament we can deduce

they did not believe in the resurrection as did the Pharisees, nor did they believe in angels. Other than this, reliable information is difficult to find. Many suppose the Sadducees did not accept the authority of the Prophets and the Writings, i.e., they held to the authority of the Pentateuch alone. It is also supposed they collaborated with the Greeks and the Romans and so were Hellenized. But actually the Sadducees were conservative Jews. It may be that the Sadducees really cooperated with the Romans only reluctantly and only because they traditionally had the power. On the other hand, they may have cooperated with the Romans because their religion was not brought up-to-date by new expressions (like the laws and traditions of the Pharisees). In any case, Jesus was surely identified with the opposing party (the Pharisees) as was Paul in Acts 26, and he must have appeared to the Sadducees a considerable threat to the delicately balanced peace in Palestine. Since no one had spoken for God since Moses, Jesus likely appeared a charlatan to them.

WHAT SHALL WE DO WITH JESUS? A Simulation Based upon John 11

THE SITUATION

You are to simulate the members of the Sanhedrin who have been called together by the high priest because of the disturbances that Jesus of Nazareth is causing throughout the land. Many in the Sanhedrin feel that something must be done immediately. You are faced with several problems:

1. You must select a chairman for the meeting.

   Since the Sadducees were largely the aristocracy of Jerusalem, it was their party which usually furnished the high priest and/or president of the Sanhedrin. However, after the purge of this group by Herod the Great in 37 B.C., Herodians, inserted into power by Herod himself, and then also Pharisees could furnish the leader of the Jewish council. Presumably the more radical Jews, such as Essenes, Qumranites, and Zealots, would not be interested in the Sanhedrin, nor would they likely be elected to office.

2. You will inevitably express your views about who Jesus is.

   The confession of Peter in Mark 8:27-30 shows that Jesus was quite differently regarded by various groups in Palestine. Herod and his followers thought Jesus was John the Baptist come back to haunt them and criticize their political policies (Mark 6:14). The apocalypticists likely thought he was the forerunner of the kingdom and so spoke of him as Elijah. Others, such as the Pharisees and Sadducees, must have seen him as a prophet (John 4:19, 44) or a rabbi (Mark 1:27). Most dangerous, however, was the belief in Jesus as a Messiah. The intent of the high priest and the Sanhedrin was to trap him into admitting he was a messianic pretender (Son of God or King of the Jews). This was finally done (Mark 15:26) and Jesus was killed as a threat to Rome.

3. You must decide what to do with Jesus.

   The meeting of the Sanhedrin, recorded in John 11:45-53, was called by the high priests to determine what they should do with this popular leader named Jesus. We can see that the high priest and the Sadducees wished

him killed, while the Pharisees were more tolerant. The Sadducees were disturbed by his growing political power, while the more faith-oriented Pharisees recognized that he might be "of God." Jesus was finally trapped when his affirmations convinced both parties that he was a political revolutionary and also a religious blasphemer. He was killed for pretending to be the King of the Jews.

4. You must decide how to carry out your plan.

   There are two basic problems in the death of Jesus:

   a. Who was responsible—the Jews or the Romans? Pro-Roman sources say it was the Jews (Luke), while pro-Jewish sources say it was the Romans (Mark). Did the Sanhedrin issue a death warrant which the Romans carried out, or did they trick the Romans into passing sentence on Jesus? We cannot say for sure.

   b. Could the Jews have held an execution? This, too, cannot be answered. Many suppose that since it was a religious court, they could not have condemned Jesus to death and then carried it out. At least a Jewish execution would have been by stoning, while crucifixion is a Roman means of execution.

TASKS OF ALL GROUPS
PRIOR TO THE SIMULATION

1. Appoint a leader who will—

   a. chair in the preparation for the simulation,

   b. lead the group during the simulation.

   For purposes of the simulation the leaders of the groups will have the following identities:

The Sadducees	Caiaphas
The Pharisees	Nicodemus
Herodians	Antipater
Apocalypticists	Saul

2. Appoint a chronicler who will—

   a. record briefly the process of the group.

   b. record the action of the simulation from the perspective of his group,

c. report to the debriefing session.

3. Examine those texts of the New Testament which establish the identity of your particular group.

4. Articulate your identity to each other by a song or a gesture or a banner.

5. Decide how your group will act in the simulated decision.

6. Discuss what means of group persuasion are available to you, given the group identity you have.

7. Assist the chronicler in recording, especially by articulating your plans as you project them prior to the simulation.

RULES OF THE SIMULATION

1. Each group will be allowed four representatives at the official Sanhedrin conference table.

2. Other members of the group will be arranged behind the four representatives.

3. Any member of the group may replace his table representative at will.

4. Each group will be allowed two roving politicians who may—

   a. discover the character and purposes of the other groups,

   b. facilitate or disrupt the procedures,

   c. consult with the background resource person.

TASKS OF THE SIMULATION

1. The coordinator will chair the meeting until a chairman of the Sanhedrin can be elected.

2. Under the guidance of the chairman of the Sanhedrin the Jewish leaders will attempt to deal with the following critical decisions:

   a. Who is Jesus and what is his purpose?

   b. What should be done with Jesus?

   c. Who will carry out the decision about Jesus?

TASKS FOR DEBRIEFING

Follow the suggestions of the coordinator. (For a detailed explanation of the debriefing process, see chapter 4, page 29.)

1. The Sadducees

Your group identity for the simulation will be that of a major party of the Jewish people at the time of Jesus, known as Sadducees. In the simulation there will be other Jewish parties with views quite different from your own. It is your task to determine how your group would deal with Jesus and what means of persuasion would be suitable for you to use in the simulation exercise. The following are some New Testament texts which will help you with your identity:

> Mark 12:18-27
> Acts 4:1-4
> Acts 5:17-28
> Acts 23:6-8
> Matthew 16:21
> Matthew 26:3-5, 14-16, 57-68

BACKGROUND DATA

The Sadducees stem from a priestly family in Jerusalem known in the intertestamental period as the Hasmoneans. Apparently they held considerable power in Jerusalem, so that the Romans continued to appoint them as high priests. From the New Testament we can deduce they did not believe in the resurrection as did the Pharisees, nor did they believe in angels. Other than this, reliable information is difficult to find. Many suppose the Sadducees did not accept the authority of the Prophets and the Writings, i.e., they held to the authority of the Pentateuch alone. It is also supposed they collaborated with the Greeks and the Romans and so were Hellenized. But actually the Sadducees were conservative Jews. It may be that the Sadducees really cooperated with the Romans only reluctantly and only because they traditionally had the power. On the other hand, they may have cooperated with the Romans because their religion was not brought up-to-date by new expressions (like the laws and traditions of the Pharisees). In any case, Jesus was surely identified with the opposing party (the Pharisees) as was Paul in Acts 26, and he must have appeared to the Sadducees a considerable threat to the delicately balanced peace in Palestine. Since no one had spoken for God since Moses, Jesus likely appeared a charlatan to them.

WHAT SHALL WE DO WITH JESUS? A Simulation Based upon John 11

THE SITUATION

You are to simulate the members of the Sanhedrin who have been called together by the high priest because of the disturbances that Jesus of Nazareth is causing throughout the land. Many in the Sanhedrin feel that something must be done immediately. You are faced with several problems:

1. You must select a chairman for the meeting.
   Since the Sadducees were largely the aristocracy of Jerusalem, it was their party which usually furnished the high priest and/or president of the Sanhedrin. However, after the purge of this group by Herod the Great in 37 B.C., Herodians, inserted into power by Herod himself, and then also Pharisees could furnish the leader of the Jewish council. Presumably the more radical Jews, such as Essenes, Qumranites, and Zealots, would not be interested in the Sanhedrin, nor would they likely be elected to office.
2. You will inevitably express your views about who Jesus is.
   The confession of Peter in Mark 8:27-30 shows that Jesus was quite differently regarded by various groups in Palestine. Herod and his followers thought Jesus was John the Baptist come back to haunt them and criticize their political policies (Mark 6:14). The apocalypticists likely thought he was the forerunner of the kingdom and so spoke of him as Elijah. Others, such as the Pharisees and Sadducees, must have seen him as a prophet (John 4:19, 44) or a rabbi (Mark 1:27). Most dangerous, however, was the belief in Jesus as a Messiah. The intent of the high priest and the Sanhedrin was to trap him into admitting he was a messianic pretender (Son of God or King of the Jews). This was finally done (Mark 15:26) and Jesus was killed as a threat to Rome.
3. You must decide what to do with Jesus.
   The meeting of the Sanhedrin, recorded in John 11:45-53, was called by the high priests to determine what they should do with this popular leader named Jesus. We can see that the high priest and the Sadducees wished

him killed, while the Pharisees were more tolerant. The Sadducees were disturbed by his growing political power, while the more faith-oriented Pharisees recognized that he might be "of God." Jesus was finally trapped when his affirmations convinced both parties that he was a political revolutionary and also a religious blasphemer. He was killed for pretending to be the King of the Jews.
4. You must decide how to carry out your plan.
   There are two basic problems in the death of Jesus:
   a. Who was responsible—the Jews or the Romans? Pro-Roman sources say it was the Jews (Luke), while pro-Jewish sources say it was the Romans (Mark). Did the Sanhedrin issue a death warrant which the Romans carried out, or did they trick the Romans into passing sentence on Jesus? We cannot say for sure.
   b. Could the Jews have held an execution? This, too, cannot be answered. Many suppose that since it was a religious court, they could not have condemned Jesus to death and then carried it out. At least a Jewish execution would have been by stoning, while crucifixion is a Roman means of execution.

TASKS OF ALL GROUPS
PRIOR TO THE SIMULATION

1. Appoint a leader who will—
   a. chair in the preparation for the simulation,
   b. lead the group during the simulation.
   For purposes of the simulation the leaders of the groups will have the following identities:

The Sadducees	Caiaphas
The Pharisees	Nicodemus
Herodians	Antipater
Apocalypticists	Saul

2. Appoint a chronicler who will—
   a. record briefly the process of the group.
   b. record the action of the simulation from the perspective of his group,

c. report to the debriefing session.

3. Examine those texts of the New Testament which establish the identity of your particular group.

4. Articulate your identity to each other by a song or a gesture or a banner.

5. Decide how your group will act in the simulated decision.

6. Discuss what means of group persuasion are available to you, given the group identity you have.

7. Assist the chronicler in recording, especially by articulating your plans as you project them prior to the simulation.

RULES OF THE SIMULATION

1. Each group will be allowed four representatives at the official Sanhedrin conference table.

2. Other members of the group will be arranged behind the four representatives.

3. Any member of the group may replace his table representative at will.

4. Each group will be allowed two roving politicians who may—
   a. discover the character and purposes of the other groups,
   b. facilitate or disrupt the procedures,
   c. consult with the background resource person.

TASKS OF THE SIMULATION

1. The coordinator will chair the meeting until a chairman of the Sanhedrin can be elected.

2. Under the guidance of the chairman of the Sanhedrin the Jewish leaders will attempt to deal with the following critical decisions:
   a. Who is Jesus and what is his purpose?
   b. What should be done with Jesus?
   c. Who will carry out the decision about Jesus?

TASKS FOR DEBRIEFING

Follow the suggestions of the coordinator. (For a detailed explanation of the debriefing process, see chapter 4, page 29.)

2. The Pharisees

Your group identity for the simulation will be that of a major party of the Jews at the time of Jesus, known as the Pharisees. In the simulation there will be other Jewish parties with views quite different from your own. It is your task to determine how your group would deal with Jesus and what means of persuasion would be suitable for you to use in the simulation exercise. The following are some New Testament texts which will help you with your identity:

> Matthew 9:10-17
> Matthew 12:1-14
> Matthew 15:1-9
> Matthew 22:15-22
> Matthew 23:1-36
> John 3:1-15
> John 7:45-52
> John 19:38-42
> Acts 5:33-42
> Acts 15:5
> Acts 23:6-10

BACKGROUND DATA

Like other parties of the Jews the Pharisees cannot be described historically with absolute certainty. It is supposed by many that they arose from the Maccabean revolt as Jews who wanted to be separate (the meaning of *pharas*) from Hellenized Jews. Their religion was very vital. They kept the laws of Moses up-to-date by reinterpreting them from age to age. They accepted the authority of later books of the Old Testament (Prophets and Writings) and were responsible for the great books of Judaism known as the Mishnah and the Talmud. In fact, one could correctly say the Pharisees were the source of modern-day Judaism. By and large the Pharisees did not cooperate with the Romans. But since the Pharisees were the most popular party, the Romans had to work through and with them. The Herod family particularly tried to utilize the power of the Pharisees. The beliefs of the Pharisees were very much like those of the later Christians. Jesus was undoubtedly of Pharisaic persuasion, and Paul claims it openly more than once. The intense quarrel between Jesus and the Pharisees was, in a sense, a lovers' quarrel. Jesus must have seen in the Pharisees those who should have responded to him, and the Pharisees must have seen in Jesus the embodiment of most of their faith and hopes. Consequently, it was the Pharisees who most consistently tried to save Jesus.

WHAT SHALL WE DO WITH JESUS? A Simulation Based upon John 11

THE SITUATION

You are to simulate the members of the Sanhedrin who have been called together by the high priest because of the disturbances that Jesus of Nazareth is causing throughout the land. Many in the Sanhedrin feel that something must be done immediately. You are faced with several problems:

1. You must select a chairman for the meeting.

   Since the Sadducees were largely the aristocracy of Jerusalem, it was their party which usually furnished the high priest and/ or president of the Sanhedrin. However, after the purge of this group by Herod the Great in 37 B.C., Herodians, inserted into power by Herod himself, and then also Pharisees could furnish the leader of the Jewish council. Presumably the more radical Jews, such as Essenes, Qumranites, and Zealots, would not be interested in the Sanhedrin, nor would they likely be elected to office.

2. You will inevitably express your views about who Jesus is.

   The confession of Peter in Mark 8:27-30 shows that Jesus was quite differently regarded by various groups in Palestine. Herod and his followers thought Jesus was John the Baptist come back to haunt them and criticize their political policies (Mark 6:14). The apocalypticists likely thought he was the forerunner of the kingdom and so spoke of him as Elijah. Others, such as the Pharisees and Sadducees, must have seen him as a prophet (John 4:19, 44) or a rabbi (Mark 1:27). Most dangerous, however, was the belief in Jesus as a Messiah. The intent of the high priest and the Sanhedrin was to trap him into admitting he was a messianic pretender (Son of God or King of the Jews). This was finally done (Mark 15:26) and Jesus was killed as a threat to Rome.

3. You must decide what to do with Jesus.

   The meeting of the Sanhedrin, recorded in John 11:45-53, was called by the high priests to determine what they should do with this popular leader named Jesus. We can see that the high priest and the Sadducees wished him killed, while the Pharisees were more tolerant. The Sadducees were disturbed by his growing political power, while the more faith-oriented Pharisees recognized that he might be "of God." Jesus was finally trapped when his affirmations convinced both parties that he was a political revolutionary and also a religious blasphemer. He was killed for pretending to be the King of the Jews.

4. You must decide how to carry out your plan.

   There are two basic problems in the death of Jesus:

   a. Who was responsible—the Jews or the Romans? Pro-Roman sources say it was the Jews (Luke), while pro-Jewish sources say it was the Romans (Mark). Did the Sanhedrin issue a death warrant which the Romans carried out, or did they trick the Romans into passing sentence on Jesus? We cannot say for sure.

   b. Could the Jews have held an execution? This, too, cannot be answered. Many suppose that since it was a religious court, they could not have condemned Jesus to death and then carried it out. At least a Jewish execution would have been by stoning, while crucifixion is a Roman means of execution.

TASKS OF ALL GROUPS
PRIOR TO THE SIMULATION

1. Appoint a leader who will—

   a. chair in the preparation for the simulation,

   b. lead the group during the simulation.

   For purposes of the simulation the leaders of the groups will have the following identities:

The Sadducees	Caiaphas
The Pharisees	Nicodemus
Herodians	Antipater
Apocalypticists	Saul

2. Appoint a chronicler who will—

   a. record briefly the process of the group.

   b. record the action of the simulation from the perspective of his group,

143

c. report to the debriefing session.

3. Examine those texts of the New Testament which establish the identity of your particular group.

4. Articulate your identity to each other by a song or a gesture or a banner.

5. Decide how your group will act in the simulated decision.

6. Discuss what means of group persuasion are available to you, given the group identity you have.

7. Assist the chronicler in recording, especially by articulating your plans as you project them prior to the simulation.

RULES OF THE SIMULATION

1. Each group will be allowed four representatives at the official Sanhedrin conference table.

2. Other members of the group will be arranged behind the four representatives.

3. Any member of the group may replace his table representative at will.

4. Each group will be allowed two roving politicians who may—
   a. discover the character and purposes of the other groups,
   b. facilitate or disrupt the procedures,
   c. consult with the background resource person.

TASKS OF THE SIMULATION

1. The coordinator will chair the meeting until a chairman of the Sanhedrin can be elected.

2. Under the guidance of the chairman of the Sanhedrin the Jewish leaders will attempt to deal with the following critical decisions:
   a. Who is Jesus and what is his purpose?
   b. What should be done with Jesus?
   c. Who will carry out the decision about Jesus?

TASKS FOR DEBRIEFING

Follow the suggestions of the coordinator. (For a detailed explanation of the debriefing process, see chapter 4, page 29.)

2. The Pharisees

Your group identity for the simulation will be that of a major party of the Jews at the time of Jesus, known as the Pharisees. In the simulation there will be other Jewish parties with views quite different from your own. It is your task to determine how your group would deal with Jesus and what means of persuasion would be suitable for you to use in the simulation exercise. The following are some New Testament texts which will help you with your identity:

> Matthew 9:10-17
> Matthew 12:1-14
> Matthew 15:1-9
> Matthew 22:15-22
> Matthew 23:1-36
> John 3:1-15
> John 7:45-52
> John 19:38-42
> Acts 5:33-42
> Acts 15:5
> Acts 23:6-10

BACKGROUND DATA

Like other parties of the Jews the Pharisees cannot be described historically with absolute certainty. It is supposed by many that they arose from the Maccabean revolt as Jews who wanted to be separate (the meaning of *pharas*) from Hellenized Jews. Their religion was very vital. They kept the laws of Moses up-to-date by reinterpreting them from age to age. They accepted the authority of later books of the Old Testament (Prophets and Writings) and were responsible for the great books of Judaism known as the Mishnah and the Talmud. In fact, one could correctly say the Pharisees were the source of modern-day Judaism. By and large the Pharisees did not cooperate with the Romans. But since the Pharisees were the most popular party, the Romans had to work through and with them. The Herod family particularly tried to utilize the power of the Pharisees. The beliefs of the Pharisees were very much like those of the later Christians. Jesus was undoubtedly of Pharisaic persuasion, and Paul claims it openly more than once. The intense quarrel between Jesus and the Pharisees was, in a sense, a lovers' quarrel. Jesus must have seen in the Pharisees those who should have responded to him, and the Pharisees must have seen in Jesus the embodiment of most of their faith and hopes. Consequently, it was the Pharisees who most consistently tried to save Jesus.

WHAT SHALL WE DO WITH JESUS? A Simulation Based upon John 11

THE SITUATION

You are to simulate the members of the Sanhedrin who have been called together by the high priest because of the disturbances that Jesus of Nazareth is causing throughout the land. Many in the Sanhedrin feel that something must be done immediately. You are faced with several problems:

1. You must select a chairman for the meeting.

   Since the Sadducees were largely the aristocracy of Jerusalem, it was their party which usually furnished the high priest and/or president of the Sanhedrin. However, after the purge of this group by Herod the Great in 37 B.C., Herodians, inserted into power by Herod himself, and then also Pharisees could furnish the leader of the Jewish council. Presumably the more radical Jews, such as Essenes, Qumranites, and Zealots, would not be interested in the Sanhedrin, nor would they likely be elected to office.

2. You will inevitably express your views about who Jesus is.

   The confession of Peter in Mark 8:27-30 shows that Jesus was quite differently regarded by various groups in Palestine. Herod and his followers thought Jesus was John the Baptist come back to haunt them and criticize their political policies (Mark 6:14). The apocalypticists likely thought he was the forerunner of the kingdom and so spoke of him as Elijah. Others, such as the Pharisees and Sadducees, must have seen him as a prophet (John 4:19, 44) or a rabbi (Mark 1:27). Most dangerous, however, was the belief in Jesus as a Messiah. The intent of the high priest and the Sanhedrin was to trap him into admitting he was a messianic pretender (Son of God or King of the Jews). This was finally done (Mark 15:26) and Jesus was killed as a threat to Rome.

3. You must decide what to do with Jesus.

   The meeting of the Sanhedrin, recorded in John 11:45-53, was called by the high priests to determine what they should do with this popular leader named Jesus. We can see that the high priest and the Sadducees wished him killed, while the Pharisees were more tolerant. The Sadducees were disturbed by his growing political power, while the more faith-oriented Pharisees recognized that he might be "of God." Jesus was finally trapped when his affirmations convinced both parties that he was a political revolutionary and also a religious blasphemer. He was killed for pretending to be the King of the Jews.

4. You must decide how to carry out your plan.

   There are two basic problems in the death of Jesus:

   a. Who was responsible—the Jews or the Romans? Pro-Roman sources say it was the Jews (Luke), while pro-Jewish sources say it was the Romans (Mark). Did the Sanhedrin issue a death warrant which the Romans carried out, or did they trick the Romans into passing sentence on Jesus? We cannot say for sure.

   b. Could the Jews have held an execution? This, too, cannot be answered. Many suppose that since it was a religious court, they could not have condemned Jesus to death and then carried it out. At least a Jewish execution would have been by stoning, while crucifixion is a Roman means of execution.

TASKS OF ALL GROUPS
PRIOR TO THE SIMULATION

1. Appoint a leader who will—
   a. chair in the preparation for the simulation,
   b. lead the group during the simulation.

   For purposes of the simulation the leaders of the groups will have the following identities:

The Sadducees	Caiaphas
The Pharisees	Nicodemus
Herodians	Antipater
Apocalypticists	Saul

2. Appoint a chronicler who will—
   a. record briefly the process of the group.
   b. record the action of the simulation from the perspective of his group,

145

c. report to the debriefing session.

3. Examine those texts of the New Testament which establish the identity of your particular group.

4. Articulate your identity to each other by a song or a gesture or a banner.

5. Decide how your group will act in the simulated decision.

6. Discuss what means of group persuasion are available to you, given the group identity you have.

7. Assist the chronicler in recording, especially by articulating your plans as you project them prior to the simulation.

RULES OF THE SIMULATION

1. Each group will be allowed four representatives at the official Sanhedrin conference table.

2. Other members of the group will be arranged behind the four representatives.

3. Any member of the group may replace his table representative at will.

4. Each group will be allowed two roving politicians who may—
   a. discover the character and purposes of the other groups,
   b. facilitate or disrupt the procedures,
   c. consult with the background resource person.

TASKS OF THE SIMULATION

1. The coordinator will chair the meeting until a chairman of the Sanhedrin can be elected.

2. Under the guidance of the chairman of the Sanhedrin the Jewish leaders will attempt to deal with the following critical decisions:
   a. Who is Jesus and what is his purpose?
   b. What should be done with Jesus?
   c. Who will carry out the decision about Jesus?

TASKS FOR DEBRIEFING

Follow the suggestions of the coordinator. (For a detailed explanation of the debriefing process, see chapter 4, page 29.)

3. The Herodians

Your group identity for the simulation will be that of a party of the Jews at the time of Jesus, known as the Herodians. In the simulation there will be other Jewish parties with views quite different from your own. It is your task to determine how your group would deal with Jesus and what means of persuasion would be suitable for you to use in the simulation exercise. The following are some New Testament texts which will help you with your identity:

> Matthew 2:1-23
> Matthew 22:15-22
> Mark 3:1-6
> Mark 6:14-29
> Acts 12:1-24

BACKGROUND DATA

The Herodian party mentioned so seldom in the New Testament must have been a group of Jews who backed the Herod family. Possibly they were even members of the Herod family who were placed in the Sanhedrin by Herod the Great in the first years of his reign (37 - 4 B.C.). The Herod family was an Idumean family (Semitic, but not totally Jewish) which continually tried to gain political control of the Jews. The work of Antipater finally resulted in the famous reign of Herod the Great during whose rule Jesus was born. After Herod died, the kingdom was divided four ways (a tetrarchy) among the family. Eventually this system failed and Judea itself was placed under direct Roman rule (the procurators). However, Herod Antipas, tetrarch of Galilee and Perea, managed to remain in power. It was he who killed John the Baptist and who later interviewed Jesus. Somewhat later a grandson of Herod the Great, Agrippa, was king of the Jews for a brief time (A.D. 41 - 44), but the situation was too violent for him to remain. While direct evidence is lacking, we can assume that the Herodians cooperated gladly with Rome and would have acted with either the Pharisees and/or the Sadducees to destroy Jesus if he threatened the peace with Rome. Since they were pro-Roman, it seems likely they would have tried to keep the matter of Jesus and his death within the Jewish ranks; i.e., they would not want the Romans to be held responsible for the death of a popular leader.

WHAT SHALL WE DO WITH JESUS? A Simulation Based upon John 11

THE SITUATION

You are to simulate the members of the Sanhedrin who have been called together by the high priest because of the disturbances that Jesus of Nazareth is causing throughout the land. Many in the Sanhedrin feel that something must be done immediately. You are faced with several problems:

1. You must select a chairman for the meeting.

   Since the Sadducees were largely the aristocracy of Jerusalem, it was their party which usually furnished the high priest and/ or president of the Sanhedrin. However, after the purge of this group by Herod the Great in 37 B.C., Herodians, inserted into power by Herod himself, and then also Pharisees could furnish the leader of the Jewish council. Presumably the more radical Jews, such as Essenes, Qumranites, and Zealots, would not be interested in the Sanhedrin, nor would they likely be elected to office.

2. You will inevitably express your views about who Jesus is.

   The confession of Peter in Mark 8:27-30 shows that Jesus was quite differently regarded by various groups in Palestine. Herod and his followers thought Jesus was John the Baptist come back to haunt them and criticize their political policies (Mark 6:14). The apocalypticists likely thought he was the forerunner of the kingdom and so spoke of him as Elijah. Others, such as the Pharisees and Sadducees, must have seen him as a prophet (John 4:19, 44) or a rabbi (Mark 1:27). Most dangerous, however, was the belief in Jesus as a Messiah. The intent of the high priest and the Sanhedrin was to trap him into admitting he was a messianic pretender (Son of God or King of the Jews). This was finally done (Mark 15:26) and Jesus was killed as a threat to Rome.

3. You must decide what to do with Jesus.

   The meeting of the Sanhedrin, recorded in John 11:45-53, was called by the high priests to determine what they should do with this popular leader named Jesus. We can see that the high priest and the Sadducees wished him killed, while the Pharisees were more tolerant. The Sadducees were disturbed by his growing political power, while the more faith-oriented Pharisees recognized that he might be "of God." Jesus was finally trapped when his affirmations convinced both parties that he was a political revolutionary and also a religious blasphemer. He was killed for pretending to be the King of the Jews.

4. You must decide how to carry out your plan.

   There are two basic problems in the death of Jesus:

   a. Who was responsible—the Jews or the Romans? Pro-Roman sources say it was the Jews (Luke), while pro-Jewish sources say it was the Romans (Mark). Did the Sanhedrin issue a death warrant which the Romans carried out, or did they trick the Romans into passing sentence on Jesus? We cannot say for sure.

   b. Could the Jews have held an execution? This, too, cannot be answered. Many suppose that since it was a religious court, they could not have condemned Jesus to death and then carried it out. At least a Jewish execution would have been by stoning, while crucifixion is a Roman means of execution.

TASKS OF ALL GROUPS
PRIOR TO THE SIMULATION

1. Appoint a leader who will—

   a. chair in the preparation for the simulation,

   b. lead the group during the simulation.

   For purposes of the simulation the leaders of the groups will have the following identities:

The Sadducees	Caiaphas
The Pharisees	Nicodemus
Herodians	Antipater
Apocalypticists	Saul

2. Appoint a chronicler who will—

   a. record briefly the process of the group.

   b. record the action of the simulation from the perspective of his group,

147

c. report to the debriefing session.

3. Examine those texts of the New Testament which establish the identity of your particular group.
4. Articulate your identity to each other by a song or a gesture or a banner.
5. Decide how your group will act in the simulated decision.
6. Discuss what means of group persuasion are available to you, given the group identity you have.
7. Assist the chronicler in recording, especially by articulating your plans as you project them prior to the simulation.

RULES OF THE SIMULATION
1. Each group will be allowed four representatives at the official Sanhedrin conference table.
2. Other members of the group will be arranged behind the four representatives.
3. Any member of the group may replace his table representative at will.

4. Each group will be allowed two roving politicians who may—
   a. discover the character and purposes of the other groups,
   b. facilitate or disrupt the procedures,
   c. consult with the background resource person.

TASKS OF THE SIMULATION
1. The coordinator will chair the meeting until a chairman of the Sanhedrin can be elected.
2. Under the guidance of the chairman of the Sanhedrin the Jewish leaders will attempt to deal with the following critical decisions:
   a. Who is Jesus and what is his purpose?
   b. What should be done with Jesus?
   c. Who will carry out the decision about Jesus?

TASKS FOR DEBRIEFING
Follow the suggestions of the coordinator. (For a detailed explanation of the debriefing process, see chapter 4, page 29.)

3. The Herodians

Your group identity for the simulation will be that of a party of the Jews at the time of Jesus, known as the Herodians. In the simulation there will be other Jewish parties with views quite different from your own. It is your task to determine how your group would deal with Jesus and what means of persuasion would be suitable for you to use in the simulation exercise. The following are some New Testament texts which will help you with your identity:

> Matthew 2:1-23
> Matthew 22:15-22
> Mark 3:1-6
> Mark 6:14-29
> Acts 12:1-24

BACKGROUND DATA
The Herodian party mentioned so seldom in the New Testament must have been a group of Jews who backed the Herod family. Possibly they were even members of the Herod family who were placed in the Sanhedrin by Herod the Great in the first years of his reign (37 - 4 B.C.). The Herod family was an Idumean family

(Semitic, but not totally Jewish) which continually tried to gain political control of the Jews. The work of Antipater finally resulted in the famous reign of Herod the Great during whose rule Jesus was born. After Herod died, the kingdom was divided four ways (a tetrarchy) among the family. Eventually this system failed and Judea itself was placed under direct Roman rule (the procurators). However, Herod Antipas, tetrarch of Galilee and Perea, managed to remain in power. It was he who killed John the Baptist and who later interviewed Jesus. Somewhat later a grandson of Herod the Great, Agrippa, was king of the Jews for a brief time (A.D. 41 - 44), but the situation was too violent for him to remain. While direct evidence is lacking, we can assume that the Herodians cooperated gladly with Rome and would have acted with either the Pharisees and/or the Sadducees to destroy Jesus if he threatened the peace with Rome. Since they were pro-Roman, it seems likely they would have tried to keep the matter of Jesus and his death within the Jewish ranks; i.e., they would not want the Romans to be held responsible for the death of a popular leader.

WHAT SHALL WE DO WITH JESUS? A Simulation Based upon John 11

THE SITUATION

You are to simulate the members of the Sanhedrin who have been called together by the high priest because of the disturbances that Jesus of Nazareth is causing throughout the land. Many in the Sanhedrin feel that something must be done immediately. You are faced with several problems:

1. You must select a chairman for the meeting.

   Since the Sadducees were largely the aristocracy of Jerusalem, it was their party which usually furnished the high priest and/or president of the Sanhedrin. However, after the purge of this group by Herod the Great in 37 B.C., Herodians, inserted into power by Herod himself, and then also Pharisees could furnish the leader of the Jewish council. Presumably the more radical Jews, such as Essenes, Qumranites, and Zealots, would not be interested in the Sanhedrin, nor would they likely be elected to office.

2. You will inevitably express your views about who Jesus is.

   The confession of Peter in Mark 8:27-30 shows that Jesus was quite differently regarded by various groups in Palestine. Herod and his followers thought Jesus was John the Baptist come back to haunt them and criticize their political policies (Mark 6:14). The apocalypticists likely thought he was the forerunner of the kingdom and so spoke of him as Elijah. Others, such as the Pharisees and Sadducees, must have seen him as a prophet (John 4:19, 44) or a rabbi (Mark 1:27). Most dangerous, however, was the belief in Jesus as a Messiah. The intent of the high priest and the Sanhedrin was to trap him into admitting he was a messianic pretender (Son of God or King of the Jews). This was finally done (Mark 15:26) and Jesus was killed as a threat to Rome.

3. You must decide what to do with Jesus.

   The meeting of the Sanhedrin, recorded in John 11:45-53, was called by the high priests to determine what they should do with this popular leader named Jesus. We can see that the high priest and the Sadducees wished him killed, while the Pharisees were more tolerant. The Sadducees were disturbed by his growing political power, while the more faith-oriented Pharisees recognized that he might be "of God." Jesus was finally trapped when his affirmations convinced both parties that he was a political revolutionary and also a religious blasphemer. He was killed for pretending to be the King of the Jews.

4. You must decide how to carry out your plan.

   There are two basic problems in the death of Jesus:

   a. Who was responsible—the Jews or the Romans? Pro-Roman sources say it was the Jews (Luke), while pro-Jewish sources say it was the Romans (Mark). Did the Sanhedrin issue a death warrant which the Romans carried out, or did they trick the Romans into passing sentence on Jesus? We cannot say for sure.

   b. Could the Jews have held an execution? This, too, cannot be answered. Many suppose that since it was a religious court, they could not have condemned Jesus to death and then carried it out. At least a Jewish execution would have been by stoning, while crucifixion is a Roman means of execution.

TASKS OF ALL GROUPS
PRIOR TO THE SIMULATION

1. Appoint a leader who will—

   a. chair in the preparation for the simulation,

   b. lead the group during the simulation.

   For purposes of the simulation the leaders of the groups will have the following identities:

The Sadducees	Caiaphas
The Pharisees	Nicodemus
Herodians	Antipater
Apocalypticists	Saul

2. Appoint a chronicler who will—

   a. record briefly the process of the group.

   b. record the action of the simulation from the perspective of his group,

c. report to the debriefing session.

3. Examine those texts of the New Testament which establish the identity of your particular group.

4. Articulate your identity to each other by a song or a gesture or a banner.

5. Decide how your group will act in the simulated decision.

6. Discuss what means of group persuasion are available to you, given the group identity you have.

7. Assist the chronicler in recording, especially by articulating your plans as you project them prior to the simulation.

RULES OF THE SIMULATION

1. Each group will be allowed four representatives at the official Sanhedrin conference table.

2. Other members of the group will be arranged behind the four representatives.

3. Any member of the group may replace his table representative at will.

4. Each group will be allowed two roving politicians who may—
   a. discover the character and purposes of the other groups,
   b. facilitate or disrupt the procedures,
   c. consult with the background resource person.

TASKS OF THE SIMULATION

1. The coordinator will chair the meeting until a chairman of the Sanhedrin can be elected.

2. Under the guidance of the chairman of the Sanhedrin the Jewish leaders will attempt to deal with the following critical decisions:
   a. Who is Jesus and what is his purpose?
   b. What should be done with Jesus?
   c. Who will carry out the decision about Jesus?

TASKS FOR DEBRIEFING

Follow the suggestions of the coordinator. (For a detailed explanation of the debriefing process, see chapter 4, page 29.)

4. The Apocalypticists

Your group identity for the simulation will be that of the party of the Jews at the time of Jesus which we are calling apocalypticists. In the simulation there will be other Jewish parties with views quite different from your own. It is your task to determine how your group would deal with Jesus and what means of persuasion would be suitable for you to use in the simulation exercise. The following are some New Testament texts which will help you with your identity:

Matthew 3:1-6
Matthew 4:1-25
Matthew 5:1-48
Matthew 9:1-17
Matthew 11:2-6
Matthew 24:1-51
Matthew 25:31-46
Matthew 26:47-56

BACKGROUND DATA

The apocalypticists are never mentioned as such in the New Testament, and in fact the term is a modern rubric for what was then a number of Baptist-like radicals within Palestinian Judaism. Thanks to recent discoveries we can now see that there were many such groups which fervently expected the kingdom to come and a radical change to occur. Most of these groups grew up out of despair that postexilic Judaism would ever consummate the ancient promises of God to Israel. The apocalypticists said that the present history would come to an end and then a new age would start with God as the sole ruler. Some apocalypticists were led by this faith to work actively for the overthrow and destruction of this age so that God's legions would come down and take over. These radical militaristic apocalypticists were called Zealots. It is now clear to us that many of Jesus' followers were Zealots. Peter carried a sword and used it. Judas likely "betrayed" Jesus in order to force that very military encounter and committed suicide when he discovered he had been mistaken. The other kind of apocalypticists did not try to destroy this age, but confidently expected the new age to come as the old died. Jesus surely belonged to this group, and Christianity is, in a sense, the continuation of such Jewish apocalypticism with its faith that in Jesus, the Messiah, the kingdom has come. The apocalypticists were very sympathetic to Jesus, but it is likely they favored an encounter between him and the ruling authorities.

WHAT SHALL WE DO WITH JESUS? A Simulation Based upon John 11

THE SITUATION

You are to simulate the members of the Sanhedrin who have been called together by the high priest because of the disturbances that Jesus of Nazareth is causing throughout the land. Many in the Sanhedrin feel that something must be done immediately. You are faced with several problems:

1. You must select a chairman for the meeting.

   Since the Sadducees were largely the aristocracy of Jerusalem, it was their party which usually furnished the high priest and/or president of the Sanhedrin. However, after the purge of this group by Herod the Great in 37 B.C., Herodians, inserted into power by Herod himself, and then also Pharisees could furnish the leader of the Jewish council. Presumably the more radical Jews, such as Essenes, Qumranites, and Zealots, would not be interested in the Sanhedrin, nor would they likely be elected to office.

2. You will inevitably express your views about who Jesus is.

   The confession of Peter in Mark 8:27-30 shows that Jesus was quite differently regarded by various groups in Palestine. Herod and his followers thought Jesus was John the Baptist come back to haunt them and criticize their political policies (Mark 6:14). The apocalypticists likely thought he was the forerunner of the kingdom and so spoke of him as Elijah. Others, such as the Pharisees and Sadducees, must have seen him as a prophet (John 4:19, 44) or a rabbi (Mark 1:27). Most dangerous, however, was the belief in Jesus as a Messiah. The intent of the high priest and the Sanhedrin was to trap him into admitting he was a messianic pretender (Son of God or King of the Jews). This was finally done (Mark 15:26) and Jesus was killed as a threat to Rome.

3. You must decide what to do with Jesus.

   The meeting of the Sanhedrin, recorded in John 11:45-53, was called by the high priests to determine what they should do with this popular leader named Jesus. We can see that the high priest and the Sadducees wished him killed, while the Pharisees were more tolerant. The Sadducees were disturbed by his growing political power, while the more faith-oriented Pharisees recognized that he might be "of God." Jesus was finally trapped when his affirmations convinced both parties that he was a political revolutionary and also a religious blasphemer. He was killed for pretending to be the King of the Jews.

4. You must decide how to carry out your plan.

   There are two basic problems in the death of Jesus:

   a. Who was responsible—the Jews or the Romans? Pro-Roman sources say it was the Jews (Luke), while pro-Jewish sources say it was the Romans (Mark). Did the Sanhedrin issue a death warrant which the Romans carried out, or did they trick the Romans into passing sentence on Jesus? We cannot say for sure.

   b. Could the Jews have held an execution? This, too, cannot be answered. Many suppose that since it was a religious court, they could not have condemned Jesus to death and then carried it out. At least a Jewish execution would have been by stoning, while crucifixion is a Roman means of execution.

TASKS OF ALL GROUPS
PRIOR TO THE SIMULATION

1. Appoint a leader who will—

   a. chair in the preparation for the simulation,

   b. lead the group during the simulation.

   For purposes of the simulation the leaders of the groups will have the following identities:

The Sadducees	Caiaphas
The Pharisees	Nicodemus
Herodians	Antipater
Apocalypticists	Saul

2. Appoint a chronicler who will—

   a. record briefly the process of the group.

   b. record the action of the simulation from the perspective of his group,

c. report to the debriefing session.
3. Examine those texts of the New Testament which establish the identity of your particular group.
4. Articulate your identity to each other by a song or a gesture or a banner.
5. Decide how your group will act in the simulated decision.
6. Discuss what means of group persuasion are available to you, given the group identity you have.
7. Assist the chronicler in recording, especially by articulating your plans as you project them prior to the simulation.

RULES OF THE SIMULATION
1. Each group will be allowed four representatives at the official Sanhedrin conference table.
2. Other members of the group will be arranged behind the four representatives.
3. Any member of the group may replace his table representative at will.

4. Each group will be allowed two roving politicians who may—
   a. discover the character and purposes of the other groups,
   b. facilitate or disrupt the procedures,
   c. consult with the background resource person.

TASKS OF THE SIMULATION
1. The coordinator will chair the meeting until a chairman of the Sanhedrin can be elected.
2. Under the guidance of the chairman of the Sanhedrin the Jewish leaders will attempt to deal with the following critical decisions:
   a. Who is Jesus and what is his purpose?
   b. What should be done with Jesus?
   c. Who will carry out the decision about Jesus?

TASKS FOR DEBRIEFING
Follow the suggestions of the coordinator. (For a detailed explanation of the debriefing process, see chapter 4, page 29.)

4. The Apocalypticists

Your group identity for the simulation will be that of the party of the Jews at the time of Jesus which we are calling apocalypticists. In the simulation there will be other Jewish parties with views quite different from your own. It is your task to determine how your group would deal with Jesus and what means of persuasion would be suitable for you to use in the simulation exercise. The following are some New Testament texts which will help you with your identity:

> Matthew 3:1-6
> Matthew 4:1-25
> Matthew 5:1-48
> Matthew 9:1-17
> Matthew 11:2-6
> Matthew 24:1-51
> Matthew 25:31-46
> Matthew 26:47-56

BACKGROUND DATA
The apocalypticists are never mentioned as such in the New Testament, and in fact the term is a modern rubric for what was then a number of Baptist-like radicals within Palestinian Judaism. Thanks to recent discoveries we can now see that there were many such groups which fervently expected the kingdom to come

and a radical change to occur. Most of these groups grew up out of despair that postexilic Judaism would ever consummate the ancient promises of God to Israel. The apocalypticists said that the present history would come to an end and then a new age would start with God as the sole ruler. Some apocalypticists were led by this faith to work actively for the overthrow and destruction of this age so that God's legions would come down and take over. These radical militaristic apocalypticists were called Zealots. It is now clear to us that many of Jesus' followers were Zealots. Peter carried a sword and used it. Judas likely "betrayed" Jesus in order to force that very military encounter and committed suicide when he discovered he had been mistaken. The other kind of apocalypticists did not try to destroy this age, but confidently expected the new age to come as the old died. Jesus surely belonged to this group, and Christianity is, in a sense, the continuation of such Jewish apocalypticism with its faith that in Jesus, the Messiah, the kingdom has come. The apocalypticists were very sympathetic to Jesus, but it is likely they favored an encounter between him and the ruling authorities.

12.   THE COUNCIL OF JERUSALEM

A Simulation Based upon Acts 15

INSTRUCTIONS TO THE COORDINATOR

Preparation

Involve some "leaders" in a discussion of goals prior to the simulation itself. It is crucial that some participants share the vision of an experiential learning situation which affords the opportunity to deal (while in a role) with some crucial issues like evangelism, basic morality, and violence. Since the longer version of the simulation requires about six hours, a meal with selected leaders prior to the event might prove useful.

Schedule

This simulation was originally devised for about six hours, although it can be done in a much briefer time. For a time breakdown see the coordinator's instructions in chapter 3 on page 19 or another "council"-type simulation, e.g., "The Taking of the Land." If the simulation must be shortened or done in sessions on separate days, see chapter 3 for alternate schedules. In case of a very short simulation the coordinator would do well to appoint the "bishop," so that more important issues can be decided.

Space and Equipment

The initial meeting should take place in a large room with conventional seating. The small groups will function best if each can have a small room. While the groups are working on their identity, the large room should be prepared for a "council" situation. A large table with nine chairs around it presents an ideal council table. The remaining places for each group should be situated behind the two chairs of their representatives.

A Bible, copies of the simulation, and note paper should be furnished for all participants. Some particular items may be desired by the small groups. All will need sign and banner materials (inexpensive oak-tag, felt pens, burlap pieces, felt scraps, scissors, glue, and pieces of wood). The Zealots may desire fake weapons and rough robes. The Hellenistic group may want choir robes and liturgical symbols. The Suffering Servants may want equipment to do acts of service, such as wash feet, serve coffee, or the like.

Facilitation

To introduce this simulation, review with everyone what a simulation is, how to participate, the purpose of this particular exercise, meeting places, materials, small-group assignments, and division into groups. Be sure there is good understanding of these points before going on (see chapter 4). During the period of small-group preparation the coordinator should circulate among the groups to clarify anything that is misunderstood.

When the groups reassemble for the council, they will be led by Paul, James, Stephen, and Peter. You can add much interest, if there is sufficient time, by calling upon two other persons: Titus and the man from Corinth who lived with his stepmother. There are two ways to produce such persons. The coordinator, who may play the role of the "Holy Spirit" as a way of starting the simulation, could take on the other two roles as needed. On the other hand, it has been successful to have those two roles played by persons in simulation, presumably from the same party in which Paul is found (the apocalypticists).

In any case these two roles can add a great deal to the mood of the simulation. If Titus belongs to the Paul party from the beginning, then the Zealot group would logically refuse to be seated at the same table. If Titus arrives later, he can make up a story which would "infuriate" the Zealots and the Suffering Servants. For example, he could admit he was in the Roman seventh legion prior to becoming a Christian. He might suggest he had helped quell riots in predominantly Jewish centers like Alexandria. This along with the problem of circumcision should make the question of his admission to the council very intense.

The problem of the man living with his stepmother can be very interesting also. Normally the groups decide this issue rather quickly. Since living with one's stepmother was immoral and illegal in all the societies involved, they conclude he should not be accepted as a Christian. If this man can tell some story which appeals to the Christian empathy of the group, then the decision can become more complicated. The following testimony has been given with considerable success:

My name is Fortunatus and I am grateful to you for the opportunity to speak to you. My mother was born in Liberia into a fairly important family; but when she was young, our village was plundered by pirates and she was sold to a wealthy merchant in Corinth. As often happens in slave situations, my mother eventually became pregnant by the merchant slave-owner. Even though I was black, my father treated me kindly and gave me considerable education and training. During my youth I fell in love with a beautiful slave girl captured in eastern Asia Minor. We both resolved that some day we would become free and marry each other. Unfortunately our hopes were dashed by a strange turn of events. The wife of our owner, my father, died suddenly. After a short time my father chose a new wife, the lovely slave girl who was to have been my wife. But then another turn of events changed everything. My father was killed in a tragic chariot accident, and according to Roman law a considerable share of his estate went to his new wife, my stepmother. Her first action, as you might imagine, was to free me. Since she was my stepmother, we could not even live together, much less become legally married. But we resolved that our dream should be realized by common consent even though the marriage could not be legally consummated. Needless to say, most of the Corinthian society would have nothing to do with us. At times I thought that was as much because I was black as because I was living with my stepmother. Still, we were fairly well-to-do and we managed to avoid legal action against us. Then Paul came to town and told us about Jesus Christ who died for all our sins—no life was too destitute to be saved. We asked Paul if Christ died for us, too, and he said, "Yes!" We accepted Christ and became a part of the Corinthian church. Paul was right! The church loved us and accepted us. Now we could hardly live without the new life Jesus has granted us. But I understand some of you have raised questions about us. Even Paul has expressed doubts. I have wanted to tell you our story. I wanted you to know how much the church meant to us before you make your final decision.

Debriefing

After the simulation has been terminated, at least two tasks remain: debriefing and articulation of the learning experience. For the debriefing a change of seating will often mark the break of the role play, but in a simulation which is as competitive as this, time must be set aside to allow everyone to express how he felt and some of the emotions aroused by the struggle. The total session could then close with an expression of what was learned. Everyone should be offered an opportunity to make a statement, but the chroniclers especially should be called on. A worshipful way to close is with prayer, a renewal of baptismal vows, and a hymn.

THE COUNCIL OF JERUSALEM A Simulation Based upon Acts 15

THE SITUATION

You are to simulate the leaders of the early church who have come together in Jerusalem to decide the next steps in your mission to the Gentile world. This is the first meeting of the various groups following Jesus, and you are faced with several important problems:

1. You will need to elect a bishop for Jerusalem who will then conduct your further deliberations.

     The problem of leadership in the first church must have been fairly intense. By all odds the leader should have been Peter, leader of the twelve. But that is either hindsight or else opposition to the apparent leader the church was forced to take as a compromise candidate (Galatians 1). The compromise was a brother of Jesus, James the Just. Oddly enough, after the martyrdom of James, another relative of Jesus, Matthias, an uncle, led the church for about thirty more years.

2. You will need to decide whether to send Paul on a mission to the Gentiles.

     The decision for Paul to cross from Asia Minor into Macedonia was one of the most momentous actions of the earliest church. It meant that Greeks who had never been exposed to Judaism would be brought into the church. Presumably previous adherents were either Jewish or at least god-fearers (non-Jews self-consciously associated with Judaism). It also meant the great antagonism between Jew and Greek, Palestinian and Roman would be erased within the church. Paul says it was the Holy Spirit appearing in a vision which caused him to cross over into Europe.

3. You need to establish minimal requirements for non-Jews who are brought into the church.

     Christianity was at first a branch of Judaism; as such it adhered to the basic laws and customs of Judaism. All were circumcised. Within limits all adhered to the formal liturgical and dietary laws of their faith. To expect this of Greeks was futile. Yet there had to be minimal expectations if Jews and Greeks were to remain in the same social structure. In Acts 15 it is recorded this problem was solved by the mother church issuing the following minimal requirements: not to commit adultery, not to commit idolatry, and not to murder.

4. In view of the possibility of riots in Ephesus you need to decide whether Paul will be allowed to go there to preach the gospel.

     Nearly everywhere Paul went on a missionary journey, conflict was created. In the early accounts (Acts 14 - 18) it is clear a riot occurred at nearly every point.

TASKS OF ALL GROUPS
PRIOR TO THE SIMULATION

1. Appoint a leader who will—
   a. chair in the preparations for the simulation,
   b. lead the group during the simulation.

     For purposes of the simulation the leaders of the groups will have the following identities:

Suffering Servants	James
Apocalypticists	Paul
Zealots	Peter
Hellenists	Stephen

2. Appoint a chronicler who will—
   a. record briefly the process of the group,
   b. record the action of the simulation from the perspective of his group,
   c. report to the debriefing session.

3. Examine those texts of the New Testament which establish the identity of this particular group.

4. Articulate your identity to each other, i.e., make a banner or a standard, etc.

5. Project your group's position regarding each of the decisions to be made.

6. Discuss what type of power you could and should use in the course of the simulated decision making.

7. Assist the chronicler in recording all pertinent data, especially your projections prior to the simulation so that you can make a later comparison.

RULES OF THE SIMULATION

1. Each group will be allowed two representatives at the Jerusalem table.
2. Other members will be arranged behind the chairs of the two representatives.
3. Any member may replace a representative as he or she chooses.
4. Each group will be allowed two roving politicians who may—
   a. discover the character and purpose of the other groups,
   b. facilitate or disrupt the procedures,
   c. consult with the background resource person.

TASKS OF THE SIMULATION

1. The coordinator will chair the session until the church is able to elect a bishop.
2. Following the guidance of the bishop, the church council will attempt to deal with the following critical decisions:
   a. Will Paul and his cohorts from Antioch be allowed to carry the gospel to the purely Gentile world, i.e., Greece? Specifically, will you allow Titus to be seated in your meeting?
   b. What minimal requirements should be established for Christianity as it spreads? Specifically, will you accept into the church the man who has been living with his stepmother?
   c. What method will be used for the spreading of the gospel?

TASKS FOR DEBRIEFING

1. Make some change of your room arrangements to symbolize the end of the simulation.
2. Discuss with one another how you felt during the simulation.
3. Hear the reports from the chroniclers.
4. Discuss any questions that may be raised by the experience together.

1. The Disciples of the Suffering Servant

Your group identity for the simulation will be that of a band of faithful followers of that Jesus who was known as the Suffering Servant. In the simulation there will be other groups who are identified with the same Jesus of Nazareth, but from a vastly different perspective. It is your task to determine how your group (church?) should utilize its power so that it can be true to your understanding of Jesus. The following are some New Testament texts which will help you with your identity:

> Mark 8:34-38
> Mark 9:33-37
> Mark 10:35-45
> Matthew 5:1-16
> Matthew 5:38-48
> Matthew 10:34-39
> Matthew 11:25-30
> Matthew 23:1-12
> Luke 10:29-37
> John 13:1-20
> 1 Corinthians 1:18-31
> 1 Corinthians 4:8-13
> Philippians 2:1-11

BACKGROUND DATA

The idea of a suffering servant in Judeo-Christianity arose after the Jews were taken into captivity by the Babylonians (586 B.C.). The political power of the state of Israel had failed. Now some writers began to interpret the role of Israel as one who enables all nations to come to God by taking on herself the turmoil and sin of international strife. We know this position best by the servant songs in Isaiah, especially Isaiah 53. It is the opinion of many people that the genius of Jesus of Nazareth was to combine this picture of the suffering servant with the more apocalyptic Son of man in order to say that the kingdom of God will come with the self-giving of men to each other. The cross, of course, would be the paradigmatic symbol of that self-sacrifice. Those who follow this Jesus would use their power and their personhood to enable others to participate in the kingdom. This picture of Jesus has been especially powerful among free churches and Catholic orders.

THE COUNCIL OF JERUSALEM A Simulation Based upon Acts 15

THE SITUATION

You are to simulate the leaders of the early church who have come together in Jerusalem to decide the next steps in your mission to the Gentile world. This is the first meeting of the various groups following Jesus, and you are faced with several important problems:

1. You will need to elect a bishop for Jerusalem who will then conduct your further deliberations.

The problem of leadership in the first church must have been fairly intense. By all odds the leader should have been Peter, leader of the twelve. But that is either hindsight or else opposition to the apparent leader the church was forced to take as a compromise candidate (Galatians 1). The compromise was a brother of Jesus, James the Just. Oddly enough, after the martyrdom of James, another relative of Jesus, Matthias, an uncle, led the church for about thirty more years.

2. You will need to decide whether to send Paul on a mission to the Gentiles.

The decision for Paul to cross from Asia Minor into Macedonia was one of the most momentous actions of the earliest church. It meant that Greeks who had never been exposed to Judaism would be brought into the church. Presumably previous adherents were either Jewish or at least god-fearers (non-Jews self-consciously associated with Judaism). It also meant the great antagonism between Jew and Greek, Palestinian and Roman would be erased within the church. Paul says it was the Holy Spirit appearing in a vision which caused him to cross over into Europe.

3. You need to establish minimal requirements for non-Jews who are brought into the church.

Christianity was at first a branch of Judaism; as such it adhered to the basic laws and customs of Judaism. All were circumcised. Within limits all adhered to the formal liturgical and dietary laws of their faith. To expect this of Greeks was futile. Yet there had to be minimal expectations if Jews and Greeks were to remain in the same social structure. In Acts 15 it is recorded this problem was solved by the mother church issuing the following minimal requirements: not to commit adultery, not to commit idolatry, and not to murder.

4. In view of the possibility of riots in Ephesus you need to decide whether Paul will be allowed to go there to preach the gospel.

Nearly everywhere Paul went on a missionary journey, conflict was created. In the early accounts (Acts 14 - 18) it is clear a riot occurred at nearly every point.

TASKS OF ALL GROUPS
PRIOR TO THE SIMULATION

1. Appoint a leader who will—
   a. chair in the preparations for the simulation,
   b. lead the group during the simulation.

For purposes of the simulation the leaders of the groups will have the following identities:

Suffering Servants	James
Apocalypticists	Paul
Zealots	Peter
Hellenists	Stephen

2. Appoint a chronicler who will—
   a. record briefly the process of the group,
   b. record the action of the simulation from the perspective of his group,
   c. report to the debriefing session.
3. Examine those texts of the New Testament which establish the identity of this particular group.
4. Articulate your identity to each other, i.e., make a banner or a standard, etc.
5. Project your group's position regarding each of the decisions to be made.
6. Discuss what type of power you could and should use in the course of the simulated decision making.
7. Assist the chronicler in recording all pertinent data, especially your projections prior to the simulation so that you can make a later comparison.

RULES OF THE SIMULATION

1. Each group will be allowed two representatives at the Jerusalem table.
2. Other members will be arranged behind the chairs of the two representatives.
3. Any member may replace a representative as he or she chooses.
4. Each group will be allowed two roving politicians who may—
   a. discover the character and purpose of the other groups,
   b. facilitate or disrupt the procedures,
   c. consult with the background resource person.

TASKS OF THE SIMULATION

1. The coordinator will chair the session until the church is able to elect a bishop.
2. Following the guidance of the bishop, the church council will attempt to deal with the following critical decisions:
   a. Will Paul and his cohorts from Antioch be allowed to carry the gospel to the purely Gentile world, i.e., Greece? Specifically, will you allow Titus to be seated in your meeting?
   b. What minimal requirements should be established for Christianity as it spreads? Specifically, will you accept into the church the man who has been living with his stepmother?
   c. What method will be used for the spreading of the gospel?

TASKS FOR DEBRIEFING

1. Make some change of your room arrangements to symbolize the end of the simulation.
2. Discuss with one another how you felt during the simulation.
3. Hear the reports from the chroniclers.
4. Discuss any questions that may be raised by the experience together.

1. The Disciples of the Suffering Servant

Your group identity for the simulation will be that of a band of faithful followers of that Jesus who was known as the Suffering Servant. In the simulation there will be other groups who are identified with the same Jesus of Nazareth, but from a vastly different perspective. It is your task to determine how your group (church?) should utilize its power so that it can be true to your understanding of Jesus. The following are some New Testament texts which will help you with your identity:

> Mark 8:34-38
> Mark 9:33-37
> Mark 10:35-45
> Matthew 5:1-16
> Matthew 5:38-48
> Matthew 10:34-39
> Matthew 11:25-30
> Matthew 23:1-12
> Luke 10:29-37
> John 13:1-20
> 1 Corinthians 1:18-31
> 1 Corinthians 4:8-13
> Philippians 2:1-11

BACKGROUND DATA

The idea of a suffering servant in Judeo-Christianity arose after the Jews were taken into captivity by the Babylonians (586 B.C.). The political power of the state of Israel had failed. Now some writers began to interpret the role of Israel as one who enables all nations to come to God by taking on herself the turmoil and sin of international strife. We know this position best by the servant songs in Isaiah, especially Isaiah 53. It is the opinion of many people that the genius of Jesus of Nazareth was to combine this picture of the suffering servant with the more apocalyptic Son of man in order to say that the kingdom of God will come with the self-giving of men to each other. The cross, of course, would be the paradigmatic symbol of that self-sacrifice. Those who follow this Jesus would use their power and their personhood to enable others to participate in the kingdom. This picture of Jesus has been especially powerful among free churches and Catholic orders.

THE COUNCIL OF JERUSALEM A Simulation Based upon Acts 15

THE SITUATION

You are to simulate the leaders of the early church who have come together in Jerusalem to decide the next steps in your mission to the Gentile world. This is the first meeting of the various groups following Jesus, and you are faced with several important problems:

1. You will need to elect a bishop for Jerusalem who will then conduct your further deliberations.

    The problem of leadership in the first church must have been fairly intense. By all odds the leader should have been Peter, leader of the twelve. But that is either hindsight or else opposition to the apparent leader the church was forced to take as a compromise candidate (Galatians 1). The compromise was a brother of Jesus, James the Just. Oddly enough, after the martyrdom of James, another relative of Jesus, Matthias, an uncle, led the church for about thirty more years.

2. You will need to decide whether to send Paul on a mission to the Gentiles.

    The decision for Paul to cross from Asia Minor into Macedonia was one of the most momentous actions of the earliest church. It meant that Greeks who had never been exposed to Judaism would be brought into the church. Presumably previous adherents were either Jewish or at least god-fearers (non-Jews self-consciously associated with Judaism). It also meant the great antagonism between Jew and Greek, Palestinian and Roman would be erased within the church. Paul says it was the Holy Spirit appearing in a vision which caused him to cross over into Europe.

3. You need to establish minimal requirements for non-Jews who are brought into the church.

    Christianity was at first a branch of Judaism; as such it adhered to the basic laws and customs of Judaism. All were circumcised. Within limits all adhered to the formal liturgical and dietary laws of their faith. To expect this of Greeks was futile. Yet there had to be minimal expectations if Jews and Greeks were to remain in the same social structure. In Acts 15 it is recorded this problem was solved by the mother church issuing the following minimal requirements: not to commit adultery, not to commit idolatry, and not to murder.

4. In view of the possibility of riots in Ephesus you need to decide whether Paul will be allowed to go there to preach the gospel.

    Nearly everywhere Paul went on a missionary journey, conflict was created. In the early accounts (Acts 14 - 18) it is clear a riot occurred at nearly every point.

TASKS OF ALL GROUPS
PRIOR TO THE SIMULATION

1. Appoint a leader who will—
    a. chair in the preparations for the simulation,
    b. lead the group during the simulation.

    For purposes of the simulation the leaders of the groups will have the following identities:

Suffering Servants	James
Apocalypticists	Paul
Zealots	Peter
Hellenists	Stephen

2. Appoint a chronicler who will—
    a. record briefly the process of the group,
    b. record the action of the simulation from the perspective of his group,
    c. report to the debriefing session.

3. Examine those texts of the New Testament which establish the identity of this particular group.

4. Articulate your identity to each other, i.e., make a banner or a standard, etc.

5. Project your group's position regarding each of the decisions to be made.

6. Discuss what type of power you could and should use in the course of the simulated decision making.

7. Assist the chronicler in recording all pertinent data, especially your projections prior to the simulation so that you can make a later comparison.

RULES OF THE SIMULATION

1. Each group will be allowed two representatives at the Jerusalem table.
2. Other members will be arranged behind the chairs of the two representatives.
3. Any member may replace a representative as he or she chooses.
4. Each group will be allowed two roving politicians who may—
   a. discover the character and purpose of the other groups,
   b. facilitate or disrupt the procedures,
   c. consult with the background resource person.

TASKS OF THE SIMULATION

1. The coordinator will chair the session until the church is able to elect a bishop.
2. Following the guidance of the bishop, the church council will attempt to deal with the following critical decisions:
   a. Will Paul and his cohorts from Antioch be allowed to carry the gospel to the purely Gentile world, i.e., Greece? Specifically, will you allow Titus to be seated in your meeting?
   b. What minimal requirements should be established for Christianity as it spreads? Specifically, will you accept into the church the man who has been living with his stepmother?
   c. What method will be used for the spreading of the gospel?

TASKS FOR DEBRIEFING

1. Make some change of your room arrangements to symbolize the end of the simulation.
2. Discuss with one another how you felt during the simulation.
3. Hear the reports from the chroniclers.
4. Discuss any questions that may be raised by the experience together.

2. The Hellenistic Believers on the Son of God

Your group identity for the simulation will be that of a band of Greeks or, more likely, Hellenistic Jews, who think of Jesus as Son of God. In the simulation there will be other groups who are identified with the same Jesus of Nazareth, but from a vastly different perspective. It is your task to determine how your group (church?) should utilize its power so as to be true to your understanding of Jesus. The following are some New Testament texts which will help you with your identity:

Mark 1:9-11
Mark 9:2-8
Mark 15:33-39
Colossians 1:15-20
Matthew 12:15-21
John 5:19-47
John 18:33-37
Revelation 5:1-14

BACKGROUND DATA

"Son of God" is primarily a monarchical or imperial term. It denotes the king. In the Old Testament the king is called the Son of God (2 Samuel 7:14) and becomes that at the time he is enthroned (Psalm 2). In the more contemporary Roman Empire the emperor was just becoming known as *filius dei* (son of god). To speak of Jesus as Son of God is to say he is your Lord rather than someone else (e.g., Nero). Those who believe in Jesus as the Son of God have seen in Jesus the ultimate Truth, the Father. They consider themselves as the true agents of God, exercising his power and proclaiming his truth. Needless to say, the church groups derive their identity primarily from this confession that Jesus is Lord, the Son of God.

Whether Jesus himself was conscious of being the Son of God is debatable. Most students of the New Testament suppose we are dealing with a term which became popular when Christianity began to compete with other Eastern religions and with the power of the emperor himself.

THE COUNCIL OF JERUSALEM   A Simulation Based upon Acts 15

THE SITUATION

You are to simulate the leaders of the early church who have come together in Jerusalem to decide the next steps in your mission to the Gentile world. This is the first meeting of the various groups following Jesus, and you are faced with several important problems:

1. You will need to elect a bishop for Jerusalem who will then conduct your further deliberations.

    The problem of leadership in the first church must have been fairly intense. By all odds the leader should have been Peter, leader of the twelve. But that is either hindsight or else opposition to the apparent leader the church was forced to take as a compromise candidate (Galatians 1). The compromise was a brother of Jesus, James the Just. Oddly enough, after the martyrdom of James, another relative of Jesus, Matthias, an uncle, led the church for about thirty more years.

2. You will need to decide whether to send Paul on a mission to the Gentiles.

    The decision for Paul to cross from Asia Minor into Macedonia was one of the most momentous actions of the earliest church. It meant that Greeks who had never been exposed to Judaism would be brought into the church. Presumably previous adherents were either Jewish or at least god-fearers (non-Jews self-consciously associated with Judaism). It also meant the great antagonism between Jew and Greek, Palestinian and Roman would be erased within the church. Paul says it was the Holy Spirit appearing in a vision which caused him to cross over into Europe.

3. You need to establish minimal requirements for non-Jews who are brought into the church.

    Christianity was at first a branch of Judaism; as such it adhered to the basic laws and customs of Judaism. All were circumcised. Within limits all adhered to the formal liturgical and dietary laws of their faith. To expect this of Greeks was futile. Yet there had to be minimal expectations if Jews and Greeks were to remain in the same social structure. In Acts 15 it is recorded this problem was solved by the mother church issuing the following minimal requirements: not to commit adultery, not to commit idolatry, and not to murder.

4. In view of the possibility of riots in Ephesus you need to decide whether Paul will be allowed to go there to preach the gospel.

    Nearly everywhere Paul went on a missionary journey, conflict was created. In the early accounts (Acts 14 - 18) it is clear a riot occurred at nearly every point.

TASKS OF ALL GROUPS
PRIOR TO THE SIMULATION

1. Appoint a leader who will—
    a. chair in the preparations for the simulation,
    b. lead the group during the simulation.

    For purposes of the simulation the leaders of the groups will have the following identities:

Suffering Servants	James
Apocalypticists	Paul
Zealots	Peter
Hellenists	Stephen

2. Appoint a chronicler who will—
    a. record briefly the process of the group,
    b. record the action of the simulation from the perspective of his group,
    c. report to the debriefing session.

3. Examine those texts of the New Testament which establish the identity of this particular group.

4. Articulate your identity to each other, i.e., make a banner or a standard, etc.

5. Project your group's position regarding each of the decisions to be made.

6. Discuss what type of power you could and should use in the course of the simulated decision making.

7. Assist the chronicler in recording all pertinent data, especially your projections prior to the simulation so that you can make a later comparison.

RULES OF THE SIMULATION

1. Each group will be allowed two representatives at the Jerusalem table.
2. Other members will be arranged behind the chairs of the two representatives.
3. Any member may replace a representative as he or she chooses.
4. Each group will be allowed two roving politicians who may—
   a. discover the character and purpose of the other groups,
   b. facilitate or disrupt the procedures,
   c. consult with the background resource person.

TASKS OF THE SIMULATION

1. The coordinator will chair the session until the church is able to elect a bishop.
2. Following the guidance of the bishop, the church council will attempt to deal with the following critical decisions:
   a. Will Paul and his cohorts from Antioch be allowed to carry the gospel to the purely Gentile world, i.e., Greece? Specifically, will you allow Titus to be seated in your meeting?
   b. What minimal requirements should be established for Christianity as it spreads? Specifically, will you accept into the church the man who has been living with his stepmother?
   c. What method will be used for the spreading of the gospel?

TASKS FOR DEBRIEFING

1. Make some change of your room arrangements to symbolize the end of the simulation.
2. Discuss with one another how you felt during the simulation.
3. Hear the reports from the chroniclers.
4. Discuss any questions that may be raised by the experience together.

2. The Hellenistic Believers on the Son of God

Your group identity for the simulation will be that of a band of Greeks or, more likely, Hellenistic Jews, who think of Jesus as Son of God. In the simulation there will be other groups who are identified with the same Jesus of Nazareth, but from a vastly different perspective. It is your task to determine how your group (church?) should utilize its power so as to be true to your understanding of Jesus. The following are some New Testament texts which will help you with your identity:

Mark 1:9-11
Mark 9:2-8
Mark 15:33-39
Colossians 1:15-20
Matthew 12:15-21
John 5:19-47
John 18:33-37
Revelation 5:1-14

BACKGROUND DATA

"Son of God" is primarily a monarchical or imperial term. It denotes the king. In the Old Testament the king is called the Son of God (2 Samuel 7:14) and becomes that at the time he is enthroned (Psalm 2). In the more contemporary Roman Empire the emperor was just becoming known as *filius dei* (son of god). To speak of Jesus as Son of God is to say he is your Lord rather than someone else (e.g., Nero). Those who believe in Jesus as the Son of God have seen in Jesus the ultimate Truth, the Father. They consider themselves as the true agents of God, exercising his power and proclaiming his truth. Needless to say, the church groups derive their identity primarily from this confession that Jesus is Lord, the Son of God.

Whether Jesus himself was conscious of being the Son of God is debatable. Most students of the New Testament suppose we are dealing with a term which became popular when Christianity began to compete with other Eastern religions and with the power of the emperor himself.

THE COUNCIL OF JERUSALEM A Simulation Based upon Acts 15

THE SITUATION

You are to simulate the leaders of the early church who have come together in Jerusalem to decide the next steps in your mission to the Gentile world. This is the first meeting of the various groups following Jesus, and you are faced with several important problems:

1. You will need to elect a bishop for Jerusalem who will then conduct your further deliberations.

   The problem of leadership in the first church must have been fairly intense. By all odds the leader should have been Peter, leader of the twelve. But that is either hindsight or else opposition to the apparent leader the church was forced to take as a compromise candidate (Galatians 1). The compromise was a brother of Jesus, James the Just. Oddly enough, after the martyrdom of James, another relative of Jesus, Matthias, an uncle, led the church for about thirty more years.

2. You will need to decide whether to send Paul on a mission to the Gentiles.

   The decision for Paul to cross from Asia Minor into Macedonia was one of the most momentous actions of the earliest church. It meant that Greeks who had never been exposed to Judaism would be brought into the church. Presumably previous adherents were either Jewish or at least god-fearers (non-Jews self-consciously associated with Judaism). It also meant the great antagonism between Jew and Greek, Palestinian and Roman would be erased within the church. Paul says it was the Holy Spirit appearing in a vision which caused him to cross over into Europe.

3. You need to establish minimal requirements for non-Jews who are brought into the church.

   Christianity was at first a branch of Judaism; as such it adhered to the basic laws and customs of Judaism. All were circumcised. Within limits all adhered to the formal liturgical and dietary laws of their faith. To expect this of Greeks was futile. Yet there had to be minimal expectations if Jews and Greeks were to remain in the same social structure. In Acts 15 it is recorded this problem was solved by the mother church issuing the following minimal requirements: not to commit adultery, not to commit idolatry, and not to murder.

4. In view of the possibility of riots in Ephesus you need to decide whether Paul will be allowed to go there to preach the gospel.

   Nearly everywhere Paul went on a missionary journey, conflict was created. In the early accounts (Acts 14 - 18) it is clear a riot occurred at nearly every point.

TASKS OF ALL GROUPS
PRIOR TO THE SIMULATION

1. Appoint a leader who will—
   a. chair in the preparations for the simulation,
   b. lead the group during the simulation.

   For purposes of the simulation the leaders of the groups will have the following identities:

Suffering Servants	James
Apocalypticists	Paul
Zealots	Peter
Hellenists	Stephen

2. Appoint a chronicler who will—
   a. record briefly the process of the group,
   b. record the action of the simulation from the perspective of his group,
   c. report to the debriefing session.

3. Examine those texts of the New Testament which establish the identity of this particular group.

4. Articulate your identity to each other, i.e., make a banner or a standard, etc.

5. Project your group's position regarding each of the decisions to be made.

6. Discuss what type of power you could and should use in the course of the simulated decision making.

7. Assist the chronicler in recording all pertinent data, especially your projections prior to the simulation so that you can make a later comparison.

RULES OF THE SIMULATION

1. Each group will be allowed two representatives at the Jerusalem table.
2. Other members will be arranged behind the chairs of the two representatives.
3. Any member may replace a representative as he or she chooses.
4. Each group will be allowed two roving politicians who may—
   a. discover the character and purpose of the other groups,
   b. facilitate or disrupt the procedures,
   c. consult with the background resource person.

TASKS OF THE SIMULATION

1. The coordinator will chair the session until the church is able to elect a bishop.
2. Following the guidance of the bishop, the church council will attempt to deal with the following critical decisions:
   a. Will Paul and his cohorts from Antioch be allowed to carry the gospel to the purely Gentile world, i.e., Greece? Specifically, will you allow Titus to be seated in your meeting?
   b. What minimal requirements should be established for Christianity as it spreads? Specifically, will you accept into the church the man who has been living with his stepmother?
   c. What method will be used for the spreading of the gospel?

TASKS FOR DEBRIEFING

1. Make some change of your room arrangements to symbolize the end of the simulation.
2. Discuss with one another how you felt during the simulation.
3. Hear the reports from the chroniclers.
4. Discuss any questions that may be raised by the experience together.

3. The Warriors of the Zealot Jesus

Your group identity for the simulation will be that of a band of armed and dangerous revolutionaries who believed Jesus had come to overthrow Rome. You are the historic Zealots. In the simulation there will be other groups who are identified with the same Jesus of Nazareth, but from a vastly different perspective. It is your task to determine how your group (church?) should utilize its power so as to be true to your understanding of Jesus. The following are some New Testament texts which will help you with your identity:

Matthew 4:1-11
Matthew 10:1-4
Matthew 19:23-30
Matthew 20:20-28
Matthew 21:12-13
Matthew 26:47-56
Luke 20:19-26
Luke 22:35-38
Luke 23:32-38

BACKGROUND DATA

The Zealots were one of several parties among the Jews at the time of Jesus. In contrast to the Sadducees who cooperated with Rome and the Pharisees who quietly resisted, the Zealots intended to bring the kingdom by triggering the new age with a violent, radical action. It is not known how they arose, but somehow they must have evolved from the militant Maccabeans. They constantly sought out leaders who appeared to be messianic hopefuls. Most of these were Galileans and most of them were killed as insurrectionists. There can be little doubt that Jesus was killed for the same reasons. It was Zealots who precipitated the Jewish War which ended in the defeat and destruction of Jerusalem by Titus (A.D. 70). Just prior to this the Christian community finally recognized it had no part in the Zealots' cause and left Jerusalem. But at the time of the Jerusalem Council, as found in Acts 15, this would not have been so clear. The presence of so much Zealot material in the Gospels would indicate this was a continuing struggle.

THE COUNCIL OF JERUSALEM A Simulation Based upon Acts 15

THE SITUATION

You are to simulate the leaders of the early church who have come together in Jerusalem to decide the next steps in your mission to the Gentile world. This is the first meeting of the various groups following Jesus, and you are faced with several important problems:

1. You will need to elect a bishop for Jerusalem who will then conduct your further deliberations.

    The problem of leadership in the first church must have been fairly intense. By all odds the leader should have been Peter, leader of the twelve. But that is either hindsight or else opposition to the apparent leader the church was forced to take as a compromise candidate (Galatians 1). The compromise was a brother of Jesus, James the Just. Oddly enough, after the martyrdom of James, another relative of Jesus, Matthias, an uncle, led the church for about thirty more years.

2. You will need to decide whether to send Paul on a mission to the Gentiles.

    The decision for Paul to cross from Asia Minor into Macedonia was one of the most momentous actions of the earliest church. It meant that Greeks who had never been exposed to Judaism would be brought into the church. Presumably previous adherents were either Jewish or at least god-fearers (non-Jews self-consciously associated with Judaism). It also meant the great antagonism between Jew and Greek, Palestinian and Roman would be erased within the church. Paul says it was the Holy Spirit appearing in a vision which caused him to cross over into Europe.

3. You need to establish minimal requirements for non-Jews who are brought into the church.

    Christianity was at first a branch of Judaism; as such it adhered to the basic laws and customs of Judaism. All were circumcised. Within limits all adhered to the formal liturgical and dietary laws of their faith. To expect this of Greeks was futile. Yet there had to be minimal expectations if Jews and Greeks were to remain in the same social structure. In Acts 15 it is recorded this problem was solved by the mother church issuing the following minimal requirements: not to commit adultery, not to commit idolatry, and not to murder.

4. In view of the possibility of riots in Ephesus you need to decide whether Paul will be allowed to go there to preach the gospel.

    Nearly everywhere Paul went on a missionary journey, conflict was created. In the early accounts (Acts 14 - 18) it is clear a riot occurred at nearly every point.

TASKS OF ALL GROUPS
PRIOR TO THE SIMULATION

1. Appoint a leader who will—
    a. chair in the preparations for the simulation,
    b. lead the group during the simulation.

    For purposes of the simulation the leaders of the groups will have the following identities:

Suffering Servants	James
Apocalypticists	Paul
Zealots	Peter
Hellenists	Stephen

2. Appoint a chronicler who will—
    a. record briefly the process of the group,
    b. record the action of the simulation from the perspective of his group,
    c. report to the debriefing session.

3. Examine those texts of the New Testament which establish the identity of this particular group.

4. Articulate your identity to each other, i.e., make a banner or a standard, etc.

5. Project your group's position regarding each of the decisions to be made.

6. Discuss what type of power you could and should use in the course of the simulated decision making.

7. Assist the chronicler in recording all pertinent data, especially your projections prior to the simulation so that you can make a later comparison.

RULES OF THE SIMULATION

1. Each group will be allowed two representatives at the Jerusalem table.
2. Other members will be arranged behind the chairs of the two representatives.
3. Any member may replace a representative as he or she chooses.
4. Each group will be allowed two roving politicians who may—
   a. discover the character and purpose of the other groups,
   b. facilitate or disrupt the procedures,
   c. consult with the background resource person.

TASKS OF THE SIMULATION

1. The coordinator will chair the session until the church is able to elect a bishop.
2. Following the guidance of the bishop, the church council will attempt to deal with the following critical decisions:
   a. Will Paul and his cohorts from Antioch be allowed to carry the gospel to the purely Gentile world, i.e., Greece? Specifically, will you allow Titus to be seated in your meeting?
   b. What minimal requirements should be established for Christianity as it spreads? Specifically, will you accept into the church the man who has been living with his stepmother?
   c. What method will be used for the spreading of the gospel?

TASKS FOR DEBRIEFING

1. Make some change of your room arrangements to symbolize the end of the simulation.
2. Discuss with one another how you felt during the simulation.
3. Hear the reports from the chroniclers.
4. Discuss any questions that may be raised by the experience together.

3. The Warriors of the Zealot Jesus

Your group identity for the simulation will be that of a band of armed and dangerous revolutionaries who believed Jesus had come to overthrow Rome. You are the historic Zealots. In the simulation there will be other groups who are identified with the same Jesus of Nazareth, but from a vastly different perspective. It is your task to determine how your group (church?) should utilize its power so as to be true to your understanding of Jesus. The following are some New Testament texts which will help you with your identity:

Matthew 4:1-11
Matthew 10:1-4
Matthew 19:23-30
Matthew 20:20-28
Matthew 21:12-13
Matthew 26:47-56
Luke 20:19-26
Luke 22:35-38
Luke 23:32-38

BACKGROUND DATA

The Zealots were one of several parties among the Jews at the time of Jesus. In contrast to the Sadducees who cooperated with Rome and the Pharisees who quietly resisted, the Zealots intended to bring the kingdom by triggering the new age with a violent, radical action. It is not known how they arose, but somehow they must have evolved from the militant Maccabeans. They constantly sought out leaders who appeared to be messianic hopefuls. Most of these were Galileans and most of them were killed as insurrectionists. There can be little doubt that Jesus was killed for the same reasons. It was Zealots who precipitated the Jewish War which ended in the defeat and destruction of Jerusalem by Titus (A.D. 70). Just prior to this the Christian community finally recognized it had no part in the Zealots' cause and left Jerusalem. But at the time of the Jerusalem Council, as found in Acts 15, this would not have been so clear. The presence of so much Zealot material in the Gospels would indicate this was a continuing struggle.

THE COUNCIL OF JERUSALEM A Simulation Based upon Acts 15

THE SITUATION

You are to simulate the leaders of the early church who have come together in Jerusalem to decide the next steps in your mission to the Gentile world. This is the first meeting of the various groups following Jesus, and you are faced with several important problems:

1. You will need to elect a bishop for Jerusalem who will then conduct your further deliberations.

    The problem of leadership in the first church must have been fairly intense. By all odds the leader should have been Peter, leader of the twelve. But that is either hindsight or else opposition to the apparent leader the church was forced to take as a compromise candidate (Galatians 1). The compromise was a brother of Jesus, James the Just. Oddly enough, after the martyrdom of James, another relative of Jesus, Matthias, an uncle, led the church for about thirty more years.

2. You will need to decide whether to send Paul on a mission to the Gentiles.

    The decision for Paul to cross from Asia Minor into Macedonia was one of the most momentous actions of the earliest church. It meant that Greeks who had never been exposed to Judaism would be brought into the church. Presumably previous adherents were either Jewish or at least god-fearers (non-Jews self-consciously associated with Judaism). It also meant the great antagonism between Jew and Greek, Palestinian and Roman would be erased within the church. Paul says it was the Holy Spirit appearing in a vision which caused him to cross over into Europe.

3. You need to establish minimal requirements for non-Jews who are brought into the church.

    Christianity was at first a branch of Judaism; as such it adhered to the basic laws and customs of Judaism. All were circumcised. Within limits all adhered to the formal liturgical and dietary laws of their faith. To expect this of Greeks was futile. Yet there had to be minimal expectations if Jews and Greeks were to remain in the same social structure. In Acts 15 it is recorded this problem was solved by the mother church issuing the following minimal requirements: not to commit adultery, not to commit idolatry, and not to murder.

4. In view of the possibility of riots in Ephesus you need to decide whether Paul will be allowed to go there to preach the gospel.

    Nearly everywhere Paul went on a missionary journey, conflict was created. In the early accounts (Acts 14 - 18) it is clear a riot occurred at nearly every point.

TASKS OF ALL GROUPS
PRIOR TO THE SIMULATION

1. Appoint a leader who will—
    a. chair in the preparations for the simulation,
    b. lead the group during the simulation.

    For purposes of the simulation the leaders of the groups will have the following identities:

Suffering Servants	James
Apocalypticists	Paul
Zealots	Peter
Hellenists	Stephen

2. Appoint a chronicler who will—
    a. record briefly the process of the group,
    b. record the action of the simulation from the perspective of his group,
    c. report to the debriefing session.

3. Examine those texts of the New Testament which establish the identity of this particular group.

4. Articulate your identity to each other, i.e., make a banner or a standard, etc.

5. Project your group's position regarding each of the decisions to be made.

6. Discuss what type of power you could and should use in the course of the simulated decision making.

7. Assist the chronicler in recording all pertinent data, especially your projections prior to the simulation so that you can make a later comparison.

RULES OF THE SIMULATION

1. Each group will be allowed two representatives at the Jerusalem table.
2. Other members will be arranged behind the chairs of the two representatives.
3. Any member may replace a representative as he or she chooses.
4. Each group will be allowed two roving politicians who may—
   a. discover the character and purpose of the other groups,
   b. facilitate or disrupt the procedures,
   c. consult with the background resource person.

TASKS OF THE SIMULATION

1. The coordinator will chair the session until the church is able to elect a bishop.
2. Following the guidance of the bishop, the church council will attempt to deal with the following critical decisions:
   a. Will Paul and his cohorts from Antioch be allowed to carry the gospel to the purely Gentile world, i.e., Greece? Specifically, will you allow Titus to be seated in your meeting?
   b. What minimal requirements should be established for Christianity as it spreads? Specifically, will you accept into the church the man who has been living with his stepmother?
   c. What method will be used for the spreading of the gospel?

TASKS FOR DEBRIEFING

1. Make some change of your room arrangements to symbolize the end of the simulation.
2. Discuss with one another how you felt during the simulation.
3. Hear the reports from the chroniclers.
4. Discuss any questions that may be raised by the experience together.

4. Apostles of the Apocalyptic Prophet

Your group identity for the simulation will be that of a band of people who, as did Jesus before them, continue to await and proclaim the coming of the kingdom of God. You are the messengers of God, the apostles. In the simulation there will be other groups who are identified with the same Jesus of Nazareth, but from a vastly different perspective. It is your task to determine how your group (church?) should utilize its power so as to be true to your understanding of Jesus. The following are some New Testament texts which will help with your identity·

>Mark 1:14-15
>Matthew 5:1-10
>Matthew 10:34-39
>Matthew 13:24-52
>Matthew 19:23-30
>Matthew 21:33-44
>Matthew 22:1-14
>Matthew 22:23-33
>Matthew 24:36-51
>Luke 9:57-62
>Luke 12:8-40
>1 Thessalonians 1:6-10
>2 Thessalonians 3:11-13
>Acts 14:1-18

BACKGROUND DATA

Apocalypticism is both a form of literature and, in the Bible, an attitude which grew up out of the despair of the Jewish exile. Essentially these were Jews who believed the promise of God would be fulfilled but that historical movements and institutions could not bring about that kingdom. Since it was both a prophetic movement and a wisdom genre, it stands to reason that eventually there were those who said the kingdom of God most likely does come when one lives as if it were coming. The historical Jesus must have been such an apocalypticist who felt himself sent by God to proclaim the coming kingdom. He gathered about him apostles who also shared that sentness (apostleship). A major aspect of the earliest church was that of continuing to proclaim this coming, even though eventually most of Christendom defined that coming by the past events which surrounded the man Jesus.

THE COUNCIL OF JERUSALEM A Simulation Based upon Acts 15

THE SITUATION

You are to simulate the leaders of the early church who have come together in Jerusalem to decide the next steps in your mission to the Gentile world. This is the first meeting of the various groups following Jesus, and you are faced with several important problems:

1. You will need to elect a bishop for Jerusalem who will then conduct your further deliberations.

    The problem of leadership in the first church must have been fairly intense. By all odds the leader should have been Peter, leader of the twelve. But that is either hindsight or else opposition to the apparent leader the church was forced to take as a compromise candidate (Galatians 1). The compromise was a brother of Jesus, James the Just. Oddly enough, after the martyrdom of James, another relative of Jesus, Matthias, an uncle, led the church for about thirty more years.

2. You will need to decide whether to send Paul on a mission to the Gentiles.

    The decision for Paul to cross from Asia Minor into Macedonia was one of the most momentous actions of the earliest church. It meant that Greeks who had never been exposed to Judaism would be brought into the church. Presumably previous adherents were either Jewish or at least god-fearers (non-Jews self-consciously associated with Judaism). It also meant the great antagonism between Jew and Greek, Palestinian and Roman would be erased within the church. Paul says it was the Holy Spirit appearing in a vision which caused him to cross over into Europe.

3. You need to establish minimal requirements for non-Jews who are brought into the church.

    Christianity was at first a branch of Judaism; as such it adhered to the basic laws and customs of Judaism. All were circumcised. Within limits all adhered to the formal liturgical and dietary laws of their faith. To expect this of Greeks was futile. Yet there had to be minimal expectations if Jews and Greeks were to remain in the same social structure. In Acts 15 it is recorded this problem was solved by the mother church issuing the following minimal requirements: not to commit adultery, not to commit idolatry, and not to murder.

4. In view of the possibility of riots in Ephesus you need to decide whether Paul will be allowed to go there to preach the gospel.

    Nearly everywhere Paul went on a missionary journey, conflict was created. In the early accounts (Acts 14 - 18) it is clear a riot occurred at nearly every point.

TASKS OF ALL GROUPS
PRIOR TO THE SIMULATION

1. Appoint a leader who will—
    a. chair in the preparations for the simulation,
    b. lead the group during the simulation.

    For purposes of the simulation the leaders of the groups will have the following identities:

Suffering Servants	James
Apocalypticists	Paul
Zealots	Peter
Hellenists	Stephen

2. Appoint a chronicler who will—
    a. record briefly the process of the group,
    b. record the action of the simulation from the perspective of his group,
    c. report to the debriefing session.

3. Examine those texts of the New Testament which establish the identity of this particular group.

4. Articulate your identity to each other, i.e., make a banner or a standard, etc.

5. Project your group's position regarding each of the decisions to be made.

6. Discuss what type of power you could and should use in the course of the simulated decision making.

7. Assist the chronicler in recording all pertinent data, especially your projections prior to the simulation so that you can make a later comparison.

RULES OF THE SIMULATION

1. Each group will be allowed two representatives at the Jerusalem table.
2. Other members will be arranged behind the chairs of the two representatives.
3. Any member may replace a representative as he or she chooses.
4. Each group will be allowed two roving politicians who may—
   a. discover the character and purpose of the other groups,
   b. facilitate or disrupt the procedures,
   c. consult with the background resource person.

TASKS OF THE SIMULATION

1. The coordinator will chair the session until the church is able to elect a bishop.
2. Following the guidance of the bishop, the church council will attempt to deal with the following critical decisions:
   a. Will Paul and his cohorts from Antioch be allowed to carry the gospel to the purely Gentile world, i.e., Greece? Specifically, will you allow Titus to be seated in your meeting?
   b. What minimal requirements should be established for Christianity as it spreads? Specifically, will you accept into the church the man who has been living with his stepmother?
   c. What method will be used for the spreading of the gospel?

TASKS FOR DEBRIEFING

1. Make some change of your room arrangements to symbolize the end of the simulation.
2. Discuss with one another how you felt during the simulation.
3. Hear the reports from the chroniclers.
4. Discuss any questions that may be raised by the experience together.

4. Apostles of the Apocalyptic Prophet

Your group identity for the simulation will be that of a band of people who, as did Jesus before them, continue to await and proclaim the coming of the kingdom of God. You are the messengers of God, the apostles. In the simulation there will be other groups who are identified with the same Jesus of Nazareth, but from a vastly different perspective. It is your task to determine how your group (church?) should utilize its power so as to be true to your understanding of Jesus. The following are some New Testament texts which will help with your identity:

Mark 1:14-15
Matthew 5:1-10
Matthew 10:34-39
Matthew 13:24-52
Matthew 19:23-30
Matthew 21:33-44
Matthew 22:1-14
Matthew 22:23-33
Matthew 24:36-51
Luke 9:57-62
Luke 12:8-40
1 Thessalonians 1:6-10
2 Thessalonians 3:11-13
Acts 14:1-18

BACKGROUND DATA

Apocalypticism is both a form of literature and, in the Bible, an attitude which grew up out of the despair of the Jewish exile. Essentially these were Jews who believed the promise of God would be fulfilled but that historical movements and institutions could not bring about that kingdom. Since it was both a prophetic movement and a wisdom genre, it stands to reason that eventually there were those who said the kingdom of God most likely does come when one lives as if it were coming. The historical Jesus must have been such an apocalypticist who felt himself sent by God to proclaim the coming kingdom. He gathered about him apostles who also shared that sentness (apostleship). A major aspect of the earliest church was that of continuing to proclaim this coming, even though eventually most of Christendom defined that coming by the past events which surrounded the man Jesus.

13. THE GIFTS OF THE SPIRIT

A Simulation Based upon 1 Corinthians 12-14

INSTRUCTIONS TO THE COORDINATOR

Preparation

"The gifts of the Spirit" is a very important question today inside and outside the church. Many people are caught up in the use of drugs, faith healing, speaking in tongues, sensitivity sessions, etc. This simulation is designed to get to the heart of the experience of the Spirit.

If the simulation is to go well, you, as coordinator, should be sure to read through all the instructions in order to be quite familiar with the various tasks. The groups will depend upon you to clarify their instructions. Furthermore you may want to call together several leaders in advance of the session to work through the instructions.

Schedule

This simulation can be adapted to a shorter or longer time schedule. The following are several possible options:

	One Hour	Two Hours	Six Hours
Introduction	10 min.	15 min.	¼ hr.
Small groups	20 min.	45 min.	2¾ hrs.
Simulation	15 min.	30 min.	2 hrs.
Debriefing	15 min.	30 min.	1 hr.

If you have only one hour available, plan to make only one decision, i.e., whether or not to accept speaking in tongues. A two-hour session may allow you to debate whether or not to have Paul's letter read. Longer periods permit fuller discussion of all issues, and we would recommend at least two hours.

Grouping

This simulation is based upon a conference model. It will go best if there are at least two persons in each small group. Groups that contain more than twelve persons should be subdivided. The recommended number of groups and the number of group representatives at the council table are as follows:

Persons present	Number of small groups	Representatives at the table
8-48	4	3 per group
49-96	8	2 per group

With more than one hundred persons you probably ought to run two simulations simultaneously.

Space and Equipment

Your preparation should include obtaining each of the following items (see chapter 3): a large room, small rooms, chairs, tables, Bibles, study aids, paper, pencils, materials for symbols, and refreshments. Special arrangements for costumes might include choir robes or clothes draped in the manner of the ancient Greek costume. Women might wear hair coverings. Anything reminiscent of Corinth as a busy, ancient marketplace, a seaport, and a center of worship of Greek Gods (e.g., Zeus) will add interest.

Facilitation

Your group's enthusiasm for the simulation will depend a great deal upon how you introduce it. Your introduction ought to include an explanation of the following items: what a biblical simulation is, how to participate, purpose and tasks of this simulation, schedule, small-group preparation, materials, and division into groups.

As a coordinator it is very important for you to distinguish sharply between the schedule on one hand, and the process on the other. It is well for you to move the scheduled events along so that they terminate at the times you have announced. However, it is not your job to control the process. What happens in the process depends upon the persons present. There are things you can do to help a lagging group, but that is much different from controlling the process. You do not know in advance what people will experience or what conclusions they will come to. However, you do know that many will gain a new appreciation for the biblical event.

This simulation will be helped if you can find someone in the group who has spoken in tongues or who has attended such a service. Such a person might wish to speak in tongues or describe the service (let us say at the church in Athens).

The problem of Paul's attitude toward women almost certainly will come up. The council may possibly spend more time on that issue than any other. The Pauline group might intentionally leave out the references to women if the council asks them to read the letter from Paul. They can assume that others do not have the letter.

Debriefing

The final part of the simulation is the debriefing, which you should handle as coordinator. You may conclude the council meeting early or late, as seems fitting. It is, however, highly important that you allow ample time for debriefing. If you must decrease time alloted any part of the simulation schedule, don't make the mistake of cutting off the debriefing period.

This simulation lends itself especially well to a concluding worship in the form of naming the gifts of the Spirit. You will notice that the debriefing instructions direct people in groups of three to name the special spiritual gifts of each person. Each person has a special unique quality which, when exercised in faithfulness, becomes a special gift of the Spirit. Paul makes it clear in 1 Corinthians 12 that there are a variety of gifts. He mentions wisdom and knowledge (verse 8), faith and healing (verse 9), working of miracles, prophecy, the ability to distinguish between spirits, various tongues, and the interpretation of tongues (verse 10). He repeats nearly the same group of gifts in verses 28 to 30. Paul's recognition of the variety of gifts that were present in the Corinthian church gives us a basis for the naming of the various gifts in our own group. We certainly may add other gifts that are not mentioned in chapter 12, but are clearly gifts of the Spirit. You may want to refer to Galatians 5:22-23, where love, joy, peace, kindness, goodness, faithfulness, gentleness, and self-control are mentioned.

The Scripture passage 1 Corinthians 12-14 is a plea from Paul to recognize how various gifts complement one another. In chapter 12 he uses the image of the body, certainly well-known to his Greek readers, to indicate that each of these gifts depends upon another. He makes the same point in a different way in chapter 13, where he writes about love as a relationship between persons with various gifts. Individual capacities may be ever so wonderful in themselves, and God may use them in the most excellent ways, but the relatedness between persons who have these gifts is more profound and fundamental than any one of the gifts themselves. Prophecy, knowledge, tongues, etc., can never be so eternal as is love between the persons who exercise these gifts.

The naming of gifts in a group can be a beautiful and moving experience. It can be done after people have been together for some time and have begun to sense the special qualities and abilities of the other persons present. The debriefing instructions offer suggestions for a celebration of the gifts of the Spirit.

THE GIFTS OF THE SPIRIT A Simulation of 1 Corinthians 12 - 14

THE SITUATION

The purpose of this simulation is to gain a greater appreciation for the gifts of the Spirit and to celebrate the working of the Spirit in your own group. You are to simulate the Corinthian church in a council meeting in which they are deciding whether to permit speaking in tongues to be a part of the regular worship service. You are then to name some of the gifts of the Spirit in your group and to celebrate their presence.

TASKS OF ALL GROUPS
PRIOR TO THE SIMULATION

For purposes of the simulation there will be four groups with the following identities. Each person is to take part in one of these groups.

1. The Paulinists—those who sympathize with Paul.
2. The Petrine group—those who follow Peter.
3. The Apollos group—those who follow Apollos.
4. The Christ group—those with knowledge in Christ.

Specific tasks which each group should perform follow:

1. Each group should appoint a leader who will chair in the preparation of the simulation.
2. Each group should appoint a chronicler who will—
   a. record briefly the process of his group,
   b. record the action of the whole simulation from the point of view of his group,
   c. report at the debriefing session.
3. Each group should carefully examine the biblical tests indicated on the guidesheet for that particular group in order to establish its own identity.
4. Each group should try to come to some common understanding about the issues to be discussed at the council meeting.
5. Each group should prepare some visible and easily recognized symbol of its point of view.
6. It is important for each group to finish preparation so that the simulation will

begin on time. The coordinator should announce how much time will be allowed.

RULES OF THE SIMULATION

1. *CHAIRMAN.* Before the simulation begins, someone will be asked to serve as chairman for the council meeting. If a man is appointed chairman for the meeting, he should take the role of Stephanas, whose household were the first converts in that region (1 Corinthians 16:15). Stephanas was also one of the few persons baptized by Paul (1 Corinthians 1:16). Paul urged that the church at Corinth be subject to Stephanas and others like him (1 Corinthians 16:16). If a woman is appointed to chair, she might take the role of Priscilla (1 Corinthians 16:19; Acts 18:1-3). The person who plays Stephanas or Priscilla should be sure to read the references just cited. During the preparation prior to the simulation, Stephanas or Priscilla should be a part of the group that is sympathetic to Paul.
2. *SEATING.* The groups will be seated in a semicircular arrangement so that the chairman can preside over the meeting. The arrangement will be such that each group can caucus among themselves and at the same time take part in the whole meeting.
3. *VOTING.* Issues will be decided by vote of the meeting. Each group should have the same number of votes. In case of a tie vote, the groups should caucus and vote again.
4. *CAUCUS.* Each group is allowed to call a brief recess for the sake of conferring, during which time each of the groups is allowed to caucus with its own members.
5. *RECOGNITION.* Anyone who has been recognized by the chairman may speak, but no one will be allowed to speak more than one minute (or some other limit, if you like). Anyone who has not spoken, or who has spoken less frequently, has priority over someone who has spoken more frequently. Here the chairman will have to use his good judgment in recognizing people.
6. *ADJOURNMENT.* The council meeting

will adjourn at the appointed time whether or not a decision has been reached. The coordinator should periodically announce how much time remains.

TASKS OF THE SIMULATION

1. During the council meeting you should decide whether to permit the speaking in tongues to be a part of the regular worship service.
2. Part of the decision about speaking in tongues should include the prior decision whether or not to read to the council meeting a portion of a letter just received from Paul, namely 1 Corinthians 14.
3. If tongues are permitted, decide in what manner they should be allowed.

TASKS FOR DEBRIEFING

1. When the council meeting has terminated, everyone should stand and rearrange the seating.
2. A few minutes should be taken to allow anyone who wishes to say how he feels and what he has learned.
3. Each person may then find two other persons from his or her study group. Within this small group the spiritual gifts of each person should be identified. Allow five to ten minutes depending upon involvement.

4. Each person should then be given the opportunity to tell everyone about the gifts that he sees in the person or persons to whom he has just been speaking.
5. Each person should be encouraged to pray publicly for one other person in the group.
6. Sing "Spirit of the Living God."
7. Read 1 Corinthians 13 in unison if you have enough Bibles of the same translation.
8. Join hands and sing a hymn, such as "We Are One in the Spirit."
9. An optional closing that we have found to be very moving is to assemble in groups of six or eight and spend as much as an hour identifying each other's gifts of the Spirit. Each small group in its turn takes its place in the midst of the whole assembly, and each person becomes a spokesman for the spiritual gift of someone else in his small group. When everyone in the small group has had his gift announced by someone else in his group, then the whole assembly gathers round, laying hands upon everyone in that small group and saying, "These are the gifts of God's Spirit to you. Go and exercise them in his name." This continues until each small group has taken part. The service closes with singing as above.

1. The Paulinists

Your group represents those persons who are most sympathetic to Paul. Many of you were converted by Paul, even if you were not baptized by him. In the simulation there will be many who do not agree with Paul. Some will question his authority to be considered an apostle and teacher. It is your task to try to persuade the others that the Pauline answer is the best one, or be persuaded by them that it is not. For your study, the whole book of First Corinthians is good background reading, but especially the following passages:

1 Corinthians 1, 2, 3, 4, 12, 13, 14
Acts 9:1-19
Acts 18:1-11

BACKGROUND DATA

Paul was only one of a number of traveling evangelists and prophets who moved through the Mediterranean world. Although Paul was apparently the founder of the church at Corinth, the people came under the influence of other traveling prophets. Many in Corinth questioned whether Paul could be genuinely considered to be an apostle. Some remembered the severe persecution he had earlier carried on against the Christians. Some felt that they had a newfound freedom in Christ that released them from all their old inhibitions. These latter persons considered speaking in tongues to be a genuine mark of the Spirit of Christ, and they insisted upon speaking in tongues at the worship services. Your group believes that Paul has special understanding about these matters. You feel that he had a genuine encounter with Christ in his conversion experience. You feel that his letter should be read and followed in the church.

THE GIFTS OF THE SPIRIT A Simulation of 1 Corinthians 12 - 14

THE SITUATION

The purpose of this simulation is to gain a greater appreciation for the gifts of the Spirit and to celebrate the working of the Spirit in your own group. You are to simulate the Corinthian church in a council meeting in which they are deciding whether to permit speaking in tongues to be a part of the regular worship service. You are then to name some of the gifts of the Spirit in your group and to celebrate their presence.

TASKS OF ALL GROUPS
PRIOR TO THE SIMULATION

For purposes of the simulation there will be four groups with the following identities. Each person is to take part in one of these groups.

1. The Paulinists—those who sympathize with Paul.
2. The Petrine group—those who follow Peter.
3. The Apollos group—those who follow Apollos.
4. The Christ group—those with knowledge in Christ.

Specific tasks which each group should perform follow:

1. Each group should appoint a leader who will chair in the preparation of the simulation.
2. Each group should appoint a chronicler who will—
   a. record briefly the process of his group,
   b. record the action of the whole simulation from the point of view of his group,
   c. report at the debriefing session.
3. Each group should carefully examine the biblical tests indicated on the guidesheet for that particular group in order to establish its own identity.
4. Each group should try to come to some common understanding about the issues to be discussed at the council meeting.
5. Each group should prepare some visible and easily recognized symbol of its point of view.
6. It is important for each group to finish preparation so that the simulation will begin on time. The coordinator should announce how much time will be allowed.

RULES OF THE SIMULATION

1. *CHAIRMAN.* Before the simulation begins, someone will be asked to serve as chairman for the council meeting. If a man is appointed chairman for the meeting, he should take the role of Stephanas, whose household were the first converts in that region (1 Corinthians 16:15). Stephanas was also one of the few persons baptized by Paul (1 Corinthians 1:16). Paul urged that the church at Corinth be subject to Stephanas and others like him (1 Corinthians 16:16). If a woman is appointed to chair, she might take the role of Priscilla (1 Corinthians 16:19; Acts 18:1-3). The person who plays Stephanas or Priscilla should be sure to read the references just cited. During the preparation prior to the simulation, Stephanas or Priscilla should be a part of the group that is sympathetic to Paul.
2. *SEATING.* The groups will be seated in a semicircular arrangement so that the chairman can preside over the meeting. The arrangement will be such that each group can caucus among themselves and at the same time take part in the whole meeting.
3. *VOTING.* Issues will be decided by vote of the meeting. Each group should have the same number of votes. In case of a tie vote, the groups should caucus and vote again.
4. *CAUCUS.* Each group is allowed to call a brief recess for the sake of conferring, during which time each of the groups is allowed to caucus with its own members.
5. *RECOGNITION.* Anyone who has been recognized by the chairman may speak, but no one will be allowed to speak more than one minute (or some other limit, if you like). Anyone who has not spoken, or who has spoken less frequently, has priority over someone who has spoken more frequently. Here the chairman will have to use his good judgment in recognizing people.
6. *ADJOURNMENT.* The council meeting

will adjourn at the appointed time whether or not a decision has been reached. The coordinator should periodically announce how much time remains.

TASKS OF THE SIMULATION
1. During the council meeting you should decide whether to permit the speaking in tongues to be a part of the regular worship service.
2. Part of the decision about speaking in tongues should include the prior decision whether or not to read to the council meeting a portion of a letter just received from Paul, namely 1 Corinthians 14.
3. If tongues are permitted, decide in what manner they should be allowed.

TASKS FOR DEBRIEFING
1. When the council meeting has terminated, everyone should stand and rearrange the seating.
2. A few minutes should be taken to allow anyone who wishes to say how he feels and what he has learned.
3. Each person may then find two other persons from his or her study group. Within this small group the spiritual gifts of each person should be identified. Allow five to ten minutes depending upon involvement.
4. Each person should then be given the opportunity to tell everyone about the gifts that he sees in the person or persons to whom he has just been speaking.
5. Each person should be encouraged to pray publicly for one other person in the group.
6. Sing "Spirit of the Living God."
7. Read 1 Corinthians 13 in unison if you have enough Bibles of the same translation.
8. Join hands and sing a hymn, such as "We Are One in the Spirit."
9. An optional closing that we have found to be very moving is to assemble in groups of six or eight and spend as much as an hour identifying each other's gifts of the Spirit. Each small group in its turn takes its place in the midst of the whole assembly, and each person becomes a spokesman for the spiritual gift of someone else in his small group. When everyone in the small group has had his gift announced by someone else in his group, then the whole assembly gathers round, laying hands upon everyone in that small group and saying, "These are the gifts of God's Spirit to you. Go and exercise them in his name." This continues until each small group has taken part. The service closes with singing as above.

1. The Paulinists

Your group represents those persons who are most sympathetic to Paul. Many of you were converted by Paul, even if you were not baptized by him. In the simulation there will be many who do not agree with Paul. Some will question his authority to be considered an apostle and teacher. It is your task to try to persuade the others that the Pauline answer is the best one, or be persuaded by them that it is not. For your study, the whole book of First Corinthians is good background reading, but especially the following passages:

    1 Corinthians 1, 2, 3, 4, 12, 13, 14
    Acts 9:1-19
    Acts 18:1-11

BACKGROUND DATA
Paul was only one of a number of traveling evangelists and prophets who moved through the Mediterranean world. Although Paul was apparently the founder of the church at Corinth, the people came under the influence of other traveling prophets. Many in Corinth questioned whether Paul could be genuinely considered to be an apostle. Some remembered the severe persecution he had earlier carried on against the Christians. Some felt that they had a newfound freedom in Christ that released them from all their old inhibitions. These latter persons considered speaking in tongues to be a genuine mark of the Spirit of Christ, and they insisted upon speaking in tongues at the worship services. Your group believes that Paul has special understanding about these matters. You feel that he had a genuine encounter with Christ in his conversion experience. You feel that his letter should be read and followed in the church.

THE GIFTS OF THE SPIRIT A Simulation of 1 Corinthians 12 - 14

THE SITUATION

The purpose of this simulation is to gain a greater appreciation for the gifts of the Spirit and to celebrate the working of the Spirit in your own group. You are to simulate the Corinthian church in a council meeting in which they are deciding whether to permit speaking in tongues to be a part of the regular worship service. You are then to name some of the gifts of the Spirit in your group and to celebrate their presence.

TASKS OF ALL GROUPS
PRIOR TO THE SIMULATION

For purposes of the simulation there will be four groups with the following identities. Each person is to take part in one of these groups.

1. The Paulinists—those who sympathize with Paul.
2. The Petrine group—those who follow Peter.
3. The Apollos group—those who follow Apollos.
4. The Christ group—those with knowledge in Christ.

Specific tasks which each group should perform follow:

1. Each group should appoint a leader who will chair in the preparation of the simulation.
2. Each group should appoint a chronicler who will—
   a. record briefly the process of his group,
   b. record the action of the whole simulation from the point of view of his group,
   c. report at the debriefing session.
3. Each group should carefully examine the biblical tests indicated on the guidesheet for that particular group in order to establish its own identity.
4. Each group should try to come to some common understanding about the issues to be discussed at the council meeting.
5. Each group should prepare some visible and easily recognized symbol of its point of view.
6. It is important for each group to finish preparation so that the simulation will

begin on time. The coordinator should announce how much time will be allowed.

RULES OF THE SIMULATION

1. *CHAIRMAN*. Before the simulation begins, someone will be asked to serve as chairman for the council meeting. If a man is appointed chairman for the meeting, he should take the role of Stephanas, whose household were the first converts in that region (1 Corinthians 16:15). Stephanas was also one of the few persons baptized by Paul (1 Corinthians 1:16). Paul urged that the church at Corinth be subject to Stephanas and others like him (1 Corinthians 16:16). If a woman is appointed to chair, she might take the role of Priscilla (1 Corinthians 16:19; Acts 18:1-3). The person who plays Stephanas or Priscilla should be sure to read the references just cited. During the preparation prior to the simulation, Stephanas or Priscilla should be a part of the group that is sympathetic to Paul.
2. *SEATING*. The groups will be seated in a semicircular arrangement so that the chairman can preside over the meeting. The arrangement will be such that each group can caucus among themselves and at the same time take part in the whole meeting.
3. *VOTING*. Issues will be decided by vote of the meeting. Each group should have the same number of votes. In case of a tie vote, the groups should caucus and vote again.
4. *CAUCUS*. Each group is allowed to call a brief recess for the sake of conferring, during which time each of the groups is allowed to caucus with its own members.
5. *RECOGNITION*. Anyone who has been recognized by the chairman may speak, but no one will be allowed to speak more than one minute (or some other limit, if you like). Anyone who has not spoken, or who has spoken less frequently, has priority over someone who has spoken more frequently. Here the chairman will have to use his good judgment in recognizing people.
6. *ADJOURNMENT*. The council meeting

will adjourn at the appointed time whether or not a decision has been reached. The coordinator should periodically announce how much time remains.

TASKS OF THE SIMULATION
1. During the council meeting you should decide whether to permit the speaking in tongues to be a part of the regular worship service.
2. Part of the decision about speaking in tongues should include the prior decision whether or not to read to the council meeting a portion of a letter just received from Paul, namely 1 Corinthians 14.
3. If tongues are permitted, decide in what manner they should be allowed.

TASKS FOR DEBRIEFING
1. When the council meeting has terminated, everyone should stand and rearrange the seating.
2. A few minutes should be taken to allow anyone who wishes to say how he feels and what he has learned.
3. Each person may then find two other persons from his or her study group. Within this small group the spiritual gifts of each person should be identified. Allow five to ten

minutes depending upon involvement.
4. Each person should then be given the opportunity to tell everyone about the gifts that he sees in the person or persons to whom he has just been speaking.
5. Each person should be encouraged to pray publicly for one other person in the group.
6. Sing "Spirit of the Living God."
7. Read 1 Corinthians 13 in unison if you have enough Bibles of the same translation.
8. Join hands and sing a hymn, such as "We Are One in the Spirit."
9. An optional closing that we have found to be very moving is to assemble in groups of six or eight and spend as much as an hour identifying each other's gifts of the Spirit. Each small group in its turn takes its place in the midst of the whole assembly, and each person becomes a spokesman for the spiritual gift of someone else in his small group. When everyone in the small group has had his gift announced by someone else in his group, then the whole assembly gathers round, laying hands upon everyone in that small group and saying, "These are the gifts of God's Spirit to you. Go and exercise them in his name." This continues until each small group has taken part. The service closes with singing as above.

2. The Petrine Group

Your group represents those who sympathize with Peter and who feel that being a Christian should make a distinct difference in your life. You will find that the other groups do not necessarily agree with you, and you will need to find ways to persuade them that your point of view is true, or you may perhaps be won over to theirs. The book of First Peter is your best source, since that is most generally accepted as the work of Peter. You may also want to look at the early chapters of Acts to get Luke's interpretation of Peter. Texts that will help you are:

    1 Peter 1, 2, 3, and 4, especially 2:21-24
    Acts 2

BACKGROUND DATA
Your group takes a definite stand against touching meat that has been dedicated to idols,

against remarrying after the death of a spouse, for having order in the worship service, and for being modestly dressed in church. You follow Peter's teaching that being a Christian should make a difference. You are a holy people, a royal priesthood, a group that is dedicated to the imitation of Christ. You are considered by some to be putting unnecessary limitations upon the gospel, but you believe that commitment to Christ should make a difference in the way a person lives. Despite the fact that Luke describes Peter's preaching to be accompanied by the speaking in tongues (Acts 2), Peter himself taught orderliness in worship, as well as modesty. Speaking in tongues violates both. You are not eager to have Paul's letter read because the Corinthians may be overly influenced by it. After all, Paul cannot claim to be an apostle in the same way as Peter.

THE GIFTS OF THE SPIRIT A Simulation of 1 Corinthians 12 - 14

THE SITUATION

The purpose of this simulation is to gain a greater appreciation for the gifts of the Spirit and to celebrate the working of the Spirit in your own group. You are to simulate the Corinthian church in a council meeting in which they are deciding whether to permit speaking in tongues to be a part of the regular worship service. You are then to name some of the gifts of the Spirit in your group and to celebrate their presence.

TASKS OF ALL GROUPS
PRIOR TO THE SIMULATION

For purposes of the simulation there will be four groups with the following identities. Each person is to take part in one of these groups.

1. The Paulinists—those who sympathize with Paul.
2. The Petrine group—those who follow Peter.
3. The Apollos group—those who follow Apollos.
4. The Christ group—those with knowledge in Christ.

Specific tasks which each group should perform follow:
1. Each group should appoint a leader who will chair in the preparation of the simulation.
2. Each group should appoint a chronicler who will—
   a. record briefly the process of his group,
   b. record the action of the whole simulation from the point of view of his group,
   c. report at the debriefing session.
3. Each group should carefully examine the biblical tests indicated on the guidesheet for that particular group in order to establish its own identity.
4. Each group should try to come to some common understanding about the issues to be discussed at the council meeting.
5. Each group should prepare some visible and easily recognized symbol of its point of view.
6. It is important for each group to finish preparation so that the simulation will begin on time. The coordinator should announce how much time will be allowed.

RULES OF THE SIMULATION

1. *CHAIRMAN*. Before the simulation begins, someone will be asked to serve as chairman for the council meeting. If a man is appointed chairman for the meeting, he should take the role of Stephanas, whose household were the first converts in that region (1 Corinthians 16:15). Stephanas was also one of the few persons baptized by Paul (1 Corinthians 1:16). Paul urged that the church at Corinth be subject to Stephanas and others like him (1 Corinthians 16:16). If a woman is appointed to chair, she might take the role of Priscilla (1 Corinthians 16:19; Acts 18:1-3). The person who plays Stephanas or Priscilla should be sure to read the references just cited. During the preparation prior to the simulation, Stephanas or Priscilla should be a part of the group that is sympathetic to Paul.
2. *SEATING*. The groups will be seated in a semicircular arrangement so that the chairman can preside over the meeting. The arrangement will be such that each group can caucus among themselves and at the same time take part in the whole meeting.
3. *VOTING*. Issues will be decided by vote of the meeting. Each group should have the same number of votes. In case of a tie vote, the groups should caucus and vote again.
4. *CAUCUS*. Each group is allowed to call a brief recess for the sake of conferring, during which time each of the groups is allowed to caucus with its own members.
5. *RECOGNITION*. Anyone who has been recognized by the chairman may speak, but no one will be allowed to speak more than one minute (or some other limit, if you like). Anyone who has not spoken, or who has spoken less frequently, has priority over someone who has spoken more frequently. Here the chairman will have to use his good judgment in recognizing people.
6. *ADJOURNMENT*. The council meeting

will adjourn at the appointed time whether or not a decision has been reached. The coordinator should periodically announce how much time remains.

TASKS OF THE SIMULATION

1. During the council meeting you should decide whether to permit the speaking in tongues to be a part of the regular worship service.
2. Part of the decision about speaking in tongues should include the prior decision whether or not to read to the council meeting a portion of a letter just received from Paul, namely 1 Corinthians 14.
3. If tongues are permitted, decide in what manner they should be allowed.

TASKS FOR DEBRIEFING

1. When the council meeting has terminated, everyone should stand and rearrange the seating.
2. A few minutes should be taken to allow anyone who wishes to say how he feels and what he has learned.
3. Each person may then find two other persons from his or her study group. Within this small group the spiritual gifts of each person should be identified. Allow five to ten minutes depending upon involvement.
4. Each person should then be given the opportunity to tell everyone about the gifts that he sees in the person or persons to whom he has just been speaking.
5. Each person should be encouraged to pray publicly for one other person in the group.
6. Sing "Spirit of the Living God."
7. Read 1 Corinthians 13 in unison if you have enough Bibles of the same translation.
8. Join hands and sing a hymn, such as "We Are One in the Spirit."
9. An optional closing that we have found to be very moving is to assemble in groups of six or eight and spend as much as an hour identifying each other's gifts of the Spirit. Each small group in its turn takes its place in the midst of the whole assembly, and each person becomes a spokesman for the spiritual gift of someone else in his small group. When everyone in the small group has had his gift announced by someone else in his group, then the whole assembly gathers round, laying hands upon everyone in that small group and saying, "These are the gifts of God's Spirit to you. Go and exercise them in his name." This continues until each small group has taken part. The service closes with singing as above.

2. The Petrine Group

Your group represents those who sympathize with Peter and who feel that being a Christian should make a distinct difference in your life. You will find that the other groups do not necessarily agree with you, and you will need to find ways to persuade them that your point of view is true, or you may perhaps be won over to theirs. The book of First Peter is your best source, since that is most generally accepted as the work of Peter. You may also want to look at the early chapters of Acts to get Luke's interpretation of Peter. Texts that will help you are:

1 Peter 1, 2, 3, and 4, especially 2:21-24
Acts 2

BACKGROUND DATA

Your group takes a definite stand against touching meat that has been dedicated to idols, against remarrying after the death of a spouse, for having order in the worship service, and for being modestly dressed in church. You follow Peter's teaching that being a Christian should make a difference. You are a holy people, a royal priesthood, a group that is dedicated to the imitation of Christ. You are considered by some to be putting unnecessary limitations upon the gospel, but you believe that commitment to Christ should make a difference in the way a person lives. Despite the fact that Luke describes Peter's preaching to be accompanied by the speaking in tongues (Acts 2), Peter himself taught orderliness in worship, as well as modesty. Speaking in tongues violates both. You are not eager to have Paul's letter read because the Corinthians may be overly influenced by it. After all, Paul cannot claim to be an apostle in the same way as Peter.

THE GIFTS OF THE SPIRIT A Simulation of 1 Corinthians 12 - 14

THE SITUATION
The purpose of this simulation is to gain a greater appreciation for the gifts of the Spirit and to celebrate the working of the Spirit in your own group. You are to simulate the Corinthian church in a council meeting in which they are deciding whether to permit speaking in tongues to be a part of the regular worship service. You are then to name some of the gifts of the Spirit in your group and to celebrate their presence.

TASKS OF ALL GROUPS
PRIOR TO THE SIMULATION
For purposes of the simulation there will be four groups with the following identities. Each person is to take part in one of these groups.

1. The Paulinists—those who sympathize with Paul.
2. The Petrine group—those who follow Peter.
3. The Apollos group—those who follow Apollos.
4. The Christ group—those with knowledge in Christ.

Specific tasks which each group should perform follow:
1. Each group should appoint a leader who will chair in the preparation of the simulation.
2. Each group should appoint a chronicler who will—
   a. record briefly the process of his group,
   b. record the action of the whole simulation from the point of view of his group,
   c. report at the debriefing session.
3. Each group should carefully examine the biblical tests indicated on the guidesheet for that particular group in order to establish its own identity.
4. Each group should try to come to some common understanding about the issues to be discussed at the council meeting.
5. Each group should prepare some visible and easily recognized symbol of its point of view.
6. It is important for each group to finish preparation so that the simulation will

begin on time. The coordinator should announce how much time will be allowed.

RULES OF THE SIMULATION
1. *CHAIRMAN.* Before the simulation begins, someone will be asked to serve as chairman for the council meeting. If a man is appointed chairman for the meeting, he should take the role of Stephanas, whose household were the first converts in that region (1 Corinthians 16:15). Stephanas was also one of the few persons baptized by Paul (1 Corinthians 1:16). Paul urged that the church at Corinth be subject to Stephanas and others like him (1 Corinthians 16:16). If a woman is appointed to chair, she might take the role of Priscilla (1 Corinthians 16:19; Acts 18:1-3). The person who plays Stephanas or Priscilla should be sure to read the references just cited. During the preparation prior to the simulation, Stephanas or Priscilla should be a part of the group that is sympathetic to Paul.
2. *SEATING.* The groups will be seated in a semicircular arrangement so that the chairman can preside over the meeting. The arrangement will be such that each group can caucus among themselves and at the same time take part in the whole meeting.
3. *VOTING.* Issues will be decided by vote of the meeting. Each group should have the same number of votes. In case of a tie vote, the groups should caucus and vote again.
4. *CAUCUS.* Each group is allowed to call a brief recess for the sake of conferring, during which time each of the groups is allowed to caucus with its own members.
5. *RECOGNITION.* Anyone who has been recognized by the chairman may speak, but no one will be allowed to speak more than one minute (or some other limit, if you like). Anyone who has not spoken, or who has spoken less frequently, has priority over someone who has spoken more frequently. Here the chairman will have to use his good judgment in recognizing people.
6. *ADJOURNMENT.* The council meeting

will adjourn at the appointed time whether or not a decision has been reached. The coordinator should periodically announce how much time remains.

TASKS OF THE SIMULATION
1. During the council meeting you should decide whether to permit the speaking in tongues to be a part of the regular worship service.
2. Part of the decision about speaking in tongues should include the prior decision whether or not to read to the council meeting a portion of a letter just received from Paul, namely 1 Corinthians 14.
3. If tongues are permitted, decide in what manner they should be allowed.

TASKS FOR DEBRIEFING
1. When the council meeting has terminated, everyone should stand and rearrange the seating.
2. A few minutes should be taken to allow anyone who wishes to say how he feels and what he has learned.
3. Each person may then find two other persons from his or her study group. Within this small group the spiritual gifts of each person should be identified. Allow five to ten minutes depending upon involvement.
4. Each person should then be given the opportunity to tell everyone about the gifts that he sees in the person or persons to whom he has just been speaking.
5. Each person should be encouraged to pray publicly for one other person in the group.
6. Sing "Spirit of the Living God."
7. Read 1 Corinthians 13 in unison if you have enough Bibles of the same translation.
8. Join hands and sing a hymn, such as "We Are One in the Spirit."
9. An optional closing that we have found to be very moving is to assemble in groups of six or eight and spend as much as an hour identifying each other's gifts of the Spirit. Each small group in its turn takes its place in the midst of the whole assembly, and each person becomes a spokesman for the spiritual gift of someone else in his small group. When everyone in the small group has had his gift announced by someone else in his group, then the whole assembly gathers round, laying hands upon everyone in that small group and saying, "These are the gifts of God's Spirit to you. Go and exercise them in his name." This continues until each small group has taken part. The service closes with singing as above.

3. The Apollos Group

Your group represents those persons who are most sympathetic to Apollos. You have been deeply moved by Apollos's power and dynamic preaching. Had it not been for him, you would not now be Christians. Other groups will not necessarily agree with you, and it is your task to persuade them of your point of view, or be persuaded by them. It is possible (not historically certain) that Apollos wrote the book of Hebrews; so that book will be your main source for developing your own point of view. Texts that will help you formulate your point of view and plan your action are as follows:

Acts 18:24 - 19:7
Hebrews, especially 11, 12, 13
1 Corinthians 1, 3, 4

BACKGROUND DATA
Like Paul, Apollos was one of a number of traveling evangelists and prophets who moved through the Mediterranean world. From Acts 18, we learn that Apollos was very eloquent and that he could interpret the Scriptures with power. The "Scriptures" in the first century would have been the Law and the Prophets, but not the other books of the Old Testament, and nothing from the New Testament. Apollos's message was one of repentance and faithful endurance to the end. From Acts 19, we learn that he did not know of the baptism of the Holy Spirit when he taught at Corinth. Apollos's message, his facility with the books of Moses, and his eloquence lead many to believe that Apollos is the author of the book of Hebrews. As followers of Apollos, you are not opposed to having Paul's letter read, but you do not consider that Paul's opinion should have undue influence. Apollos would be far more helpful in these matters, but there is nothing in the book of Hebrews that applies directly to the subject of speaking in tongues. The stress on disciplined faithfulness found in Acts 19 and Hebrews leads us to believe that Apollos would not favor speaking in tongues as a part of the worship service. Therefore, you are to oppose speaking in tongues.

THE GIFTS OF THE SPIRIT A Simulation of 1 Corinthians 12 - 14

THE SITUATION

The purpose of this simulation is to gain a greater appreciation for the gifts of the Spirit and to celebrate the working of the Spirit in your own group. You are to simulate the Corinthian church in a council meeting in which they are deciding whether to permit speaking in tongues to be a part of the regular worship service. You are then to name some of the gifts of the Spirit in your group and to celebrate their presence.

TASKS OF ALL GROUPS
PRIOR TO THE SIMULATION

For purposes of the simulation there will be four groups with the following identities. Each person is to take part in one of these groups.

1. The Paulinists—those who sympathize with Paul.
2. The Petrine group—those who follow Peter.
3. The Apollos group—those who follow Apollos.
4. The Christ group—those with knowledge in Christ.

Specific tasks which each group should perform follow:

1. Each group should appoint a leader who will chair in the preparation of the simulation.
2. Each group should appoint a chronicler who will—
    a. record briefly the process of his group,
    b. record the action of the whole simulation from the point of view of his group,
    c. report at the debriefing session.
3. Each group should carefully examine the biblical tests indicated on the guidesheet for that particular group in order to establish its own identity.
4. Each group should try to come to some common understanding about the issues to be discussed at the council meeting.
5. Each group should prepare some visible and easily recognized symbol of its point of view.
6. It is important for each group to finish preparation so that the simulation will begin on time. The coordinator should announce how much time will be allowed.

RULES OF THE SIMULATION

1. *CHAIRMAN.* Before the simulation begins, someone will be asked to serve as chairman for the council meeting. If a man is appointed chairman for the meeting, he should take the role of Stephanas, whose household were the first converts in that region (1 Corinthians 16:15). Stephanas was also one of the few persons baptized by Paul (1 Corinthians 1:16). Paul urged that the church at Corinth be subject to Stephanas and others like him (1 Corinthians 16:16). If a woman is appointed to chair, she might take the role of Priscilla (1 Corinthians 16:19; Acts 18:1-3). The person who plays Stephanas or Priscilla should be sure to read the references just cited. During the preparation prior to the simulation, Stephanas or Priscilla should be a part of the group that is sympathetic to Paul.
2. *SEATING.* The groups will be seated in a semicircular arrangement so that the chairman can preside over the meeting. The arrangement will be such that each group can caucus among themselves and at the same time take part in the whole meeting.
3. *VOTING.* Issues will be decided by vote of the meeting. Each group should have the same number of votes. In case of a tie vote, the groups should caucus and vote again.
4. *CAUCUS.* Each group is allowed to call a brief recess for the sake of conferring, during which time each of the groups is allowed to caucus with its own members.
5. *RECOGNITION.* Anyone who has been recognized by the chairman may speak, but no one will be allowed to speak more than one minute (or some other limit, if you like). Anyone who has not spoken, or who has spoken less frequently, has priority over someone who has spoken more frequently. Here the chairman will have to use his good judgment in recognizing people.
6. *ADJOURNMENT.* The council meeting

will adjourn at the appointed time whether or not a decision has been reached. The coordinator should periodically announce how much time remains.

TASKS OF THE SIMULATION

1. During the council meeting you should decide whether to permit the speaking in tongues to be a part of the regular worship service.
2. Part of the decision about speaking in tongues should include the prior decision whether or not to read to the council meeting a portion of a letter just received from Paul, namely 1 Corinthians 14.
3. If tongues are permitted, decide in what manner they should be allowed.

TASKS FOR DEBRIEFING

1. When the council meeting has terminated, everyone should stand and rearrange the seating.
2. A few minutes should be taken to allow anyone who wishes to say how he feels and what he has learned.
3. Each person may then find two other persons from his or her study group. Within this small group the spiritual gifts of each person should be identified. Allow five to ten minutes depending upon involvement.

4. Each person should then be given the opportunity to tell everyone about the gifts that he sees in the person or persons to whom he has just been speaking.
5. Each person should be encouraged to pray publicly for one other person in the group.
6. Sing "Spirit of the Living God."
7. Read 1 Corinthians 13 in unison if you have enough Bibles of the same translation.
8. Join hands and sing a hymn, such as "We Are One in the Spirit."
9. An optional closing that we have found to be very moving is to assemble in groups of six or eight and spend as much as an hour identifying each other's gifts of the Spirit. Each small group in its turn takes its place in the midst of the whole assembly, and each person becomes a spokesman for the spiritual gift of someone else in his small group. When everyone in the small group has had his gift announced by someone else in his group, then the whole assembly gathers round, laying hands upon everyone in that small group and saying, "These are the gifts of God's Spirit to you. Go and exercise them in his name." This continues until each small group has taken part. The service closes with singing as above.

3. The Apollos Group

Your group represents those persons who are most sympathetic to Apollos. You have been deeply moved by Apollos's power and dynamic preaching. Had it not been for him, you would not now be Christians. Other groups will not necessarily agree with you, and it is your task to persuade them of your point of view, or be persuaded by them. It is possible (not historically certain) that Apollos wrote the book of Hebrews; so that book will be your main source for developing your own point of view. Texts that will help you formulate your point of view and plan your action are as follows:

    Acts 18:24 - 19:7
    Hebrews, especially 11, 12, 13
    1 Corinthians 1, 3, 4

BACKGROUND DATA

Like Paul, Apollos was one of a number of traveling evangelists and prophets who moved through the Mediterranean world. From Acts 18, we learn that Apollos was very eloquent and that he could interpret the Scriptures with power. The "Scriptures" in the first century would have been the Law and the Prophets, but not the other books of the Old Testament, and nothing from the New Testament. Apollos's message was one of repentance and faithful endurance to the end. From Acts 19, we learn that he did not know of the baptism of the Holy Spirit when he taught at Corinth. Apollos's message, his facility with the books of Moses, and his eloquence lead many to believe that Apollos is the author of the book of Hebrews. As followers of Apollos, you are not opposed to having Paul's letter read, but you do not consider that Paul's opinion should have undue influence. Apollos would be far more helpful in these matters, but there is nothing in the book of Hebrews that applies directly to the subject of speaking in tongues. The stress on disciplined faithfulness found in Acts 19 and Hebrews leads us to believe that Apollos would not favor speaking in tongues as a part of the worship service. Therefore, you are to oppose speaking in tongues.

THE GIFTS OF THE SPIRIT   A Simulation of 1 Corinthians 12 - 14

THE SITUATION

The purpose of this simulation is to gain a greater appreciation for the gifts of the Spirit and to celebrate the working of the Spirit in your own group. You are to simulate the Corinthian church in a council meeting in which they are deciding whether to permit speaking in tongues to be a part of the regular worship service. You are then to name some of the gifts of the Spirit in your group and to celebrate their presence.

TASKS OF ALL GROUPS
PRIOR TO THE SIMULATION

For purposes of the simulation there will be four groups with the following identities. Each person is to take part in one of these groups.

1. The Paulinists—those who sympathize with Paul.
2. The Petrine group—those who follow Peter.
3. The Apollos group—those who follow Apollos.
4. The Christ group—those with knowledge in Christ.

Specific tasks which each group should perform follow:

1. Each group should appoint a leader who will chair in the preparation of the simulation.
2. Each group should appoint a chronicler who will—
   a. record briefly the process of his group,
   b. record the action of the whole simulation from the point of view of his group,
   c. report at the debriefing session.
3. Each group should carefully examine the biblical tests indicated on the guidesheet for that particular group in order to establish its own identity.
4. Each group should try to come to some common understanding about the issues to be discussed at the council meeting.
5. Each group should prepare some visible and easily recognized symbol of its point of view.
6. It is important for each group to finish preparation so that the simulation will

begin on time. The coordinator should announce how much time will be allowed.

RULES OF THE SIMULATION

1. *CHAIRMAN.* Before the simulation begins, someone will be asked to serve as chairman for the council meeting. If a man is appointed chairman for the meeting, he should take the role of Stephanas, whose household were the first converts in that region (1 Corinthians 16:15). Stephanas was also one of the few persons baptized by Paul (1 Corinthians 1:16). Paul urged that the church at Corinth be subject to Stephanas and others like him (1 Corinthians 16:16). If a woman is appointed to chair, she might take the role of Priscilla (1 Corinthians 16:19; Acts 18:1-3). The person who plays Stephanas or Priscilla should be sure to read the references just cited. During the preparation prior to the simulation, Stephanas or Priscilla should be a part of the group that is sympathetic to Paul.
2. *SEATING.* The groups will be seated in a semicircular arrangement so that the chairman can preside over the meeting. The arrangement will be such that each group can caucus among themselves and at the same time take part in the whole meeting.
3. *VOTING.* Issues will be decided by vote of the meeting. Each group should have the same number of votes. In case of a tie vote, the groups should caucus and vote again.
4. *CAUCUS.* Each group is allowed to call a brief recess for the sake of conferring, during which time each of the groups is allowed to caucus with its own members.
5. *RECOGNITION.* Anyone who has been recognized by the chairman may speak, but no one will be allowed to speak more than one minute (or some other limit, if you like). Anyone who has not spoken, or who has spoken less frequently, has priority over someone who has spoken more frequently. Here the chairman will have to use his good judgment in recognizing people.
6. *ADJOURNMENT.* The council meeting

will adjourn at the appointed time whether or not a decision has been reached. The coordinator should periodically announce how much time remains.

TASKS OF THE SIMULATION

1. During the council meeting you should decide whether to permit the speaking in tongues to be a part of the regular worship service.
2. Part of the decision about speaking in tongues should include the prior decision whether or not to read to the council meeting a portion of a letter just received from Paul, namely 1 Corinthians 14.
3. If tongues are permitted, decide in what manner they should be allowed.

TASKS FOR DEBRIEFING

1. When the council meeting has terminated, everyone should stand and rearrange the seating.
2. A few minutes should be taken to allow anyone who wishes to say how he feels and what he has learned.
3. Each person may then find two other persons from his or her study group. Within this small group the spiritual gifts of each person should be identified. Allow five to ten minutes depending upon involvement.
4. Each person should then be given the opportunity to tell everyone about the gifts that he sees in the person or persons to whom he has just been speaking.
5. Each person should be encouraged to pray publicly for one other person in the group.
6. Sing "Spirit of the Living God."
7. Read 1 Corinthians 13 in unison if you have enough Bibles of the same translation.
8. Join hands and sing a hymn, such as "We Are One in the Spirit."
9. An optional closing that we have found to be very moving is to assemble in groups of six or eight and spend as much as an hour identifying each other's gifts of the Spirit. Each small group in its turn takes its place in the midst of the whole assembly, and each person becomes a spokesman for the spiritual gift of someone else in his small group. When everyone in the small group has had his gift announced by someone else in his group, then the whole assembly gathers round, laying hands upon everyone in that small group and saying, "These are the gifts of God's Spirit to you. Go and exercise them in his name." This continues until each small group has taken part. The service closes with singing as above.

4. The Christ Group

Your group represents those who have become "free" in Jesus Christ. You know that you are no longer bound by the ancient religious laws and you know the ecstasy of being born again by the Spirit of Christ. You speak in tongues and feel that such freedom is the center of worship. Many will disagree with you, and it is your task to persuade them that you are right, or you might be persuaded by them. You can find background passages describing your point of view scattered throughout the book of First Corinthians. You can also appeal to the doctrine of the Spirit in Acts. Helpful passages are the following:

      1 Corinthians 1, 2, 3, 4
      1 Corinthians 12, 13, 14
      Acts 2:1-13

BACKGROUND DATA

The Christ group consisted of those who had been released in Jesus Christ, who had a new knowledge and understanding of their freedom. They openly ate meat dedicated to idols, because they knew that there was no reality to an idol (1 Corinthians 8). They dressed as they pleased because they knew that dress neither makes nor breaks one's faith (1 Corinthians 11). They spoke in tongues because they knew the ecstasy of faith and the depth of freedom that comes with such speech (1 Corinthians 14). Much of what Paul wrote in the letter to the Corinthians is directed to the Christ group. As members of the Christ group, you do not favor the reading of Paul's letter. You do not feel that he has wisdom on such matters as speaking in tongues, and you do not believe that his claim to be an apostle is better founded than your own experience of freedom in Christ. Furthermore, you feel strongly that worship must include the freedom to speak in tongues. Not to do so would limit the Spirit of Christ beyond recognition.

THE GIFTS OF THE SPIRIT A Simulation of 1 Corinthians 12 - 14

THE SITUATION

The purpose of this simulation is to gain a greater appreciation for the gifts of the Spirit and to celebrate the working of the Spirit in your own group. You are to simulate the Corinthian church in a council meeting in which they are deciding whether to permit speaking in tongues to be a part of the regular worship service. You are then to name some of the gifts of the Spirit in your group and to celebrate their presence.

TASKS OF ALL GROUPS
PRIOR TO THE SIMULATION

For purposes of the simulation there will be four groups with the following identities. Each person is to take part in one of these groups.

1. The Paulinists—those who sympathize with Paul.
2. The Petrine group—those who follow Peter.
3. The Apollos group—those who follow Apollos.
4. The Christ group—those with knowledge in Christ.

Specific tasks which each group should perform follow:

1. Each group should appoint a leader who will chair in the preparation of the simulation.
2. Each group should appoint a chronicler who will—
   a. record briefly the process of his group,
   b. record the action of the whole simulation from the point of view of his group,
   c. report at the debriefing session.
3. Each group should carefully examine the biblical tests indicated on the guidesheet for that particular group in order to establish its own identity.
4. Each group should try to come to some common understanding about the issues to be discussed at the council meeting.
5. Each group should prepare some visible and easily recognized symbol of its point of view.
6. It is important for each group to finish preparation so that the simulation will

begin on time. The coordinator should announce how much time will be allowed.

RULES OF THE SIMULATION

1. *CHAIRMAN*. Before the simulation begins, someone will be asked to serve as chairman for the council meeting. If a man is appointed chairman for the meeting, he should take the role of Stephanas, whose household were the first converts in that region (1 Corinthians 16:15). Stephanas was also one of the few persons baptized by Paul (1 Corinthians 1:16). Paul urged that the church at Corinth be subject to Stephanas and others like him (1 Corinthians 16:16). If a woman is appointed to chair, she might take the role of Priscilla (1 Corinthians 16:19; Acts 18:1-3). The person who plays Stephanas or Priscilla should be sure to read the references just cited. During the preparation prior to the simulation, Stephanas or Priscilla should be a part of the group that is sympathetic to Paul.
2. *SEATING*. The groups will be seated in a semicircular arrangement so that the chairman can preside over the meeting. The arrangement will be such that each group can caucus among themselves and at the same time take part in the whole meeting.
3. *VOTING*. Issues will be decided by vote of the meeting. Each group should have the same number of votes. In case of a tie vote, the groups should caucus and vote again.
4. *CAUCUS*. Each group is allowed to call a brief recess for the sake of conferring, during which time each of the groups is allowed to caucus with its own members.
5. *RECOGNITION*. Anyone who has been recognized by the chairman may speak, but no one will be allowed to speak more than one minute (or some other limit, if you like). Anyone who has not spoken, or who has spoken less frequently, has priority over someone who has spoken more frequently. Here the chairman will have to use his good judgment in recognizing people.
6. *ADJOURNMENT*. The council meeting

will adjourn at the appointed time whether or not a decision has been reached. The coordinator should periodically announce how much time remains.

TASKS OF THE SIMULATION

1. During the council meeting you should decide whether to permit the speaking in tongues to be a part of the regular worship service.
2. Part of the decision about speaking in tongues should include the prior decision whether or not to read to the council meeting a portion of a letter just received from Paul, namely 1 Corinthians 14.
3. If tongues are permitted, decide in what manner they should be allowed.

TASKS FOR DEBRIEFING

1. When the council meeting has terminated, everyone should stand and rearrange the seating.
2. A few minutes should be taken to allow anyone who wishes to say how he feels and what he has learned.
3. Each person may then find two other persons from his or her study group. Within this small group the spiritual gifts of each person should be identified. Allow five to ten minutes depending upon involvement.

4. Each person should then be given the opportunity to tell everyone about the gifts that he sees in the person or persons to whom he has just been speaking.
5. Each person should be encouraged to pray publicly for one other person in the group.
6. Sing "Spirit of the Living God."
7. Read 1 Corinthians 13 in unison if you have enough Bibles of the same translation.
8. Join hands and sing a hymn, such as "We Are One in the Spirit."
9. An optional closing that we have found to be very moving is to assemble in groups of six or eight and spend as much as an hour identifying each other's gifts of the Spirit. Each small group in its turn takes its place in the midst of the whole assembly, and each person becomes a spokesman for the spiritual gift of someone else in his small group. When everyone in the small group has had his gift announced by someone else in his group, then the whole assembly gathers round, laying hands upon everyone in that small group and saying, "These are the gifts of God's Spirit to you. Go and exercise them in his name." This continues until each small group has taken part. The service closes with singing as above.

4. The Christ Group

Your group represents those who have become "free" in Jesus Christ. You know that you are no longer bound by the ancient religious laws and you know the ecstasy of being born again by the Spirit of Christ. You speak in tongues and feel that such freedom is the center of worship. Many will disagree with you, and it is your task to persuade them that you are right, or you might be persuaded by them. You can find background passages describing your point of view scattered throughout the book of First Corinthians. You can also appeal to the doctrine of the Spirit in Acts. Helpful passages are the following:

> 1 Corinthians 1, 2, 3, 4
> 1 Corinthians 12, 13, 14
> Acts 2:1-13

BACKGROUND DATA

The Christ group consisted of those who had been released in Jesus Christ, who had a new knowledge and understanding of their freedom. They openly ate meat dedicated to idols, because they knew that there was no reality to an idol (1 Corinthians 8). They dressed as they pleased because they knew that dress neither makes nor breaks one's faith (1 Corinthians 11). They spoke in tongues because they knew the ecstasy of faith and the depth of freedom that comes with such speech (1 Corinthians 14). Much of what Paul wrote in the letter to the Corinthians is directed to the Christ group. As members of the Christ group, you do not favor the reading of Paul's letter. You do not feel that he has wisdom on such matters as speaking in tongues, and you do not believe that his claim to be an apostle is better founded than your own experience of freedom in Christ. Furthermore, you feel strongly that worship must include the freedom to speak in tongues. Not to do so would limit the Spirit of Christ beyond recognition.

14. THE UPPER ROOM

A Simulation Based upon the Accounts of the Lord's Supper

INSTRUCTIONS TO THE COORDINATOR

Preparation

Read through the whole simulation to get a good understanding of its purpose and direction. If you expect a large number of persons to take part, then you ought to involve some "leaders" in a discussion of goals prior to the simulation itself. You and they should read through the chapter "How to Conduct a Biblical Simulation" if you have not already done so.

Schedule

This simulation can very profitably fill a whole day or it can be done in an hour or two. The time can be continuous or split up over several different sessions (see chapter 3). The following are possible options:

	One Hour	Two Hours	Six Hours
Introduction	10 min.	15 min.	¼ hr.
Small groups	20 min.	45 min.	2¾ hrs.
Simulation	15 min.	30 min.	2 hrs.
Debriefing	15 min.	30 min.	1 hr.

If only a single hour is available, decide only what parts of the upper-room account are going to be included in your service. We have found it helpful to focus only upon whether or not to have a meal, and if so, what will be served. With two hours of time available you may also include still other parts of the service, e.g., the bread and the cup and how they will be handled. With six hours you can make all the decisions. If you are breaking the time into three sessions, begin with the introduction and small groups. During the second session you should begin by giving the small groups a few minutes for preparation. Then move to the council meeting, deciding only upon what parts of the

service to include, and concluding with a few minutes of debriefing. During the third session begin by giving the small groups a few minutes and then proceed to work together on the order of the service in the council meeting. Allow ample time for debriefing. An additional session will be needed if you carry out the Communion service that you have planned.

Grouping

You will need two or three persons working in each small group or a total of eight to twelve persons. From the following list you can decide upon the number of small groups and the number of representatives from each small group to be seated at the table during the simulation:

Persons present	Number of small groups	Representatives at the table
8- 48	4	3 per group
49- 96	8	2 per group
97-144	16	1 per group

More than one hundred persons may require two simultaneous simulations. If you hope to conclude with the Communion service which you have planned, then we suggest that everyone be included in the same simulation even though the group be very large.

Space and Equipment

Your preparation should include obtaining each of the following items (see chapter 3 for fuller explanation): a large room, small rooms, chairs, tables, Bibles, study aids, paper, pencils, materials for symbols (optional), and refreshments. Other special materials and resources will help this simulation:

1. A sufficient number of Bibles is important, and various translations will be helpful.

2. Concordances, Bible dictionaries, and commentaries must be available.
3. A harmony of the Gospels will be very helpful.
4. Special interesting touches can include veils for women and draped cloth or choir robes to represent clothing that was worn in the second century.

Facilitation

Refer to the suggestions in chapter 4 on how to introduce a simulation. There you will find an explanation of the following items: what a biblical simulation is, how to participate, schedule, small-group tasks, materials, and division into groups. In your introduction you will also want to include an explanation of the purpose and tasks of this particular simulation. Allow people time to ask questions. Appoint someone to serve as chairman of the council meeting.

The simulation is designed to give people a better understanding of the events in the upper room just before Jesus' betrayal. It brings worship and simulation together. The most effective way to use this simulation is actually to conduct the service of Breaking of Bread that the group has planned. You may need to allow additional time to fill out the outline of the service that results from the council meeting. Perhaps the study groups can be assigned to develop one or another parts of the order of service. In any event you should decide whether you are actually going to hold the ceremony and announce the plan during your introductory remarks.

During the council meeting focus first of all upon what events from the upper room are to be included. This may be a difficult enough problem that you may not get beyond one item, e.g., the meal. If the group reaches agreement, then it should move on to the order of the service. Privately you may want to encourage some in the Johannine group to question whether there should be any order to the service at all. They may argue that such structures destroy the Spirit. If you have enough time, the group can try to agree upon a prayer of anticipation to be used at the service.

Debriefing

As coordinator you should conduct the debriefing session. Here is a list of suggestions to be followed:
1. Rearrange the chairs so that everyone is aware that all have dropped their roles.
2. In groups of four discuss what you have learned. A different group might take each of the following questions. Why are there differences in the New Testament accounts? Can these differences be reconciled? Do you prefer the name Breaking of Bread, Lord's Supper, or Eucharist? How ought the church celebrate the events in the upper room? How free are we to substitute new forms for the old? How do you feel now about this experience? What did you learn? You may have other and much better questions of your own.
3. Ask volunteers to share their observations with the whole group.
4. Ask the chroniclers to share their observations.
5. Try to summarize what you have been hearing.

This simulation is designed to conclude with the actual ceremony of Breaking of Bread. Perhaps a committee of representatives from each study group could agree upon an order of service, and the different study groups could then be assigned to prepare one part or another of the ceremony. It may take many hours to make the preparation, depending upon how brief or elaborate your service is. The group members ought then to conduct the service that they have planned.

THE UPPER ROOM A Simulation Based upon the Accounts of the Lord's Supper

THE SITUATION

The purpose of this simulation is to gain insight into the celebration which is variously called the Lord's Supper, the Breaking of Bread, and the Eucharist. You are to take the part of Christians from across the Roman Empire, gathering in Antioch. The time is near the end of the second century, say A.D. 190. You are gathered together to plan a celebration in which you reenact the events of the upper room on the evening that Jesus was betrayed. You do not simply want to mimic those events; rather you want to catch up their true meaning and significance.

Many of you have come at the special invitation of the church at Antioch. You are not acquainted with some of the other believers present, and you soon find that your beliefs are based upon different accounts of the Gospels. Some of you have been using one Gospel account; some, another; and some, the letters of Paul. As you attempt to catch the significance of the events of the upper room, you want above all to be true to the version of the Gospel that has been your guide for many years. The setting is a council meeting in which you are voting on what shall be included in your upper-room ceremony.

For purposes of the simulation you must remember that you may refer to only the Gospel with which you are acquainted. Much before the year A.D. 200 the use of the Four Gospels was well established in the churches, even though the canon of the New Testament was not completed until late in the fourth century. We will assume that each group has been somewhat isolated and is not familiar with any Gospel other than its own. You may refer to the Old Testament as we know it, which was likely well established by the time of the Council of Jamnia, *ca.* A.D. 90. The letters of Paul were also well established by A.D. 140, but it is possible that some isolated groups had not heard of them. You represent an assembly in Antioch of several groups who had been so isolated.

Your decision about how to celebrate the events of the upper room will probably focus first of all upon the meal. You will need to decide whether the meal is to follow the tradition of the Passover. A critical question will be what to serve, e.g., lamb or fish? You may then consider whether to portray the disciples' concern about who had betrayed Jesus, a period of what might be called self-examination. All of the accounts refer to the Old Testament, the bread and the cup. You should decide which to include and in what manner. Another issue is Jesus' reference to what is to come. Shall you include this "anticipation"? Should you include a hymn?

TASKS OF ALL GROUPS
PRIOR TO THE SIMULATION

For the purposes of the simulation there will be four groups with the following identities:

The Markan group—those who have only the Gospels of Matthew and Mark;

The Lukan group—those who have only the Gospel of Luke and Acts;

The Johannine group—those who have only the Gospel of John;

The Paulinists—those who have only the letters of Paul.

Following are specific tasks which each group should perform:

1. Each group should appoint a leader who will chair in the preparation of the simulation.

2. Each group should appoint a chronicler who will—

   a. record briefly the process of his group,

   b. record the action of the whole simulation from the point of view of his group,

   c. report at the debriefing session.

3. Each group should carefully examine the biblical texts indicated on the guidesheet for that group to establish its own identity.

4. Each group should come to some common understanding about issues to be discussed at the council meeting.

5. Each group should prepare some visible symbol of its point of view.

6. Each group should consider how it may persuade others of its own point of view.

RULES OF THE SIMULATION

1. Before the simulation begins, someone should be asked to serve as chairman.
2. The seating arrangement should be such that members of each group can caucus among themselves and at the same time take part in the whole meeting.
3. Issues will be decided by majority vote. In case of a tie vote the groups are to caucus and vote again. The chairperson may not break a vote.
4. Each group is to have an equal number of votes (e.g., two). Each group will decide which of its members may cast their votes.
5. Each group may caucus prior to any vote. The chair should grant a brief recess for caucusing upon request.
6. The council meeting will adjourn at the appointed time whether or not a decision has been reached.

TASKS OF THE SIMULATION

1. The council is to decide what parts to include in the upper-room ceremony. For example, will the ceremony include a meal, self-examination, Scripture, the bread, the cup, anticipation, and/or a hymn?
2. The council is to decide how each part of the ceremony shall be conducted. For example, if there should be a meal, will it consist of lamb or fish?
3. The council should decide in what order the parts of the ceremony should come. For example, should the cup precede or follow the breaking of bread?

TASKS FOR DEBRIEFING

1. Rearrange the room to symbolize the termination of the simulation.
2. Let everyone, including each chronicler, share his observations with the whole group.
3. Let everyone express his feelings about what happened.
4. Discuss whether you can carry out the ceremony together. Perhaps you can conclude the debriefing with the service you have just planned.

1. The Markan Group

You represent a group of early Christians who have only the Gospels of Matthew and Mark to work from. Your understanding of the events of the upper room is taken from those accounts, and you are not aware of other Gospel accounts. You will find that persons in other groups do not always agree with you, and it is your task to persuade them that your view is correct, or be persuaded by them. In preparing for the council meeting, consult the following sources:

Mark 14:17-26
Matthew 26:20-30

BACKGROUND DATA

Mark is generally considered to be the first of the Four Gospels to be written, and therefore it should carry great authority in deciding what may have actually happened during the Last Supper. In both Matthew and Mark the bread is broken and the wine is taken as a memorial or remembrance of Jesus's broken body and his shed blood. These passages point to an early tradition in which faith was celebrated by a common meal in memory of those events that occurred during the passion of Jesus. The heart of the passion week was the Last Supper, the taking of bread and wine, the memory of what had happened. Both Matthew and Mark are set within the framework of the Passover meal with its lamb and unleavened bread. The Passover was itself a memorial of what God had done to release Israel from Egyptian slavery. Some of the occurrences described in Mark 14 are the meal (verse 18), self-examination (verse 19), Scripture (verse 21), bread (verse 22), cup (verses 23, 24), anticipation (verse 25), and the hymn (verse 26).

THE UPPER ROOM A Simulation Based upon the Accounts of the Lord's Supper

THE SITUATION

The purpose of this simulation is to gain insight into the celebration which is variously called the Lord's Supper, the Breaking of Bread, and the Eucharist. You are to take the part of Christians from across the Roman Empire, gathering in Antioch. The time is near the end of the second century, say A.D. 190. You are gathered together to plan a celebration in which you reenact the events of the upper room on the evening that Jesus was betrayed. You do not simply want to mimic those events; rather you want to catch up their true meaning and significance.

Many of you have come at the special invitation of the church at Antioch. You are not acquainted with some of the other believers present, and you soon find that your beliefs are based upon different accounts of the Gospels. Some of you have been using one Gospel account; some, another; and some, the letters of Paul. As you attempt to catch the significance of the events of the upper room, you want above all to be true to the version of the Gospel that has been your guide for many years. The setting is a council meeting in which you are voting on what shall be included in your upper-room ceremony.

For purposes of the simulation you must remember that you may refer to only the Gospel with which you are acquainted. Much before the year A.D. 200 the use of the Four Gospels was well established in the churches, even though the canon of the New Testament was not completed until late in the fourth century. We will assume that each group has been somewhat isolated and is not familiar with any Gospel other than its own. You may refer to the Old Testament as we know it, which was likely well established by the time of the Council of Jamnia, ca. A.D. 90. The letters of Paul were also well established by A.D. 140, but it is possible that some isolated groups had not heard of them. You represent an assembly in Antioch of several groups who had been so isolated.

Your decision about how to celebrate the events of the upper room will probably focus first of all upon the meal. You will need to decide whether the meal is to follow the tradition of the Passover. A critical question will be what to serve, e.g., lamb or fish? You may then consider whether to portray the disciples' concern about who had betrayed Jesus, a period of what might be called self-examination. All of the accounts refer to the Old Testament, the bread and the cup. You should decide which to include and in what manner. Another issue is Jesus' reference to what is to come. Shall you include this "anticipation"? Should you include a hymn?

TASKS OF ALL GROUPS
PRIOR TO THE SIMULATION

For the purposes of the simulation there will be four groups with the following identities:

The Markan group—those who have only the Gospels of Matthew and Mark;

The Lukan group—those who have only the Gospel of Luke and Acts;

The Johannine group—those who have only the Gospel of John;

The Paulinists—those who have only the letters of Paul.

Following are specific tasks which each group should perform:

1. Each group should appoint a leader who will chair in the preparation of the simulation.
2. Each group should appoint a chronicler who will—
   a. record briefly the process of his group,
   b. record the action of the whole simulation from the point of view of his group,
   c. report at the debriefing session.
3. Each group should carefully examine the biblical texts indicated on the guidesheet for that group to establish its own identity.
4. Each group should come to some common understanding about issues to be discussed at the council meeting.
5. Each group should prepare some visible symbol of its point of view.
6. Each group should consider how it may persuade others of its own point of view.

RULES OF THE SIMULATION

1. Before the simulation begins, someone should be asked to serve as chairman.
2. The seating arrangement should be such that members of each group can caucus among themselves and at the same time take part in the whole meeting.
3. Issues will be decided by majority vote. In case of a tie vote the groups are to caucus and vote again. The chairperson may not break a vote.
4. Each group is to have an equal number of votes (e.g., two). Each group will decide which of its members may cast their votes.
5. Each group may caucus prior to any vote. The chair should grant a brief recess for caucusing upon request.
6. The council meeting will adjourn at the appointed time whether or not a decision has been reached.

TASKS OF THE SIMULATION

1. The council is to decide what parts to include in the upper-room ceremony. For example, will the ceremony include a meal, self-examination, Scripture, the bread, the cup, anticipation, and/or a hymn?
2. The council is to decide how each part of the ceremony shall be conducted. For example, if there should be a meal, will it consist of lamb or fish?
3. The council should decide in what order the parts of the ceremony should come. For example, should the cup precede or follow the breaking of bread?

TASKS FOR DEBRIEFING

1. Rearrange the room to symbolize the termination of the simulation.
2. Let everyone, including each chronicler, share his observations with the whole group.
3. Let everyone express his feelings about what happened.
4. Discuss whether you can carry out the ceremony together. Perhaps you can conclude the debriefing with the service you have just planned.

1. The Markan Group

You represent a group of early Christians who have only the Gospels of Matthew and Mark to work from. Your understanding of the events of the upper room is taken from those accounts, and you are not aware of other Gospel accounts. You will find that persons in other groups do not always agree with you, and it is your task to persuade them that your view is correct, or be persuaded by them. In preparing for the council meeting, consult the following sources:

Mark 14:17-26
Matthew 26:20-30

BACKGROUND DATA

Mark is generally considered to be the first of the Four Gospels to be written, and therefore it should carry great authority in deciding what may have actually happened during the Last Supper. In both Matthew and Mark the bread is broken and the wine is taken as a memorial or remembrance of Jesus's broken body and his shed blood. These passages point to an early tradition in which faith was celebrated by a common meal in memory of those events that occurred during the passion of Jesus. The heart of the passion week was the Last Supper, the taking of bread and wine, the memory of what had happened. Both Matthew and Mark are set within the framework of the Passover meal with its lamb and unleavened bread. The Passover was itself a memorial of what God had done to release Israel from Egyptian slavery. Some of the occurrences described in Mark 14 are the meal (verse 18), self-examination (verse 19), Scripture (verse 21), bread (verse 22), cup (verses 23, 24), anticipation (verse 25), and the hymn (verse 26).

THE UPPER ROOM A Simulation Based upon the Accounts of the Lord's Supper

THE SITUATION

The purpose of this simulation is to gain insight into the celebration which is variously called the Lord's Supper, the Breaking of Bread, and the Eucharist. You are to take the part of Christians from across the Roman Empire, gathering in Antioch. The time is near the end of the second century, say A.D. 190. You are gathered together to plan a celebration in which you reenact the events of the upper room on the evening that Jesus was betrayed. You do not simply want to mimic those events; rather you want to catch up their true meaning and significance.

Many of you have come at the special invitation of the church at Antioch. You are not acquainted with some of the other believers present, and you soon find that your beliefs are based upon different accounts of the Gospels. Some of you have been using one Gospel account; some, another; and some, the letters of Paul. As you attempt to catch the significance of the events of the upper room, you want above all to be true to the version of the Gospel that has been your guide for many years. The setting is a council meeting in which you are voting on what shall be included in your upper-room ceremony.

For purposes of the simulation you must remember that you may refer to only the Gospel with which you are acquainted. Much before the year A.D. 200 the use of the Four Gospels was well established in the churches, even though the canon of the New Testament was not completed until late in the fourth century. We will assume that each group has been somewhat isolated and is not familiar with any Gospel other than its own. You may refer to the Old Testament as we know it, which was likely well established by the time of the Council of Jamnia, ca. A.D. 90. The letters of Paul were also well established by A.D. 140, but it is possible that some isolated groups had not heard of them. You represent an assembly in Antioch of several groups who had been so isolated.

Your decision about how to celebrate the events of the upper room will probably focus first of all upon the meal. You will need to decide whether the meal is to follow the tradition of the Passover. A critical question will be what to serve, e.g., lamb or fish? You may then consider whether to portray the disciples' concern about who had betrayed Jesus, a period of what might be called self-examination. All of the accounts refer to the Old Testament, the bread and the cup. You should decide which to include and in what manner. Another issue is Jesus' reference to what is to come. Shall you include this "anticipation"? Should you include a hymn?

TASKS OF ALL GROUPS
PRIOR TO THE SIMULATION

For the purposes of the simulation there will be four groups with the following identities:

The Markan group—those who have only the Gospels of Matthew and Mark;

The Lukan group—those who have only the Gospel of Luke and Acts;

The Johannine group—those who have only the Gospel of John;

The Paulinists—those who have only the letters of Paul.

Following are specific tasks which each group should perform:

1. Each group should appoint a leader who will chair in the preparation of the simulation.

2. Each group should appoint a chronicler who will—
   a. record briefly the process of his group,
   b. record the action of the whole simulation from the point of view of his group,
   c. report at the debriefing session.

3. Each group should carefully examine the biblical texts indicated on the guidesheet for that group to establish its own identity.

4. Each group should come to some common understanding about issues to be discussed at the council meeting.

5. Each group should prepare some visible symbol of its point of view.

6. Each group should consider how it may persuade others of its own point of view.

195

RULES OF THE SIMULATION

1. Before the simulation begins, someone should be asked to serve as chairman.
2. The seating arrangement should be such that members of each group can caucus among themselves and at the same time take part in the whole meeting.
3. Issues will be decided by majority vote. In case of a tie vote the groups are to caucus and vote again. The chairperson may not break a vote.
4. Each group is to have an equal number of votes (e.g., two). Each group will decide which of its members may cast their votes.
5. Each group may caucus prior to any vote. The chair should grant a brief recess for caucusing upon request.
6. The council meeting will adjourn at the appointed time whether or not a decision has been reached.

TASKS OF THE SIMULATION

1. The council is to decide what parts to include in the upper-room ceremony. For example, will the ceremony include a meal, self-examination, Scripture, the bread, the cup, anticipation, and/or a hymn?
2. The council is to decide how each part of the ceremony shall be conducted. For example, if there should be a meal, will it consist of lamb or fish?
3. The council should decide in what order the parts of the ceremony should come. For example, should the cup precede or follow the breaking of bread?

TASKS FOR DEBRIEFING

1. Rearrange the room to symbolize the termination of the simulation.
2. Let everyone, including each chronicler, share his observations with the whole group.
3. Let everyone express his feelings about what happened.
4. Discuss whether you can carry out the ceremony together. Perhaps you can conclude the debriefing with the service you have just planned.

2. The Lukan Group

You represent a group of early Christians who have only the Gospel of Luke and the book of Acts to work from. Your understanding of the events of the upper room is taken from those accounts, and you are not aware of any other account. You will find that persons from other groups do not always agree with you, and it is your task to persuade them that your view is correct, or be persuaded by them. In preparing for the council meeting, consult the following sources:

> Luke 22:14-38
> Luke 24:13-35, note 28-35
> Luke 9:10-17
> Acts 2:42-46

BACKGROUND DATA

Luke considers the "breaking of bread" a celebration of the unity that Christ is bringing into the world. It is an anticipation of the final unity that God is bringing among all people in Jesus Christ. The meal is not so much a sorrowful memory as a hopeful expectancy of what is to come. It opens people's eyes to the forward expansion of the kingdom of God. It is for Luke clearly a "resurrection meal."

The feeding of the five thousand, Luke 9:10-17, was also an anticipation of the coming kingdom, a resurrection meal. As members of the early church you see in it Jesus conducting a service of Breaking of Bread. This means that the meal might include fish rather than lamb. The account in Luke 22 includes a meal (verse 15), anticipation (verses 16, 30), cup (verses 17, 18), bread (verse 19), betrayal (verse 21), self-examination (verses 23, 33), instruction (verses 26, 27), and Scripture (verse 37). The resurrection meal has the cup before the breaking of bread. The words of interpretation look forward (verse 18) rather than backward; thus the mention of the kingdom rather than of blood.

THE UPPER ROOM A Simulation Based upon the Accounts of the Lord's Supper

THE SITUATION

The purpose of this simulation is to gain insight into the celebration which is variously called the Lord's Supper, the Breaking of Bread, and the Eucharist. You are to take the part of Christians from across the Roman Empire, gathering in Antioch. The time is near the end of the second century, say A.D. 190. You are gathered together to plan a celebration in which you reenact the events of the upper room on the evening that Jesus was betrayed. You do not simply want to mimic those events; rather you want to catch up their true meaning and significance.

Many of you have come at the special invitation of the church at Antioch. You are not acquainted with some of the other believers present, and you soon find that your beliefs are based upon different accounts of the Gospels. Some of you have been using one Gospel account; some, another; and some, the letters of Paul. As you attempt to catch the significance of the events of the upper room, you want above all to be true to the version of the Gospel that has been your guide for many years. The setting is a council meeting in which you are voting on what shall be included in your upper-room ceremony.

For purposes of the simulation you must remember that you may refer to only the Gospel with which you are acquainted. Much before the year A.D. 200 the use of the Four Gospels was well established in the churches, even though the canon of the New Testament was not completed until late in the fourth century. We will assume that each group has been somewhat isolated and is not familiar with any Gospel other than its own. You may refer to the Old Testament as we know it, which was likely well established by the time of the Council of Jamnia, ca. A.D. 90. The letters of Paul were also well established by A.D. 140, but it is possible that some isolated groups had not heard of them. You represent an assembly in Antioch of several groups who had been so isolated.

Your decision about how to celebrate the events of the upper room will probably focus first of all upon the meal. You will need to decide whether the meal is to follow the tradition of the Passover. A critical question will be what to serve, e.g., lamb or fish? You may then consider whether to portray the disciples' concern about who had betrayed Jesus, a period of what might be called self-examination. All of the accounts refer to the Old Testament, the bread and the cup. You should decide which to include and in what manner. Another issue is Jesus' reference to what is to come. Shall you include this "anticipation"? Should you include a hymn?

TASKS OF ALL GROUPS
PRIOR TO THE SIMULATION

For the purposes of the simulation there will be four groups with the following identities:

The Markan group—those who have only the Gospels of Matthew and Mark;

The Lukan group—those who have only the Gospel of Luke and Acts;

The Johannine group—those who have only the Gospel of John;

The Paulinists—those who have only the letters of Paul.

Following are specific tasks which each group should perform:

1. Each group should appoint a leader who will chair in the preparation of the simulation.
2. Each group should appoint a chronicler who will—
   a. record briefly the process of his group,
   b. record the action of the whole simulation from the point of view of his group,
   c. report at the debriefing session.
3. Each group should carefully examine the biblical texts indicated on the guidesheet for that group to establish its own identity.
4. Each group should come to some common understanding about issues to be discussed at the council meeting.
5. Each group should prepare some visible symbol of its point of view.
6. Each group should consider how it may persuade others of its own point of view.

RULES OF THE SIMULATION

1. Before the simulation begins, someone should be asked to serve as chairman.
2. The seating arrangement should be such that members of each group can caucus among themselves and at the same time take part in the whole meeting.
3. Issues will be decided by majority vote. In case of a tie vote the groups are to caucus and vote again. The chairperson may not break a vote.
4. Each group is to have an equal number of votes (e.g., two). Each group will decide which of its members may cast their votes.
5. Each group may caucus prior to any vote. The chair should grant a brief recess for caucusing upon request.
6. The council meeting will adjourn at the appointed time whether or not a decision has been reached.

TASKS OF THE SIMULATION

1. The council is to decide what parts to include in the upper-room ceremony. For example, will the ceremony include a meal, self-examination, Scripture, the bread, the cup, anticipation, and/or a hymn?
2. The council is to decide how each part of the ceremony shall be conducted. For example, if there should be a meal, will it consist of lamb or fish?
3. The council should decide in what order the parts of the ceremony should come. For example, should the cup precede or follow the breaking of bread?

TASKS FOR DEBRIEFING

1. Rearrange the room to symbolize the termination of the simulation.
2. Let everyone, including each chronicler, share his observations with the whole group.
3. Let everyone express his feelings about what happened.
4. Discuss whether you can carry out the ceremony together. Perhaps you can conclude the debriefing with the service you have just planned.

2. The Lukan Group

You represent a group of early Christians who have only the Gospel of Luke and the book of Acts to work from. Your understanding of the events of the upper room is taken from those accounts, and you are not aware of any other account. You will find that persons from other groups do not always agree with you, and it is your task to persuade them that your view is correct, or be persuaded by them. In preparing for the council meeting, consult the following sources:

> Luke 22:14-38
> Luke 24:13-35, note 28-35
> Luke 9:10-17
> Acts 2:42-46

BACKGROUND DATA

Luke considers the "breaking of bread" a celebration of the unity that Christ is bringing into the world. It is an anticipation of the final unity that God is bringing among all people in Jesus Christ. The meal is not so much a sorrowful memory as a hopeful expectancy of what is to come. It opens people's eyes to the forward expansion of the kingdom of God. It is for Luke clearly a "resurrection meal."

The feeding of the five thousand, Luke 9:10-17, was also an anticipation of the coming kingdom, a resurrection meal. As members of the early church you see in it Jesus conducting a service of Breaking of Bread. This means that the meal might include fish rather than lamb. The account in Luke 22 includes a meal (verse 15), anticipation (verses 16, 30), cup (verses 17, 18), bread (verse 19), betrayal (verse 21), self-examination (verses 23, 33), instruction (verses 26, 27), and Scripture (verse 37). The resurrection meal has the cup before the breaking of bread. The words of interpretation look forward (verse 18) rather than backward; thus the mention of the kingdom rather than of blood.

THE UPPER ROOM A Simulation Based upon the Accounts of the Lord's Supper

THE SITUATION

The purpose of this simulation is to gain insight into the celebration which is variously called the Lord's Supper, the Breaking of Bread, and the Eucharist. You are to take the part of Christians from across the Roman Empire, gathering in Antioch. The time is near the end of the second century, say A.D. 190. You are gathered together to plan a celebration in which you reenact the events of the upper room on the evening that Jesus was betrayed. You do not simply want to mimic those events; rather you want to catch up their true meaning and significance.

Many of you have come at the special invitation of the church at Antioch. You are not acquainted with some of the other believers present, and you soon find that your beliefs are based upon different accounts of the Gospels. Some of you have been using one Gospel account; some, another; and some, the letters of Paul. As you attempt to catch the significance of the events of the upper room, you want above all to be true to the version of the Gospel that has been your guide for many years. The setting is a council meeting in which you are voting on what shall be included in your upper-room ceremony.

For purposes of the simulation you must remember that you may refer to only the Gospel with which you are acquainted. Much before the year A.D. 200 the use of the Four Gospels was well established in the churches, even though the canon of the New Testament was not completed until late in the fourth century. We will assume that each group has been somewhat isolated and is not familiar with any Gospel other than its own. You may refer to the Old Testament as we know it, which was likely well established by the time of the Council of Jamnia, ca. A.D. 90. The letters of Paul were also well established by A.D. 140, but it is possible that some isolated groups had not heard of them. You represent an assembly in Antioch of several groups who had been so isolated.

Your decision about how to celebrate the events of the upper room will probably focus first of all upon the meal. You will need to decide whether the meal is to follow the tradition of the Passover. A critical question will be what to serve, e.g., lamb or fish? You may then consider whether to portray the disciples' concern about who had betrayed Jesus, a period of what might be called self-examination. All of the accounts refer to the Old Testament, the bread and the cup. You should decide which to include and in what manner. Another issue is Jesus' reference to what is to come. Shall you include this "anticipation"? Should you include a hymn?

TASKS OF ALL GROUPS
PRIOR TO THE SIMULATION

For the purposes of the simulation there will be four groups with the following identities:

The Markan group—those who have only the Gospels of Matthew and Mark;

The Lukan group—those who have only the Gospel of Luke and Acts;

The Johannine group—those who have only the Gospel of John;

The Paulinists—those who have only the letters of Paul.

Following are specific tasks which each group should perform:

1. Each group should appoint a leader who will chair in the preparation of the simulation.
2. Each group should appoint a chronicler who will—
   a. record briefly the process of his group,
   b. record the action of the whole simulation from the point of view of his group,
   c. report at the debriefing session.
3. Each group should carefully examine the biblical texts indicated on the guidesheet for that group to establish its own identity.
4. Each group should come to some common understanding about issues to be discussed at the council meeting.
5. Each group should prepare some visible symbol of its point of view.
6. Each group should consider how it may persuade others of its own point of view.

RULES OF THE SIMULATION

1. Before the simulation begins, someone should be asked to serve as chairman.
2. The seating arrangement should be such that members of each group can caucus among themselves and at the same time take part in the whole meeting.
3. Issues will be decided by majority vote. In case of a tie vote the groups are to caucus and vote again. The chairperson may not break a vote.
4. Each group is to have an equal number of votes (e.g., two). Each group will decide which of its members may cast their votes.
5. Each group may caucus prior to any vote. The chair should grant a brief recess for caucusing upon request.
6. The council meeting will adjourn at the appointed time whether or not a decision has been reached.

TASKS OF THE SIMULATION

1. The council is to decide what parts to include in the upper-room ceremony. For example, will the ceremony include a meal, self-examination, Scripture, the bread, the cup, anticipation, and/or a hymn?
2. The council is to decide how each part of the ceremony shall be conducted. For example, if there should be a meal, will it consist of lamb or fish?
3. The council should decide in what order the parts of the ceremony should come. For example, should the cup precede or follow the breaking of bread?

TASKS FOR DEBRIEFING

1. Rearrange the room to symbolize the termination of the simulation.
2. Let everyone, including each chronicler, share his observations with the whole group.
3. Let everyone express his feelings about what happened.
4. Discuss whether you can carry out the ceremony together. Perhaps you can conclude the debriefing with the service you have just planned.

3. The Johannine Group

You represent a group of early Christians who have only the Gospel of John to study from. Your understanding of the events of the upper room must be taken from this account, since you are not aware of other Gospel accounts. You will find that persons from other groups do not always agree with you, and it is your task to persuade them that your view is correct, or be persuaded by them. In preparing for the council meeting, consult the following sources:

> John 13
> John 14
> John 6

BACKGROUND DATA

John's account of the upper room is much different from that of the other Gospels. The meal takes place before the Passover (John 13:1; 18:28; 19:31) and may have included fish (6:11; 21:13). It was not a Passover meal as in the other Gospels. The washing of feet is set within the context of Judas's plan to betray Jesus (13:11) and is a change of the Jewish purification rites (13:10, 2:6).

The receiving of bread is not in itself sufficient to be in Christ, for it did not suffice for Judas (13:26). Contrast the receiving of bread from Jesus (13:18, 13:30) and being close to him (13:25). John's emphasis is not upon receiving bread, but upon being close to Jesus, abiding in him, loving one another. Not in some outward symbol, but in their love for one another will Christians be known (13:35). However, John does consider the bread and the cup (6:55-56), but they must be more than physical (6:58). The Spirit of love and truth must be present.

The emphasis upon the Spirit comes in a series of instructions in which the disciples are told to be faithful in adversity, to love one another, and to await the Spirit of truth. Possibly they leave the upper room with verse 31 in chapter 14, although Jesus' instruction goes on without a break. The prayer in chapter 17 may be in the upper room, or it may represent the prayer in Gethsemane.

In summary, John's account includes a meal (13:2), awareness of betrayal (13:2), washing of feet (13:5), Scripture (13:18), pointing out Judas (13:26), predicting Peter's denial (13:38), and instructions about the Spirit (chapter 14). Possibly the further instructions of chapters 15 and 16 and the prayer of chapter 17 should be included.

THE UPPER ROOM A Simulation Based upon the Accounts of the Lord's Supper

THE SITUATION

The purpose of this simulation is to gain insight into the celebration which is variously called the Lord's Supper, the Breaking of Bread, and the Eucharist. You are to take the part of Christians from across the Roman Empire, gathering in Antioch. The time is near the end of the second century, say A.D. 190. You are gathered together to plan a celebration in which you reenact the events of the upper room on the evening that Jesus was betrayed. You do not simply want to mimic those events; rather you want to catch up their true meaning and significance.

Many of you have come at the special invitation of the church at Antioch. You are not acquainted with some of the other believers present, and you soon find that your beliefs are based upon different accounts of the Gospels. Some of you have been using one Gospel account; some, another; and some, the letters of Paul. As you attempt to catch the significance of the events of the upper room, you want above all to be true to the version of the Gospel that has been your guide for many years. The setting is a council meeting in which you are voting on what shall be included in your upper-room ceremony.

For purposes of the simulation you must remember that you may refer to only the Gospel with which you are acquainted. Much before the year A.D. 200 the use of the Four Gospels was well established in the churches, even though the canon of the New Testament was not completed until late in the fourth century. We will assume that each group has been somewhat isolated and is not familiar with any Gospel other than its own. You may refer to the Old Testament as we know it, which was likely well established by the time of the Council of Jamnia, *ca.* A.D. 90. The letters of Paul were also well established by A.D. 140, but it is possible that some isolated groups had not heard of them. You represent an assembly in Antioch of several groups who had been so isolated.

Your decision about how to celebrate the events of the upper room will probably focus first of all upon the meal. You will need to decide whether the meal is to follow the tradition of the Passover. A critical question will be what to serve, e.g., lamb or fish? You may then consider whether to portray the disciples' concern about who had betrayed Jesus, a period of what might be called self-examination. All of the accounts refer to the Old Testament, the bread and the cup. You should decide which to include and in what manner. Another issue is Jesus' reference to what is to come. Shall you include this "anticipation"? Should you include a hymn?

TASKS OF ALL GROUPS
PRIOR TO THE SIMULATION

For the purposes of the simulation there will be four groups with the following identities:

The Markan group—those who have only the Gospels of Matthew and Mark;

The Lukan group—those who have only the Gospel of Luke and Acts;

The Johannine group—those who have only the Gospel of John;

The Paulinists—those who have only the letters of Paul.

Following are specific tasks which each group should perform:

1. Each group should appoint a leader who will chair in the preparation of the simulation.
2. Each group should appoint a chronicler who will—
   a. record briefly the process of his group,
   b. record the action of the whole simulation from the point of view of his group,
   c. report at the debriefing session.
3. Each group should carefully examine the biblical texts indicated on the guidesheet for that group to establish its own identity.
4. Each group should come to some common understanding about issues to be discussed at the council meeting.
5. Each group should prepare some visible symbol of its point of view.
6. Each group should consider how it may persuade others of its own point of view.

RULES OF THE SIMULATION

1. Before the simulation begins, someone should be asked to serve as chairman.
2. The seating arrangement should be such that members of each group can caucus among themselves and at the same time take part in the whole meeting.
3. Issues will be decided by majority vote. In case of a tie vote the groups are to caucus and vote again. The chairperson may not break a vote.
4. Each group is to have an equal number of votes (e.g., two). Each group will decide which of its members may cast their votes.
5. Each group may caucus prior to any vote. The chair should grant a brief recess for caucusing upon request.
6. The council meeting will adjourn at the appointed time whether or not a decision has been reached.

TASKS OF THE SIMULATION

1. The council is to decide what parts to include in the upper-room ceremony. For example, will the ceremony include a meal, self-examination, Scripture, the bread, the cup, anticipation, and/or a hymn?
2. The council is to decide how each part of the ceremony shall be conducted. For example, if there should be a meal, will it consist of lamb or fish?
3. The council should decide in what order the parts of the ceremony should come. For example, should the cup precede or follow the breaking of bread?

TASKS FOR DEBRIEFING

1. Rearrange the room to symbolize the termination of the simulation.
2. Let everyone, including each chronicler, share his observations with the whole group.
3. Let everyone express his feelings about what happened.
4. Discuss whether you can carry out the ceremony together. Perhaps you can conclude the debriefing with the service you have just planned.

3. The Johannine Group

You represent a group of early Christians who have only the Gospel of John to study from. Your understanding of the events of the upper room must be taken from this account, since you are not aware of other Gospel accounts. You will find that persons from other groups do not always agree with you, and it is your task to persuade them that your view is correct, or be persuaded by them. In preparing for the council meeting, consult the following sources:

John 13
John 14
John 6

BACKGROUND DATA

John's account of the upper room is much different from that of the other Gospels. The meal takes place before the Passover (John 13:1; 18:28; 19:31) and may have included fish (6:11; 21:13). It was not a Passover meal as in the other Gospels. The washing of feet is set within the context of Judas's plan to betray Jesus (13:11) and is a change of the Jewish purification rites (13:10, 2:6).

The receiving of bread is not in itself sufficient to be in Christ, for it did not suffice for Judas (13:26). Contrast the receiving of bread from Jesus (13:18, 13:30) and being close to him (13:25). John's emphasis is not upon receiving bread, but upon being close to Jesus, abiding in him, loving one another. Not in some outward symbol, but in their love for one another will Christians be known (13:35). However, John does consider the bread and the cup (6:55-56), but they must be more than physical (6:58). The Spirit of love and truth must be present.

The emphasis upon the Spirit comes in a series of instructions in which the disciples are told to be faithful in adversity, to love one another, and to await the Spirit of truth. Possibly they leave the upper room with verse 31 in chapter 14, although Jesus' instruction goes on without a break. The prayer in chapter 17 may be in the upper room, or it may represent the prayer in Gethsemane.

In summary, John's account includes a meal (13:2), awareness of betrayal (13:2), washing of feet (13:5), Scripture (13:18), pointing out Judas (13:26), predicting Peter's denial (13:38), and instructions about the Spirit (chapter 14). Possibly the further instructions of chapters 15 and 16 and the prayer of chapter 17 should be included.

THE UPPER ROOM A Simulation Based upon the Accounts of the Lord's Supper

THE SITUATION

The purpose of this simulation is to gain insight into the celebration which is variously called the Lord's Supper, the Breaking of Bread, and the Eucharist. You are to take the part of Christians from across the Roman Empire, gathering in Antioch. The time is near the end of the second century, say A.D. 190. You are gathered together to plan a celebration in which you reenact the events of the upper room on the evening that Jesus was betrayed. You do not simply want to mimic those events; rather you want to catch up their true meaning and significance.

Many of you have come at the special invitation of the church at Antioch. You are not acquainted with some of the other believers present, and you soon find that your beliefs are based upon different accounts of the Gospels. Some of you have been using one Gospel account; some, another; and some, the letters of Paul. As you attempt to catch the significance of the events of the upper room, you want above all to be true to the version of the Gospel that has been your guide for many years. The setting is a council meeting in which you are voting on what shall be included in your upper-room ceremony.

For purposes of the simulation you must remember that you may refer to only the Gospel with which you are acquainted. Much before the year A.D. 200 the use of the Four Gospels was well established in the churches, even though the canon of the New Testament was not completed until late in the fourth century. We will assume that each group has been somewhat isolated and is not familiar with any Gospel other than its own. You may refer to the Old Testament as we know it, which was likely well established by the time of the Council of Jamnia, ca. A.D. 90. The letters of Paul were also well established by A.D. 140, but it is possible that some isolated groups had not heard of them. You represent an assembly in Antioch of several groups who had been so isolated.

Your decision about how to celebrate the events of the upper room will probably focus first of all upon the meal. You will need to decide whether the meal is to follow the tradition of the Passover. A critical question will be what to serve, e.g., lamb or fish? You may then consider whether to portray the disciples' concern about who had betrayed Jesus, a period of what might be called self-examination. All of the accounts refer to the Old Testament, the bread and the cup. You should decide which to include and in what manner. Another issue is Jesus' reference to what is to come. Shall you include this "anticipation"? Should you include a hymn?

TASKS OF ALL GROUPS
PRIOR TO THE SIMULATION

For the purposes of the simulation there will be four groups with the following identities:

> The Markan group—those who have only the Gospels of Matthew and Mark;
> The Lukan group—those who have only the Gospel of Luke and Acts;
> The Johannine group—those who have only the Gospel of John;
> The Paulinists—those who have only the letters of Paul.

Following are specific tasks which each group should perform:

1. Each group should appoint a leader who will chair in the preparation of the simulation.
2. Each group should appoint a chronicler who will—
   a. record briefly the process of his group,
   b. record the action of the whole simulation from the point of view of his group,
   c. report at the debriefing session.
3. Each group should carefully examine the biblical texts indicated on the guidesheet for that group to establish its own identity.
4. Each group should come to some common understanding about issues to be discussed at the council meeting.
5. Each group should prepare some visible symbol of its point of view.
6. Each group should consider how it may persuade others of its own point of view.

RULES OF THE SIMULATION

1. Before the simulation begins, someone should be asked to serve as chairman.
2. The seating arrangement should be such that members of each group can caucus among themselves and at the same time take part in the whole meeting.
3. Issues will be decided by majority vote. In case of a tie vote the groups are to caucus and vote again. The chairperson may not break a vote.
4. Each group is to have an equal number of votes (e.g., two). Each group will decide which of its members may cast their votes.
5. Each group may caucus prior to any vote. The chair should grant a brief recess for caucusing upon request.
6. The council meeting will adjourn at the appointed time whether or not a decision has been reached.

TASKS OF THE SIMULATION

1. The council is to decide what parts to include in the upper-room ceremony. For example, will the ceremony include a meal, self-examination, Scripture, the bread, the cup, anticipation, and/or a hymn?
2. The council is to decide how each part of the ceremony shall be conducted. For example, if there should be a meal, will it consist of lamb or fish?
3. The council should decide in what order the parts of the ceremony should come. For example, should the cup precede or follow the breaking of bread?

TASKS FOR DEBRIEFING

1. Rearrange the room to symbolize the termination of the simulation.
2. Let everyone, including each chronicler, share his observations with the whole group.
3. Let everyone express his feelings about what happened.
4. Discuss whether you can carry out the ceremony together. Perhaps you can conclude the debriefing with the service you have just planned.

4. The Pauline Group

You represent a group of early Christians who have only the letters of Paul to guide you. Your understanding of the events of the upper room must be taken from those letters, and not from any other source. You may find that persons in other groups do not agree with you. It is your task to persuade them that your view is correct, or be persuaded by them. For your study use the following selections:

> 1 Corinthians 11:17-34
> 1 Corinthians 10:14-22
> 1 Corinthians 12:12-27

BACKGROUND DATA

Paul's account of the events of the upper room may be the earliest account to be recorded in the New Testament. Paul's letters were probably circulated before any of the Gospels were written down. His description is therefore probably nearest to the event itself.

Parts of the ceremony that Paul mentions are the meal (11:20-21), the betrayal (11:23), the bread (11:24), the cup (11:25), anticipation (11:26), self-examination (11:28), and judgment (11:29). With the bread there is the giving of thanks, the breaking of the loaf, and the interpretation (11:24). With the cup there is perhaps the giving of thanks (unmentioned) and the interpretation (11:25).

Paul considers it very important that eating and drinking be done in relation to the body (11:29), and the body is made up of every believer individually and all believers together (12:27). When we bicker and form factions, we are breaking the body of Christ (11:27). The one loaf is the symbol of the one body of believers (10:17). Apparently the Corinthians were eating in separate little groups and even getting drunk (11:21).

THE UPPER ROOM A Simulation Based upon the Accounts of the Lord's Supper

THE SITUATION

The purpose of this simulation is to gain insight into the celebration which is variously called the Lord's Supper, the Breaking of Bread, and the Eucharist. You are to take the part of Christians from across the Roman Empire, gathering in Antioch. The time is near the end of the second century, say A.D. 190. You are gathered together to plan a celebration in which you reenact the events of the upper room on the evening that Jesus was betrayed. You do not simply want to mimic those events; rather you want to catch up their true meaning and significance.

Many of you have come at the special invitation of the church at Antioch. You are not acquainted with some of the other believers present, and you soon find that your beliefs are based upon different accounts of the Gospels. Some of you have been using one Gospel account; some, another; and some, the letters of Paul. As you attempt to catch the significance of the events of the upper room, you want above all to be true to the version of the Gospel that has been your guide for many years. The setting is a council meeting in which you are voting on what shall be included in your upper-room ceremony.

For purposes of the simulation you must remember that you may refer to only the Gospel with which you are acquainted. Much before the year A.D. 200 the use of the Four Gospels was well established in the churches, even though the canon of the New Testament was not completed until late in the fourth century. We will assume that each group has been somewhat isolated and is not familiar with any Gospel other than its own. You may refer to the Old Testament as we know it, which was likely well established by the time of the Council of Jamnia, ca. A.D. 90. The letters of Paul were also well established by A.D. 140, but it is possible that some isolated groups had not heard of them. You represent an assembly in Antioch of several groups who had been so isolated.

Your decision about how to celebrate the events of the upper room will probably focus first of all upon the meal. You will need to decide whether the meal is to follow the tradition of the Passover. A critical question will be what to serve, e.g., lamb or fish? You may then consider whether to portray the disciples' concern about who had betrayed Jesus, a period of what might be called self-examination. All of the accounts refer to the Old Testament, the bread and the cup. You should decide which to include and in what manner. Another issue is Jesus' reference to what is to come. Shall you include this "anticipation"? Should you include a hymn?

TASKS OF ALL GROUPS
PRIOR TO THE SIMULATION

For the purposes of the simulation there will be four groups with the following identities:

The Markan group—those who have only the Gospels of Matthew and Mark;

The Lukan group—those who have only the Gospel of Luke and Acts;

The Johannine group—those who have only the Gospel of John;

The Paulinists—those who have only the letters of Paul.

Following are specific tasks which each group should perform:

1. Each group should appoint a leader who will chair in the preparation of the simulation.
2. Each group should appoint a chronicler who will—
   a. record briefly the process of his group,
   b. record the action of the whole simulation from the point of view of his group,
   c. report at the debriefing session.
3. Each group should carefully examine the biblical texts indicated on the guidesheet for that group to establish its own identity.
4. Each group should come to some common understanding about issues to be discussed at the council meeting.
5. Each group should prepare some visible symbol of its point of view.
6. Each group should consider how it may persuade others of its own point of view.

RULES OF THE SIMULATION

1. Before the simulation begins, someone should be asked to serve as chairman.
2. The seating arrangement should be such that members of each group can caucus among themselves and at the same time take part in the whole meeting.
3. Issues will be decided by majority vote. In case of a tie vote the groups are to caucus and vote again. The chairperson may not break a vote.
4. Each group is to have an equal number of votes (e.g., two). Each group will decide which of its members may cast their votes.
5. Each group may caucus prior to any vote. The chair should grant a brief recess for caucusing upon request.
6. The council meeting will adjourn at the appointed time whether or not a decision has been reached.

TASKS OF THE SIMULATION

1. The council is to decide what parts to include in the upper-room ceremony. For example, will the ceremony include a meal, self-examination, Scripture, the bread, the cup, anticipation, and/or a hymn?
2. The council is to decide how each part of the ceremony shall be conducted. For example, if there should be a meal, will it consist of lamb or fish?
3. The council should decide in what order the parts of the ceremony should come. For example, should the cup precede or follow the breaking of bread?

TASKS FOR DEBRIEFING

1. Rearrange the room to symbolize the termination of the simulation.
2. Let everyone, including each chronicler, share his observations with the whole group.
3. Let everyone express his feelings about what happened.
4. Discuss whether you can carry out the ceremony together. Perhaps you can conclude the debriefing with the service you have just planned.

4. The Pauline Group

You represent a group of early Christians who have only the letters of Paul to guide you. Your understanding of the events of the upper room must be taken from those letters, and not from any other source. You may find that persons in other groups do not agree with you. It is your task to persuade them that your view is correct, or be persuaded by them. For your study use the following selections:

> 1 Corinthians 11:17-34
> 1 Corinthians 10:14-22
> 1 Corinthians 12:12-27

BACKGROUND DATA

Paul's account of the events of the upper room may be the earliest account to be recorded in the New Testament. Paul's letters were probably circulated before any of the Gospels were written down. His description is therefore probably nearest to the event itself.

Parts of the ceremony that Paul mentions are the meal (11:20-21), the betrayal (11:23), the bread (11:24), the cup (11:25), anticipation (11:26), self-examination (11:28), and judgment (11:29). With the bread there is the giving of thanks, the breaking of the loaf, and the interpretation (11:24). With the cup there is perhaps the giving of thanks (unmentioned) and the interpretation (11:25).

Paul considers it very important that eating and drinking be done in relation to the body (11:29), and the body is made up of every believer individually and all believers together (12:27). When we bicker and form factions, we are breaking the body of Christ (11:27). The one loaf is the symbol of the one body of believers (10:17). Apparently the Corinthians were eating in separate little groups and even getting drunk (11:21).

15. WHAT'S IN A WORD?

A Simulation Based upon Mark 8:35

INSTRUCTIONS TO THE COORDINATOR

Preparation

The special significance of this simulation is that it will give people an insight into not only translation but also the interpretation of Scripture. It is written in such a way that no previous knowledge of Greek is necessary. Read through the whole simulation to get a sense of its purpose and direction. Involve other leaders in the preparation if you will be working with a large group.

Schedule

You will want to adapt this simulation to the time you have available. It is very difficult to have a satisfying experience in a session of less than two hours. The following table itemizes three different schedules:

	One Hour	Two Hours	Six Hours
Introduction	10 min.	15 min.	¼ hr.
Preparation	20 min.	45 min.	3¾ hrs.
Simulation	15 min.	30 min.	1 hr.
Debriefing	15 min.	30 min.	1 hr.

For a single-hour session we recommend that you work only on the translation of *psuche.* For two-, three-, or four-hour periods (whether in separate sessions or in a single block of time) decide upon the text and the translation of *psuche.* For a six-hour period try to resolve all the problems of the text.

Grouping

You need two or three persons working in each small group, or a total of eight to twelve persons for the simulation to work well.

Persons present	Number of groups	Representatives at table
8-48	4	3 per group
49-96	8	2 per group

If more than one hundred people are involved, consider conducting two simulations simultaneously.

An alternate plan is to have everyone in each group serve as a representative at one or another table, using as many tables as are needed. Each table would then produce its own translation. This has the special advantage of illustrating why we have various translations.

Space and Equipment

Your preparation should include obtaining each of the following items (see chapter 3): a large room, small rooms, chairs, tables, Bibles, Bible study aids, paper and pencils, art materials for symbols, and refreshments. Certain other special materials and preparations will help this simulation:

1. Robert Young's *Analytical Concordance to the Bible* will help with the Greek words.
2. Several copies of the Greek New Testament will be useful. The text printed on poster board in large Greek letters will add a genuine note.
3. Provide a good lexicon, such as W. F. Arndt and F. W. Gingrich, eds., *A Greek-English Lexicon of the New Testament and Other Early Christian Literature* (Grand Rapids: Zondervan Publishing House, 1963).
4. Bring many translations: e.g., King James, American, Revised Standard, Phillips, New English, Jerusalem, Moffatt, etc.
5. Invite one or several persons who read Greek and also Hebrew to serve as consultants.

Facilitation

The group's enthusiasm for the simulation will depend a great deal upon how you introduce it. In addition to helping people get a feel for simulation you will need to help them

207

understand the purpose and situation of this simulation. Items to be covered are as follows: what a simulation is, how to participate, purposes and tasks of this simulation, schedule, small-group tasks, materials, division into groups, and duties of the small-group chairmen. Allow time for questions. Find someone who will serve as chairman of the simulated council meeting.

During the small-group period circulate among the groups to see that everyone understands the task and is using the materials available. It is important that anyone who reads Greek does not intimidate others by what he knows. This simulation is designed for people who have had no previous experience with Greek, and anyone who has such knowledge should not be "giving answers."

During the simulation itself the group will want first of all to establish the text and then to work at the translation. There should be no sense of failure if the translation is not completed. Simply establishing the text is a sufficient exercise in itself. It will likely take a six-hour period to complete the whole assignment.

The group may spend its time debating the merits of one or another text. See the article "Text of the New Testament" in *The Interpreter's Dictionary of the Bible* (Nashville: Abingdon Press, 1962). On the other hand, they may spend time debating about the translation of *psuche*, the meaning of which is the central question of the passage. You may need to encourage the group to come to this point.

Debriefing

When the council meeting is completed, you, as coordinator, should conduct the interpretation session. Here are the suggestions to be followed:

1. Change seating so that everyone is aware that all have dropped their roles.
2. Divide into groups of four and talk about what you have learned. A different group might take each of these questions: How important is the problem of a correct text? Should a translation be very literal, or should it use paraphrase a great deal? How did your understanding of the passage change? What does it mean to follow Christ? How close can we come to the words of Jesus? How did the differences in the Gospels come about?
3. Ask volunteers to share their observations with the whole group.
4. Ask the chroniclers to share their observations.
5. Pass out various translations of the Bible and compare the different groups' translations with those.
6. Attempt to summarize what people are learning (optional conclusion).
7. Lead a prayer in which people voice what they have learned about being Christians.
8. As a concluding benediction, read the translations you have produced.

WHAT'S IN A WORD? A Simulation Based upon Mark 8:35

THE SITUATION

The purpose of this simulation is to help you gain a new understanding of the reasons for various versions of Scripture by actually translating a familiar passage from the original Greek. You are to simulate a group of translators who have been commissioned by various churches to produce a new translation of the Bible to be called the International Standard Version. Just now you are at the point of trying to agree upon a translation for Mark 8:35.

TASKS OF ALL GROUPS
PRIOR TO THE SIMULATION

Everyone is assigned to one of four study groups to prepare a preliminary translation: the Markan group, the Hebrew group, the Johannine group, and the Jesus group.

Specific tasks which each group should perform follow:

1. Appoint a chairman for your group who will lead in the preparation of the simulation.
2. Appoint a chronicler who will—
   a. record the process of his or her own group,
   b. record the action of the simulation from the perspective of his or her group,
   c. report during the debriefing session.
3. Establish the text, i.e., decide upon the version of the original that has a stronger claim to be considered the proper text.
4. Use the lexicon to make a word by word translation.
5. Rephrase the translation to make good idiomatic English:
   a. put the words in proper order;
   b. rephrase the words to catch the original meaning.
6. Discuss how you will persuade the other groups that they should adopt your translation.

RULES OF THE SIMULATION

1. The chairman should see that the whole group works on the tasks of the simulation and that the rules are followed. The chairman decides who may speak.
2. Three people from each study group may sit around the table with the others from that group seated behind them. Only those at the table may take part in the debate.
3. Anyone from a study group may replace one of the three persons at the table merely by indicating his wish to do so.
4. All decisions are to be made by two-thirds vote of all involved in the simulation.
5. Any study group may request a caucus just prior to a vote.
6. Anyone not at the table may lobby to change the minds of persons from other groups.

TASKS OF THE SIMULATION

1. Reach a decision about which Greek words will be included in the text.
2. Decide upon the English words and phrases to be used to translate the text.

TASKS FOR DEBRIEFING

Follow the coordinator's instructions for debriefing found in this chapter.

GREEK TEXT OF MARK 8:35

hos gar ean thelé tén (   )[1] sōsai, apolesei autén. hos d' an (   )[2] tén psuchén autou heneken (   )[3] tou euaggeliou, sōsei autén.

1. The Greek phrase to be inserted in the space marked [1] is one of the following:
   a. *psuchén autou*. Most manuscripts have this phrase.
   b. *eautou psuchén*. A few insignificant manuscripts have this alternate form.
2. The Greek phrase to be inserted in the space marked [2] is one of the following:
   a. *apolesei*. Most manuscripts have this form.
   b. *apolese*. The important Byzantine group of manuscripts which come from Antioch through Constantinople have this.
3. The space marked [3] is either filled with a Greek phrase or left blank as indicated in the choices below:

a. *emou kai.* Most manuscripts contain this phrase.

b. The phrase is omitted in the oldest known manuscript fragment of this verse, a fragment from the Chester Beatty Papyri dating back to the third century. It is also omitted in several old Italian manuscripts and in a Syriac translation dating back to the fourth century.

LEXICON

an. Under the circumstances, in that case, anyhow, would, if. The word has the effect of making a statement contingent that would otherwise be definite.

apollumi. Lose, destroy, perish. *Apolesei* is the future, 3rd person, singular, and means will lose, will destroy, etc. *Apolese'* is the 3rd person singular of the subjunctive and means would or might lose, etc.

autos. He, self, the very, the same. The possessive form is *autou,* his, his own, its, self, or the same. The accusative form is *autén,* him, it, self, or the same.

de. But, on the other hand, and. A weak adversative particle, generally placed second in its clause. Before a vowel it is written as *d'.*

ean. If, when introducing a clause. The meaning of *hos* changes to who, whoever, or whosoever when accompanied by *ean.*

?autou. His own, its own.

emos. Mine, of me. After some prepositions it is written as *emou.*

euaggeliou. The good news, the gospel.

gar. For. A conjunction relating the phrase to previous ideas.

heneken. For the sake of, on account of, in behalf of.

ho, hé, to. The. Other forms with the same meaning are *ten* and *tou.*

hos. Who, which. A definite relative pronoun. With *an* or *ean* it may mean whoever or whosoever.

kai. And, even. A conjunction.

psuche'. Appetite, desire, soul, self, life, breath of life, person, individual, identity. It is often used to translate the Hebrew word *nephesh.* The form *psuchen* is used as the object of the verb.

sodzo. Save, rescue, preserve from danger or from death. Sometimes it refers to physical danger and sometimes to spiritual death. Other forms are *sōsei,* 3rd person, singular, future, will save, etc.; and *sosai,* past infinitive, to save (in a single complete action), to rescue, etc.

ten, tou. See *ho, hé, to.*

thelō. To will, to stick resolutely to, to wish, to desire. The 3rd person, singular, subjunctive is *thele',* would or might will, etc.

1. The Markan Group

Your group bases its argument upon Mark. You believe that the translation should reflect Mark's point of view, since the verse occurs in that Gospel. Those in other groups will not always agree with you. It is your task to try to persuade them that your view is correct, or be persuaded by them. Passages you should study are the following:

> Mark 10:32-45
> Mark 8:31-33
> Mark 14:66-72
> Isaiah 53:10-12

BACKGROUND DATA

Mark is likely the earliest of the Gospels to be written and therefore carries much authority in discussions about original meanings. Both Matthew and Luke borrow heavily from Mark. It is not critical that *emou kai* be included in the text since giving up life for the sake of the gospel

is itself following after Jesus. Mark places great emphasis upon Jesus giving up his life and upon the disciples following him in that act (8:34), drinking of the cup of his blood and being baptized in his death (10:38-39). In view of Mark's emphasis throughout his Gospel and in a preceding verse (8:31), it would seem that *psuche'* ought to be translated "life," i.e., physical life. The Hebrew word behind *psuche'* is *nephesh.* The use of *psuche'* in our passage may refer to Isaiah 53. Mark 10:45 is so close to Isaiah 53:12 that the relationship can hardly be denied. Isaiah 53:12 says, "he poured out his (*psuche', nephesh*) to death, and was numbered with the transgressors." We also find that *apollumi* sometimes (not always) means to die or to lose one's life. See Mark 4:38 where in the midst of the storm the disciples wake Jesus to ask, "Do you not care if we perish?"

WHAT'S IN A WORD? A Simulation Based upon Mark 8:35

THE SITUATION

The purpose of this simulation is to help you gain a new understanding of the reasons for various versions of Scripture by actually translating a familiar passage from the original Greek. You are to simulate a group of translators who have been commissioned by various churches to produce a new translation of the Bible to be called the International Standard Version. Just now you are at the point of trying to agree upon a translation for Mark 8:35.

TASKS OF ALL GROUPS
PRIOR TO THE SIMULATION

Everyone is assigned to one of four study groups to prepare a preliminary translation: the Markan group, the Hebrew group, the Johannine group, and the Jesus group.

Specific tasks which each group should perform follow:

1. Appoint a chairman for your group who will lead in the preparation of the simulation.
2. Appoint a chronicler who will—
   a. record the process of his or her own group,
   b. record the action of the simulation from the perspective of his or her group,
   c. report during the debriefing session.
3. Establish the text, i.e., decide upon the version of the original that has a stronger claim to be considered the proper text.
4. Use the lexicon to make a word by word translation.
5. Rephrase the translation to make good idiomatic English:
   a. put the words in proper order;
   b. rephrase the words to catch the original meaning.
6. Discuss how you will persuade the other groups that they should adopt your translation.

RULES OF THE SIMULATION

1. The chairman should see that the whole group works on the tasks of the simulation and that the rules are followed. The chairman decides who may speak.
2. Three people from each study group may sit around the table with the others from that group seated behind them. Only those at the table may take part in the debate.
3. Anyone from a study group may replace one of the three persons at the table merely by indicating his wish to do so.
4. All decisions are to be made by two-thirds vote of all involved in the simulation.
5. Any study group may request a caucus just prior to a vote.
6. Anyone not at the table may lobby to change the minds of persons from other groups.

TASKS OF THE SIMULATION

1. Reach a decision about which Greek words will be included in the text.
2. Decide upon the English words and phrases to be used to translate the text.

TASKS FOR DEBRIEFING

Follow the coordinator's instructions for debriefing found in this chapter.

GREEK TEXT OF MARK 8:35

hos gar ean thelé tén (   )[1] sōsai, apolesei autén. hos d' an (   )[2] tén psuchén autou heneken (   )[3] tou euaggeliou, sōsei autén.

1. The Greek phrase to be inserted in the space marked [1] is one of the following:
   a. *psuchén autou.* Most manuscripts have this phrase.
   b. *eautou psuchén.* A few insignificant manuscripts have this alternate form.
2. The Greek phrase to be inserted in the space marked [2] is one of the following:
   a. *apolesei.* Most manuscripts have this form.
   b. *apolese.* The important Byzantine group of manuscripts which come from Antioch through Constantinople have this.
3. The space marked [3] is either filled with a Greek phrase or left blank as indicated in the choices below:

a. *emou kai.* Most manuscripts contain this phrase.

b. The phrase is omitted in the oldest known manuscript fragment of this verse, a fragment from the Chester Beatty Papyri dating back to the third century. It is also omitted in several old Italian manuscripts and in a Syriac translation dating back to the fourth century.

LEXICON

an. Under the circumstances, in that case, anyhow, would, if. The word has the effect of making a statement contingent that would otherwise be definite.

apollumi. Lose, destroy, perish. *Apolesei* is the future, 3rd person, singular, and means will lose, will destroy, etc. *Apolese* is the 3rd person singular of the subjunctive and means would or might lose, etc.

autos. He, self, the very, the same. The possessive form is *autou,* his, his own, its, self, or the same. The accusative form is *autén,* him, it, self, or the same.

de. But, on the other hand, and. A weak adversative particle, generally placed second in its clause. Before a vowel it is written *d'.*

ean. If, when introducing a clause. The meaning of *hos* changes to who, whoever, or whosoever when accompanied by *ean.*

eautou. His own, its own.

emos. Mine, of me. After some prepositions it is written as *emou.*

euaggeliou. The good news, the gospel.

gar. For. A conjunction relating the phrase to previous ideas.

heneken. For the sake of, on account of, in behalf of.

ho, he, to. The. Other forms with the same meaning are *ten* and *tou.*

hos. Who, which. A definite relative pronoun. With *an* or *ean* it may mean whoever or whosoever.

kai. And, even. A conjunction.

psuche. Appetite, desire, soul, self, life, breath of life, person, individual, identity. It is often used to translate the Hebrew word *nephesh.* The form *psuchen* is used as the object of the verb.

sodzo. Save, rescue, preserve from danger or from death. Sometimes it refers to physical danger and sometimes to spiritual death. Other forms are *sosei,* 3rd person, singular, future, will save, etc.; and *sosai,* past infinitive, to save (in a single complete action), to rescue, etc.

ten, tou. See *ho, he, to.*

thelo. To will, to stick resolutely to, to wish, to desire. The 3rd person, singular, subjunctive is *thele,* would or might will, etc.

1. The Markan Group

Your group bases its argument upon Mark. You believe that the translation should reflect Mark's point of view, since the verse occurs in that Gospel. Those in other groups will not always agree with you. It is your task to try to persuade them that your view is correct, or be persuaded by them. Passages you should study are the following:

> Mark 10:32-45
> Mark 8:31-33
> Mark 14:66-72
> Isaiah 53:10-12

BACKGROUND DATA

Mark is likely the earliest of the Gospels to be written and therefore carries much authority in discussions about original meanings. Both Matthew and Luke borrow heavily from Mark. It is not critical that *emou kai* be included in the text since giving up life for the sake of the gospel is itself following after Jesus. Mark places great emphasis upon Jesus giving up his life and upon the disciples following him in that act (8:34), drinking of the cup of his blood and being baptized in his death (10:38-39). In view of Mark's emphasis throughout his Gospel and in a preceding verse (8:31), it would seem that *psuche* ought to be translated "life," i.e., physical life. The Hebrew word behind *psuche* is *nephesh.* The use of *psuche* in our passage may refer to Isaiah 53. Mark 10:45 is so close to Isaiah 53:12 that the relationship can hardly be denied. Isaiah 53:12 says, "he poured out his *(psuche, nephesh)* to death, and was numbered with the transgressors." We also find that *apollumi* sometimes (not always) means to die or to lose one's life. See Mark 4:38 where in the midst of the storm the disciples wake Jesus to ask, "Do you not care if we perish?"

WHAT'S IN A WORD? A Simulation Based upon Mark 8:35

THE SITUATION
The purpose of this simulation is to help you gain a new understanding of the reasons for various versions of Scripture by actually translating a familiar passage from the original Greek. You are to simulate a group of translators who have been commissioned by various churches to produce a new translation of the Bible to be called the International Standard Version. Just now you are at the point of trying to agree upon a translation for Mark 8:35.

TASKS OF ALL GROUPS
PRIOR TO THE SIMULATION
Everyone is assigned to one of four study groups to prepare a preliminary translation: the Markan group, the Hebrew group, the Johannine group, and the Jesus group.

Specific tasks which each group should perform follow:
1. Appoint a chairman for your group who will lead in the preparation of the simulation.
2. Appoint a chronicler who will—
   a. record the process of his or her own group,
   b. record the action of the simulation from the perspective of his or her group,
   c. report during the debriefing session.
3. Establish the text, i.e., decide upon the version of the original that has a stronger claim to be considered the proper text.
4. Use the lexicon to make a word by word translation.
5. Rephrase the translation to make good idiomatic English:
   a. put the words in proper order;
   b. rephrase the words to catch the original meaning.
6. Discuss how you will persuade the other groups that they should adopt your translation.

RULES OF THE SIMULATION
1. The chairman should see that the whole group works on the tasks of the simulation and that the rules are followed. The chairman decides who may speak.
2. Three people from each study group may sit around the table with the others from that group seated behind them. Only those at the table may take part in the debate.
3. Anyone from a study group may replace one of the three persons at the table merely by indicating his wish to do so.
4. All decisions are to be made by two-thirds vote of all involved in the simulation.
5. Any study group may request a caucus just prior to a vote.
6. Anyone not at the table may lobby to change the minds of persons from other groups.

TASKS OF THE SIMULATION
1. Reach a decision about which Greek words will be included in the text.
2. Decide upon the English words and phrases to be used to translate the text.

TASKS FOR DEBRIEFING
Follow the coordinator's instructions for debriefing found in this chapter.

GREEK TEXT OF MARK 8:35
hos gar ean thele ten (   )[1] sosai, apolesei auten. hos d' an (   )[2] ten psuchen autou heneken (   )[3] tou euaggeliou, sosei auten.
1. The Greek phrase to be inserted in the space marked [1] is one of the following:
   a. *psuchen autou.* Most manuscripts have this phrase.
   b. *eautou psuchen.* A few insignificant manuscripts have this alternate form.
2. The Greek phrase to be inserted in the space marked [2] is one of the following:
   a. *apolesei.* Most manuscripts have this form.
   b. *apolese.* The important Byzantine group of manuscripts which come from Antioch through Constantinople have this.
3. The space marked [3] is either filled with a Greek phrase or left blank as indicated in the choices below:

a. *emou kai*. Most manuscripts contain this phrase.

b. The phrase is omitted in the oldest known manuscript fragment of this verse, a fragment from the Chester Beatty Papyri dating back to the third century. It is also omitted in several old Italian manuscripts and in a Syriac translation dating back to the fourth century.

LEXICON

an. Under the circumstances, in that case, anyhow, would, if. The word has the effect of making a statement contingent that would otherwise be definite.

apollumi. Lose, destroy, perish. *Apolesei* is the future, 3rd person, singular, and means will lose, will destroy, etc. *Apolese'* is the 3rd person singular of the subjunctive and means would or might lose, etc.

autos. He, self, the very, the same. The possessive form is *autou*, his, his own, its, self, or the same. The accusative form is *auten*, him, it, self, or the same.

de. But, on the other hand, and. A weak adversative particle, generally placed second in its clause. Before a vowel it is written as *d'*.

ean. If, when introducing a clause. The meaning of *hos* changes to who, whoever, or whosoever when accompanied by *ean*.

eautou. His own, its own.

emos. Mine, of me. After some prepositions it is written as *emou*.

euaggeliou. The good news, the gospel.

gar. For. A conjunction relating the phrase to previous ideas.

heneken. For the sake of, on account of, in behalf of.

ho, he', to. The. Other forms with the same meaning are *ten* and *tou*.

hos. Who, which. A definite relative pronoun. With *an* or *ean* it may mean whoever or whosoever.

kai. And, even. A conjunction.

psuche'. Appetite, desire, soul, self, life, breath of life, person, individual, identity. It is often used to translate the Hebrew word *nephesh*. The form *psuchen* is used as the object of the verb.

sodzo. Save, rescue, preserve from danger or from death. Sometimes it refers to physical danger and sometimes to spiritual death. Other forms are *sōsei*, 3rd person, singular, future, will save, etc.; and *sosai*, past infinitive, to save (in a single complete action), to rescue, etc.

ten, tou. See *ho, he', to*.

thelō. To will, to stick resolutely to, to wish, to desire. The 3rd person, singular, subjunctive is *thele'*, would or might will, etc.

2. The Hebrew Group

Your group believes that the Hebrew tradition is the key to translating the passage. Other groups will probably not agree with you. It is your task to persuade them that your view is correct, or be persuaded by them. The following passages are for background study:

Deuteronomy 6:4-9
Deuteronomy 11:13-18
Exodus 1:5
Mark 12:28-34
Mark 14:34

BACKGROUND DATA

Jesus and the earliest disciples were Hebrews, and only later did the church come under Greek influence. While Jesus and the disciples may have spoken Syriac, it was the Hebrew tradition that was the overwhelming influence behind the Gospel accounts. The Hebrew word behind *psuche'* is *nephesh*, which may refer to persons casually, as in Exodus 1:5, "All the offspring *(nepheshim)* of Jacob were seventy persons *(nepheshim)*." However, it often refers to the deepest desires of the heart of a person. Deuteronomy 6:5, "You shall love the Lord your God with all your heart, and with all your soul *(nephesh)*, and with all your might." When Jesus quoted this passage in Mark 12:30, the Greek word *psuche'* is used to translate *nephesh*. Deuteronomy 11:13 and 18 are two more examples of *nephesh* used to mean fundamental intention or personal identity. In Mark 14:34 again we find Mark quoting Jesus as he refers to his deepest selfhood, identity, or will. You are wary of the influence upon the text of a martyrdom theology that developed during the second- and third-century persecutions of the church. You also oppose any arbitrary division of body and soul.

214

WHAT'S IN A WORD? A Simulation Based upon Mark 8:35

THE SITUATION
The purpose of this simulation is to help you gain a new understanding of the reasons for various versions of Scripture by actually translating a familiar passage from the original Greek. You are to simulate a group of translators who have been commissioned by various churches to produce a new translation of the Bible to be called the International Standard Version. Just now you are at the point of trying to agree upon a translation for Mark 8:35.

TASKS OF ALL GROUPS
PRIOR TO THE SIMULATION
Everyone is assigned to one of four study groups to prepare a preliminary translation: the Markan group, the Hebrew group, the Johannine group, and the Jesus group.

Specific tasks which each group should perform follow:
1. Appoint a chairman for your group who will lead in the preparation of the simulation.
2. Appoint a chronicler who will—
   a. record the process of his or her own group,
   b. record the action of the simulation from the perspective of his or her group,
   c. report during the debriefing session.
3. Establish the text, i.e., decide upon the version of the original that has a stronger claim to be considered the proper text.
4. Use the lexicon to make a word by word translation.
5. Rephrase the translation to make good idiomatic English:
   a. put the words in proper order;
   b. rephrase the words to catch the original meaning.
6. Discuss how you will persuade the other groups that they should adopt your translation.

RULES OF THE SIMULATION
1. The chairman should see that the whole group works on the tasks of the simulation

and that the rules are followed. The chairman decides who may speak.
2. Three people from each study group may sit around the table with the others from that group seated behind them. Only those at the table may take part in the debate.
3. Anyone from a study group may replace one of the three persons at the table merely by indicating his wish to do so.
4. All decisions are to be made by two-thirds vote of all involved in the simulation.
5. Any study group may request a caucus just prior to a vote.
6. Anyone not at the table may lobby to change the minds of persons from other groups.

TASKS OF THE SIMULATION
1. Reach a decision about which Greek words will be included in the text.
2. Decide upon the English words and phrases to be used to translate the text.

TASKS FOR DEBRIEFING
Follow the coordinator's instructions for debriefing found in this chapter.

GREEK TEXT OF MARK 8:35
hos gar ean thelé tén ( )[1] sōsai, apolesei autén. hos d' an ( )[2] tén psuchén autou heneken ( )[3] tou euaggeliou, sōsei autén.
1. The Greek phrase to be inserted in the space marked [1] is one of the following:
   a. *psuchén autou.* Most manuscripts have this phrase.
   b. *eautou psuchén.* A few insignificant manuscripts have this alternate form.
2. The Greek phrase to be inserted in the space marked [2] is one of the following:
   a. *apolesei.* Most manuscripts have this form.
   b. *apolese.* The important Byzantine group of manuscripts which come from Antioch through Constantinople have this.
3. The space marked [3] is either filled with a Greek phrase or left blank as indicated in the choices below:

a. *emou kai*. Most manuscripts contain this phrase.

b. The phrase is omitted in the oldest known manuscript fragment of this verse, a fragment from the Chester Beatty Papyri dating back to the third century. It is also omitted in several old Italian manuscripts and in a Syriac translation dating back to the fourth century.

LEXICON

an. Under the circumstances, in that case, anyhow, would, if. The word has the effect of making a statement contingent that would otherwise be definite.

apollumi. Lose, destroy, perish. *Apolesei* is the future, 3rd person, singular, and means will lose, will destroy, etc. *Apolese* is the 3rd person singular of the subjunctive and means would or might lose, etc.

autos. He, self, the very, the same. The possessive form is *autou*, his, his own, its, self, or the same. The accusative form is *auten*, him, it, self, or the same.

de. But, on the other hand, and. A weak adversative particle, generally placed second in its clause. Before a vowel it is written as *d'*.

ean. If, when introducing a clause. The meaning of *hos* changes to who, whoever, or whosoever when accompanied by *ean*.

eautou. His own, its own.

emos. Mine, of me. After some prepositions it is written as *emou*.

euaggeliou. The good news, the gospel.

gar. For. A conjunction relating the phrase to previous ideas.

heneken. For the sake of, on account of, in behalf of.

ho, he, to. The. Other forms with the same meaning are *ten* and *tou*.

hos. Who, which. A definite relative pronoun. With *an* or *ean* it may mean whoever or whosoever.

kai. And, even. A conjunction.

psuche. Appetite, desire, soul, self, life, breath of life, person, individual, identity. It is often used to translate the Hebrew word *nephesh*. The form *psuchen* is used as the object of the verb.

sodzo. Save, rescue, preserve from danger or from death. Sometimes it refers to physical danger and sometimes to spiritual death. Other forms are *sosei*, 3rd person, singular, future, will save, etc.; and *sosai*, past infinitive, to save (in a single complete action), to rescue, etc.

ten, tou. See *ho, he, to*.

thelo. To will, to stick resolutely to, to wish, to desire. The 3rd person, singular, subjunctive is *thele*, would or might will, etc.

2. The Hebrew Group

Your group believes that the Hebrew tradition is the key to translating the passage. Other groups will probably not agree with you. It is your task to persuade them that your view is correct, or be persuaded by them. The following passages are for background study:

Deuteronomy 6:4-9
Deuteronomy 11:13-18
Exodus 1:5
Mark 12:28-34
Mark 14:34

BACKGROUND DATA

Jesus and the earliest disciples were Hebrews, and only later did the church come under Greek influence. While Jesus and the disciples may have spoken Syriac, it was the Hebrew tradition that was the overwhelming influence behind the Gospel accounts. The Hebrew word behind *psuche* is *nephesh*, which may refer to persons casually, as in Exodus 1:5, "All the offspring *(nepheshim)* of Jacob were seventy persons *(nepheshim)*." However, it often refers to the deepest desires of the heart of a person. Deuteronomy 6:5, "You shall love the Lord your God with all your heart, and with all your soul *(nephesh)*, and with all your might." When Jesus quoted this passage in Mark 12:30, the Greek word *psuche* is used to translate *nephesh*. Deuteronomy 11:13 and 18 are two more examples of *nephesh* used to mean fundamental intention or personal identity. In Mark 14:34 again we find Mark quoting Jesus as he refers to his deepest selfhood, identity, or will. You are wary of the influence upon the text of a martyrdom theology that developed during the second- and third-century persecutions of the church. You also oppose any arbitrary division of body and soul.

WHAT'S IN A WORD? A Simulation Based upon Mark 8:35

THE SITUATION
The purpose of this simulation is to help you gain a new understanding of the reasons for various versions of Scripture by actually translating a familiar passage from the original Greek. You are to simulate a group of translators who have been commissioned by various churches to produce a new translation of the Bible to be called the International Standard Version. Just now you are at the point of trying to agree upon a translation for Mark 8:35.

TASKS OF ALL GROUPS
PRIOR TO THE SIMULATION
Everyone is assigned to one of four study groups to prepare a preliminary translation: the Markan group, the Hebrew group, the Johannine group, and the Jesus group.

Specific tasks which each group should perform follow:
1. Appoint a chairman for your group who will lead in the preparation of the simulation.
2. Appoint a chronicler who will—
   a. record the process of his or her own group,
   b. record the action of the simulation from the perspective of his or her group,
   c. report during the debriefing session.
3. Establish the text, i.e., decide upon the version of the original that has a stronger claim to be considered the proper text.
4. Use the lexicon to make a word by word translation.
5. Rephrase the translation to make good idiomatic English:
   a. put the words in proper order;
   b. rephrase the words to catch the original meaning.
6. Discuss how you will persuade the other groups that they should adopt your translation.

RULES OF THE SIMULATION
1. The chairman should see that the whole group works on the tasks of the simulation and that the rules are followed. The chairman decides who may speak.
2. Three people from each study group may sit around the table with the others from that group seated behind them. Only those at the table may take part in the debate.
3. Anyone from a study group may replace one of the three persons at the table merely by indicating his wish to do so.
4. All decisions are to be made by two-thirds vote of all involved in the simulation.
5. Any study group may request a caucus just prior to a vote.
6. Anyone not at the table may lobby to change the minds of persons from other groups.

TASKS OF THE SIMULATION
1. Reach a decision about which Greek words will be included in the text.
2. Decide upon the English words and phrases to be used to translate the text.

TASKS FOR DEBRIEFING
Follow the coordinator's instructions for debriefing found in this chapter.

GREEK TEXT OF MARK 8:35
hos gar ean thele ten (   )[1] sōsai, apolesei autén. hos d' an (   )[2] tén psuchén autou heneken (   )[3] tou euaggeliou, sōsei autén.
1. The Greek phrase to be inserted in the space marked [1] is one of the following:
   a. *psuchén autou.* Most manuscripts have this phrase.
   b. *eautou psuchén.* A few insignificant manuscripts have this alternate form.
2. The Greek phrase to be inserted in the space marked [2] is one of the following:
   a. *apolesei.* Most manuscripts have this form.
   b. *apolese.* The important Byzantine group of manuscripts which come from Antioch through Constantinople have this.
3. The space marked [3] is either filled with a Greek phrase or left blank as indicated in the choices below:

a. *emou kai*. Most manuscripts contain this phrase.

b. The phrase is omitted in the oldest known manuscript fragment of this verse, a fragment from the Chester Beatty Papyri dating back to the third century. It is also omitted in several old Italian manuscripts and in a Syriac translation dating back to the fourth century.

LEXICON

an. Under the circumstances, in that case, anyhow, would, if. The word has the effect of making a statement contingent that would otherwise be definite.

apollumi. Lose, destroy, perish. *Apolesei* is the future, 3rd person, singular, and means will lose, will destroy, etc. *Apolese'* is the 3rd person singular of the subjunctive and means would or might lose, etc.

autos. He, self, the very, the same. The possessive form is *autou*, his, his own, its, self, or the same. The accusative form is *auten*, him, it, self, or the same.

de. But, on the other hand, and. A weak adversative particle, generally placed second in its clause. Before a vowel it is written *d'*.

ean. If, when introducing a clause. The meaning of *hos* changes to who, whoever, or whosoever when accompanied by *ean*.

eautou. His own, its own.

emos. Mine, of me. After some prepositions it is written as *emou*.

euaggeliou. The good news, the gospel.

gar. For. A conjunction relating the phrase to previous ideas.

heneken. For the sake of, on account of, in behalf of.

ho, he', to. The. Other forms with the same meaning are *ten* and *tou*.

hos. Who, which. A definite relative pronoun. With *an* or *ean* it may mean whoever or whosoever.

kai. And, even. A conjunction.

psuche'. Appetite, desire, soul, self, life, breath of life, person, individual, identity. It is often used to translate the Hebrew word *nephesh*. The form *psuchen* is used as the object of the verb.

sodzo. Save, rescue, preserve from danger or from death. Sometimes it refers to physical danger and sometimes to spiritual death. Other forms are *sosei*, 3rd person, singular, future, will save, etc.; and *sosai*, past infinitive, to save (in a single complete action), to rescue, etc.

ten, tou. See *ho, he', to*.

thelo. To will, to stick resolutely to, to wish, to desire. The 3rd person, singular, subjunctive is *thele'*, would or might will, etc.

3. The Johannine Group

Your group bases its argument upon the Johannine understanding of *psuche'*. You believe that while the body is perishable, the soul is imperishable. Those in other groups may not agree with you. It is your task to try to persuade them that your view is correct, or be persuaded by them. Passages you should study are the following:

> John 12:24-26
> John 11:20-27
> John 15:1-14
> John 21:18-23

BACKGROUND DATA

You believe that each person is a unity of body and soul. While the body can be killed, the soul can be injured only in other ways (Matthew 10:28). It may fall into lustful passions (1 Peter 2:11), or it can be lost in the cares of the world (John 12:25). Only as the soul abides in Jesus (John 15:1-7) does it realize its eternal possibilities. This is brought out most clearly in John 11:25-26 where the one who believes in Jesus shall live even when he dies (i.e., his body dies). The same point is made in John 21:18-23 where Peter's martyrdom gains him no advantage over the natural death of John (the disciple whom Jesus loved). The person who loves his soul's involvement in flesh and blood (John 1:13) lives in darkness, but the one who hates the entanglements of this life will realize the eternal life of the soul (John 12:25). Unless some word or phrase can be found to catch up the meaning above, you prefer to translate *psuche'* as soul. Life sounds too much as though the gospel is primarily a call to martyrdom. Furthermore, verses 36 and 37 of Mark 8 call for a stronger word than life. Mark 9:1 also indicates that physical death is not necessary in order to "see the kingdom of God." Finally you do not want to eliminate *emou kai* without very good reason, since the soul lives on in Christ. To remove *emou kai* corrupts the essential meaning.

WHAT'S IN A WORD? A Simulation Based upon Mark 8:35

THE SITUATION
The purpose of this simulation is to help you gain a new understanding of the reasons for various versions of Scripture by actually translating a familiar passage from the original Greek. You are to simulate a group of translators who have been commissioned by various churches to produce a new translation of the Bible to be called the International Standard Version. Just now you are at the point of trying to agree upon a translation for Mark 8:35.

TASKS OF ALL GROUPS
PRIOR TO THE SIMULATION
Everyone is assigned to one of four study groups to prepare a preliminary translation: the Markan group, the Hebrew group, the Johannine group, and the Jesus group.

Specific tasks which each group should perform follow:
1. Appoint a chairman for your group who will lead in the preparation of the simulation.
2. Appoint a chronicler who will—
   a. record the process of his or her own group,
   b. record the action of the simulation from the perspective of his or her group,
   c. report during the debriefing session.
3. Establish the text, i.e., decide upon the version of the original that has a stronger claim to be considered the proper text.
4. Use the lexicon to make a word by word translation.
5. Rephrase the translation to make good idiomatic English:
   a. put the words in proper order;
   b. rephrase the words to catch the original meaning.
6. Discuss how you will persuade the other groups that they should adopt your translation.

RULES OF THE SIMULATION
1. The chairman should see that the whole group works on the tasks of the simulation and that the rules are followed. The chairman decides who may speak.
2. Three people from each study group may sit around the table with the others from that group seated behind them. Only those at the table may take part in the debate.
3. Anyone from a study group may replace one of the three persons at the table merely by indicating his wish to do so.
4. All decisions are to be made by two-thirds vote of all involved in the simulation.
5. Any study group may request a caucus just prior to a vote.
6. Anyone not at the table may lobby to change the minds of persons from other groups.

TASKS OF THE SIMULATION
1. Reach a decision about which Greek words will be included in the text.
2. Decide upon the English words and phrases to be used to translate the text.

TASKS FOR DEBRIEFING
Follow the coordinator's instructions for debriefing found in this chapter.

GREEK TEXT OF MARK 8:35
hos gar ean thelé tén (   )[1] sōsai, apolesei autén. hos d' an (   )[2] tén psuchén autou heneken (   )[3] tou euaggeliou, sōsei autén.
1. The Greek phrase to be inserted in the space marked [1] is one of the following:
   a. *psuchén autou.* Most manuscripts have this phrase.
   b. *eautou psuchén.* A few insignificant manuscripts have this alternate form.
2. The Greek phrase to be inserted in the space marked [2] is one of the following:
   a. *apolesei.* Most manuscripts have this form.
   b. *apolese.* The important Byzantine group of manuscripts which come from Antioch through Constantinople have this.
3. The space marked [3] is either filled with a Greek phrase or left blank as indicated in the choices below:

a. *emou kai.* Most manuscripts contain this phrase.

b. The phrase is omitted in the oldest known manuscript fragment of this verse, a fragment from the Chester Beatty Papyri dating back to the third century. It is also omitted in several old Italian manuscripts and in a Syriac translation dating back to the fourth century.

LEXICON

an. Under the circumstances, in that case, anyhow, would, if. The word has the effect of making a statement contingent that would otherwise be definite.

apollumi. Lose, destroy, perish. *Apolesei* is the future, 3rd person, singular, and means will lose, will destroy, etc. *Apolese* is the 3rd person singular of the subjunctive and means would or might lose, etc.

autos. He, self, the very, the same. The possessive form is *autou,* his, his own, its, self, or the same. The accusative form is *autén,* him, it, self, or the same.

de. But, on the other hand, and. A weak adversative particle, generally placed second in its clause. Before a vowel it is written *d'.*

ean. If, when introducing a clause. The meaning of *hos* changes to who, whoever, or whosoever when accompanied by *ean.*

eautou. His own, its own.

emos. Mine, of me. After some prepositions it is written as *emou.*

euaggeliou. The good news, the gospel.

gar. For. A conjunction relating the phrase to previous ideas.

heneken. For the sake of, on account of, in behalf of.

ho, he, to. The. Other forms with the same meaning are *ten* and *tou.*

hos. Who, which. A definite relative pronoun. With *an* or *ean* it may mean whoever or whosoever.

kai. And, even. A conjunction.

psuche. Appetite, desire, soul, self, life, breath of life, person, individual, identity. It is often used to translate the Hebrew word *nephesh.* The form *psuchen* is used as the object of the verb.

sodzo. Save, rescue, preserve from danger or from death. Sometimes it refers to physical danger and sometimes to spiritual death. Other forms are *sōsei,* 3rd person, singular, future, will save, etc.; and *sosai,* past infinitive, to save (in a single complete action), to rescue, etc.

ten, tou. See *ho, he, to.*

thelō. To will, to stick resolutely to, to wish, to desire. The 3rd person, singular, subjunctive is *thele,* would or might will, etc.

3. The Johannine Group

Your group bases its argument upon the Johannine understanding of *psuche.* You believe that while the body is perishable, the soul is imperishable. Those in other groups may not agree with you. It is your task to try to persuade them that your view is correct, or be persuaded by them. Passages you should study are the following:

> John 12:24-26
> John 11:20-27
> John 15:1-14
> John 21:18-23

BACKGROUND DATA

You believe that each person is a unity of body and soul. While the body can be killed, the soul can be injured only in other ways (Matthew 10:28). It may fall into lustful passions (1 Peter 2:11), or it can be lost in the cares of the world (John 12:25). Only as the soul abides in Jesus (John 15:1-7) does it realize its eternal possibilities. This is brought out most clearly in John 11:25-26 where the one who believes in Jesus shall live even when he dies (i.e., his body dies). The same point is made in John 21:18-23 where Peter's martyrdom gains him no advantage over the natural death of John (the disciple whom Jesus loved). The person who loves his soul's involvement in flesh and blood (John 1:13) lives in darkness, but the one who hates the entanglements of this life will realize the eternal life of the soul (John 12:25). Unless some word or phrase can be found to catch up the meaning above, you prefer to translate *psuche* as soul. Life sounds too much as though the gospel is primarily a call to martyrdom. Furthermore, verses 36 and 37 of Mark 8 call for a stronger word than life. Mark 9:1 also indicates that physical death is not necessary in order to "see the kingdom of God." Finally you do not want to eliminate *emou kai* without very good reason, since the soul lives on in Christ. To remove *emou kai* corrupts the essential meaning.

WHAT'S IN A WORD? A Simulation Based upon Mark 8:35

THE SITUATION

The purpose of this simulation is to help you gain a new understanding of the reasons for various versions of Scripture by actually translating a familiar passage from the original Greek. You are to simulate a group of translators who have been commissioned by various churches to produce a new translation of the Bible to be called the International Standard Version. Just now you are at the point of trying to agree upon a translation for Mark 8:35.

TASKS OF ALL GROUPS
PRIOR TO THE SIMULATION

Everyone is assigned to one of four study groups to prepare a preliminary translation: the Markan group, the Hebrew group, the Johannine group, and the Jesus group.

Specific tasks which each group should perform follow:

1. Appoint a chairman for your group who will lead in the preparation of the simulation.
2. Appoint a chronicler who will—
   a. record the process of his or her own group,
   b. record the action of the simulation from the perspective of his or her group,
   c. report during the debriefing session.
3. Establish the text, i.e., decide upon the version of the original that has a stronger claim to be considered the proper text.
4. Use the lexicon to make a word by word translation.
5. Rephrase the translation to make good idiomatic English:
   a. put the words in proper order;
   b. rephrase the words to catch the original meaning.
6. Discuss how you will persuade the other groups that they should adopt your translation.

RULES OF THE SIMULATION

1. The chairman should see that the whole group works on the tasks of the simulation and that the rules are followed. The chairman decides who may speak.
2. Three people from each study group may sit around the table with the others from that group seated behind them. Only those at the table may take part in the debate.
3. Anyone from a study group may replace one of the three persons at the table merely by indicating his wish to do so.
4. All decisions are to be made by two-thirds vote of all involved in the simulation.
5. Any study group may request a caucus just prior to a vote.
6. Anyone not at the table may lobby to change the minds of persons from other groups.

TASKS OF THE SIMULATION

1. Reach a decision about which Greek words will be included in the text.
2. Decide upon the English words and phrases to be used to translate the text.

TASKS FOR DEBRIEFING

Follow the coordinator's instructions for debriefing found in this chapter.

GREEK TEXT OF MARK 8:35

hos gar ean thele' tén (   )[1] sōsai, apolesei autén. hos d' an (   )[2] tén psuchén autou heneken (   )[3] tou euaggeliou, sōsei autén.

1. The Greek phrase to be inserted in the space marked [1] is one of the following:
   a. *psuchén autou.* Most manuscripts have this phrase.
   b. *eautou psuchén.* A few insignificant manuscripts have this alternate form.
2. The Greek phrase to be inserted in the space marked [2] is one of the following:
   a. *apolesei.* Most manuscripts have this form.
   b. *apolese.* The important Byzantine group of manuscripts which come from Antioch through Constantinople have this.
3. The space marked [3] is either filled with a Greek phrase or left blank as indicated in the choices below:

a. *emou kai.* Most manuscripts contain this phrase.

b. The phrase is omitted in the oldest known manuscript fragment of this verse, a fragment from the Chester Beatty Papyri dating back to the third century. It is also omitted in several old Italian manuscripts and in a Syriac translation dating back to the fourth century.

LEXICON

an. Under the circumstances, in that case, anyhow, would, if. The word has the effect of making a statement contingent that would otherwise be definite.

apollumi. Lose, destroy, perish. *Apolesei* is the future, 3rd person, singular, and means will lose, will destroy, etc. *Apolese'* is the 3rd person singular of the subjunctive and means would or might lose, etc.

autos. He, self, the very, the same. The possessive form is *autou,* his, his own, its, self, or the same. The accusative form is *auten,* him, it, self, or the same.

de. But, on the other hand, and. A weak adversative particle, generally placed second in its clause. Before a vowel it is written *d'*

ean. If. when introducing a clause. The meaning of *hos* changes to who, whoever, or whosoever when accompanied by *ean.*

eautou. His own, its own.

emos. Mine, of me. After some prepositions it is written as *emou.*

euaggeliou. The good news, the gospel.

gar. For. A conjunction relating the phrase to previous ideas.

heneken. For the sake of, on account of, in behalf of.

ho, he', to. The. Other forms with the same meaning are *ten* and *tou.*

hos. Who, which. A definite relative pronoun. With *an* or *ean* it may mean whoever or whosoever.

kai. And, even. A conjunction.

psuche'. Appetite, desire, soul, self, life, breath of life, person, individual, identity. It is often used to translate the Hebrew word *nephesh.* The form *psuchen* is used as the object of the verb.

sodzo. Save, rescue, preserve from danger or from death. Sometimes it refers to physical danger and sometimes to spiritual death. Other forms are *sōsei,* 3rd person, singular, future, will save, etc.; and *sosai,* past infinitive, to save (in a single complete action), to rescue, etc.

ten, tou. See *ho, he', to.*

thelō. To will, to stick resolutely to, to wish, to desire. The 3rd person, singular, subjunctive is *thele',* would or might will, etc.

4. The Jesus Group

Your group wants as nearly as possible to recover the words of Jesus. You believe that any translation has to take account of each of the Synoptic Gospels (Matthew, Mark, and Luke). Those in other groups may not agree with you. It is your task to try to persuade them that your view is correct, or be persuaded by them. Passages you should study are the following:

Matthew 16:25
Luke 9:24
Matthew 10:39
Luke 17:33

BACKGROUND DATA

It is generally thought that the Synoptic Gospels refer to an earlier collection of the sayings of Jesus. Whereas Matthew and Luke may have borrowed many of the sayings of Jesus from Mark, it is also possible that Matthew or Luke, or both, had access to the sayings of Jesus independently from Mark. In the latter case Matthew's or Luke's version of the sayings of Jesus could be more original. You believe that it is important to compare the different versions of a quotation from Jesus before making a translation. In the parallel passage in Matthew 16:25 all manuscripts agree to the form *apolese',* not *apolesei,* in the second appearance of that verb. Furthermore *emou* is present, but there is no reference to *tou euaggeliou.* The parallel passage in Luke 9:24 also has *apolese'* rather than *apolesei.* It also has *emou,* but without reference to *tou euaggeliou.* Before *sōsei* is the word *outos,* which means "he, that person, or such a person." The saying also occurs in Matthew 10:39 as a part of Jesus' instruction to the twelve before sending them out. Again we find *emou,* but no reference to *tou euaggeliou.* Finally in Luke 17:33 there is no mention of either *emou* or *tou euaggeliou.*

WHAT'S IN A WORD? A Simulation Based upon Mark 8:35

THE SITUATION

The purpose of this simulation is to help you gain a new understanding of the reasons for various versions of Scripture by actually translating a familiar passage from the original Greek. You are to simulate a group of translators who have been commissioned by various churches to produce a new translation of the Bible to be called the International Standard Version. Just now you are at the point of trying to agree upon a translation for Mark 8:35.

TASKS OF ALL GROUPS
PRIOR TO THE SIMULATION

Everyone is assigned to one of four study groups to prepare a preliminary translation: the Markan group, the Hebrew group, the Johannine group, and the Jesus group.

Specific tasks which each group should perform follow:

1. Appoint a chairman for your group who will lead in the preparation of the simulation.
2. Appoint a chronicler who will—
   a. record the process of his or her own group,
   b. record the action of the simulation from the perspective of his or her group,
   c. report during the debriefing session.
3. Establish the text, i.e., decide upon the version of the original that has a stronger claim to be considered the proper text.
4. Use the lexicon to make a word by word translation.
5. Rephrase the translation to make good idiomatic English:
   a. put the words in proper order;
   b. rephrase the words to catch the original meaning.
6. Discuss how you will persuade the other groups that they should adopt your translation.

RULES OF THE SIMULATION

1. The chairman should see that the whole group works on the tasks of the simulation

and that the rules are followed. The chairman decides who may speak.
2. Three people from each study group may sit around the table with the others from that group seated behind them. Only those at the table may take part in the debate.
3. Anyone from a study group may replace one of the three persons at the table merely by indicating his wish to do so.
4. All decisions are to be made by two-thirds vote of all involved in the simulation.
5. Any study group may request a caucus just prior to a vote.
6. Anyone not at the table may lobby to change the minds of persons from other groups.

TASKS OF THE SIMULATION

1. Reach a decision about which Greek words will be included in the text.
2. Decide upon the English words and phrases to be used to translate the text.

TASKS FOR DEBRIEFING

Follow the coordinator's instructions for debriefing found in this chapter.

GREEK TEXT OF MARK 8:35

hos gar ean thelé tén (   )[1] sōsai, apolesei autén. hos d' an (   )[2] tén psuchén autou heneken (   )[3] tou euaggeliou, sōsei autén.

1. The Greek phrase to be inserted in the space marked [1] is one of the following:
   a. psuchén autou. Most manuscripts have this phrase.
   b. eautou psuchén. A few insignificant manuscripts have this alternate form.
2. The Greek phrase to be inserted in the space marked [2] is one of the following:
   a. apolesei. Most manuscripts have this form.
   b. apolese. The important Byzantine group of manuscripts which come from Antioch through Constantinople have this.
3. The space marked [3] is either filled with a Greek phrase or left blank as indicated in the choices below:

a. *emou kai*. Most manuscripts contain this phrase.

b. The phrase is omitted in the oldest known manuscript fragment of this verse, a fragment from the Chester Beatty Papyri dating back to the third century. It is also omitted in several old Italian manuscripts and in a Syriac translation dating back to the fourth century.

LEXICON

an. Under the circumstances, in that case, anyhow, would, if. The word has the effect of making a statement contingent that would otherwise be definite.

apollumi. Lose, destroy, perish. *Apolesei* is the future, 3rd person, singular, and means will lose, will destroy, etc. *Apolese'* is the 3rd person singular of the subjunctive and means would or might lose, etc.

autos. He, self, the very, the same. The possessive form is *autou*, his, his own, its, self, or the same. The accusative form is *auten*, him, it, self, or the same.

de. But, on the other hand, and. A weak adversative particle, generally placed second in its clause. Before a vowel it is written as *d'*.

ean. If, when introducing a clause. The meaning of *hos* changes to who, whoever, or whosoever when accompanied by *ean*.

eautou. His own, its own.

emos. Mine, of me. After some prepositions it is written as *emou*.

euaggeliou. The good news, the gospel.

gar. For. A conjunction relating the phrase to previous ideas.

heneken. For the sake of, on account of, in behalf of.

ho, he', to. The. Other forms with the same meaning are *ten* and *tou*.

hos. Who, which. A definite relative pronoun. With *an* or *ean* it may mean whoever or whosoever.

kai. And, even. A conjunction.

psuche'. Appetite, desire, soul, self, life, breath of life, person, individual, identity. It is often used to translate the Hebrew word *nephesh*. The form *psuchen* is used as the object of the verb.

sodzo. Save, rescue, preserve from danger or from death. Sometimes it refers to physical danger and sometimes to spiritual death. Other forms are *sosei*, 3rd person, singular, future, will save, etc.; and *sosai*, past infinitive, to save (in a single complete action), to rescue, etc.

ten, tou. See *ho, he', to*.

thelo. To will, to stick resolutely to, to wish, to desire. The 3rd person, singular, subjunctive is *thele'*, would or might will, etc.

4. The Jesus Group

Your group wants as nearly as possible to recover the words of Jesus. You believe that any translation has to take account of each of the Synoptic Gospels (Matthew, Mark, and Luke). Those in other groups may not agree with you. It is your task to try to persuade them that your view is correct, or be persuaded by them. Passages you should study are the following:

> Matthew 16:25
> Luke 9:24
> Matthew 10:39
> Luke 17:33

BACKGROUND DATA

It is generally thought that the Synoptic Gospels refer to an earlier collection of the sayings of Jesus. Whereas Matthew and Luke may have borrowed many of the sayings of Jesus from Mark, it is also possible that Matthew or Luke, or both, had access to the sayings of Jesus independently from Mark. In the latter case Matthew's or Luke's version of the sayings of Jesus could be more original. You believe that it is important to compare the different versions of a quotation from Jesus before making a translation. In the parallel passage in Matthew 16:25 all manuscripts agree to the form *apolese'*, not *apolesei*, in the second appearance of that verb. Furthermore *emou* is present, but there is no reference to *tou euaggeliou*. The parallel passage in Luke 9:24 also has *apolese'* rather than *apolesei*. It also has *emou*, but without reference to *tou euaggeliou*. Before *sosei* is the word *outos*, which means "he, that person, or such a person." The saying also occurs in Matthew 10:39 as a part of Jesus' instruction to the twelve before sending them out. Again we find *emou*, but no reference to *tou euaggeliou*. Finally in Luke 17:33 there is no mention of either *emou* or *tou euaggeliou*.